D0681654

EXAM✓CRAM

CompTIA®
Security+™
SYO-301

Third Edition

**Diane Barrett,
Kalani K. Hausman,
and Martin Weiss**

CompTIA Security+™ SY0-301 Authorized Exam Cram, Third Edition

ISBN-13: 978-0-7897-4829-4

ISBN-10: 0-7897-4829-0

Library of Congress Cataloging-in-Publication data is on file.

Printed in the United States of America

First Printing: December 2011

14   13   4

Trademarks

Warning and Disclaimer

Bulk Sales

Pearson IT Certification offers excellent discounts on this book when ordered in quantity for bulk purchases or special sales. For more –information, please contact

U.S. Corporate and Government Sales
1-800-382-3419
corpsales@pearsontechgroup.com

For sales outside of the U.S., please contact

International Sales
international@pearson.com

Associate Publisher
David Dusthimer

Acquisitions Editor
Betsy Brown

Development Editor
Andrew Cupp

Managing Editor
Sandra Schroeder

Project Editor
Mandie Frank

Copy Editor
Charlotte Kughen,
The Wordsmithery LLC

Indexer
Tim Wright

Proofreader
Megan Wade

Technical Editor
Chris Crayton

Publishing Coordinator
Vanessa Evans

Multimedia Developer
Tim Warner

Book Designer
Gary Adair

Composition
TnT Design, Inc.

Contents at a Glance

Table of Contents

Part II: Compliance and Operational Security

Part III: Threats and Vulnerabilities

About the Authors

Diane Barrett is the director of training for Paraben Corporation and an adjunct professor for American Military University. She has done contract forensic and security assessment work for several years and has authored other security and forensic books. She is a regular committee member for ADFSL's Conference on Digital Forensics, Security, and Law as well as an academy director for Edvancement Solutions. She holds many industry certifications, including CISSP, ISSMP, DFCP, PCME, and Security+. Diane's education includes an MS in information technology with a specialization in information security. She expects to complete a PhD in business administration with a specialization in information security.

Kalani Kirk Hausman is an author, enterprise and security architect, ISO, and consultant with experience including medium- to large-scale globally deployed networks in governmental, higher-education, health-care, and corporate settings. Kalani's professional certifications include the CISSP, CGEIT, CRISC, CISA, CISM, GIAC-GHSC, PMP, and CCP. He is active within the FBI InfraGard, Information Systems Audit and Control Association (ISACA), and ISSA. Kalani is currently employed as the assistant commandant for Strategic Communications, Information Technology, and Public Relations at TAMU and as an adjunct professor of InfoSec at UMUC. Kalani can be reached at kkhausman@hotmail.com or followed on Twitter at @kkhausman.

Martin Weiss lives within a triangle of sales, engineering, and marketing, providing information security solutions for organizations of all sizes. He is currently most interested in governance, risk, compliance, and how to secure elastic cloud environments. He is also an adjunct professor with the University of Maryland University College focusing on security classes. Marty is the author of several other books. His work has been compared to literary greats. His mother, upon reviewing a recent book, described it as riveting as anything by Dostoevsky. Marty holds several certifications, including Security+, CISSP, CISA, and CCSK. He received his M.B.A. from the Isenberg School of Management at the University of Massachusetts and currently lives in Connecticut with his wife, three sons, and iPhone. Marty can be reached at martyweiss@gmail.com or stalked on Twitter @martyweiss.

Dedication

To my husband, Bill, for his patience and understanding.
—Diane Barrett

To Susan and our wonderful children, Jonathan and Cassandra,
who inspire me every moment to greater deeds.
—Kalani K. Hausman

vp,[yos drvitoyu [;id rcs, vts, drvpmf rfoyopm eo;; ntrsl yjr vpfr 2521202 0861704
3330307 3251403
—Martin Weiss

Acknowledgments

Publishing a book takes the collaboration and teamwork of many individuals. Thanks to everyone involved in this process from Waterside Productions and Pearson Education (and thanks to those who purchase this book in their quest for certification). Betsy, thanks for keeping us all on track. To our editorial and technical reviewers, thank you for making sure that our work was sound and on target. Special thanks to my coauthors, Marty and Kirk: You made this project interesting and enjoyable.

—Diane Barrett

Thanks go to my extraordinary agent Carole McClendon, to Betsy Brown, and the Pearson editorial staff. Special thanks go to my coauthors Martin Weiss and Diane Barrett, whose strengths and knowledge produced a remarkable product in this text. As always, the unflagging support of Susan and our wonderful children (Jonathan and Cassandra) was instrumental in completing this book.

—Kalani K. Hausman

Thank you to the entire team that helped bring this book together, including all the folks at Waterside Productions and Pearson. Special thanks to Carole Jelen, Betsy Brown, Andrew Cupp, and, of course, Diane and Kirk. Most importantly I thank you, the reader of this book. Finally, I'd like to acknowledge my family. Thank you to my boys—Ollie, Max, and Kobe; you inspire me. I'm especially thankful to my wife Kelly, who provided a lot of understanding and support during a particularly busy time for me.

—Martin Weiss

We Want to Hear from You!

As the reader of this book, *you* are our most important critic and commentator. We value your opinion and want to know what we're doing right, what we could do better, what areas you'd like to see us publish in, and any other words of wisdom you're willing to pass our way.

As an Associate Publisher for Pearson IT Certification, I welcome your comments. You can email or write me directly to let me know what you did or didn't like about this book—as well as what we can do to make our books better.

Please note that I cannot help you with technical problems related to the topic of this book. We do have a User Services group, however, where I will forward specific technical questions related to the book.

When you write, please be sure to include this book's title and authors as well as your name, email address, and phone number. I will carefully review your comments and share them with the authors and editors who worked on the book.

Email: feedback@pearsonitcertification.com

Mail: David Dusthimer
Associate Publisher
800 East 96th Street
Indianapolis, IN 46240 USA

CompTIA.

CompTIA Security+

Designed for IT professionals focused on system security.

Covers network infrastructure, cryptography, assessments, and audits.

Security+ is mandated by the U.S. Department of Defense and is recommended by top companies such as Microsoft, HP, and Cisco.

It Pays to Get Certified

In a digital world, digital literacy is an essential survival skill—
Certification proves you have the knowledge and skill to solve business problems in virtually any business environment. Certifications are highly valued credentials that qualify you for jobs, increased compensation and promotion.

Security is one of the highest demand job categories—growing in importance as the frequency and severity of security threats continues to be a major concern for organizations around the world.

Jobs for security administrators are expected to increase by 18%—the skill set required for these types of jobs map to CompTIA Security+ certification.

Network Security Administrators—can earn as much as $106,000 per year.

CompTIA Security+ is the first step—in starting your career as a Network Security Administrator or Systems Security Administrator.

CompTIA Security+ is regularly used in organizations—such as Hitachi Information Systems, Trendmicro, the McAfee Elite Partner program, the U.S. State Department, and U.S. government contractors such as EDS, General Dynamics, and Northrop Grumman.

How Certification Helps Your Career

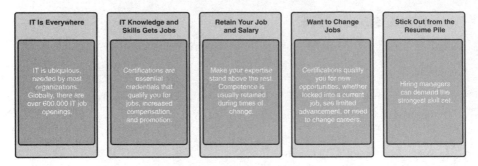

IT Is Everywhere	IT Knowledge and Skills Gets Jobs	Retain Your Job and Salary	Want to Change Jobs	Stick Out from the Resume Pile
IT is ubiquitous, needed by most organizations. Globally, there are over 600,000 IT job openings.	Certifications are essential credentials that qualify you for jobs, increased compensation, and promotion.	Make your expertise stand above the rest. Competence is usually retained during times of change.	Certifications qualify you for new opportunities, whether locked into a current job, see limited advancement, or need to change careers.	Hiring managers can demand the strongest skill set.

CompTIA Career Pathway

CompTIA offers a number of credentials that form a foundation for your career in technology and allow you to pursue specific areas of concentration. Depending on the path you choose to take, CompTIA certifications help you build upon your skills and knowledge, supporting learning throughout your entire career.

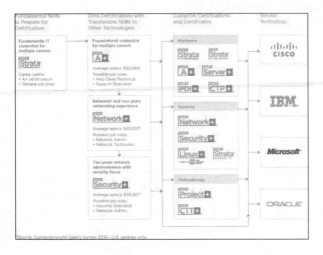

Steps to Getting Certified and Staying Certified

Review Exam Objectives	Review the certification objectives to make sure you know what is covered in the exam. http://certification.comptia.org/Training/testingcenters/examobjectives.aspx
Practice for the Exam	After you have studied for the certification, take a free assessment and sample test to get an idea of what type of questions might be on the exam. http://certification.comptia.org/Training/testingcenters/samplequestions.aspx
Purchase an Exam Voucher	Purchase your exam voucher on the CompTIA Marketplace, which is located at: http://www.comptiastore.com/
Take the Test!	Select a certification exam provider and schedule a time to take your exam. You can find exam providers at the following link: http://certification.comptia.org/Training/testingcenters.aspx
Stay Certified! Continuing education	Effective January 1, 2011, new CompTIA Security+ certifications are valid for three years from the date of your certification. There are a number of ways the certification can be renewed. For more information go to: http://certification.comptia.org/getCertified/steps_to_certification/stayCertified.aspx

Join the Professional Community

Join IT Pro Community http://itpro.comptia.org	The free IT Pro online community provides valuable content to students and professionals. Career IT Job Resources ▶ Where to start in IT ▶ Career Assessments ▶ Salary Trends ▶ US Job Board Forums on Networking, Security, Computing and Cutting Edge Technologies Access to blogs written by Industry Experts Current information on Cutting Edge Technologies Access to various industry resource links and articles related to IT and IT careers

Content Seal of Quality

This courseware bears the seal of **CompTIA Approved Quality Content.** This seal signifies this content covers 100% of the exam objectives and implements important instructional design principles. CompTIA recommends multiple learning tools to help increase coverage of the learning objectives.

Why CompTIA?

Global Recognition—CompTIA is recognized globally as the leading IT non-profit trade association and has enormous credibility. Plus, CompTIA's certifications are vendor-neutral and offer proof of foundational knowledge that translates across technologies.

Valued by Hiring Managers—Hiring managers value CompTIA certification, because it is vendor- and technology-independent validation of your technical skills.

Recommended or Required by Government and Businesses—Many government organizations and corporations either recommend or require technical staff to be CompTIA certified. (For example, Dell, Sharp, Ricoh, the U.S. Department of Defense, and many more.)

Three CompTIA Certifications ranked in the top 10—In a study by DICE of 17,000 technology professionals, certifications helped command higher salaries at all experience levels.

How to obtain more information

Visit CompTIA online—www.comptia.org to learn more about getting CompTIA certified.

Contact CompTIA—Call 866-835-8020 ext. 5 or email questions@comptia.org.

Join the IT Pro Community—http://itpro.comptia.org to join the IT community to get relevant career information.

Connect with us—

Introduction

Welcome to *CompTIA Security+ Exam Cram*, Third Edition. This book aims to help you get ready to take and pass the CompTIA Security+ exam, number SY0-301.

Chapters 1–13 are designed to remind you of everything you need to know to pass the SY0-301 certification exam. The two practice exams at the end of this book should give you a reasonably accurate assessment of your knowledge, and, yes, we've provided the answers and their explanations for these practice exams. Read this book, understand the material, and you'll stand a very good chance of passing the real test.

Exam Cram books help you understand and appreciate the subjects and materials you need to know to pass CompTIA certification exams. *Exam Cram* books are aimed strictly at test preparation and review. They do not teach you everything you need to know about a subject. Instead, the authors streamline and highlight the pertinent information by presenting and dissecting the questions and problems they've discovered that you're likely to encounter on a CompTIA test.

We strongly recommend that you spend some time installing, configuring, and working with the latest operating systems to patch and maintain them for the best and most current security possible because the Security+ exam focuses on such activities and the knowledge and skills they can provide for you. Nothing beats hands-on experience and familiarity when it comes to understanding the questions you're likely to encounter on a certification test. Book learning is essential, but, without doubt, hands-on experience is the best teacher of all!

Taking a Certification Exam

After you prepare for your exam, you need to register with a testing center. At the time of this writing, the cost to take the Security+ exam is $266 USD for individuals ($226 for CompTIA members). CompTIA corporate members receive discounts on nonmember pricing. For more information about these discounts, a local CompTIA sales representative can provide answers to any questions you might have. If you don't pass, you can take the exam again for the same cost as the first attempt, for each attempt until you pass. In the United States and Canada, tests are administered by Prometric or VUE.

After you sign up for a test, you are told when and where the test is scheduled. You should arrive at least 15 minutes early. To be admitted into the testing room, you must supply two forms of identification, one of which must be a photo ID.

About This Book

We've structured the topics in this book to build on one another. Therefore, some topics in later chapters make the most sense after you've read earlier chapters. That's why we suggest that you read this book from front to back for your initial test preparation. If you need to brush up on a topic or if you have to bone up for a second try, you can use the index, table of contents, or Table I-1 to go straight to the topics and questions that you need to study. Beyond helping you prepare for the test, we think you'll find this book useful as a tightly focused reference to some of the most important aspects of the Security+ certification.

Chapter Format and Conventions

Every *Exam Cram* chapter follows a standard structure and contains graphical clues about important information. The structure of each chapter includes the following:

▶ **Opening objectives list:** This defines the official CompTIA Security+ exam objectives covered in the chapter.

▶ **Cram Saver questions:** Each major section begins with a Cram Saver to help you determine your current level of knowledge of the topics in that section.

▶ **Topical coverage:** The heart of the chapter. Explains the topics from a hands-on and a theory-based standpoint. This includes in-depth descriptions geared to build your knowledge so that you can pass the exam.

▶ **Exam Alerts:** These are interspersed throughout the book. They include important information on test topics. Watch out for them!

> ### Exam**Alert**
>
> This is what an Exam Alert looks like. Normally, an alert stresses concepts, terms, hardware, software, or activities that are likely to relate to one or more certification test questions.

▶ **Cram Quiz questions:** At the end of each topic is a quiz. The quizzes, and ensuing explanations, are meant to gauge your knowledge of the subjects. If the answers to the questions don't come readily to you, consider reviewing the section.

Additional Elements

Beyond the chapters there are a few more elements:

- ▶ **Practice Exams:** There are two practice exams. They are printed in the book and included with the Pearson IT Certification Practice Test Engine on the CD.

- ▶ **Cram Sheet:** The tear-out Cram Sheet is located right in the beginning of the book. This is designed to jam some of the most important facts you need to know for the exam into one small sheet, allowing for easy memorization.

- ▶ **Glossary:** Definitions of key CompTIA Security+ exam terms.

Exam Objectives

Table I-1 lists the skills measured by the SY0-301 exam and the chapter in which the objective is discussed. Some objectives are covered in other chapters, too.

TABLE I-1 **CompTIA SY0-301 Exam Objectives**

Exam Objective	Chapter
Domain 1: Network Security	
Explain the security function and purpose of network	1
Apply and implement secure network administration principles	1
Distinguish and differentiate network design elements and compounds	1
Implement and use common protocols	2
Identify commonly used default network ports	2
Implement wireless network in a secure manner	2
Domain 2: Compliance and Operational Security	
Explain risk-related concepts	3
Carry out appropriate risk-mitigation strategies	3
Execute appropriate incident response procedures	4
Explain the importance of security-related awareness and training	3
Compare and contrast aspects of business continuity	4
Explain the impact and proper use of environmental controls	4
Execute disaster recovery plans and procedures	4
Exemplify the concepts of confidentiality, integrity, and availability (CIA)	3
Domain 3: Threats and Vulnerabilities	
Analyze and differentiate among types of malware	5
Analyze and differentiate among types of attacks	5
Analyze and differentiate among types of social engineering attacks	5

Pearson IT Certification Practice Test Engine and Questions on the CD

The CD in the back of the book includes the Pearson IT Certification Practice Test engine—software that displays and grades a set of exam-realistic multiple-choice questions. Using the Pearson IT Certification Practice Test engine, you can either study by going through the questions in Study Mode or take a simulated exam that mimics real exam conditions.

The installation process requires two major steps: installing the software and then activating the exam. The CD in the back of this book has a recent copy of the Pearson IT Certification Practice Test engine. The practice exam—the database of exam questions—is not on the CD.

> **Note**
>
> The cardboard CD case in the back of this book includes the CD and a piece of paper. The paper lists the activation code for the practice exam associated with this book. Do not lose the activation code. On the opposite side of the paper from the activation code is a unique, one-time use coupon code for the purchase of the Premium Edition eBook and Practice Test.

Install the Software from the CD

The Pearson IT Certification Practice Test is a Windows-only desktop application. You can run it on a Mac using a Windows Virtual Machine, but it was built specifically for the PC platform. The minimum system requirements are the following:

- ▶ Windows XP (SP3), Windows Vista (SP2), or Windows 7

- ▶ Microsoft .NET Framework 4.0 Client

- ▶ Microsoft SQL Server Compact 4.0

- ▶ Pentium class 1GHz processor (or equivalent)

- ▶ 512MB RAM

- ▶ 650MB disc space plus 50MB for each downloaded practice exam

The software installation process is routine compared to other software installation processes. If you have already installed the Pearson IT Certification Practice Test software from another Pearson product, there is no need for you to reinstall the software. Simply launch the software on your desktop and proceed to activate the practice exam from this book by using the activation code included in the CD sleeve.

The following steps outline the installation process:

1. Insert the CD into your PC.

2. The software that automatically runs is the Pearson software to access and use all CD-based features. From the main menu, click the option to **Install the Exam Engine**.

3. Respond to windows prompts as with any typical software installation process.

The installation process gives you the option to activate your exam with the activation code supplied on the paper in the CD sleeve. This process requires that you establish a Pearson website login. You need this login in order to activate the exam, so please do register when prompted. If you already have a Pearson website login, there is no need to register again. Just use your existing login.

Activate and Download the Practice Exam

After the exam engine is installed, you should then activate the exam associated with this book (if you did not do so during the installation process) as follows:

1. Start the Pearson IT Certification Practice Test software from the Windows **Start** menu or from your desktop shortcut icon.

2. To activate and download the exam associated with this book, from the **My Products** or **Tools** tab, select the **Activate** button.

3. At the next screen, enter the Activation Key from the paper inside the cardboard CD holder in the back of the book. Once entered, click the **Activate** button.

4. The activation process will download the practice exam. Click **Next** and then click **Finish.**

After you've completed the activation process, the **My Products** tab should list your new exam. If you do not see the exam, make sure you have selected the **My Products** tab on the menu. At this point, the software and practice exam are ready to use. Simply select the exam and click the **Open Exam** button.

To update a particular exam you have already activated and downloaded, simply select the **Tools** tab and select the **Update Products** button. Updating your exams ensures you have the latest changes and updates to the exam data.

If you want to check for updates to the Pearson Cert Practice Test exam engine software, simply select the **Tools** tab and select the **Update Application** button. This ensures you are running the latest version of the software engine.

Activating Other Exams

The exam software installation process and the registration process only has to happen once. Then, for each new exam, only a few steps are required. For instance, if you buy another new Pearson IT Certification Cert Guide or Cisco Press Official Cert Guide, extract the activation code from the CD sleeve in the back of that book—you don't even need the CD at this point. From there, all you have to do is start the exam engine (if it is not still up and running) and perform steps 2–4 from the previous list.

Premium Edition

In addition to the free practice exams provided with your purchase, you can purchase one additional exam with expanded functionality directly from Pearson IT Certification. The Premium Edition eBook and Practice Test for this title contains an additional full practice exam as well as an eBook (in both PDF and ePub format). In addition, the Premium Edition title also has remediation for each question to the specific part of the eBook that relates to that question.

If you have purchased the print version of this title, you can purchase the Premium Edition at a deep discount. There is a coupon code in the CD sleeve that contains a one-time use code as well as instructions for where you can purchase the Premium Edition.

To view the premium edition product page, go to: http://www.pearsonitcertification.com/store/product.aspx?isbn=0132939592

CHAPTER 1

Network Design

This chapter covers the following official CompTIA Security+, SY0-301 exam objectives:

▶ Explain the security function and purpose of network devices and technologies

▶ Apply and implement secure network administration principles

▶ Distinguish and differentiate network design elements and compounds

(For more information on the official CompTIA Security+, SY0-301 exam topics, see the "About the CompTIA Security+, SY0-301 Exam" section in the Introduction.)

The easiest way to keep a computer safe is by physically isolating it from outside contact. With the way organizations do business today, this is virtually impossible. We have a global economy, and our networks are becoming increasingly more complex. Securing the devices on the network is imperative to protecting the environment. In order to secure those devices, one must know the different functions of each device. To secure devices, you must also understand the basic security concepts of network design.

Although we describe the design elements and components such as firewalls, VLANs, and perimeter network boundaries that distinguish between private networks, intranets, and the Internet, it is also essential to know how to use these components. Network compromises now carry an increased threat with the spread of botnets and malware. This means an entire corporate network can be used for spam relay, phishing systems, and launching distributed denial-of-service (DDoS) attacks. It is important to not only know how to use the proper elements in design, but also how to position and apply these tools to facilitate security. This chapter discusses just that.

Explain the Security Function and Purpose of Network Devices and Technologies

- ▶ Firewalls
- ▶ Routers
- ▶ Switches
- ▶ Load balancers
- ▶ Proxies
- ▶ Web security gateways
- ▶ VPN concentrators
- ▶ NIDS and NIPS (behavior based, signature based, anomaly based, heuristic)
- ▶ Protocol analyzers
- ▶ Sniffers
- ▶ Spam filter, all-in-one security appliances
- ▶ Web application firewall versus network firewall
- ▶ URL filtering, content inspection, malware inspection

Cram**Saver**

If you can correctly answer these questions before going through this section, save time by skimming the Exam Alerts in this section and then completing the Cram Quiz at the end of the section.

1. What purpose does an application–level gateway serve?

2. When an insider threat is detected and you want to implement a solution that monitors the internal network activity as well as incoming external traffic, what two types of devices could you use?

3. Explain the functions that a proxy server can perform.

Answers

1. An application-level gateway understands services and protocols. All traffic is examined to check for OSI application layer (Layer 7) protocols that are allowed. Examples of this type of traffic are File Transfer Protocol (FTP), Simple Mail Transfer Protocol (SMTP), and Hypertext Transfer Protocol (HTTP). Because the filtering is application-specific, it adds overhead to the transmissions but is more secure than packet filtering.

Answers

2. Network-based intrusion-detection systems monitor the packet flow and try to locate packets that are not allowed for one reason or another and might have gotten through the firewall. Host-based intrusion-detection systems monitor communications on a host-by-host basis and try to filter malicious data. These types of IDSs are good at detecting unauthorized file modifications and user activity.

3. Proxy servers can be placed between the private network and the Internet for Internet connectivity or internally for web content caching. If the organization is using the proxy server for both Internet connectivity and web content caching, the proxy server should be placed between the internal network and the Internet, with access for users who are requesting the web content. In some proxy server designs, the proxy server is placed in parallel with IP routers. This allows for network load balancing by forwarding of all HTTP and FTP traffic through the proxy server and all other IP traffic through the router.

Before you can properly secure a network, you must understand the security function and purpose of network devices and technologies. This section introduces security concepts as they apply to the design of physical security devices used to form the protection found on most networks.

Firewalls

A *firewall* is a component placed on computers and networks to help eliminate undesired access by the outside world. It can be composed of hardware, software, or a combination of both. A firewall is the first line of defense for the network. The primary function of a firewall is to mitigate threats by monitoring all traffic entering or leaving a network. How firewalls are configured is important, especially for large companies where a compromised firewall might spell disaster in the form of bad publicity or a lawsuit, not only for the company, but also for the companies it does business with. For smaller companies, a firewall is an excellent investment because most small companies don't have a full-time technology staff and an intrusion could easily put them out of business. All things considered, a firewall is an important part of your defense, but you should not rely on it exclusively for network protection. Figure 1.1 shows a network with a firewall in place.

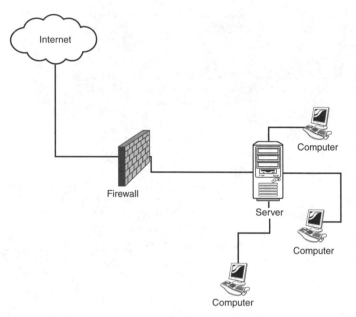

FIGURE 1.1   **A network with a firewall.**

Routers

Routers operate at the Network layer of the OSI model. They are the items that receive information from a host and forward that information to its destination on the network or the Internet. Routers maintain tables that are checked each time a packet needs to be redirected from one interface to another. The tables inside the router help speed up request resolution so packets can reach their destination quicker. The routes may be added manually to the routing table or may be updated automatically using the following protocols:

- ▶ Routing Information Protocol (RIP/RIPv2)

- ▶ Interior Gateway Routing Protocol (IGRP)

- ▶ Enhanced Interior Gateway Routing Protocol (EIGRP)

- ▶ Open Shortest Path First (OSPF)

- ▶ Border Gateway Protocol (BGP)

- ▶ Exterior Gateway Protocol (EGP)

- ▶ Intermediate System–Intermediate System (IS-IS)

Although routers are primarily used to segment traffic, they have some good security features. One of the best features of a router is its ability to filter packets, by source address, destination address, protocol, or port. These filters are referred to as *access control lists (ACLs)*. Routers can also be configured to help prevent IP spoofing by using strong protocol authentication. In IP spoofing, an attacker gains unauthorized access to a network by making it appear that traffic has come from a trusted source by faking the IP address. Keep in mind that no matter how secure the routing protocol of choice is, if you never change the default password on the router, you have left yourself wide open to attacks.

Switches

Switches are the most common choice when it comes to connecting desktops to the wiring closet. Switches operate at the Data Link layer (layer 2) of the OSI model. Their packet-forwarding decisions are based on MAC addresses. They allow LANs to be segmented, thus increasing the amount of bandwidth that goes to each device. Each segment is a separate collision domain, but all segments are in the same broadcast domain. Here are the basic functions of a switch:

▶ Filtering and forwarding frames

▶ Learning Media Access Control (MAC) addresses

▶ Preventing loops

Because most switches are configurable, you can implement sound security with your switches very similarly to configuring security on a firewall or a router. In general, you don't want to deploy switches using their default configuration because many times their default configuration does not provide the most suitable network design. Designing the network the proper way from the start is important to ensure that the network is stable, reliable, and scalable. Physical and virtual security controls must be in place. Place switches in a physically secured area if possible. Be sure that strong authentication and password policies are in place to secure access to the operating system and configuration files.

Load Balancers

Network *load balancers* are servers configured in a cluster to provide scalability and high availability. Load balancing distributes IP traffic to multiple copies of a TCP/IP service, such as a web server, each running on a host within the cluster. This is used for enterprise-wide services, such as Internet sites with high traffic requirements, web, FTP, media streaming, and content delivery networks or hosted applications using thin-client architectures, such as Windows Terminal Services. Network load balancing distributes the workload among multiple servers while providing a mechanism for server availability. From the client's point of view, the cluster appears to be a single server. As enterprise traffic increases, network administrators can simply plug another server into the cluster. In the event of server or application failure, a load balancer can provide automatic failover to ensure continuous availability.

Some load balancers integrate IP load balancing and network intrusion prevention into one appliance. This provides failover capabilities in case of server failure, distribution of traffic across multiple servers, and integrated protection from network intrusions along with optimizing performance for other IP services such as SMTP, DNS, RADIUS, and TFTP. In order to mitigate risks associated with failures of the load balancers themselves, you can deploy two appliances in what is called an active/passive configuration. In this type of configuration, all traffic is sent to the active server. The passive server is promoted to active if the active server fails or is taken down for maintenance.

Proxies

A *proxy server* operates on the same principle as a proxy-level firewall in that it is a go-between for the network and the Internet. Proxy servers are used for security, logging, and caching. When the proxy server receives a request for an Internet service, it passes through filtering requirements and checks its local cache for previously downloaded web pages. Because web pages are stored locally, response times for web pages are faster, and traffic to the Internet is substantially reduced. The web cache can also be used to block content from websites that you don't want employees to access, such as pornography, social, or peer-to-peer networks. This type of server can be used to rearrange web content to work for mobile devices. It also provides better utilization of bandwidth because it stores all your results from requests for a period of time.

ExamAlert

An exposed server that provides public access to a critical service, such as a proxy, web, or email server, may be configured to isolate it from an organization's internal network and to report attack attempts to the network administrator. Such an isolated server is referred to as a *bastion host*, named for the isolated towers that were used to provide castles advanced notice of pending assault.

Proxy servers are used for a variety of reasons, so the placement depends on the usage. You can place proxy servers between the private network and the Internet for Internet connectivity or internally for web content caching. If the organization is using the proxy server for both Internet connectivity and web content caching, you should place the proxy server between the internal network and the Internet with access for users who are requesting the web content. In some proxy server designs, the proxy server is placed in parallel with IP routers. This design allows for network load balancing by forwarding of all HTTP and FTP traffic through the proxy server and all other IP traffic through the router.

Every proxy server in your network must have at least one network interface. Proxy servers with a single network interface can provide web content caching and IP gateway services. To provide Internet connectivity, you must specify two or more network interfaces for the proxy server.

Web Security Gateways

With the advent of Web 2.0, social-networking sites, video-sharing sites, wikis, and blogs became popular. Web 2.0 enables users to interact with other users. Although this interactivity might have increased collaboration, it can cause losses in productivity, vulnerabilities to data leaks, and inherent increased security risks.

A *web security gateway* offers a single point of policy control and management for web-based content access. A web security gateway can be either software or hardware and is most often marketed as an appliance. Web security gateways can provide URL filtering, web traffic malware detection, and application control. Managed web security gateway services are another option. Gateways can offer a scalable platform that enables organizations to maintain critical up-time when an attack happens. The advantages of using a web security gateway include protection across multiple protocols for inbound and outbound web traffic, the ability to detect botnets, broad web reporting and alerting, and the ability to monitor and control web application usage by end users.

VPN Concentrators

In the world of a mobile workforce, employers require a secure method for employees to access corporate resources while on the road or working from home. One of the most common methods implemented for this type of access is a VPN (virtual private network). A *VPN concentrator* is used to allow multiple external users to access internal network resources using secure features that are built into the device and are deployed where the requirement is for a single device to handle a very large number of VPN tunnels. Remote Access VPN connectivity is provided using either IPsec (Internet Protocol Security) or SSL for the VPN. User authentication can be via RADIUS, Kerberos, MS Active Directory, RSA SDI, digital certificates, or the built-in authentication server. The function and purpose of authentication services is covered in detail in Chapter 10, "Authentication and Authorization."

A typical scenario is where the VPN concentrator allows users to utilize an encrypted tunnel to securely access a corporate or other network via the Internet. Another use is internally, to encrypt WLAN or wired traffic, where there is concern about protecting the security of login and password information for high-level user and sensitive information. You can implement a VPN concentrator to prevent login and password information from being captured. It also allows ACLs to be applied to remote user sessions.

VPN concentrators come in various models that can be used for the numbers of simultaneous users, amount of throughput needed, and amount of protection required. For example, Cisco VPN concentrators include components, called Scalable Encryption Processing (SEP) modules, that allow for increased capacity and throughput.

NIDS and NIPS (Behavior Based, Signature Based, Anomaly Based, Heuristic)

IDS stands for *intrusion-detection system*. Intrusion-detection systems are designed to analyze data, identify attacks, and respond to the intrusion. They are different from firewalls in that firewalls control the information that gets in and out of the network, whereas IDSs can identify unauthorized activity. IDSs are also designed to catch attacks in progress within the network, not just on the boundary between private and public networks.

NIDS and HIDS

The two basic types of IDSs are *network-based* and *host-based*. As the names suggest, network-based IDSs (NIDSs) look at the information exchanged between machines, and host-based IDSs (HIDSs) look at information that originates on the individual machines. Here are some basics:

- ▶ NIDSs monitor the packet flow and try to locate packets that might have gotten through the firewall and are not allowed for one reason or another. They are best at detecting DoS attacks and unauthorized user access.

▶ HIDSs monitor communications on a host-by-host basis and try to filter malicious data. These types of IDSs are good at detecting unauthorized file modifications and user activity.

> ### ExamAlert
>
> NIDSs try to locate packets not allowed on the network that the firewall missed. HIDSs collect and analyze data that originates on the local machine or a computer hosting a service. NIDSs tend to be more distributed.

You should use NIDSs and HIDSs together to ensure a truly secure environment. IDSs can be located anywhere on the network. You can place them internally or between firewalls. Many different types of IDSs are available, all with different capabilities, so make sure they meet the needs of your company before committing to using them.

Network Intrusion Prevention System

Network intrusion-prevention systems (*NIPSs*) are sometimes considered to be an extension of IDSs. NIPSs can be either hardware or software based, like many other network-protection devices. Intrusion prevention differs from intrusion detection in that it actually prevents attacks instead of only detecting the occurrence of an attack. Intrusion-detection software is reactive—scanning for configuration weaknesses and detecting attacks after they occur. By the time an alert has been issued, the attack has usually occurred and has damaged the network or desktop. NIPSs are designed to sit inline with traffic flows and prevent attacks in real time. An inline NIPS works like a Layer 2 bridge. It sits between the systems that need to be protected and the rest of the network. They proactively protect machines against damage from attacks that signature-based technologies cannot detect because most NIPS solutions can look at application layer protocols such HTTP, FTP, and SMTP.

When implementing a NIPS, keep in mind that the sensors must be physically inline to function properly. This adds single points of failure to the network. A good way to prevent this issue is to use fail-open technology. This means that if the device fails, it doesn't cause a complete network outage; instead, it acts like a patch cable.

Host Intrusion Prevention System

Host Intrusion Prevention System (*HIPS*) are a necessity in any enterprise environment. HIPSs protect hosts against known and unknown malicious attacks from the network layer up through the application layer. HIPS technologies can be categorized by what they scan for, how they recognize for an attack, and at what layer they attempt to detect the attack. HIPSs encompass many technologies to protect servers, desktops, and laptops. They are often used as an all-in-one solution that includes everything from traditional signature-based antivirus to behavior analysis.

Protocol Analyzers

Protocol analyzers help you troubleshoot network issues by gathering packet-level information across the network. These applications capture packets and can conduct protocol decoding, putting the information into readable data for analysis. Protocol analyzers can do more than just look at packets. They prove useful in many other areas of network management, such as monitoring the network for unexpected, unwanted, and unnecessary traffic. For example, if the network is running slowly, a protocol analyzer can tell you whether unnecessary protocols are running on the network. You can also filter specific port numbers and types of traffic so that you can keep an eye on indicators that might cause you problems. Many protocol analyzers can be run on multiple platforms and do live traffic captures and offline analysis. Software USB protocol analyzers are also available for the development of USB devices and analysis of USB traffic.

You can place protocol analyzers inline or in between the devices from which you want to capture the traffic. If you are analyzing SAN (storage area network) traffic, you can place the analyzer outside the direct link with the use of an optical splitter. The analyzer is placed to capture traffic between the host and the monitored device.

Sniffers

Sniffer is a registered trademark of NAI (Network Associates) Packet capture. A packet sniffer is similar to a protocol analyzer. In the strictest sense, sniffers are used to capture traffic whereas protocol analyzers are used for protocol analysis. So the capture happens first and the analysis occurs afterward. For example, Snort, an open source network intrusion prevention and detection system (IDS/IPS), has many different modules. By itself, it can capture packets but the analysis part happens when the IDSCenter is added to it. A packet sniffer simply captures all of the packets of data that pass through a given network interface. Typically, the packet sniffer would only capture packets that were intended for the machine unless the application is used in promiscuous mode. By placing a packet sniffer on a network in promiscuous mode, all of the network traffic can be captured and analyzed. Another possible distinction is that protocol analyzers tend to be stateful and are typically able to use information from one packet to analyze another that is part of the same context whereas packet sniffers typically analyze each packet in isolation.

Spam Filter, All-in-one Security Appliances

Based on a Symantec study, *InformationWeek* reported that, as of July 2010, spam made up 92% of all email messages. This has become an enormous problem for corporations. Vendors have responded by offering all-in-one security appliances that contain spam-filtering functions and can also provide antivirus protection. For example, the Barracuda Spam & Virus Firewall has antivirus protection as a built-in feature along with spam filtering. Updates are posted hourly to ensure the latest virus definitions are in place. Messages are checked when they arrive and directed to the user's mailbox or quarantined based on a score value. In addition to the keyword scanning methods that include scoring systems for emails based on multiple criteria, all-in-one spam filter appliances allow for checksum technology that tracks the number of times a particular message has appeared, and message authenticity checking which uses multiple algorithms to verify authenticity of a message. Additionally, the appliance performs file type attachment blocking and scanning using the built-in antivirus protection. As with any all-in-one appliance, it is a single point of failure. In order to maintain availability, organizations might need to have two units deployed in automatic failover mode.

Web Application Firewall versus Network Firewall

The main objective for the placement of network firewalls is to allow only traffic that the organization deems necessary and provide notification of suspicious behavior. Most organizations deploy, at a minimum, two firewalls. The first firewall is placed in front of the *demilitarized zone* (*DMZ*) to allow requests destined for servers in the DMZ or to route requests to an authentication proxy. The second firewall is placed between the DMZ and the internal network to allow outbound requests. All initial necessary connections are located on the DMZ machines. For example, a RADIUS server might be running in the DMZ for improved performance and enhanced security, even though its database resides inside the company intranet. DMZ is covered in more detail later in this chapter and RADIUS is covered in Chapter 10. Most organizations have many firewalls with the level of protection at its strongest where it's closest to the outside edge of the environment. Figure 1.2 shows an example.

ExamAlert

Watch for scenarios that ask you to select the proper firewall placement based on organizational need.

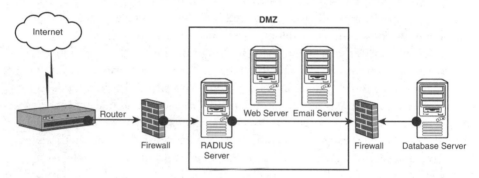

FIGURE 1.2   **A network with two firewalls.**

When deploying multiple firewalls, you might experience network latency. If you do, check the placement of the firewalls and possibly reconsider the topology to be sure you get the most out of the firewalls. Another factor to think about is the use of a SAN or network-area storage (NAS) behind a firewall. Because most storage environments span multiple networks, this creates a virtual bridge that can counteract a firewall, providing a channel into the storage environment if a system is compromised in the DMZ.

In response to the onslaught of web-based attacks, many organizations have implemented a web application firewall in addition to network firewalls. Put simply, a web application firewall is software or a hardware appliance used to protect the organization's web server from attack. A web application firewall can be an appliance, server plug-in, or filter that is used specifically for preventing execution of common web-based attacks such as Cross-site Scripting (XSS) and SQL Injection on a web server. These and other attack methods are covered in Chapter 5, "Attacks." Web application firewalls can be either signature based or anomaly based. This means some look for particular attack signatures to try to identify an attack whereas others look for abnormal behavior outside the website's normal traffic patterns. The device sits between a web client and a web server and analyzes communication at the application layer, much like a network stateful-inspection firewall. Web application firewalls are placed in front of a web server in an effort to try and shield it from incoming attacks. Web application firewalls are sometimes referred to as *deep packet inspection firewalls* due to their ability to look at every request and response within Web Service layers.

URL Filtering, Content Inspection, Malware Inspection

Spyware, malware, worms, and viruses pose a serious threat to both system integrity and user privacy. The prevalence of such malicious programs could also threaten the stability of critical systems and networks. Internet content filters use a collection of terms, words, and phrases that are compared to content from browsers and applications. This type of software can filter content from various types of Internet activity and applications, such as instant messaging, email, and office documents. Content filtering will report only on violations identified in the specified applications listed for the filtering application. In other words, if the application filters only Microsoft Office documents and a user chooses to use Office, the content are not filtered. Internet content filtering works by analyzing data against a database contained in the software. If a match occurs, the data can be addressed in one of several ways, including filtering, capturing, or blocking the content and closing the application. An example of such software is Vista's Parental Controls.

A malware inspection filter is basically a web filter applied to traffic that uses the HTTP protocol. The body of all HTTP requests and responses is inspected. Malicious content is blocked, and legitimate content passes through unaltered. Passing files may be hashed and matched against the signatures stored in a malware signature database. Other approaches include caching files for running a heuristic scan later within the file cache. If a file within the file cache is found to be malicious by the heuristic scan, the signature is inserted in the malware signature database so that it can be blocked in the future. The context for malware inspection is scanning downloaded content allowed by web access rules to inspect web pages and files downloaded over HTTP from external websites.

Internet content filters can be hardware or software. Many network solutions combine both. Hardware appliances are usually connected to the same network segment as the users they monitor. Other configurations include being deployed behind a firewall or in a DMZ with public addresses behind a packet-filtering router. These appliances use access control filtering software on the dedicated filtering appliance. The device monitors every packet of traffic that passes over a network. Unlike antivirus and antispyware applications, content monitoring does not require daily updates to keep the database effective and current. On the downside, content filtering needs to be "trained." For example, to filter non-pornographic material, the terminology must be input and defined in the database.

Cram Quiz

Answer these questions. The answers follow the last question. If you cannot answer these questions correctly, consider reading this section again until you can.

1. You want to implement a solution that offers a single point of policy control and management for web-based content access. Which of the following devices would best fit this requirement?

   ○ **A.** Proxy gateway

   ○ **B.** Web security gateway

   ○ **C.** Application-level gateway

   ○ **D.** URL filtering

2. You have recently had some security breaches in the network. You suspect the cause might be a small group of employees. You want to implement a solution that monitors the internal network activity and incoming external traffic. Which of the following devices would you use? (Choose two correct answers.)

   ○ **A.** A router

   ○ **B.** A network-based IDS

   ○ **C.** A firewall

   ○ **D.** A host-based IDS

3. Which of the following are uses for proxy servers? (Choose all correct answers.)

   ○ **A.** Intrusion detection

   ○ **B.** Internet connectivity

   ○ **C.** Load balancing

   ○ **D.** Web content caching

Cram Quiz Answers

1. B. A Web security gateway offers a single point of policy control and management for web-based content access. Answer A is too generic to be a proper answer. Answer C is incorrect because, although an application-level gateway understands services and protocols, the requirement is specifically for web-based content. Answer D is incorrect because content filtering reports only on violations identified in the specified applications listed for the filtering application.

2. B, D. Because you want to monitor both types of traffic, the IDSs should be used together. Network-based intrusion-detection systems monitor the packet flow and try to locate packets that are not allowed for one reason or another and might have gotten through the firewall. Host-based intrusion-detection systems monitor communications on a host-by-host basis and try to filter malicious data. These types of IDSs are good at detecting unauthorized file modifications and user activity. Answer A is incorrect because a router forwards information to its destination on the network or the Internet. A firewall protects computers and networks from undesired access by the outside world; therefore, Answer C is incorrect.

3. B, C, and D. You can place proxy servers between the private network and the Internet for Internet connectivity or internally for web content caching. If the organization is using the proxy server for both Internet connectivity and web content caching, you should place the proxy server between the internal network and the Internet, with access for users who are requesting the Web content. In some proxy server designs, the proxy server is placed in parallel with IP routers. This allows for network load balancing by forwarding of all HTTP and FTP traffic through the proxy server and all other IP traffic through the router. Answer A is incorrect because proxy servers are not used for intrusion detection.

Apply and Implement Secure Network Administration Principles

▶ Rule-based management

▶ Firewall rules

▶ VLAN management

▶ Secure router configuration

▶ Access control lists

▶ Port security

▶ 802.1X

▶ Flood guards

▶ Loop protection

▶ Implicit deny

▶ Prevent network bridging by network separation

▶ Log analysis

CramSaver

If you can correctly answer these questions before going through this section, save time by skimming the Exam Alerts in this section and then completing the Cram Quiz at the end of the section.

1. What is the purpose of loop protection?

2. Explain implicit deny.

3. Explain the principle behind network bridging.

Answers

1. The loop guard feature makes additional checks in Layer 2 switched networks. If BPDUs are not received on a non-designated port and loop guard is enabled, that port is moved into the STP loop-inconsistent blocking state, instead of the listening/learning/forwarding state. Without the loop guard feature, the port assumes the designated port role.

2. *Implicit deny* is an access control practice wherein resource availability is restricted to only those logons explicitly granted access, remaining unavailable even when not explicitly denied access.

3. With interconnected networks, the potential for damage greatly increases because one compromised system on one network can easily spread to other networks. Networks that are shared by partners, vendors, or departments should have clear separation boundaries.

Network security goes beyond just knowing the risks and vulnerabilities. To mitigate threats and risks, you must also know how to assess your environment and protect it. This section discusses how to implement security applications to help mitigate risk and how to use security groups, roles, rights, and permissions in accordance with industry best practices.

Rule-based Management

Rule-Based Access Control is based on ACLs. The basis of this type of access is to determine what can happen to an object based on a set of rules. The most common use of this is on routers and firewalls. Access is determined by looking at a request to see whether it matches a predefined set of conditions. An example would be if you configured your router to deny any IP addresses from the 10.10.0.0 subnet and allow addresses from the 192.168.10.0 network. When a machine with an address of 192.168.10.15 requests access, the router looks at the rules and accepts the request. In Rule-Based Access Control, the administrator sets the rules. This is considered a type of mandatory control because the users cannot change these rules. In other words, if the administrator sets the aforementioned router conditions, you, as a user, cannot have the router accept requests from a 10.10.0.25 address.

> **ExamAlert**
>
> Rule-Based Access Control is based on a predefined set of rules that determines the object's access.

In a Rule-Based Access Control solution, accounts may be granted varying levels of access, such as Read, Write, or Execute. An example of this would be setting the filtering of IP packets on a proxy server or firewall. Say you want to keep the production staff from downloading BMP files, but you want to allow the development staff to do so. Before you allow any file to be downloaded, you check conditions such as the file type and the access list configuration. Remember that the most common form of Rule-Based Access Control involves testing against an ACL that details systems and accounts with access rights and the limits of their access for the resources. In addition to firewalls and routers, ACLs are used in operating systems.

Firewall Rules

Firewall rules are configured to allow traffic associated with programs or services to be sent or received. A firewall rule set is similar to an ACL in that the rules determine parameters for each connection based on a set of conditions. Firewall rules specify what services are allowed or not allowed through the firewall. Rules consist of a source address, a destination address, a service, and an associated action. For example, a firewall rule to allow FTP traffic might look like this:

```
ipfw add allow tcp from any to any 21 keep-state
```

You can also specify the type of network adapter the rule is applied to, such as local area network (LAN), wireless, or remote access.

Generally speaking, you can create firewall rules to take one of three actions for all connections that match the rule's criteria. These actions are allow the connection, allow the connection if it is secured, or block the connection. Rules can be created for either inbound traffic or outbound traffic. Inbound rules explicitly allow, or explicitly block, inbound network traffic that matches the criteria in the rule. Outbound rules explicitly allow, or explicitly block, network traffic originating from the computer that matches the criteria in the rule.

In many firewalls the rules can be granulized and configured to specify the computers or users, program, service, or port and protocol. Rules can be configured to be applied when profiles are used. As soon as a network packet matches a rule, that rule is applied and processing stops. The more restrictive rules should be listed first, and the least restrictive rules should follow. Otherwise, if a less restrictive rule is placed before a more restrictive rule, the checking is stopped at the first rule.

VLAN Management

VLANs provide a way to limit broadcast traffic in a switched network. This creates a boundary and, in essence, creates multiple, isolated LANs on one switch. VLANs are a logical separation of a physical network. Ideally, limit a VLAN to one access switch or switch stack. However, it might be necessary to extend a VLAN across multiple access switches within a switch block to support a capability such as wireless mobility. In this situation, if you are using multiple switches from various vendors to be connected, some switch features might only be supported on one vendor's switches while other vendors' switches do not. There are things to consider such as VTP Domain management and inter-VLAN routing when there are two or more switches in the network.

There are various configurations and considerations when working with VLANs. For example, when mapping VLANs onto a new hierarchical network design, check the subnetting scheme that has been applied to the network and associate a VLAN to each subnet. By allocating IP address spaces in contiguous blocks, it allows each switch block to be summarized into one large address block. Additionally, different types of traffic may exist on the network, and that should be considered before device placement and VLAN configuration.

VLAN Trunk Protocol (VTP) reduces administration in a switched network. One way of setting up the network is to have all switches in the same VTP Domain. This reduces the need to configure the same VLAN everywhere. VTP is a Cisco-proprietary protocol. Another option for VLAN management in a Cisco environment is the use of a VLAN Management Policy Server (VMPS). This is a network switch that contains a mapping of device information to VLAN.

Secure Router Configuration

Because routers are the lifeblood of the network, it is important that they are properly secured. The security that is configured when setting up and managing routers can make the difference between keeping data secure and providing an open invitation to hackers. You can find what is perhaps the most useful information on router security in the NSA/SNAC Router Security Configuration Guide version 1.1 located at http://www.nsa.gov/ia/guidance/security_configuration_guides/cisco_router_guides.shtml. The following are general recommendations for router security:

▶ Create and maintain a written router security policy. The policy should identify who is allowed to log in to the router, who is allowed to configure and update it, and outline the logging and management practices for it.

▶ Comment and organize offline master editions of your router configuration files. Keep the offline copies of all router configurations in sync with the actual configurations running on the routers.

▶ Implement access lists that allow only those protocols, ports, and IP addresses that are required by network users and services and that deny everything else.

▶ Test the security of your routers regularly, especially after any major configuration changes.

A router that is too tightly locked down can turn a functional network into a completely isolated network that does not allow access to anyone.

Access Control Lists

Access control generally refers to the process of making resources available to accounts that should have access, while limiting that access to only what is required. In its broadest sense, an ACL is the underlying data associated with a network resource that defines the access permissions. The most common privileges are read, write to, delete, and execute a file. ACLs can apply to routers and other devices. In Microsoft operating systems, each ACL has one or more access control entries (ACEs). The access privileges are stated in a string of bits called an *access mask*. Generally, the object owner or the system administrator creates the ACL for an object.

Port Security

Port security is a Layer 2 traffic control feature on Cisco Catalyst switches. It enables individual switch ports to be configured to allow only a specified number of source MAC addresses coming in through the port. Its primary use is to keep two or three users from sharing a single access port. You can use the port security feature to restrict input to an interface by limiting and identifying MAC addresses of the workstations that are allowed to access the port. When you assign secure MAC addresses to a secure port, the port does not forward packets with source addresses outside the group of defined addresses. If you limit the number of secure MAC addresses to one and assign a single secure MAC address, the workstation attached to that port is assured the full bandwidth of the port. By default, a port security violation forces the interface into the error-disabled state. Port security can be configured to take one of three actions upon detecting a violation. In addition to the default shutdown, protect and restrict modes can be set. In protect mode, frames from MAC addresses other than the allowed addresses are dropped and restrict is similar to protect mode but generates a syslog message and increases the violation counter.

> **ExamAlert**
>
> Although a deterrent, port security is not a reliable security feature. MAC addresses can be spoofed, and multiple hosts can still easily be hidden behind a small router.

802.1X

The IEEE 802.1X standard passes Extensible Authentication Protocol (EAP) over a wired or wireless LAN. It is used for access control, providing the capability to permit or deny network connectivity, control VLAN access and apply traffic policy, based on user or machine identity. 802.1X, ideal for wireless access points and the authentication process, helps mitigate many of the risks involved in using WEP. 802.1X keeps the network port disconnected until authentication is completed. If authentication is successful, the port is made available to the user; otherwise, the user is denied access to the network. The communication process is as follows:

▶ The authenticator sends an EAP-Request/Identity packet to the supplicant when it detects the active link.

▶ The supplicant sends an EAP-Response/Identity packet to the authenticator, which is then passed on to the authentication (RADIUS) server.

▶ The authenticator sends an EAP-Request/EAP-Packet packet of the desired authentication type.

▶ The supplicant responds to the challenge via the authenticator and passes the response onto the authentication server.

Flood Guards

Flood Guard is most commonly associated with the Cisco PIX Firewall. It is an advanced firewall guard feature used to control network activity associated with DoS attacks. Flood guard controls how the authentication, accounting, and authorization (AAA) service handles bad login attempts that are tying up connections. It allows the PIX Firewall resources to automatically be reclaimed if the authentication subsystem runs out of resources, thereby defeating DoS attacks. The PIX actively reclaims TCP user resources when an inbound or outbound authorization connection is being attacked. The floodguard command is enabled by default.

In addition to the flood guard feature in PIX firewalls, there is a name brand device called FloodGuard. This is a distributed software application combined with a network appliance used for detecting and blocking DDoS attacks in an enterprise data center or a service provider's network.

Loop Protection

A major feature in Layer 2 managed switches is the spanning tree protocol (STP). STP is a link management protocol that provides path redundancy while preventing undesirable loops in the network. Multiple active paths between stations cause loops in the network. When loops occur, some switches see stations that appear on both sides of the switch. This condition confuses the forwarding algorithm and allows duplicate frames to be forwarded.

A bridge loop occurs when data units can travel from a first LAN segment to a second LAN segment through more than one path. In order to eliminate bridge loops, existing bridge devices typically employ a technique referred to as the *spanning tree algorithm*. The spanning tree algorithm is implemented by bridges interchanging special messages known as Bridge Protocol Data Units (BPDUs). The STP loop guard feature provides additional protection against STP loops. An STP loop is created when an STP blocking port in a redundant topology erroneously transitions to the forwarding state. This usually happens because one of the ports of a physically redundant topology no longer receives STP BPDUs. In its operation, STP relies on continuous reception or transmission of BPDUs based on the port role. The loop guard feature makes additional checks. If BPDUs are not received on a non-designated port and loop guard is enabled, that port is moved into the STP loop-inconsistent blocking state, instead of the listening/learning/forwarding state. Without the loop guard feature, the port assumes the designated port role. The port moves to the STP forwarding state and creates a loop.

Implicit Deny

Implicit deny is an access control practice wherein resource availability is restricted to only those logons explicitly granted access, remaining unavailable even when not explicitly denied access. This practice is used commonly in Cisco networks, where most ACLs have a default setting of "implicit deny." By default, there is an implicit deny all clause at the end of every ACL. Anything that is not explicitly permitted is denied. Essentially, an implicit deny is the same as finishing the ACL with `deny ip any any`. This ensures that when access is not explicitly granted, it is automatically denied by default.

Prevent Network Bridging by Network Separation

Besides securing ports and protocols from outside attacks, you should secure connections between interconnecting networks. This situation might come into play when an organization establishes network interconnections with partners as in an extranet or an actual connection between the involved organizations because of a merger, acquisition, or joint project. Business partners can include government agencies and commercial organizations. Although this type of interconnection increases functionality and reduces costs, it can result in security risks. These risks include compromise of all connected systems and any network connected to those systems, along with exposure of data the systems handle. With interconnected networks, the potential for damage greatly

increases because one compromised system on one network can easily spread to other networks. Networks that are shared by partners, vendors, or departments should have clear separation boundaries.

Log Analysis

Logging is the process of collecting data to be used for monitoring and auditing purposes. The log files themselves are documentation, but how do you set up a log properly? You should develop standards for each platform, application, and server type to make this a checklist or monitoring function. When choosing what to log, be sure you choose carefully. Logs take up disk space and use system resources. They also have to be read; if you log too much, the system bogs down, and it takes a long time to weed through the log files to determine what is important. You should mandate a common storage location for all logs, and documentation should state proper methods for archiving and reviewing logs.

All devices, operating systems, and applications have log files. For example, application log files contain error messages, operational data, and usage information that can help manage applications and servers. Analysis of web application logs enables you to understand who visited the application, on what pages, and how often, and it also provides information on errors and performance problems of the web application. Analyzing logs from web servers such as Apache, IIS, ISA, Tomcat, and others is automatic and can contribute important insight into website and web application quality and availability. Web server logs are usually access logs, common error logs, custom logs, and W3C logs. W3C logs are used mainly by web servers to log web-related events including web logs.

Cram Quiz

Answer these questions. The answers follow the last question. If you cannot answer these questions correctly, consider reading this section again until you can.

1. Which of the following is a switch feature that makes additional checks in Layer 2 networks to prevent STP issues?

   ○ **A.** Loop protection

   ○ **B.** Flood guard

   ○ **C.** Implicit deny

   ○ **D.** Port security

2. Which of the following is an access control practice to limit resource availability to only specific traffic?

   ○ **A.** Loop protection

   ○ **B.** Flood guard

   ○ **C.** Implicit deny

   ○ **D.** Port security

3. You are implementing network access to a new business partner that will work with the development team on a new product. Which of the following would best mitigate risk associated with allowing this new partner access to the network?

   ○ **A.** Log analysis

   ○ **B.** ACLs

   ○ **C.** Network segmentation

   ○ **D.** VPN implementation

Cram Quiz Answers

1. A. The loop guard feature makes additional checks in Layer 2 switched networks. Answer B is incorrect because a flood guard is a firewall feature to control network activity associated with DoS attacks. Answer C is incorrect because implicit deny is an access control practice wherein resource availability is restricted to only those logons explicitly granted access. Answer D is incorrect because port security is a Layer 2 traffic control feature on Cisco Catalyst switches. It enables individual switch ports to be configured to allow only a specified number of source MAC addresses coming in through the port.

2. C. Implicit deny is an access control practice wherein resource availability is restricted to only those logons explicitly granted access. Answer A is incorrect because the loop guard feature makes additional checks in Layer 2 switched networks. Answer B is incorrect because a flood guard is a firewall feature to control network activity associated with DoS attacks. Answer D is incorrect because port security is a layer 2 traffic control feature on Cisco Catalyst switches. It enables individual switch ports to be configured to allow only a specified number of source MAC addresses coming in through the port.

3. C. With interconnected networks, the potential for damage greatly increases because one compromised system on one network can easily spread to other networks. Networks that are shared by partners, vendors, or departments should have clear separation boundaries. Answer A is incorrect because logging is the process of collecting data to be used for monitoring and auditing purposes. Answer B is incorrect because access control generally refers to the process of making resources available to accounts that should have access, while limiting that access to only what is required. Answer D is incorrect because implementing a VPN does not separate the networks.

Distinguish and Differentiate Network Design Elements and Compounds

- ▶ DMZ
- ▶ Subnetting
- ▶ VLAN
- ▶ NAT
- ▶ Remote Access

- ▶ Telephony
- ▶ NAC
- ▶ Virtualization
- ▶ Cloud Computing

Cram**Saver**

If you can correctly answer these questions before going through this section, save time by skimming the Exam Alerts in this section and then completing the Cram Quiz at the end of the section.

1. You are setting up a switched network and want to group users by department. Which network design element would you implement?

2. You are setting up a web server that needs to be accessed by both the employees and by external customers. What type of architecture should you implement?

3. You are the administrator of a small organization with 50 users. Which internal address range and subnet mask should you use on the network?

Answers

1. The purpose of a VLAN is to unite network nodes logically into the same broadcast domain regardless of their physical attachment to the network. VLANs provide a way to limit broadcast traffic in a switched network. This creates a boundary and, in essence, creates multiple, isolated LANs on one switch, allowing the users to be grouped by department. Because switches operate on Layer 2 (data link layer) of the OSI model, a router is required if data is to be passed from one VLAN to another.

2. The DMZ is an area that allows external users to access information that the organization deems necessary but will not compromise any internal organizational information. This configuration allows outside access yet prevents external users from directly accessing a server that holds internal organizational data.

3. Class C addresses are network addresses with the first byte between 192 and 223 and can have about 250 hosts. The non-routable internal address range for a Class C network is from 192.168.1.1 to 192.168.1.254. The default subnet mask for a Class C address is 255.255.255.0.

As you create a network security policy, you must define procedures to defend your network and users against harm and loss. With this objective in mind, a network design and the included components play an important role in implementing the overall security of the organization.

An overall security solution includes design elements and components such as firewalls, VLANs, and perimeter network boundaries that distinguish between private networks, intranets, and the Internet. This section discusses these elements and helps you tell them apart and understand their function in the security of the network.

DMZ

A *demilitarized zone (DMZ)* is a small network between the internal network and the Internet that provides a layer of security and privacy. Both internal and external users may have limited access to the servers in the DMZ. Figure 1.3 depicts a DMZ.

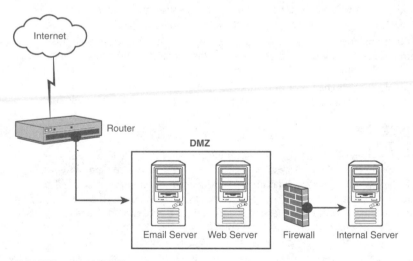

FIGURE 1.3   **A DMZ.**

Often, web and mail servers are placed in the DMZ. Because these devices are exposed to the Internet, it is important that they are hardened and patches are kept current. Table 1.1 lists the most common services and ports that are run on servers inside the DMZ.

TABLE 1.1 **Commonly Used Ports on Servers in the DMZ**

Port	Service
21	FTP
22	SSH
25	SMTP
53	DNS
80	HTTP
110	POP3
443	HTTPS

The DMZ is an area that allows external users to access information that the organization deems necessary but will not compromise any internal organizational information. This configuration allows outside access, yet prevents external users from directly accessing a server that holds internal organizational data.

Intranet

An *intranet* is a portion of the internal network that uses web-based technologies. The information is stored on web servers and accessed using browsers. Although web servers are used, they don't necessarily have to be accessible to the outside world. This is possible because the IP addresses of the servers are reserved for private, internal use. You learn more about private IP addresses in the "NAT" section later in this chapter. If the intranet can be accessed from public networks, it should be through a virtual private network (VPN) for security reasons. VPNs and VPN concentrators were discussed earlier in this chapter.

Extranet

An *extranet* is the public portion of the company's IT infrastructure that allows resources to be used by authorized partners and resellers that have proper authorization and authentication. This type of arrangement is commonly used for business-to-business relationships. Because an extranet can provide liability for a company, care must be taken to ensure that VPNs and firewalls are configured properly and that security policies are strictly enforced.

Subnetting

Subnetting can be done for several reasons. If you have an IPv4 Class C address and 1,000 clients, you will have to subnet the network or use a custom subnet mask to accommodate all the hosts. The most common reason networks are subnetted is to control network traffic. Splitting one network into two or more and using routers to connect each subnet together means that broadcasts can be limited to each subnet. However, often networks are subnetted to improve network security, not just performance. Subnetting allows you to arrange hosts into the different logical groups that isolate each subnet into its own mini network. Subnet divisions can be based on business goals and security policy objectives. For example, perhaps you use contract workers and want to keep them separated from the organizational employees. Often, organizations with branches use subnets to keep each branch separate. When your computers are on separate physical networks, you can divide your network into subnets that enable you to use one block of addresses on multiple physical networks. If an incident happens and you notice it quickly, you can usually contain the issue to that particular subnet.

When subnetting for IPv4 is done, an IP address usually originates from one of the IP address classes and default subnet masks listed in Table 1.2.

TABLE 1.2 **IPv4 Address Class, IP Range, and Default Subnet Mask**

Address Class	IP Address Range	Default Subnet Mask
Class A	0.0.0.0 to 126.255.255.255	255.0.0.0
Class B	128.0.0.0 to 191.255.255.255	255.255.0.0
Class C	192.0.0.0 to 223.255.255.255	255.255.255.0

Notice that the 127 network address is missing. Although the 127.0.0.0 network is in technically in the Class A area, using addresses in this range causes the protocol software to return data without sending traffic across a network. For example, the address 127.0.0.1 is used for TCP/IPv4 loopback testing, and the address 127.0.0.2 is used by most DNS black lists for testing purposes.

In order to denote the network prefix for the subnet mask, the number of bits in the prefix is appended to the address with a slash (/) separator. This type of notation is called Classless Inter-Domain Routing (CIDR). Here is an example: A Class C internal address of 192.168.0.0 with a subnet mask of 255.255.255.0 is written as 192.168.0.0/24.

IPv6 is designed to replace IPv4. Addresses are 128 bits rather than the 32 bits used in IPv4. IPv6 addresses are represented in hexadecimal. In IPv6, subnets uses IPv6 addresses with 64 bits for the host portion. These addresses can be further subnetted just as in IPv4. IPv6 is based on the concepts of variable length subnet masking (VLSM) and (CIDR). A Variable Length Subnet Mask (VLSM) allocates IP addresses to subnets based on individual need rather than a general network-wide rule. An example of CIDR notation for IPv6 would be 2001:db8::/32 designating the address 2001:db8:: with a network prefix consisting of the most significant 32 bits. For more information about IPv6, visit http://ipv6.com/.

Should you need additional review on IP addressing and subnetting, a wide variety of information is available. One such website is Learntosubnet.com. Figure 1.4 shows an internal network with two different subnets. Notice the IP addresses, subnet masks, and default gateway.

ExamAlert

Watch for scenarios or examples such as Figure 1.4 asking you to identify a correct/incorrect subnet mask, default gateway address, or router.

IP address: 192.168.1.15
Subnet mask: 255.255.255.0
Default Gateway: 192.168.1.1

IP address: 192.168.2.15
Subnet mask: 255.255.255.0
Default Gateway: 192.168.2.1

Subnet
192.168.1.0

Subnet
192.168.2.0

IP address: 192.168.1.25
Subnet mask: 255.255.255.0
Default Gateway: 192.168.1.1

IP address: 192.168.2.25
Subnet mask: 255.255.255.0
Default Gateway: 192.168.2.1

FIGURE 1.4   **A segmented network. Notice the subnets 192.168.1.0 and 192.168.2.0 identified next to the router. These are not valid IP addresses for a network router and are used to identify the 192.168.1.x and 192.168.2.x networks in routing tables.**

VLAN

As you create a network security policy, you must define procedures to defend your network and users against harm and loss. With this objective in mind, a network design and the included components play an important role in implementing the overall security of the organization.

An overall security solution includes design elements and components such as firewalls, VLANs, and perimeter network boundaries that distinguish between private networks, intranets, and the Internet. This section discusses these elements and helps you tell them apart and understand their function in the security of the network.

The purpose of a *virtual local area network* (*VLAN*) is to unite network nodes logically into the same broadcast domain regardless of their physical attachment to the network. VLANs provide a way to limit broadcast traffic in a switched network. This creates a boundary and, in essence, creates multiple, isolated LANs on one switch. Because switches operate on Layer 2 (data link layer) of the OSI model, a router is required if data is to be passed from one VLAN to another.

> **ExamAlert**
>
> The purpose of a VLAN is to logically group network nodes regardless of their physical location.

Frame tagging is the technology used for VLANs. The IEEE 802.1Q standard defines a mechanism that encapsulates the frames with headers, which then tags them with a VLAN ID. VLAN-aware network devices look for these tags in frames and make appropriate forwarding decisions. A VLAN is basically a software solution that allows creating unique tag identifiers to be assigned to different ports on the switch.

The most notable benefit of using a VLAN is that it can span multiple switches. Because users on the same VLAN don't have to be associated by physical location, they can be grouped by department or function. Here are the benefits that VLANs provide:

► Users can be grouped by department rather than physical location.

► Moving and adding users is simplified. No matter where a user physically moves, changes are made to the software configuration in the switch.

► Because VLANs allow users to be grouped, applying security policies becomes easier.

Keep in mind that use of a VLAN is not an absolute safeguard against security infringements. It does not provide the same level of security as a router. A VLAN is a software solution and cannot take the place of a well subnetted or routed network. It is possible to make frames hop from one VLAN to another. This takes skill and knowledge on the part of an attacker, but it is possible. For more information about frame tagging and VLANs, reference IEEE standard 802.1Q.

NAT

Network Address Translation (NAT) acts as a liaison between an internal network and the Internet. It allows multiple computers to connect to the Internet using one IP address. An important security aspect of NAT is that it hides the internal network from the outside world. In this situation, the internal network uses a private IP address. Special ranges in each IP address class are used specifically for private addressing. These addresses are considered nonroutable on the Internet.

Here are the private address ranges:

▶ *Class A*: 10.0.0.0 network. Valid host IDs are from 10.0.0.1 to 10.255.255.254.

▶ *Class B*: 172.16.0.0 through 172.31.0.0 networks. Valid host IDs are from 172.16.0.1 through 172.31.255.254.

▶ *Class C*: 192.168.0.0 network. Valid host IDs are from 192.168.0.1 to 192.168.255.254.

Just as in IPv4, blocks of addresses are set aside in IPv6 for private addresses. In IPv6, internal addresses are called unique local addresses (ULA). Addresses starting with fe80: are called link-local addresses and are routable only in the local link area.

For smaller companies, NAT can be used in the form of Windows Internet Connection Sharing (ICS), where all machines share one Internet connection, such as a dial-up modem. NAT can also be used for address translation between multiple protocols, which improves security and provides for more interoperability in heterogeneous networks.

NAT and IPsec may not work well together. IPsec uses cryptography to protect communications. NAT has to replace the headers of the incoming packet with its own headers before sending the packet. This might not be possible because IPsec information is encrypted.

IPv6 was developed before NAT was in general use. Because IPv6 has an almost infinite number of addresses, having to provide renumbering makes NAT unnecessary. However Network Address Translation - Protocol Translation (NAT-PT, RFC 2766) was developed as a means for hosts that run IPv6 to communicate with hosts that run IPv4. For more information on how NAT works, you can go to http://www.cisco.com/en/US/tech/tk648/tk361/technologies_tech_note09186a0080094831.shtml.

ExamAlert

Another address range to keep in mind when designing IP address space is Automatic Private IP Addressing (APIPA). In the event that no Dynamic Host Configuration Protocol (DHCP) server is available at the time that the client issues a DHCP lease request, the client is automatically configured with an address from the 169.254.0.1 through 169.254.255.254 range.

Remote Access

Broadband solutions such as cable modems and Digital Subscriber Line (DSL) connections are readily available. Most Internet service providers (ISPs) offer this type of network connectivity for their users. Remote Access Services (RAS) lets you connect your computer from a remote location, such as your home or any on-the-road location, to a corporate network. Many organizations maintain the use of RAS servers to provide direct connectivity for remote users or administrators. Due to concerns about "always-on" connections, RAS is achieved primarily through VPNs using IPsec or SSL or other Remote Access software. By using a remote-access VPN, secure access to corporate resources can be provided using an encrypted tunnel over the Internet. In addition to using hardware such as VPN concentrators discussed earlier in the chapter, you can establish remote access with Routing and Remote Access (RRAS). RRAS is a network service available on Microsoft Server installations that allows the deployment of VPNs and dial-up remote access services. The type of service you choose depends on many factors such as cost, connect and transfer speeds, reliability, availability, and so on.

Telephony

The transmission of data through equipment in a telecommunications environment is known as *telephony*. Telephony includes transmission of voice, fax, or other data. This section describes the components that need to be considered when securing the environment. Often, these components are neglected because they are not really network components. However, they use communications equipment that is susceptible to attack and therefore must be secured.

Telecom/PBX

The telecommunications (telecom) system and Private Branch Exchange (PBX) are a vital part of an organization's infrastructure. Besides the standard block, there are also PBX servers, where the PBX board plugs into the server and is configured through software on the computer. Many companies have moved to Voice over IP (VoIP) to integrate computer telephony, videoconferencing, and document sharing.

For years PBX-type systems have been targeted by hackers, mainly to get free long-distance service. The vulnerabilities that phone networks are subject to include social engineering, long-distance toll fraud, and breach of data privacy.

To protect your network, make sure the PBX is in a secure area, any default passwords have been changed, and only authorized maintenance is done. Many times, hackers can gain access to the phone system via social engineering because this device is usually serviced through a remote maintenance port.

Voice over Internet Protocol

VoIP uses the Internet to transmit voice data. A VoIP system might be composed of many different components, including VoIP phones, desktop systems, PBX servers, and gateways. VoIP PBX servers are susceptible to the same type of exploits as other network servers. These attacks include DoS and buffer overflows, with DoS being the most prevalent. In addition, there are voice-specific attacks and threats. H.323 and Inter Asterisk eXchange (IAX) are specifications and protocols for audio/video. They enable VoIP connections between servers and enable client/server communication. H.323 and IAX protocols can be vulnerable to sniffing during authentication. This allows an attacker to obtain passwords that might be used to compromise the voice network. Session Initiation Protocol (SIP) is commonly used in instant messaging, but it can also be used as an alternative for VoIP. Using SIP can leave VoIP networks open to unauthorized transport of data. Man-in-the-middle attacks between the SIP phone and SIP proxy allow the audio to be manipulated, causing dropped, rerouted, or playback calls. In a man-in-the-middle attack, the attacker intercepts and relays communications between two entities, making the entities believe that they are talking directly to each other when in fact the entire conversation is controlled by the attacker. Many components comprise a VoIP network, and VoIP security is built upon many layers of traditional data security. Therefore, access can be gained in a lot of areas.

Modems

Modems are used via the phone line to dial in to a server or computer. They are gradually being replaced by high-speed cable and Digital Subscriber Line (DSL) solutions, which are faster than dial-up access. However, some companies still use modems for employees to dial into the network and work from home. The modems on network computers or servers are usually configured to take incoming calls. Leaving modems open for incoming calls with little to no authentication for users who are dialing in can be a clear security vulnerability in the network. For example, war-dialing attacks take advantage of this situation. War-dialing is the process by which an automated software application is used to dial numbers in a given range to determine whether any of the numbers are serviced by modems that accept dial-in requests. This attack can be set to target connected modems that are set to receive calls without any authentication, thus allowing attackers an easy path into the network. You can resolve this problem area in several ways:

▶ Set the callback features to have the modem call the user back at a preset number.

▶ Make sure authentication is required using strong passwords.

▶ Be sure employees have not set up modems at their workstations with remote-control software installed.

NAC

One the most effective ways to protect the network from malicious hosts is to use *network access control* (*NAC*). NAC offers a method of enforcement that helps ensure computers are properly configured. The premise behind NAC is to secure the environment by examining the user's machine and based on the results grant (or not grant) access accordingly. It is based on assessment and enforcement. For example, if the user's computer patches are not up-to-date, and no desktop firewall software is installed, you can decide whether to limit access to network resources. Any host machine that doesn't comply with your defined policy could be relegated to a remediation server, or put on a guest VLAN. The basic components of NAC products are

▶ **Access requestor (AR):** This is the device that requests access. The assessment of the device can be self-performed or delegated to another system.

▶ **Policy decision point (PDP)**: This is the system that assigns a policy based on the assessment. The PDP determines what access should be granted and may be the NAC's product-management system.

▶ **Policy enforcement point (PEP)**: This is the device that enforces the policy. This device may be a switch, firewall, or router.

The four ways NAC systems can be integrated into the network are the following:

▶ **Inline**: An appliance in the line, usually between the access and the distribution switches

▶ **Out-of-band**: Intervenes and performs an assessment as hosts come online and then grants appropriate access

▶ **Switch based**: Similar to inline NAC except enforcement occurs on the switch itself

▶ **Host based**: Relies on an installed host agent to assess and enforce access policy

In addition to providing the ability to enforce security policy, contain non-compliant users, and mitigate threats, NAC offers a number of business benefits. The business benefits include compliance, a better security posture, and operational cost management.

Virtualization

With more emphasis being placed on going green and power becoming more expensive, virtualization offers cost benefits by decreasing the number of physical machines required within an environment. This applies to both servers and desktops. On the client side, the ability to run multiple operating environments allows a machine to support applications and services for an operating environment other than the primary environment. Currently, many implementations of virtual environments are available to run on just about everything from servers and routers to USB thumb drives.

The security concerns of virtual environments begin with the guest operating system. If a virtual machine is compromised, an intruder can gain control of all the guest operating systems. In addition, because hardware is shared, most virtual machines run with very high privileges. This can allow an intruder who compromises a virtual machine to compromise the host machine, too.

Vulnerabilities also come into play. For example, a few years ago, VMware's NAT service had a buffer-overflow vulnerability that allowed remote attackers to execute malicious code by exploiting the virtual machine itself. Virtual machine environments need to be patched just like host environments and are susceptible to the same issues as a host operating system. You should be cognizant of share files among guest and host operating systems.

> **ExamAlert**
>
> Virtualized environments, if compromised, can provide access to not only the network, but also any virtualization infrastructure. This puts a lot of data at risk.

Security policy should address virtual environments. Any technology software without a defined business need should not be allowed on systems. This applies to all systems, including virtual environments. To secure a virtualized environment, machines should be segmented by the sensitivity of the information they contain. A policy should be in place that specifies that hardware is not shared for test environments and sensitive data. Another way to secure a virtualized environment is to use standard locked-down images. Other areas that present issues for a virtualized environment and need special consideration are deploying financial applications on virtualized shared hosting and secure storage on storage-area network (SAN) technologies.

Cloud Computing

Cloud computing as it is used today is a very general term which basically describes anything that involves delivering hosted computing services over the Internet. The term *cloud* computing came from the cloud symbol that is commonly used to represent the Internet in network diagrams. Although cloud computing has come to the forefront over the past couple of years, the concepts of cloud computing can be traced back to the mainframe computing where multiple users were given small slices of the computer's time to run whatever program they needed at that time. Today, the typical cloud computing provider delivers computing power, storage, and common applications online to users who access them from a web browser or portal. In essence, cloud computing is the blending of virtualization, distributed computing, and prevalent high-speed bandwidth.

Platform-as-a-Service

Platform-as-a-Service (PaaS) is the delivery of a computing platform, often an operating system with associated services, that is delivered over the Internet without downloads or installation. Often PaaS systems are development platforms designed to operate specifically in the cloud environment. Google Apps are examples of PaaS. PaaS implementations typically have integrated development environment services, interface creation tools, and Web and database integration.

Software-as-a-Service

Software-as-a-Service (SaaS) is the delivery of a licensed application to customers over the Internet for use as a service on demand. A SaaS vendor hosts an application and allows the customer to download the application for a set period of time, after which the application becomes inactive. This model is useful for individuals and businesses to have the right to access a certain application without having to purchase a full license. This creates an on-demand licensing environment that allows for all the benefits of the full application without the up-front costs and maintenance associated with traditional software purchases.

Infrastructure-as-a-Service

Infrastructure-as-a-Service (IaaS) is the delivery of computer infrastructure in a hosted service model over the Internet. This method of cloud computing allows the client to literally outsource everything that would normally be in a typical IT department. Data center space, servers, networking equipment, and software can all be purchased as a service. IaaS follows the same model as power and water; you're billed for how much you use, so it falls under the category of "utility computing." IaaS implementations typically have Internet connectivity, computer networking, servers or grid computing, and hardware virtualization.

Cram Quiz

Answer these questions. The answers follow the last question. If you cannot answer these questions correctly, consider reading this section again until you can.

1. You are the administrator of a small organization with 50 users. Which IPv4 internal address range should you use on the network?

   ○ **A.** 10.x.x.x

   ○ **B.** 172.16.x.x

   ○ **C.** 172.31.x.x

   ○ **D.** 192.168.x.x

2. You are setting up a switched network and want to group users by department. Which technology would you implement?

   ○ **A.** DMZ

   ○ **B.** VPN

   ○ **C.** VLAN

   ○ **D.** NAT

3. You are setting up a web server that needs to be accessed by both the employees and external customers. What type of architecture should you implement?

   ○ **A.** VLAN

   ○ **B.** DMZ

   ○ **C.** NAT

   ○ **D.** VPN

Cram Quiz Answers

1. **D.** In A Class C network, valid host IDs are from 192.168.0.1 to 192.168.255.254 allowing for a maximum of 254 hosts on the network. Answer A is incorrect because it is a Class A address. Valid host IDs are from 10.0.0.1 to 10.255.255.254, which allows a far greater number of IP addresses than are possibly needed. Answers B and C are incorrect because they are both Class B addresses; valid host IDs are from 172.16.0.1 through 172.31.255.254, which allows a far greater number of IP addresses than are possibly needed.

2. C. The purpose of a VLAN is to unite network nodes logically into the same broadcast domain regardless of their physical attachment to the network. Answer A is incorrect because a DMZ is a small network between the internal network and the Internet that provides a layer of security and privacy. Answer B is incorrect because a VPN is a network connection that allows you access via a secure tunnel created through an Internet connection. Answer D is incorrect because NAT acts as a liaison between an internal network and the Internet.

3. B. A DMZ is a small network between the internal network and the Internet that provides a layer of security and privacy. Answer A is incorrect. The purpose of a VLAN is to unite network nodes logically into the same broadcast domain regardless of their physical attachment to the network. Answer C is incorrect because NAT acts as a liaison between an internal network and the Internet. Answer D is incorrect because a VPN is a network connection that allows you access via a secure tunnel created through an Internet connection.

What Next?

If you want more practice on this chapter's exam objectives before you move on, remember that you can access all of the Cram Quiz questions on the CD. You can also create a custom exam by objective with the practice exam software. Note any objective you struggle with and go to that objective material in this chapter.

CHAPTER 2

Network Implementation

This chapter covers the following official CompTIA Security+, SY0-301 exam objectives:

▶ Implement and use common protocols

▶ Identify commonly used default network ports

▶ Implement wireless networks in a secure manner

(For more information on the official CompTIA Security+, SY0-301 exam topics, see the "About the CompTIA Security+, SY0-301 Exam" section in the Introduction.)

The network infrastructure is subject to myriad internal and external attacks through services, protocols, and open ports. It is imperative that you understand how to properly implement services and protocols, especially if the network has been in existence for some period of time and some services are no longer needed or have been forgotten. To stop many would-be attackers, you must understand how protocols are used on the network, what common ports are used by network protocols, and how to securely implement a wireless network.

This chapter discusses these concepts to help you understand how to use the proper network implementation of protocols and services as a tool to protect and mitigate threats against network infrastructure.

Implement and Use Common Protocols

- ► IPsec
- ► SNMP
- ► SSH
- ► DNS
- ► TLS
- ► SSL
- ► TCP/IP

- ► FTPS
- ► HTTPS
- ► SFTP
- ► SCP
- ► ICMP
- ► IPv4 versus IPv6

CramSaver

If you can correctly answer these questions before going through this section, save time by skimming the Exam Alerts in this section and then completing the Cram Quiz at the end of the section.

1. Explain how IPsec is used, including the OSI model layer it operates on.

2. Explain what ICMP is and how it is used in a networking environment.

3. What are the major differences between IPv4 and IPv6?

Answers

1. The Internet Protocol Security (IPsec) authentication and encapsulation standard is widely used to establish secure VPN communications. The use of IPsec can secure transmissions between critical servers and clients. This helps prevent attacks from taking place. Unlike most security systems that function within the application layer of the Open Systems Interconnection (OSI) model, IPsec functions within the network layer.

2. ICMP is a protocol meant to be used as an aid for other protocols and system administrators to test for connectivity and search for configuration errors in a network. Ping uses the ICMP echo function and is the lowest-level test of whether a remote host is alive. A small packet containing an ICMP echo message is sent through the network to a particular IP address. The computer that sent the packet then waits for a return packet. If the connections are good and the target computer is up, the echo message return packet will be received.

3. The differences between IPv4 and IPv6 are in five major areas: addressing and routing, security, network address translation, administrative workload, and support for mobile devices.

Internet Protocol Security

The Internet Protocol Security (IPsec) authentication and encapsulation standard is widely used to establish secure VPN communications. The use of IPsec can secure transmissions between critical servers and clients. This helps prevent network-based attacks from taking place. Unlike most security systems that function within the application layer of the Open Systems Interconnection (OSI) model, IPsec functions within the network layer.

ExamAlert

You should be very familiar with the OSI model as well as the common protocols and network hardware that function within each level. For example, you should know that hubs operate at the physical layer of the OSI model. Intelligent hubs, bridges, and network switches operate at the data link layer, and Layer 3 switches and routers operate at the network layer. The *Network+ Exam Cram* and *Exam Prep* books cover the OSI model in much more detail. If you will be working extensively with network protocols and hardware, you should also look at these texts.

The layers of the OSI model are as follows:

7. Application layer

6. Presentation layer

5. Session layer

4. Transport layer

3. Network layer

2. Data link layer (subdivided into the logical-link control (LLC) and Media Access Control (MAC) sublayers)

1. Physical layer

IPsec provides authentication services and encapsulation of data through support of the Internet Key Exchange (IKE) protocol.

IPsec Services

The asymmetric key standard defining IPsec provides two primary security services:

▶ **Authentication Header (AH)**: This provides authentication of the data's sender, along with integrity and nonrepudiation. RFC2402 states that AH provides authentication for as much of the IP header as possible, as well as for upper-level protocol data. However, some IP header fields might change in transit, and when the packet arrives at the receiver, the value of these fields might not be predictable by the sender. The values of such fields cannot be protected by AH. Thus the protection provided to the IP header by AH is somewhat piecemeal.

▶ **Encapsulating Security Payload (ESP)**: This supports authentication of the data's sender and encryption of the data being transferred along with confidentiality and integrity protection. ESP is used to provide confidentiality, data origin authentication, connectionless integrity, an anti-replay service (a form of partial sequence integrity), and limited traffic-flow confidentiality. The set of services provided depends on options selected at the time of security association establishment and on the placement of the implementation. Confidentiality may be selected independently of all other services. However, the use of confidentiality without integrity/authentication (either in ESP or separately in AH) might subject traffic to certain forms of active attacks that could under-mine the confidentiality service.

Protocols 51 and 50 are the well-known port numbers assigned to the Authentication Header and Encapsulating Security Payload components of the IPsec protocol. IPsec inserts ESP or AH (or both) as protocol headers into an IP datagram that immediately follows an IP header.

The protocol field of the IP header will be 50 for ESP or 51 for AH. If IPsec is configured to do authentication rather than encryption, you must configure an IP filter to let protocol 51 traffic pass. If IPsec uses nested AH and ESP, you can configure an IP filter to let only protocol 51 (AH) traffic pass.

Internet Key Exchange Protocol

IPsec supports the Internet Key Exchange (IKE) protocol, which is a key management standard used to allow specification of separate key protocols to be used during data encryption. IKE functions within the Internet Security Association and Key Management Protocol (ISAKMP), which defines the payloads used to exchange key and authentication data appended to each packet.

The common key exchange protocols and standard encryption algorithms—including asymmetric key solutions such as the Diffie-Hellman Key Agreement and Rivest-Shamir-Adleman (RSA) standards; symmetric key solu-tions such as the International Data Encryption Algorithm (IDEA) and Digital Encryption Standard (DES); Triple DES (3DES) and hashing algo-rithms, such as the Message Digest 5 (MD5) and Secure Hash Algorithm (SHA)—are covered in detail in Chapter 12, "Cryptography Tools and Techniques."

IPsec and Wireless Access

Although IPsec by itself does not control access to the WLAN (wireless local area network), it can be used in conjunction with 802.1x to provide security for data being sent to client computers that are roaming between access points on the same network. For better security, segment the wireless network by placing a firewall between the WLAN and the remainder of the network. Because IPsec is a solution to securely authenticate and encrypt network IP packets, you can use IPsec to provide strong security between a Remote Authentication Dial-in User Service (RADIUS) server and a domain controller, or to secure traffic to a partner organization's RADIUS servers. RADIUS provides authentication and access control within an enterprise network and is explained in greater detail in Chapter 10, "Authentication and Authorization." Many of the VPN solutions use IPsec, and, like a VPN, IPsec is an excellent solution in many circumstances. However, it should not be a direct alternative for WLAN protection implemented at the network hardware layer.

SNMP

Older protocols that are still in use might leave the network vulnerable. Protocols such as Simple Network Management Protocol (SNMP) and domain name service (DNS) that were developed a long time ago and have been widely deployed can pose security risks, too. SNMP is an application layer protocol whose purpose is to collect statistics from TCP/IP devices. SNMP is used for monitoring the health of network equipment, computer equipment, and devices such as uninterruptible power supplies (UPSs). Many of the vulnerabilities associated with SNMP stem from using SNMPv1. Although these vulnerabilities were discovered in 2002, vulnerabilities are still being reported with current SNMP components. A recent Gentoo Linux Security Advisory noted that multiple vulnerabilities in Net-SNMP allow for authentication bypass and execution of arbitrary code in Perl applications using Net-SNMP.

The SNMP management infrastructure consists of three components:

- ▶ SNMP managed node
- ▶ SNMP agent
- ▶ SNMP network management station

The device loads the agent, which in turn collects the information and forwards it to the management station. Network management stations collect a massive amount of critical network information and are likely targets of intruders because SNMPv1 is not secure. The only security measure it has in place is its community name, which is similar to a password. By default, this is "public" and many times is not changed, thus leaving the information wide open to intruders. SNMPv2 uses Message Digest Version 5 (MD5) for authentication. The transmissions can also be encrypted. SNMPv3 is the current standard, but some devices are likely to still be using SNMPv1 or SNMPv2.

SNMP can help malicious users learn a lot about your system, making password-guessing attacks a bit easier than brute-force attacks. SNMP is often overlooked when checking for vulnerabilities because it uses User Datagram Protocol (UDP) ports 161 and 162. Make sure network management stations are secure physically and secure on the network. You might even consider using a separate management subnet and protecting it using a router with an access list. Unless this service is required, it should be turned off.

Secure Shell Connections

As a more secure replacement for the common command-line terminal utility Telnet, the Secure Shell (SSH) utility establishes a session between the client and host computers using an authenticated and encrypted connection. SSH requires encryption of all data, including the login portion. SSH uses the asymmetric (public key) Rivest-Shamir-Adleman (RSA) cryptography method to provide both connection and authentication.

Data encryption is accomplished using one of the following algorithms:

▸ **International Data Encryption Algorithm (IDEA)**: The default encryption algorithm used by SSH, which uses a 128-bit symmetric key block cipher.

▸ **Blowfish**: A symmetric (private key) encryption algorithm using a variable 32- to 448-bit secret key.

▸ **Data Encryption Standard (DES)**: A symmetric key encryption algorithm using a random key selected from a large number of shared keys. Most forms of this algorithm cannot be used in products meant for export from the United States.

▸ **Triple Data Encryption Standard (3DES)**: A symmetric key encryption algorithm that dramatically improves upon the DES by using the DES algorithm three times with three distinct keys.

Using SSH helps guard against attacks such as eavesdropping, man-in-the-middle attacks, and spoofing. Attempts to spoof the identity of either side of a communication can be thwarted because each packet is encrypted using a key known only by the local and remote systems.

> **ExamAlert**
>
> Some versions of SSH, including the Secure Shell for Windows Server, provide a secure version of the File Transfer Protocol (SFTP) along with the other common SSH utilities.

Domain Name Service

Domain Name Service (DNS) was originally designed as an open protocol. DNS servers are organized in a hierarchy. At the top level of the hierarchy, root servers store the complete database of Internet domain names and their corresponding IP addresses. There are different types of DNS servers. The most common types are the following:

▶ **Authoritative servers**: Definitive for particular domains providing information about only those domains. An authoritative-only name server only returns answers to queries about domain names that have been specifically configured.

▶ **Caching servers**: Uses recursion to resolve a given name starting with the DNS root through to the authoritative name servers of the queried domain.

Internal DNS servers can be less susceptible to attacks than external DNS servers, but they still need to be secured. In order to stop outside intruders from accessing the internal network of your company, use separate DNS servers for internal and Internet name resolution. To provide Internet name resolution for internal hosts, you can have your internal DNS servers use a forwarder.

The following are some considerations for internal DNS servers:

▶ Eliminate any single point of failure by making sure that the structure is planned properly. Analyze where the clients of each DNS zone are located and how they will resolve names if the DNS server is unavailable.

▶ Prevent unauthorized access to your servers by implementing integrated zones with secure dynamic updates. Keep the list of DNS servers that are allowed to obtain a zone transfer small.

▶ Monitor the server events and DNS logs. Proper monitoring of logs and server events can help prevent unauthorized access as well as diagnose problems.

Transport Layer Security

Another asymmetric key encapsulation currently considered the successor to SSL is the Transport Layer Security (TLS) protocol based on Netscape's Secure Sockets Layer 3.0 (SSL3) transport protocol, which provides encryption using stronger encryption methods, such as the Data Encryption Standard (DES), or without encryption altogether if desired for authentication only. SSL and TLS transport are similar, but not entirely interoperable. TLS also provides confidentiality and data integrity.

TLS has two layers of operation:

- ▶ **TLS Record Protocol**: This protocol allows the client and server to communicate using some form of encryption algorithm (or without encryption if desired).

- ▶ **TLS Handshake Protocol**: This protocol allows the client and server to authenticate one another and exchange encryption keys to be used during the session.

Secure Sockets Layer

Secure Sockets Layer (SSL) protocol communications occur between the HTTP (application) and TCP (transport) layers of Internet communications. SSL is used by millions of websites in the protection of their online transactions with their customers. SSL is a public key-based security protocol that is used by Internet services and clients for authentication, message integrity, and confidentiality. The SSL process uses certificates for authentication and encryption for message integrity and confidentiality. SSL establishes what is called a stateful connection. In a stateful connection, both ends set up and maintain information about the session itself during its life. This is different than a stateless connection where there is not any prior connection setup. The SSL stateful connection is negotiated by a handshaking procedure between client and server. During this handshake, the client and server exchange the specifications for the cipher that will be used for that session. SSL communicates using an asymmetric key with cipher strength of 40 or 128 bits.

SSL works by establishing a secure channel using Public Key Infrastructure (PKI). This can eliminate a vast majority of attacks, such as session hijackings and information theft.

You can secure communications when performing administration on wireless access points (AP) by leveraging protocols such as Secure Shell (SSH) or HTTP with SSL or TLS. A wireless AP can implement access control functions to allow or deny access to the network and provides the capability of encrypting wireless traffic. It also has the means to query an authentication and authorization service for authorization decisions and securely exchange encryption keys with the client to secure the network traffic.

As a general rule, SSL is not as flexible as IPsec from an application perspective but is more flexible for access from any location. One must determine the usage requirements for each class of user and determine the best approach.

TCP/IP

The core of TCP/IP is comprised of four main protocols: the Internet Protocol (IP), the Transmission Control Protocol (TCP), the User Datagram Protocol (UDP), and the Internet Control Message Protocol (ICMP). IP is responsible for providing essential routing functions for all traffic on a TCP/IP network. TCP provides connection-oriented communication. UDP provides connectionless communications. TCP connections are initiated and terminated with a three-way handshake process. ICMP provides administrative services to TCP/IP networks.

TCP/IP's implementation of the OSI model makes functionality simpler by mapping the same seven layers of the OSI model to a four-layer model instead. Unlike the OSI reference model, the TCP/IP model focuses more on delivering interconnectivity than on functional layers. It does this by acknowledging the importance of a structured hierarchical sequence of functions, yet leaves protocol designers flexibility for implementation. Table 2.1 compares the OSI and TCP/IP models.

TABLE 2.1   **OSI and TCP/IP Model Comparison**

OSI Reference Model	TCP/IP Reference Model
Application Presentation Session	Application
Transport	Transport
Network	Internet
Data Link Physical	Network Access

FTPS

FTP passes the username and password in a plain-text form, allowing packet sniffing of the network traffic to read these values, which may then be used for unauthorized access to the server. FTPS, also known as FTP Secure and FTP-SSL, is an FTP extension that adds support for TLS and SSL. FTPS supports channel encryption as defined in RFC 2228.

With FTPS, data transfers take place in a way designed to allow both parties to authenticate each other and to prevent eavesdropping, tampering, and forgery on the messages exchanged. FTPS includes full support for the TLS and SSL cryptographic protocols, including the use of server-side public key authentication certificates and client-side authorization certificates. It also supports compatible ciphers, including AES, RC4, RC2, Triple DES and DES, hash functions SHA, MD5, MD4, and MD2.

You should use FTPS when there is a need to transfer sensitive or confidential data between a client and a server that is configured to use SSL for secure transactions.

Secure variations of the FTP protocol ensure that data cannot be intercepted during transfer and allow the use of more secure transfer of user access credentials during FTP logon. However, the same certificate vulnerabilities discussed earlier in this chapter apply here, too.

Hypertext Transport Protocol over Secure Sockets Layer

Basic web connectivity using Hypertext Transport Protocol (HTTP) occurs over TCP port 80, providing no security against interception of transacted data sent in clear text. An alternative to this involves the use of SSL transport protocols operating on port 443, which creates an encrypted pipe through which HTTP traffic can be conducted securely. To differentiate a call to port 80 (http://*servername*/), HTTP over SSL calls on port 443 using HTTPS as the URL port designator (https://*servername*/).

HTTPS was originally created by the Netscape Corporation and used a 40-bit RC4 stream encryption algorithm to establish a secured connection encapsulating data transferred between the client and web server, although it can also support the use of X.509 digital certificates to allow the user to authenticate the sender. Now, 128-bit encryption keys are possible and have become the accepted level of secure connectivity for online banking and electronic commerce transactions.

> **ExamAlert**
>
> An alternative to HTTPS is the Secure Hypertext Transport Protocol (S-HTTP), which was developed to support connectivity for banking transactions and other secure web communications. S-HTTP supports DES, 3DES, RC2, and RSA2 encryption, along with CHAP authentication, but was not adopted by the early web browser developers (for example, Netscape and Microsoft) and so remains less common than the HTTPS standard.

Although HTTPS encrypts communication between the client and server, it doesn't guarantee that the merchant is trustworthy or that the merchant's server is secure. SSL/TLS is designed to positively identify the merchant's server and encrypt communication between the client and server.

Secure FTP

SFTP, or secure FTP, is a program that uses SSH to transfer files. Unlike standard FTP, it encrypts both commands and data, preventing passwords and sensitive information from being transmitted in the clear over the network. It is functionally similar to FTP, but because it uses a different protocol you can't use a standard FTP client to talk to an SFTP server, nor can you connect to an FTP server with a client that supports only SFTP.

> **ExamAlert**
>
> A more secure version of FTP (SFTP) has been developed that includes SSL encapsulation. This version is referred to as FTP over SSH and uses the Secure Shell (SSH) TCP port 22. Do not confuse it with FTPS (FTP over SSL), which uses TCP port 21. Either may be used within a modern enterprise network.

Secure Copy Protocol

The Secure Copy protocol (SCP) is a network protocol that supports file transfers. SCP is a combination of RCP and SSH. It uses the BSD RCP protocol tunneled through the Secure Shell (SSH) protocol to provide encryption and authentication. The RCP protocol performs the file transfer and the SSH protocol performs authentication and encryption. SCP runs on port 22 and protects the authenticity and confidentiality of the data in transit. It thwarts the ability for packet sniffers to extract information from data packets.

An SCP download request is server-driven, which imposes a security risk when connected to a malicious server. The SCP protocol has been mostly superseded by the more comprehensive SFTP protocol and some implementations of the SCP utility actually use SFTP instead.

Internet Control Message Protocol

Internet Control Message Protocol (ICMP) is a protocol meant to be used as an aid for other protocols and system administrators to test for connectivity and search for configuration errors in a network. Ping uses the ICMP echo function and is the lowest-level test of whether a remote host is alive. A small packet containing an ICMP echo message is sent through the network to a particular IP address. The computer that sent the packet then waits for a return packet. If the connections are good and the target computer is up, the echo message return packet will be received. It is one of the most useful network tools available because it tests the most basic function of an IP network. It also shows the Time To Live (TTL) value and the amount of time it takes for a packet to make the complete trip, also known as round-trip time (RTT), in milliseconds (ms). One caveat with using ICMP: It can be manipulated by malicious users so some administrators block ICMP traffic. If that is the case, you will receive a request timeout even though the host is available.

Traceroute is a computer network diagnostic tool for displaying the route (path) and measuring transit delays of packets across an Internet Protocol (IP) network. Traceroute outputs the list of traversed routers in simple text format, together with timing information. Traceroute is available on most operating systems. On Microsoft Windows operating systems it is named tracert. Traceroute uses an ICMP echo request packet to find the path. It sends an echo reply with the TTL value set to 1. When the first router sees the packet with TTL 1, it decreases it by 1 to 0 and discards the packet. As a result, it sends an ICMP Time Exceeded message back to the source address. The source address of the ICMP error message is the first router address. Now the source knows the address of the first router. Generally, three packets are sent at each TTL, and the RTT is measured for each one. Most implementations of traceroute keep working until they have gone 30 hops, but this can be extended up to 254 routers.

Pathping is a Windows route-tracing tool that combines features of the ping and tracert commands with additional information. The pathping command uses traceroute to identify which routers are on the path. When the traceroute is complete, pathping sends pings periodically to all the routers over a given time period and computes statistics based on the number of packets returned from each hop. By default, pathping pings each router 100 times, with a single ping every 0.25 seconds. Consequently, a default query requires 25 seconds per router hop. This is especially helpful in identifying routers that cause delays or other latency problems on a connection between two IP hosts.

IPv4 versus IPv6

Due to the increased demand of devices requiring IP addresses, IPv4 was not able to keep up with such an expansive demand. As a result, a new method was needed to address all the new devices requiring IP addresses. The Internet Engineering Task Force (IETF) published a new standard for IP addresses in RFC 2460. The new standard, IPv6, makes several changes to the older IPv4 standard. IPv6 increases the address size from IPv4 32 bits to 128 bits.

The differences between IPv6 and IPv4 are in five major areas: addressing and routing, security, network address translation, administrative workload, and support for mobile devices. Table 2.2 provides a comparison of some of the differences between IPv4 and IPv6.

TABLE 2.2　**IPv4 and IPv6 Comparison**

IPv4	IPv6
Addresses are 32 bits (4 bytes) in length.	Addresses are 128 bits (16 bytes) in length.
Header includes a checksum and options.	Header does not include a checksum, and all optional data is moved to IPv6 extension headers.
ARP uses broadcast request frames to resolve an IP address to a link-layer address.	Multicast Neighbor Solicitation messages are used to resolve IP addresses to link-layer addresses.
IPv4 header does not identify packet flow for QoS.	IPv6 header identifies packet flow for QoS.
IPsec support is optional.	IPsec support is required.
IPv4 limits packets to 64-KB of payload.	IPv6 has optional support for jumbograms, which can be as large as 4-GB.
Must be configured either manually or through DHCP.	Does not require manual configuration or DHCP.

In addition to the difference in the address structure in IPv6, there are IPv6 versions of protocols and commands. The following are some of the more prevalent ones:

▶ **DHCPv6**: Provides stateful address configuration or stateless configuration settings to IPv6 hosts.

▶ **EIGRPv6**: Enhanced Interior Gateway Routing Protocol (EIGRP) is a routing protocol that was developed by Cisco. EIGRPv6 runs on IPv6 networks. It operates in the same manner as the IPv4 version, except that is routes IPv6 addresses.

▶ **ICMPv6**: Used by IPv6 nodes to report packet processing errors and diagnostics.

▶ **Pingv6**: Used in the same capacity as Ping except for IPv6 addresses. On Windows-based machines Ping -6 is used, and on Linux/Unix-based machines Ping6 is used.

Cram Quiz

Answer these questions. The answers follow the last question. If you cannot answer these questions correctly, consider reading this section again until you can.

1. Which of the following is the correct address size for IPv6 addresses?

   ○ **A.** 32 bit

   ○ **B.** 64 bit

   ○ **C.** 128 bit

   ○ **D.** 256 bit

2. Which of the following protocols runs on port 22 and protects the authenticity and confidentiality of file transfer data in transit?

   ○ **A.** DHCP

   ○ **B.** SSL

   ○ **C.** FTP

   ○ **D.** SCP

3. You are troubleshooting connectivity issues on the network. Which of the following would be most helpful in determining where the connectivity issues lie?

   ○ **A.** SNMP

   ○ **B.** ICMP

   ○ **C.** SSL

   ○ **D.** IPsec

Cram Answers

1. **C.** IPv6 increases the address size from IPv4 32 bits to 128 bits. Answers A, B, and D are incorrect because IPv6 addresses sizes are 128 bit.

2. **D.** SCP runs on port 22 and protects the authenticity and confidentiality of the data in transit. Answer A is incorrect because DHCP is used to automatically assign IP addresses. Answer B is incorrect because SSL is a public key-based security protocol that is used by Internet services and clients for authentication, message integrity, and confidentiality. The standard port for SSL is port 443. Answer C is incorrect because in FTP, the data is not protected.

3. **B.** Traceroute uses an ICMP echo request packet to find the path between two addresses. Answer A is incorrect because SNMP is an application layer protocol whose purpose is to collect statistics from TCP/IP devices. SNMP is used for monitoring the health of network equipment, computer equipment, and devices such as uninterruptible power supplies (UPSs). Answer C is incorrect because SSL is a public key-based security protocol that is used by Internet services and clients for authentication, message integrity, and confidentiality. Answer D is incorrect because Internet Protocol Security (IPsec) authentication and encapsulation standard is widely used to establish secure VPN communications.

Identify Commonly Used Default Network Ports

- ▶ FTP
- ▶ SFTP
- ▶ FTPS
- ▶ TFTP
- ▶ TELNET

- ▶ HTTP
- ▶ HTTPS
- ▶ SCP
- ▶ SSH
- ▶ NetBIOS

CramSaver

If you can correctly answer these questions before going through this section, save time by skimming the Exam Alerts in this section and then completing the Cram Quiz at the end of the section.

1. Explain the purpose of ports 137, 138, and 139.

2. Explain what services/protocols operate on Port 22.

Answers

1. These are NetBIOS ports that are required for certain Windows network functions such as file sharing. But these ports also provide information about your computer that can be exploited by attackers. They also contain vulnerabilities that are widely used to break into systems and exploit them in various ways.

2. SSH, SFTP, and SCP are all protocols that operate on port 22. SSH is used to securely access a remote computer. SFTP is used for FTP access and encrypts both commands and data. SCP is used to securely transfer files to a remote host.

There are 65,535 TCP and UDP ports on which a computer can communicate. The port numbers are divided into three ranges:

- ▶ **Well-known ports**: The well-known ports are those from 0 through 1,023.

- ▶ **Registered ports**: The registered ports are those from 1,024 through 49,151.

- ▶ **Dynamic/private ports**: The dynamic/private ports are those from 49,152 through 65,535.

Often, many of these ports are not secured and, as a result, are used for exploitation. Table 2.3 lists some of the most commonly used ports and the services and protocols that use them. Many of these ports and services have vulnerabilities associated with them. It is important that you know what common ports are used by network protocols and how to securely implement services on these ports.

ExamAlert

Know the difference between the various ports that are used for network services and protocols.

TABLE 2.3 **Commonly Used Ports**

Port	Service/Protocol
15	Netstat
20	FTP-Data transfer
21	FTP-Control (command)
22	SSH/SFTP/SCP
23	Telnet
25	SMTP
53	DNS
69	TFTP
80	HTTP
110	POP3
111	Portmap
137, 138, 139	NetBIOS
161/162	SNMP
443	HTTPS
445	SMB
990	FTPS
1,812	RADIUS

Table 2.3 includes a list of protocols that may be currently in use on a network. These protocols, along with some older or antiquated protocols, may be configured open by default by the machine manufacturer or when an operating system is installed. Every operating system requires different services for it to operate properly. If ports are open for manufacturer-installed tools, the manufacturer should have the services listed in the documentation. Ports for older protocols such as Chargen (port 19) and Telnet (port 23) may still be

accessible. For example, Finger, which uses port 79, was widely used during the early days of Internet, and today's sites no longer offer the service. However, you might still find some old implementations of Eudora mail that use the Finger protocol, or worse, the mail clients have long since been upgraded, but the port used 10 years ago was somehow left open. The quickest way to tell which ports are open and which services are running is to do a Netstat on the machine. You can also run local or online port scans.

The best way to protect the network infrastructure from attacks aimed at antiquated or unused ports and protocols is to remove any unnecessary protocols and create access control lists to allow traffic on necessary ports only. By doing so, you eliminate the possibility of unused and antiquated protocols being exploited and minimize the threat of an attack.

Cram Quiz

Answer these questions. The answers follow the last question. If you cannot answer these questions correctly, consider reading this section again until you can.

1. You want to be sure that the NetBIOS ports that are required for certain Windows network functions have been secured. Which of the following ports would you check?

   ○ **A.** 25/110/143

   ○ **B.** 161/162

   ○ **C.** 137/138/139

   ○ **D.** 20/21

2. Your company is in the process of setting up a management system on your network, and you want to use SNMP. You have to allow this traffic through the router. Which UDP ports do you have to open? (Choose two correct answers.)

   ○ **A.** 161

   ○ **B.** 139

   ○ **C.** 138

   ○ **D.** 162

3. Which standard port is used to establish a web connection using the 40-bit RC4 encryption protocol?

   ○ **A.** 21

   ○ **B.** 80

   ○ **C.** 443

   ○ **D.** 8,250

Cram Answers

1. **C**. There are NetBIOS ports that are required for certain Windows network functions, such as file sharing, which are 137, 138, and 139. Answer A is incorrect because these ports are used for email. Answer B is incorrect because these ports are used for SNMP. Answer D is incorrect because these ports are used for FTP.

2. **A** and **D**. UDP ports 161 and 162 are used by SNMP. Answer B is incorrect because UDP port 139 is used by the NetBIOS session service. Answer C is incorrect because port 138 is used to allow NetBIOS traffic for name resolution.

3. **C**. A connection using the HTTP protocol over SSL (HTTPS) is made using the RC4 cipher and port 443. Answer A is incorrect because port 21 is used for FTP connections. Answer B is incorrect because port 80 is used for unsecure plaintext HTTP communications. Answer D is incorrect because port 8,250 is not designated to a particular TCP/IP protocol.

Implement Wireless Networks in a Secure Manner

- ▶ WPA
- ▶ WPA2
- ▶ WEP
- ▶ EAP
- ▶ PEAP
- ▶ LEAP

- ▶ MAC filter
- ▶ SSID broadcast
- ▶ TKIP
- ▶ CCMP
- ▶ Antenna Placement
- ▶ Power level controls

CramSaver

If you can correctly answer these questions before going through this section, save time by skimming the Exam Alerts in this section and then completing the Cram Quiz at the end of the section.

1. Explain the difference between PEAP and LEAP.

2. Explain how to improve the security of wireless networks with regard to SSIDs.

3. Explain what CCMP is.

Answers

1. PEAP provides several benefits within TLS including an encrypted authentication channel, dynamic keying material from TLS, fast reconnect using cached session keys, and server authentication that protects against the setting up of unauthorized access points. LEAP is a proprietary EAP method because it requires the use of a Cisco AP. It features mutual authentication, secure session key derivation, and dynamic per user, per session WEP keys.

2. In order to improve the security of your network, change the SSID. Using the default SSID poses a security risk even if the AP is not broadcasting it. When changing default SSIDs don't change the SSID to reflect your company's main names, divisions, products, or address. Turning off SSID broadcast does not effectively protect the network from attacks.

3. Counter Mode with Cipher Block Chaining Message Authentication Code Protocol (CCMP) is an encryption protocol that forms part of the 802.11i standard for wireless local area networks (WLANs). CCMP uses 128-bit keys with a 48-bit initialization vector (IV) that reduces vulnerability to replay attacks.

Wi-Fi Protected Access (WPA)

Wireless security comes in two major varieties: Wired Equivalent Privacy (WEP) and Wi-Fi Protected Access (WPA). Both include methods to encrypt wireless traffic between wireless clients and APs. WEP has been included in 802.11–based products for some time and includes a strategy for restricting network access and encrypting network traffic based upon a shared key. The Wi-Fi Protected Access (WPA and WPA2) standards were developed by the Wi-Fi Alliance to replace the WEP protocol. WPA was developed after security flaws were found in WEP. WPA protects networks by incorporating a set of enhanced security features. WPA-protected networks require users to enter a passkey in order to access a wireless network. There are two different modes of WPA: WPA-PSK (Personal Shared Key) mode and WPA-802.1x mode, which is sometimes referred to as WPA-RADIUS or WPA-Enterprise. For the PSK mode, a passphrase consisting of 8–63 ASCII characters is all that is required. The Enterprise mode requires the use of security certificates. WPA includes many of the functions of the 802.11i protocol but relies on Rivest Cipher 4 (RCA4), which is considered vulnerable to keystream attacks.

WPA2

WPA2 is based on the IEEE 802.11i standard and provides government-grade security by implementing the AES encryption algorithm and 802.1x-based authentication. AES is a block cipher that encrypts 128-bit blocks of data at a time with a 128-bit encryption key. WPA2 incorporates stricter security standards and is configurable in either the PSK or Enterprise mode. There are two versions of WPA2: WPA2-Personal and WPA2-Enterprise. WPA2-Personal protects unauthorized network access via a password. WPA2-Enterprise verifies network users through a server. WPA2 is backward compatible with WPA and supports strong encryption and authentication for both infrastructure and ad-hoc networks. Additionally, it has support for the CCMP (Counter Mode with Cipher Block Chaining Message Authentication Code Protocol) encryption mechanism based on the Advanced Encryption Standard (AES) cipher as an alternative to the Temporal Key Integrity Protocol (TKIP) protocol. TKIP is an encryption protocol included as part of the IEEE 802.11i standard for WLANs.

Wired Equivalent Privacy

Wired Equivalent Privacy (WEP) is the most basic form of encryption that can be used on 802.11-based wireless networks to provide privacy of data sent between a wireless client and its access point. Originally, many wireless networks were based on the IEEE 802.11 standard, which had serious data transmission security shortcomings. When this standard was put into place, the 802.11 committee adopted an encryption protocol called WEP. In order to discuss WEP's shortcomings, we have to understand how it operates. WEP uses a stream cipher for encryption called RC4. RC4 uses a shared secret key to generate a long sequence of bytes from what is called a *generator*. This stream is then used to produce the encrypted ciphertext. Early 802.11b networks used 40-bit encryption because of government restrictions. Hackers can crack a 40-bit key in a few hours. It is much easier to break RC4 encryption if a second instance of encryption with a single key can be isolated. In other words, the weakness is that the same keys are used repeatedly. Specifications for the Wired Equivalent Privacy (WEP) standard are detailed within the 802.11b (Wi-Fi) specification. This specification details a method of data encryption and authentication that may be used to establish a more secured wireless connection.

> **ExamAlert**
>
> Developments in the field of cryptography have revealed the WEP encryption method to be less secure than originally intended and vulnerable to cryptographic analysis of network traffic. More advanced protocols such as WPA and the 802.11i standard supersede WEP, but recommendations for a more secure wireless network may also include the use of IPsec and virtual private network (VPN) connectivity to tunnel data communications through a secured connection.

Although using WEP is much better than no encryption at all, it's important to understand its limitations so that you have an accurate picture of the consequences and what you must do to properly protect your wireless environment.

Extensible Authentication Protocol

The 802.1x standard is a means of wireless authentication. The 802.1x authentication standard is an extension of point-to-point protocol (PPP) that relies on the Extensible Authentication Protocol (EAP) for its authentication needs. EAP is a challenge response protocol that can be run over secured transport mechanisms. It is a flexible authentication technology and can be used with smart cards, one-time passwords, and public key encryption. It also allows for support of public certificates deployed using auto enrollment or smart cards. These security improvements enable access control to Ethernet networks in public places such as malls and airports. EAP-Transport Layer Security (EAP-TLS) uses certificate-based mutual authentication, negotiation of the encryption method, and encrypted key determination between the client and the authenticating server.

EAP messages are encapsulated into 802.1x packets and are marked as EAP over LAN (EAPOL). After the client sends a connection request to a wireless access point, the authenticator marks all initial communication with the client as unauthorized, and only EAPOL messages are accepted while in this mode. All other types of communication are blocked until credentials are verified with an authentication server. Upon receiving an EAPOL request from the client, the wireless access point requests logon credentials and passes them on to an authentication server. Remote Authentication Dial-In User Service (RADIUS) is usually employed for authentication purposes; however, 802.1x does not make it mandatory.

Protected EAP

Protected EAP (PEAP) was co-developed by Cisco; Microsoft Corporation; and RSA Security, Inc. PEAP provides several additional benefits within TLS including an encrypted authentication channel, dynamic keying material from TLS, fast reconnect using cached session keys, and server authentication that protects against the setting up of unauthorized access points. PEAP is a means of protecting another EAP method (such as MS-CHAP v2) within a secure channel. The use of PEAP is essential to prevent attacks on password-based EAP methods. As part of the PEAP negotiation the client establishes a Transport Layer Security (TLS) session with the RADIUS server. Using a TLS session as part of PEAP serves a number of purposes:

▶ It allows the client to authenticate the RADIUS server; this means that the client only establishes the session with a server holding a certificate that is trusted by the client.

▶ It protects the MS-CHAP v2 authentication protocol against packet snooping.

▶ The negotiation of the TLS session generates a key that can be used by the client and RADIUS server to establish common master keys. These keys are used to derive the keys used to encrypt the WLAN traffic.

Secured within the PEAP channel, the client authenticates itself to the RADIUS server using the MS-CHAP v2 EAP protocol. During this exchange, the traffic within the TLS tunnel is only visible to the client and RADIUS server and is never exposed to the wireless AP.

LEAP

LEAP combines centralized two-way authentication with dynamically generated wireless equivalent privacy keys or WEP keys. LEAP was developed by Cisco for use on WLANs that use Cisco 802.11 wireless devices. LEAP is a proprietary EAP method because it requires the use of a Cisco AP. It features mutual authentication, secure session key derivation, and dynamic per user, per session WEP keys. However, because it uses unencrypted challenges and responses, LEAP is vulnerable to dictionary attacks. Still, when LEAP is combined with a rigorous user password policy, it can offer strong authentication security without the use of certificates. LEAP can only authenticate the user to the WLAN, not the computer. Without computer authentication, machine group policies will not execute correctly.

Media Access Control Filter

Most wireless network routers and access points contain the ability to filter devices based on their Media Access Control (MAC) address. The MAC address is a unique identifier for network adapters. MAC filtering is a security access control method whereby the MAC address is used to determine access to the network. When MAC address filtering is used, only the devices with MAC addresses configured in the wireless router or access point are allowed to connect. MAC filtering permits and denies network access through the use of blacklists and whitelists.

While giving a wireless network some additional protection, it is possible to spoof the MAC address. An attacker could potentially capture details about a MAC address from the network and pretend to be that device in order to connect. MAC filtering can be circumvented by scanning a valid MAC using a tool such as airodump-ng and then spoofing one's own MAC into a validated MAC address. After an attacker knows a MAC address that is out of the blacklist or within the whitelist, MAC filtering is virtually useless.

Service Set Identifier Broadcast

A Service Set Identifier (SSID) is used to identify wireless access points on a network. The SSID is transmitted so that wireless stations searching for a network connection can find it. By default SSID broadcast is enabled. This means that it accepts any SSID. When you disable this feature, the SSID configured in the client must match the SSID of the access point or the client does not connect to the AP. Having SSID broadcast enabled essentially makes your Access Point (AP) visible to any device searching for a wireless connection.

In order to improve the security of your network, change the SSIDs on your APs. Using the default SSID poses a security risk even if the AP is not broadcasting it. When changing default SSIDs, don't change the SSID to reflect your company's main names, divisions, products, or address. This just makes you an easy target for attacks such as wardriving and warchalking. *Wardriving* is the act of searching for Wi-Fi wireless networks by a person in a moving vehicle, using a portable computer or PDA. *Warchalking* is the drawing of symbols in public places to advertise an open Wi-Fi wireless network. Keep in mind that if an SSID name is enticing enough, it might attract hackers.

Turning off SSID broadcast does not effectively protect the network from attacks. Tools such as Kismet enable non-broadcasting networks to be discovered almost as easily as broadcasting networks. From a security standpoint it is much better to secure a wireless network using protocols that are designed specifically to address wireless network threats than to disable SSID broadcast.

Temporal Key Integrity Protocol

Temporal Key Integrity Protocol (TKIP) is the security protocol designed to replace WEP and is also known by its later iterations of Wi-Fi Protected Access (WPA) or even WPA2. Similar to WEP, TKIP uses the RC4 algorithm and does not require an upgrade to existing hardware, whereas more recent protocols, such as Counter Mode with Cipher Block Chaining Message Authentication Code Protocol (CCMP), which use the AES algorithm, do require an upgrade. TKIP was designed to provide more secure encryption than WEP by using the original WEP programming, but it wraps additional code at the beginning and end to encapsulate and modify it. To increase key strength, TKIP includes four additional algorithms: a cryptographic message integrity check, an initialization-vector sequencing mechanism, a per-packet key-mixing function and a re-keying mechanism.

TKIP is useful for upgrading security on devices originally equipped with WEP but does not address all security issues and might not be reliable enough for sensitive transmission. AES is a better choice and has become the accepted encryption standard for WLAN security.

CCMP

Counter Mode with Cipher Block Chaining Message Authentication Code Protocol (CCMP) is an encryption protocol that forms part of the 802.11i standard for WLANs. CCMP offers enhanced security compared with similar technologies such as TKIP. AES is a block cipher that encrypts 128-bit blocks of data at a time with a 128-bit encryption key. The AES cipher suite uses the Counter-Mode Cipher Block Chaining (CBC) Message Authentication Code (MAC) Protocol (CCMP) as defined in RFC 3610. CCMP uses 128-bit keys with a 48-bit initialization vector (IV) that reduces vulnerability to replay attacks. To provide for replay protection, a packet number (PN) field is used. CCMP produces a message integrity code (MIC) that provides data origin authentication and data integrity for the packet payload data. The PN is included in the CCMP header and incorporated into the encryption and MIC calculations. Counter mode makes it difficult for an eavesdropper to spot patterns, and the CBC-MAC message integrity method ensures that messages have not been tampered with.

Antenna Placement

When designing wireless networks, antenna placement and power output should be configured for maximum coverage and minimum interference. Four basic types of antennas are commonly used in 802.11 wireless networking applications: parabolic grid, yagi, dipole, and vertical. APs with factory-default omni antennas cover an area that's roughly circular and are affected by RF obstacles such as walls. When using this type of antenna, it is common to place APs in central locations or divide an office into quadrants. Some 802.11n APs use Multiple Input Multiple Output (MIMO) antennas. This type of antenna takes advantage of multipath signal reflections. Ideally, locate the AP as close as possible to the antennas. The farther the signal has to travel across the cabling between the AP and the antenna, the more signal loss that occurs. Loss is an important factor when deploying a wireless network, especially at higher power levels. Loss occurs as a result of the signal traveling between the wireless base unit and the antenna.

APs that require external antennas need additional consideration. You need to configure the antennas properly, consider what role the AP serves (AP or bridge), and consider where the antennas are placed. When the antenna is mounted on the outside of the building or the interface between the wired network and the transceiver is placed in a corner, it puts the network signal in an area where it is easy to intercept. Antenna placement should not be used as a security mechanism.

Professional site surveys for wireless network installations and proper AP placement are sometimes used to ensure coverage area and security concerns. Up-front planning takes more time and effort but can pay off in the long run, especially for large WLANs. Physical placement and transmit power adjustments can make it harder for intruders to stay connected to your APs. But never count on physical placement alone to stop attackers.

Power Level Controls

One of the principle requirements for wireless communication is that the transmitted wave must reach the receiver with ample power to allow the receiver to distinguish the wave from the background noise. An antenna that is too strong raises security concerns. Strong omni-directional Wi-Fi signals are radiated to a greater distance into neighboring areas where the signals can be readily detected and viewed. Minimizing transmission power reduces the chances your data will leak out. Companies such as Cisco and Nortel have implemented dynamic power controls in their products. The system dynamically adjusts the power output of individual access points to accommodate changing network conditions, helping ensure predictable wireless performance and availability.

Reducing the energy consumption by wireless communication devices is an important issue in WLANs. Transmit Power Control is a mechanism used to prevent too much unwanted interference between different wireless networks. Adaptive transmit power control in 802.11 Wireless LANs (WLANs) on a per-link basis helps increase network capacity and improves battery life of Wi-Fi-enabled mobile devices.

Cram Quiz

Answer these questions. The answers follow the last question. If you cannot answer these questions correctly, consider reading this section again until you can.

1. You want to implement non-vendor-specific strong authentication protocols for wireless communications. Which of the following would best meet your requirements? (Select two.)

   ○ **A.** EAP

   ○ **B.** PEAP

   ○ **C.** LEAP

   ○ **D.** WEP

2. Which of the following uses 128-bit keys, with a 48-bit initialization vector (IV) that reduces vulnerability to replay attacks?

   ○ **A.** ICMP

   ○ **B.** WEP

   ○ **C.** WPA

   ○ **D.** CCMP

3. Which encryption standard is currently considered the best for Wi-Fi connections?

   ○ **A.** WAP

   ○ **B.** WEP

   ○ **C.** WPA

   ○ **D.** WPA2

Cram Answers

1. **A** and **B**. The IEEE specifies 802.1X and EAP as the standard for secure wireless networking, and Protected EAP (PEAP) is standards based. PEAP provides mutual authentication and uses a certificate for server authentication by the client, while users have the convenience of entering password-based credentials. Answer C is incorrect because LEAP is a Cisco-proprietary protocol. Answer D is incorrect because WEP is the most basic form of encryption that can be used on 802.11-based wireless networks to provide privacy of data sent between a wireless client and its access point.

2. **D**. CCMP uses 128-bit keys with a 48-bit initialization vector (IV) that reduces vulnerability to replay attacks. Answer A is incorrect because ICMP is a network troubleshooting protocol. Answer B is incorrect because WEP is the most basic form of encryption that can be used on 802.11-based wireless networks. Answer C is incorrect because WPA protects networks by incorporating a set of enhanced security features. WPA-protected networks require users to enter a passkey in order to access a wireless network.

3. **D**. The WPA2 standard implements the 802.11i protocols and is currently the highest standard for Wi-Fi communication security. Answer A is incorrect because a WAP refers to a wireless access point, which is the wireless network hardware that functions in the place of a wired switch. Answer B is incorrect because the WEP standard was proven to be unsecure and has been replaced by the newer WPA standards. Answer C is incorrect because the early WPA standard has been superseded by the WPA2 standard, implementing the full 802.11i.

What Next?

If you want more practice on this chapter's exam objectives before you move on, remember that you can access all of the Cram Quiz questions on the CD. You can also create a custom exam by objective with the practice exam software. Note any objective you struggle with and go to that objective's material in this chapter.

CHAPTER 3
Risk Management

This chapter covers the following official CompTIA Security+, SY0-301 exam objectives:

▶ Exemplify the concepts of confidentiality, integrity, and availability (CIA)

▶ Explain risk-related concepts

▶ Carry out appropriate risk mitigation strategies

▶ Explain the importance of security-related awareness and training

(For more information on the official CompTIA Security+, SY0-301 exam topics, see the "About the CompTIA Security+, SY0-301 Exam" section in the Introduction.)

The traditional "C-I-A Triad" of security directives includes maintaining the confidentiality, integrity, and availability of data and services. Threats to these three principles are constantly present and evolving. Defensive measures must be put into place to mitigate risk within the enterprise. This chapter examines risk, mitigation strategies, and the value of security-awareness training in managing risk.

Exemplify the Concepts of Confidentiality, Integrity, and Availability

CramSaver

If you can correctly answer these questions before going through this section, save time by skimming the Exam Alerts in this section and then completing the Cram Quiz at the end of the section.

1. Which element of the C-I-A Triad is addressed by biometric controls?

2. Off-site backup tapes ensure which element of the C-I-A Triad?

3. Battery backup power supplies (UPSs) support which element of the C-I-A Triad?

Answers

1. Confidentiality. Access control mechanisms such as biometric authentication systems ensure that data confidentiality is maintained.

2. Availability. Backup media is used to restore data lost, corrupted, or otherwise at risk of becoming unavailable.

3. Availability. Loss of power prevents services from remaining available to authorized access requests.

Confidentiality

The first principle of information security is that of confidentiality. Confidentiality involves controls to ensure that security is maintained when data is both at rest (stored) and in use (during processing and transport) to protect against unauthorized access or disclosure.

Confidentiality controls include physical access controls, data encryption, logical access controls, and management controls to put in place policies to protect against shoulder surfing, social engineering, and other forms of observational disclosure. We discuss individual access control mechanisms later in this book; this chapter addresses them only in terms of risk mitigation.

> **ExamAlert**
>
> Some questions might include controls that fulfill more than one principle of security, such as access controls that protect both confidentiality and integrity by limiting unauthorized access to examine data (confidentiality) and to modify data (integrity), or malware defenses that protect against key loggers (confidentiality) as well as drive deletion logic bombs (integrity). In these cases, it is best to look for additional details that can reveal the best answer.

Integrity

The second principle of information security is that of integrity. Integrity involves controls to preserve the reliability and accuracy of data and processes against unauthorized modification. Integrity controls include malware defenses protecting against data corruption or elimination, validation code that protects against code injection or malformed data input, data hashing validation identifying modifications, and limited user interface options controlling the types of access available to data.

> **ExamAlert**
>
> Integrity is focused on preserving data against unauthorized modification, which might include deletion, but controls for recovery in the case of deletion might fall more accurately into the Availability arena.

Availability

The final principle of information security is that of availability. Availability involves controls to preserve operations and data in the face of service outages, disaster, or capacity variation. Availability controls include load balancing systems, redundant services and hardware, backup solutions, and environmental controls intended to overcome outages affecting networking, power, system, and service outages.

Cram Quiz

Answer these questions. The answers follow the last question. If you cannot answer these questions correctly, consider reading this section again until you can.

1. Which two of the following support the preservation of data availability?
   - ○ **A.** Anti-static carpet
   - ○ **B.** Firewall
   - ○ **C.** Mirrored windows
   - ○ **D.** Physical access control

2. Antivirus software preserves which two elements of data security?
   - ○ **A.** Confidentiality and Integrity
   - ○ **B.** Integrity and Availability
   - ○ **C.** Availability and Confidentiality
   - ○ **D.** Accuracy and Reliability

3. Regularly expiring passwords preserves data _____ and _____.
   - ○ **A.** Confidentiality
   - ○ **B.** Integrity
   - ○ **C.** Availability
   - ○ **D.** Longevity

Cram Quiz Answers

1. **A** and **D**. Environmental controls such as anti-static carpeting aid in protecting against system failure and so preserve availability of data and services. Physical access controls protect against system theft, destruction, or damage. Answer B is incorrect because firewalls restrict access data and services, and although deletion is possible, this control is focused on preserving confidentiality and integrity. Answer C is incorrect because mirrored windows protect confidentiality by preventing observation of displayed data, user keystrokes, and other information of potential interest.

2. **A**. Malware defenses such as antivirus services protect the confidentiality and integrity of data by eliminating viral agents that could otherwise capture keystrokes, relay webcam audio/video, or modify data and services. Answers B and C are incorrect because malware defenses are not focused on the preservation of data and service availability beyond preventing outright wipe of the infected system. Answer D is incorrect because accuracy and reliability are data qualities within the Integrity principle, not directly parts of the C-I-A Triad.

3. **A** and **B**. Regular password expiration protects against reuse of compromised passwords and mitigates brute-force attacks by changing keys before all combinations can be tested. These actions protect access controls over data review and modification, preserving confidentiality and integrity of data. Answer C is incorrect because password expiration does not directly affect data and service availability. Similarly, answer D is incorrect because data longevity is unrelated to passwords and exists only as business operations allow. Some data might be updated many times every minute whereas other data remains static for years.

Explain Risk-Related Concepts

▶ **Control types**

▶ **False positives**

▶ **Importance of policies in reducing risk**

▶ **Risk calculation**

▶ **Quantitative versus qualitative**

▶ **Risk-avoidance, transference, acceptance, mitigation, deterrence**

▶ **Risks associated to cloud computing and virtualization**

Cram**Saver**

If you can correctly answer these questions before going through this section, save time by skimming the Exam Alerts in this section and then completing the Cram Quiz at the end of the section.

1. Purchasing an insurance plan to cover the costs of a stolen computer is an example of which risk management strategy?

2. If a risk has an ALE of $25,000 and an ARO of 50%, what is the value of its SLE?

3. What are the three categories commonly used to identify the likelihood of a risk?

Answers

1. Transference. The costs if the risk is actualized are transferred to the insurance company. The risk, however, is not reduced; only its cost effect has been transferred, and other issues, such as client loss of trust, might produce second-order effects.

2. The single loss expectancy (SLE) is $50,000 per event. With an annualize rate of occurrence (ARO) of 50%, this risk is expected to occur once every other year on average, so the annualized loss expectancy (ALE) is equal to the SLE ($50,000) times the ARO (.5) or $25,000.

3. Likelihood is commonly assigned as High (1.0), Medium (0.5), or Low (0.1) values for risk comparison.

Risk Responses

Risk management deals with the alignment of five potential responses with an identified risk:

▶ **Acceptance:** Recognizing a risk, identifying it, and then accepting that it is sufficiently unlikely or of such limited impact that corrective controls are not warranted. Risk acceptance must be a conscious choice, documented, approved by senior administration, and regularly reviewed.

▶ **Avoidance:** Elimination of the vulnerability that gives rise to a particular risk so that it is avoided altogether. This is the most effective solution, but often not possible due to organizational requirements. Eliminating email to avoid the risk of email-borne viruses is an effective solution but not likely to be a realistic approach in the modern enterprise.

▶ **Mitigation/Deterrence:** Risk mitigation involves the reduction in likelihood or impact of a risk's exposure. Risk deterrence involves putting into place systems and policies to mitigate a risk by protecting against the exploitation of vulnerabilities that cannot be eliminated. Most risk management decisions focus on mitigation and deterrence, balancing costs and resources against the level of risk and mitigation that will result.

▶ **Transference:** A risk or the effect of its exposure may be transferred by moving to hosted providers who assume the responsibility for recovery and restoration or by acquiring insurance to cover the costs emerging from equipment theft or data exposure.

Exam Alert

Risk management employs several terms that you should familiarize yourself with before the exam:

▶ **Vulnerability:** A vulnerability is a weakness in hardware, software, process, or people that can be employed or engaged to affect enterprise security.

▶ **Exploit:** An exploit is a mechanism of taking advantage of an identified vulnerability.

▶ **Threat:** A threat is the potential that a vulnerability will be identified and exploited.

▶ **Risk:** A risk is the likelihood that a threat will occur and the measure of its effect.

▶ **Control:** Controls act to close vulnerabilities, prevent exploitation, reduce threat potential, and/or reduce the likelihood of a risk or its impact.

Types of Controls

You can apply three general types of controls to mitigate risks, typically by layering defensive controls to protect data with multiple control types when possible. This technique is called a layered defensive strategy or "defense in depth."

The three types of controls include the following:

▶ **Management:** Management or administrative controls include business and organizational processes and procedures, such as security policies and procedures, personnel background checks, security awareness training, and formal change-management procedures.

▶ **Technical:** Technical controls include logical access control systems, security systems, encryption, and data classification solutions.

▶ **Operational:** Operational controls include organizational culture as well as physical controls that form the outer line of defense against direct access to data, such as protection of backup media; securing output and mobile file storage devices; and facility design details including layout, doors, guards, locks, and surveillance systems.

Exam Alert

Controls are intended to mitigate risk in some manner, but at times they might fail in operation. You should be familiar with the following terms for the exam:

▶ **False Positive:** A control that allows unauthorized access, falsely identifying the access as valid.

▶ **False Negative:** A control that refuses authorized access, falsely identifying the access as invalid.

Identifying Vulnerabilities

Many risks to enterprise networks relate to vulnerabilities present in system and service configurations and to network and user logon weaknesses. For the exam, you should be familiar with some of the more common tools used to conduct vulnerability assessments, including the following:

▶ **Port scanners:** This software utility scans a single machine or a range of IP addresses, checking for a response on service ports. A response on port 80, for example, might reveal the operation of an HTTP host. Port scanners are useful in creating an inventory of services hosted on networked systems. When applied to test ports on a single system, this is termed a *port scan*, whereas a scan across multiple hosts is referred to as a *port sweep*.

▶ **Vulnerability scanners:** This software utility scans a range of IP addresses, testing for the presence of known vulnerabilities in software configuration and accessible services. Unlike port scanners, which only test for the availability of services, vulnerability scanners may check for the particular version or patch level of a service to determine its level of vulnerability.

▶ **Protocol analyzers:** This software utility is used on a hub, a switch supervisory port, or in line with network connectivity to enable the analysis of network communications. Individual protocols, specific endpoints, or sequential access attempts can be identified using this utility, which is often referred to as a *packet sniffer*.

▶ **Network mappers:** Another software utility used to conduct network assessments over a range of IP addresses, the network mapper compiles a listing of all systems, devices, and network hardware present within a network segment. This information can be used to identify simple points of failure, to conduct a network inventory, and to create graphical details suitable for reporting on network configurations.

▶ **Password crackers:** This software utility allows direct testing of user logon password strength by conducting a brute-force password test using dictionary terms, specialized lexicons, or mandatory complexity guidelines. Password crackers should provide only the relative strength of a password, rather than the password itself, to avoid weakening logon responsibility under evidentiary discovery actions.

Identifying Risk

Risk is the possibility of loss or danger. Risk management is the process of identifying and reducing risk to a level that is comfortable and then implementing controls to maintain that level. Risk analysis helps align security objectives with business objectives. Here, we deal with how to calculate risk and return on investment. Risk comes in a variety of forms. Risk analysis identifies risks, estimates the effect of potential threats, and identifies ways to reduce the risk without the cost of the prevention outweighing the risk.

Measuring Risk

The annual cost of prevention against threats is compared to the expected cost of loss—a cost/benefit comparison. To calculate costs and return on investment, you must first identify your assets, the threats to your network, your vulnerabilities, and what risks result. For example, a virus is a threat; the vulnerability would be not having antivirus software; and the resulting risk would be the effects of a virus infection. All risks have loss potential. Because security resources will always be limited in some manner, it is important to determine what resources are present that may need securing. Then, you need to determine the threat level of exposure that each resource creates and plan your network defenses accordingly.

Asset Identification

Before you can determine which resources are most in need of protection, it is important to properly document all available resources. A resource can refer to a physical item (such as a server or piece of networking equipment), a logical object (such as a website or financial report), or even a business procedure (such as a distribution strategy or marketing scheme). Sales demographics, trade secrets, customer data, and even payroll information could be considered sensitive resources within an organization. When evaluating assets, consider the following factors:

▶ The original cost

▶ The replacement cost

▶ Its worth to the competition

▶ Its value to the organization

▶ Maintenance costs

▶ The amount it generates in profit

After you have identified and valued assets, an appropriate dollar amount can be spent to help protect those assets from loss.

The Risk and Threat Assessment

After assets have been identified, you must determine the assets' order of importance and which assets pose significant security risks. During the process of risk assessment, it is necessary to review many areas, such as the following:

▶ Methods of access

▶ Authentication schemes

▶ Audit policies

▶ Hiring and release procedures

▶ Isolated and non-redundant systems and services that may provide a single point of failure or avenue of compromise

▶ Data or services requiring special backup or automatic failover support

Risk assessment should include planning against both external and internal threats. An insider familiar with an organization's procedures can pose a very dangerous risk to network security.

During a risk assessment, it is important to identify potential threats and document standard response policies for each. Threats may include the following:

▶ Direct access attempts

▶ Automated cracking agents

▶ Viral agents, including worms and Trojan horses

▶ Released or dissatisfied employees

▶ Denial-of-service (DoS) attacks or overloaded capacity on critical services

▶ Hardware or software failure, including facility-related issues such as power or plumbing failures

Likelihood

When examining threat assessment, you have to consider the likelihood that the threats you've identified might actually occur. To gauge the probability of an event occurring as accurately as possible, you can use a combination of estimation and historical data. Most risk analyses use a fiscal year to set a time limit of probability and confine proposed expenditures, budget, and depreciation.

The National Institute of Standards and Technology (NIST) 800.30 document suggests measuring likelihood as High, Medium, or Low based on the motivation and capability of the threat source, the nature of the vulnerability, and the existence and effectiveness of current controls to mitigate the threat. Often the three values are translated into numerical equivalents for use in quantitative analytical processes: High (1.0), Medium (0.5), Low (0.1).

Responses must be coupled to the likelihood determined in the risk analysis, such as identifying the need to put corrective measures in place as soon as possible for all High-level threats, whereas Medium-level threats might only require an action plan for implementation as soon as is reasonable, and Low-level threats might be dealt with as possible or simply accepted.

Calculating Risk

To calculate risk, use this formula:

Risk = Threat × Vulnerability

To help you understand this, let's look at an example using DoS attacks. Firewall logs indicate that the organization was hit hard one time per month by a DoS attack in each of the past six months. You can use this historical data to estimate that it's likely you will be hit 12 times per year. This information helps you calculate the single loss expectancy (SLE) and the annual loss expectancy (ALE).

SLE equals asset value multiplied by the threat exposure factor or probability. The formula looks like this:

Asset value × Probability = SLE

The exposure factor or probability is the percentage of loss that a realized threat could have on a certain asset. In the DoS example, let's say that if a DoS were successful, 25% of business would be lost. The daily sales from the website are $100,000, so the SLE would be $25,000 (SLE = $100,000 × .25). The possibility of certain threats is greater than that of others. Historical data presents the best method of estimating these possibilities.

After you calculate the SLE, you can calculate the ALE. This gives you the probability of an event happening over a single year's time. This is done by calculating the product of the SLE and the value of the asset. ALE equals the SLE times the ARO (annualized rate of occurrence):

SLE × ARO = ALE

The ARO is the estimated possibility of a specific threat taking place in a one-year time frame. When the probability that a DoS attack will occur is 50%, the ARO is 0.5. Going back to the example, if the SLE is estimated at $25,000 and the ARO is .5, our ALE is 12,500. ($25,000 × .5 = $12,500). Spending more than $12,500 might not be prudent because the cost would outweigh the risk.

ExamAlert

Other risk models for calculating risk include the cumulative loss expectancy (CLE) and Iowa risk model. The cumulative loss expectancy (CLE) model calculates risk based on single systems. It takes into account all the threats that are likely to happen to this system over the next year, such as natural disasters, malicious code outbreak, sabotage, and backup failure. The Iowa risk model determines risk based on criticality and vulnerability.

Calculating Reduced Risk on Investment

Return on investment is the ratio of money realized or unrealized on an investment relative to the amount of money invested. Because there are so many vulnerabilities to consider and so many different technologies available, calculating the ROI for security spending can prove difficult. The formulas present too many unknowns. Many organizations don't know how many actual security incidents have occurred, nor have they tracked the cost associated with them.

One method that might be helpful in this area is called *reduced risk on investment (RROI)*. This method enables you to rank security investments based on the amount of risk they reduce. Risk is calculated by multiplying potential loss by the probability of an incident happening and dividing the result by the total expense:

RROI = Potential loss × (Probability without expense – Probability with expense) / Total expense

By using this formula, you can base alternative security investments on their projected business value.

Another approach is to look at security as loss prevention. It can be equated to loss prevention in that attacks can be prevented. ROI is calculated using the following formula:

ROI = Loss prevented – Cost of solution

If the result of this formula is a negative number, you spent more than the loss prevented.

Qualitative versus Quantitative Measures

Quantitative measures allow for the clearest measure of relative risk and expected return on investment or risk reduction on investment. Not all risk can be measured quantitatively, though, requiring qualitative risk assessment strategies. The culture of an organization greatly affects whether its risk assessments can be performed via quantitative (numerical) or qualitative (subjective/relative) measures.

Qualitative risk assessment can involve brainstorming, focus groups, surveys, and other similar processes to determine asset worth and valuation to the organization. Uncertainty is also estimated, allowing for a relative projection of qualitative risk for each threat based on its position in a risk matrix plotting the Probability (Low to High) and Impact (Low to High) of each. It is possible to assign numerical values to each state (Very Low = 1, Low = 2, Moderate = 3, and so on) so that a quasi-quantitative analysis can be performed, but because the categories are subjectively assigned, the result remains a qualitative measure.

Quantitative measures tend to be more difficult for management to understand, require very intensive labor to gather all related measurements, and are more time consuming to determine. Qualitative measures tend to be less precise, more subjective, and difficult to assign direct costs for measuring ROI/RROI.

Exam**Alert**

Because risks within cloud and virtualized hosting systems require knowledge of location, host system, shared tenancy, and other operational details subject to regular and ongoing change as data is migrated within the hosting environment, risk assessment of these environments depends on subjective assessment and service-level contractual expectations. The subjective and uncertain nature of assessments within these environments falls into the qualitative form of risk assessment.

Cloud computing solutions except for a private cloud (meaning both public and hybrid clouds) encompass all of the normal concerns of enterprise resources, together with those for outsourced resources. And because cloud computing is built atop virtualized computing models, the same factors apply to virtualized as well as cloud-based computing systems and services.

These considerations include the following:

▶ **Secure data transfer:** Because data must travel over public Internet connections for both hosted and hybrid clouds, data must be encrypted and authenticated between endpoints.

▶ **Secure APIs:** Application interfaces must be protected against unauthorized access as well as flood attacks intended to deny legitimate access to remote resources.

▶ **Secure data storage:** Data must be encrypted at rest and in backup media to protect against unauthorized access even with physical server access.

▶ **User access controls:** Logging and audit provisions for all access should be implemented to ensure that all access, both organizational and host-side, is limited to authorized requests.

▶ **Data separation:** Shared hosting creates the potential for resource competition on the host server and its network connections. Compartmentalization of data storage and service function may also be mandated by regulatory directives in some industries.

Risk Reduction Policies

To ensure that proper risk management and incident response planning is coordinated, updated, communicated, and maintained, it is important to establish clear and detailed security policies that are ratified by an organization's management and brought to the attention of its users through regular security-awareness training. Policies of which the users have no knowledge are rarely effective, and those that lack management support can prove to be unenforceable.

A number of policies support risk-management practices within the enterprise, including the following:

- ▶ Privacy

- ▶ Acceptable use

- ▶ Storage and retention

- ▶ Secure disposal

- ▶ Account provisioning

- ▶ Least privilege

- ▶ Separation of duties

- ▶ Mandatory vacations

- ▶ Job rotation

Privacy

Privacy-sensitive information is referred to as *personally identifiable information (PII)*. This is any information that identifies or can be used to identify, contact, or locate the person to whom such information pertains. Examples of PII are name, address, phone number, fax number, email address, financial profiles, Social Security number, and credit card information. For many organizations, privacy policies are mandatory, have detailed requirements, and carry significant legal penalties (for example, entities covered under the Health Insurance Privacy and Portability Act).

To be considered PII, information must be specifically associated with an individual person. Information provided either anonymously or not associated with its owner before collection is not considered PII. Unique information, such as a personal profile, unique identifier, biometric information, and IP address that is associated with PII, can also be considered PII.

The California Online Privacy Protection Act of 2003 (OPPA), which became effective on July 1, 2004, requires owners of commercial websites or online services to post a privacy policy. OPPA requires that each operator of a commercial website conspicuously post a privacy policy on its website. The privacy policy itself must contain the following features:

- ▶ A list of the categories of PII the operator collects

- ▸ A list of the categories of third parties with whom the operator might share such PII

- ▸ A description of the process by which the consumer can review and request changes to his or her PII collected by the operator

- ▸ A description of the process by which the operator notifies consumers of material changes to the operator's privacy policy

- ▸ The effective date of the privacy policy

Other federal and state laws might apply to PII. In addition, other countries have laws as to what information can be collected and stored by organizations. As with most of the information in this chapter, it is imperative that you know the regulations that govern the digital terrain in which your organization operates. The organization then has an obligation to put proper policies and procedures in place.

Acceptable Use

An organization's acceptable use policy must provide details that specify what users may do with their network access. This includes email and instant messaging usage for personal purposes, limitations on access times, and the storage space available to each user. It is important to provide users the least possible access rights while allowing them to fulfill legitimate actions.

An acceptable use policy should contain these main components:

- ▸ Clear, specific language

- ▸ Detailed standards of behavior

- ▸ Detailed enforcement guidelines and standards

- ▸ Outline of acceptable and not acceptable uses

- ▸ Consent forms

- ▸ Privacy statement

- ▸ Disclaimer of liability

The organization should be sure the acceptable use policy complies with current state and federal legislation and does not create unnecessary business risk to the company by employee misuse of resources. Upon logon, show a statement to the effect that network access is granted under certain conditions and that all activities may be monitored. This way you can be sure that any legal ramifications are covered.

Storage and Retention

Retention and storage documentation should outline the standards for storing each classification level of data. Take, for example, the military levels of data classification used in their mandatory access control strategy (MAC). Here, documentation would include directions and requirements for handling and storing the following types of data:

- ▶ Unclassified
- ▶ Sensitive
- ▶ Confidential
- ▶ Secret
- ▶ Top secret

Policies for data should include how to classify, handle, store, and destroy it. The important point to remember here is to document your security objectives. Then, change and adjust that policy when and as needed. There might be a reason to make new classifications as business goals change, but make sure this gets into your documentation. This is an ongoing, ever-changing process.

Log files, physical records, security evaluations, and other operational documentation should be managed within an organization's retention and disposal policies. These should include specifications for access authorization, term of retention, and requirements for disposal. Depending on the relative level of data sensitivity, retention and disposal requirements can become extensive and detailed.

The organization should have a legal hold policy in place, have an understanding of statutory and regulatory document retention requirements, understand the varying statutes of limitations, and maintain a records-retention and destruction schedule.

Secure Disposal

ISO 17799, particularly sections 7 and 8, has established standards for dealing with the proper disposal of obsolete hardware. Standards dictate that equipment owned or used by the organization should be disposed of only in accordance with approved procedures, including independent verification that the relevant security risks have been mitigated. This policy addresses issues that you should consider when disposing of old computer hardware, for recycle, disposal, donation, or resale.

The most prominent example of a security risk involved is that the hard disk inside the computer has not been completely or properly wiped. There are some concerns about data erasure sufficiency in new solid-state drives (SSDs) that might require organizations to totally destroy drivers rather than simply erasing them for normal disposal channels.

When implementing a policy on the secure disposal of outdated equipment, you need to consider a wide range of scenarios, such as the following:

▶ Breaches of health and safety requirements.

▶ Inadequate disposal planning results in severe business loss.

▶ Remnants of legacy data from old systems might still be accessible.

▶ Disposal of old equipment that is necessary to read archived data.

▶ Theft of equipment in use during clean-up of unwanted equipment.

Besides properly disposing of old hardware, removable media disposal is just as important. There is a proper way to handle removable media when either the data should be overwritten or is no longer useful or pertinent to the organization.

The following methods are acceptable to use for some forms of media sanitation:

▶ **Declassification:** A formal process of assessing the risk involved in discarding particular information.

▶ **Sanitization:** The process of removing the contents from the media as fully as possible, making it extremely difficult to restore.

▶ **Degaussing:** This method uses an electrical device to reduce the magnetic flux density of the storage media to zero.

▶ **Overwriting:** This method is applicable to magnetic storage devices.

▶ **Destruction:** The process of physically destroying the media and the information stored on it. For flash drives and other solid-state non-ferric removable storage, this might prove to be the only solution acceptable under certain controls and legal mandates.

Data Labeling, Handling, and Disposal

An organization's information sensitivity policy defines requirements for the classification and security of data and hardware resources based on their relative level of sensitivity. Some resources, such as hard drives, might require very extensive preparations before they can be discarded. Data labeling and cataloguing of information stored on each storage device, tape, or removable storage system becomes critical to identifying valuable and sensitive information requiring special handling.

Organizational data assets might also fall under legal discovery mandates, so a careful accounting is vital to ensure that data can be located if requested and is protected against destruction or recycling if it must be provided at a later time. Proper labeling also ensures that data storage media can be properly processed for reuse or disposal, where special requirements for sensitive data might require outright destruction of the storage device and logging of its destruction in the inventory catalog.

Account Provisioning

Human resources (HR) policies and practices should reduce the risk of theft, fraud, or misuse of information facilities by employees, contractors, and third-party users. The primary legal and HR representatives should review all policies, especially privacy issues, legal issues, and HR enforcement language. Legal and HR review of policies is required in many, if not most, organizations.

Security planning must include procedures for the creation and authorization of accounts (provisioning) for newly hired personnel and the planned removal of privileges (de-provisioning) following employment termination. When termination involves power users with high-level access rights or knowledge of service administrator passwords, it is critical to institute password and security updates to exclude known avenues of access while also increasing security monitoring for possible reprisals against the organization.

The hiring process should also include provisions for making new employees aware of acceptable use and disposal policies and the sanctions that might be enacted if violations occur. An organization should also institute a formal code of ethics to which all employees should subscribe, particularly power users with broad administrative rights.

Least Privilege

Policies addressing access rights for user accounts must mandate that only the minimum permissions necessary to perform work should be assigned to a user. This protects against unauthorized internal review of information as well as protecting against inadvertently enacted viral agents running with elevated permissions.

Separation of Duties

Too much power can lead to corruption, whether it is in politics or network administration. Most governments and other organizations implement some type of a balance of power through a separation of duties. It is important to include a separation of duties when planning for security policy compliance. Without this separation, all areas of control and compliance may be left in the hands of a single individual. The idea of separation of duties hinges on the concept that multiple people conspiring to corrupt a system is less likely than a single person corrupting it. Often, you will find this in financial institutions, where to violate the security controls all the participants in the process have to agree to compromise the system.

> **Exam**Alert
>
> For physical or operational security questions, avoid having one individual who has complete control of a transaction or process from beginning to end and implement policies such as job rotation, mandatory vacations, and cross-training. These practices also protect against the loss of a critical skill set due to injury, death, or another form of personnel separation.

Mandatory Vacations and Job Rotation

Users should be required to take mandatory vacations and rotate positions or functional duties as part of the organization's security policy. These policies outline the manner in which a user is associated with necessary information and system resources and that access is rotated between individuals. There must be other employees who can do the job of each employee so that corruption does not occur, cross-checks can be validated, and the effect of personnel loss is minimized. It is imperative that all employees are adequately cross-trained and only have the level of access necessary to perform normal duties (least privilege).

Cram Quiz

Answer these questions. The answers follow the last question. If you cannot answer these questions correctly, consider reading this section again until you can.

1. A risk has the following calculated values (SLE = $1,500, ARO = 5). What is the maximum amount that should be spent to fully mitigate the costs of this risk?

    ○ **A.** $300

    ○ **B.** $500

    ○ **C.** $1,500

    ○ **D.** $7,500

2. Regarding qualitative versus quantitative measures, which of the following statements is true?

   O **A.** Quantitative measures evaluate risk based on a subjective assessment.

   O **B.** Qualitative measures are less precise.

   O **C.** Qualitative measures are easier to measure for ROI/RROI.

   O **D.** Quantitative measures are always better than qualitative measures.

3. If a risk has the following measures (Asset value = $50, Probability = 10%, ARO = 100), and the mitigation costs $100 per year, what is the expected ROI?

   O **A.** $400

   O **B.** $500

   O **C.** $600

   O **D.** $700

4. What is the likelihood of a risk requiring corrective actions planned for implementation in a reasonable period of time?

   O **A.** Very High

   O **B.** High

   O **C.** Medium

   O **D.** Low

Cram Quiz Answers

1. **D.** The ALE = SLE ($1,500) × ARO (5) = $7,500. Spending more than $7,500 to mitigate the threat without other cause such as a regulatory or legal mandate would be without return. Answers A, B, and C present too low a figure and are all incorrect.

2. **B.** Because qualitative measures are based on subjective values, they are less precise than quantitative measures. Answer A is incorrect because quantitative measures rely on numerical values rather than subjective ones. Answer C is incorrect because qualitative measures are harder to assign numerical values and so more difficult to determine ROI. Answer D is incorrect because each form of analysis has its own benefits and neither is always better in all situations than the other.

3. **A.** The single loss expectancy (SLE) can be calculated as the product of the asset value ($50) times the probability of loss (.1) or SLE=$5/year. The annualized rate of occurrence (ARO) is 100 times per year, so the annualized loss expectancy (ALE) is SLE ($5) times the ARO (100) or ALE=$500/year. Because the cost of mitigation is $100 per year, the ROI is equal to the loss prevented (ALF = $500) less the cost of the solution ($100) or ROI = $400. Answers B, C, and D all present potential values higher than $400 and are incorrect.

4. **C**. A Medium-level risk likelihood warrants implementation of controls as soon as is reasonable. Answer A is incorrect because variations between High and Very High are not based on recognized standards such as the NIST 800.30 and instead reflect categories assigned within an organization based on its own criteria. Answer B is incorrect because High-level threats should be corrected as soon as possible, whereas Low-level threats can be dealt with when time allows or be simply accepted, making answer D incorrect as well.

Carry Out Appropriate Risk-Mitigation Strategies

▶ **Implement security controls based on risk**

▶ **Change management**

▶ **Incident management**

▶ **User rights and permissions reviews**

▶ **Perform routine audits**

▶ **Implement policies and procedures to prevent data loss or theft**

CramSaver

If you can correctly answer these questions before going through this section, save time by skimming the Exam Alerts in this section and then completing the Cram Quiz at the end of the section.

1. What is the name of the process of removing the contents from media as fully as possible?

2. What is the first step to developing an audit plan for your organization?

3. What two functions should be reviewed during a user access and rights audit?

Answers

1. Sanitization. The fully cleared media is extremely difficult if not impossible to restore.

2. Identification of resources at risk must occur before auditing of controls is possible. Resources include data and services such as sensitive files, financial applications, and personnel files.

3. Both user privilege and usage should be monitored to ensure that access controls are working properly.

As discussed earlier in this chapter, alignment between security controls, policies, and the risks they mitigate requires an assessment of relative risks and the costs associated with mitigation strategies for each. You must put controls in place based on the relative impact of each risk, with legal mandates considered absolute requirements unless designated as "addressable" and properly documented as part of the risk management plan. You should also formulate organizational policies to include change- and incident-management guidelines as well as audit review expectations.

Change Management

You should document all configuration changes. Many companies are lacking in this area. We are often in a hurry to make changes and say we will do the documentation later—most of the time, that doesn't happen. You should realize that documentation is critical. It eliminates misunderstandings and serves as a trail if something goes wrong down the road. Change documentation should include the following:

- ▶ Specific details, such as the files being replaced, the configuration being changed, the machines or operating systems affected, and so on

- ▶ The name of the authority who approved the changes

- ▶ A list of the departments that are involved in performing the changes and the names of the supervisors in those departments

- ▶ What the immediate effect of the change will be

- ▶ What the long-term effect of the change will be

- ▶ The date and time the change will occur

After the change has occurred, the following should be added to the documentation:

- ▶ Specific problems and issues that occurred during the process

- ▶ Any known workarounds if issues have occurred

- ▶ Recommendations and notes on the event

After the change has been requested, documented, and approved, you should then send out notification to the users so that they know what to expect when the change has been implemented.

Incident Management

Incidents do happen from time to time in most organizations no matter how strict security policies and procedures are. It is important to realize that proper incident handling is just as vital as the planning stage, and its presence may make the difference between being able to recover quickly and ruining a business and damaging customer relations. Customers need to see that the company has enough expertise to deal with the problem.

Incident response guidelines, change-management procedures, security procedures, and many other security-related factors require extensive planning and documentation. Incident response documentation should include the identification of required forensic and data-gathering procedures and proper reporting and recovery procedures for each type of security-related incident.

The components of an incidence-response plan should include preparation, roles, rules, and procedures. Incident-response procedures should define how to maintain business continuity while defending against further attacks. Although many organizations have an incident response team (IRT), which is a specific group of technical and security investigators that respond to and investigate security incidents, many do not. In the event there is no IRT, first responders need to handle the scene and the response. Systems should be secured to prevent as many incidents as possible and monitored to detect security breaches as they occur. The National Institute of Standards and Technology (NIST) has issued a report on incident response guidelines that can help an organization spell out its own internal procedures.

First Responders

First responders are the first ones to arrive at the incident scene. The success of data recovery and potential prosecution depends on the actions of the individual who initially discovers a computer incident. How the evidence scene is handled can severely affect the ability of the organization to prosecute if need be.

Damage and Loss Control

After the response team has determined that an incident occurred, the next step in incident analysis involves taking a comprehensive look at the incident activity to determine the scope, priority, and threat of the incident. This aids with researching possible response and mitigation strategies. In keeping with the severity of the incident, the organization can act to mitigate the effect of the incident by containing it and eventually restoring operations back to normal.

Depending on the severity of the incident and the organizational policy, incident response functions can take many forms. The response team may send out recommendations for recovery, containment, and prevention to systems and network administrators at sites who then complete the response steps. The team may perform the remediation actions themselves. The follow-up response can involve sharing information and lessons learned with other response teams and other appropriate organizations and sites.

After the incident is appropriately handled, the organization might issue a report that details the cause of the incident, the cost of the incident, and the steps the organization should take to prevent future incidents.

It is important to accurately determine the cause of each incident so that it can be fully contained and the exploited vulnerabilities can be mitigated to prevent similar incidents from occurring in the future.

Regular Audits

How much you should audit depends on how much information you want to store. Keep in mind that auditing should be a clear-cut plan built around goals and policies. Without proper planning and policies, you probably will quickly fill your log files and hard drives with useless or unused information.

The more quickly you fill up your log files, the more frequently you need to check the logs; otherwise, important security events might be deleted unnoticed.

Audit Policy

Here are some items to consider when you are ready to implement an audit policy:

> ▶ Identify potential resources at risk within your networking environment. These resources might typically include sensitive files, financial applications, and personnel files.

> ▶ After the resources are identified, set up the audit policy through the operating system tools. Each operating system will have its own method for tracking and logging access.

> ▶ Auditing can easily add an additional 25% load or more on a server. If the policy incorporates auditing large amounts of data, be sure that the hardware has the additional space needed and processing power and memory.

After you have auditing turned on, log files are generated. Schedule regular time to view the logs.

User Access and Rights Review

After you have established the proper access control scheme, it is important to monitor changes in access rights. Auditing user privileges is generally a two-step process that involves turning auditing on within the operating system and then specifying the resources to be audited. After enabling auditing, you also need to monitor the logs that are generated. Auditing should include both privilege and usage. Auditing of access use and rights changes should be implemented to prevent unauthorized or unintentional access or escalation of privileges, which might allow a guest or restricted user account access to sensitive or protected resources.

Some of the user activities that can be audited include the following:

▶ Reading, modifying, or deleting files

▶ Logging on or off the network

▶ Using services such as remote access or terminal services

▶ Using devices such as printers

When configuring an audit policy, it is important to monitor successful and failed access attempts. Failure events enable you to identify unauthorized access attempts; successful events can reveal an accidental or intentional escalation of access rights.

> ## ExamAlert
>
> The roles of the computers also determine which events or processes you need to audit and log. For example, auditing a developer's computer might include auditing process tracking, whereas auditing a desktop computer might include auditing directory services access. To audit objects on a member server or a workstation, turn on the audit object access. To audit objects on a domain controller, turn on the audit directory service access. Do not audit the use of user rights unless it is strictly necessary for your environment. If you must audit the use of user rights, it is advisable to purchase or write an event-analysis tool that can filter only the user rights of interest to you. The following user rights are never audited mainly because they are used by processes. However, the assignment of them might be monitored
>
> ▶ Bypass traverse checking
>
> ▶ Generate security audits
>
> ▶ Create a token object
>
> ▶ Debug programs
>
> ▶ Replace a process-level token

System and Service Audits

In addition to auditing events on domain controllers and user computers, servers that perform specific roles, such as a DNS, DHCP, SQL, or Exchange server, should have certain events audited. For example, you should enable audit logging for DHCP servers on your network and check the log files for an unusually high number of lease requests from clients. DHCP servers running Windows Server 2008 include several logging features and server parameters that provide enhanced auditing capabilities, such as specifying the following:

▶ The directory path in which the DHCP server stores audit log files. By default, the DHCP audit logs are located in the %windir%\System32\Dhcp directory.

▶ A minimum and maximum size for the total amount of disk space that is available for audit log files created by the DHCP service.

▶ A disk-checking interval that determines how many times the DHCP server writes audit log events to the log file before checking for available disk space on the server.

Turning on all possible audit counters for all objects could significantly affect server performance, so plan your audit settings and test them regularly.

Cram Quiz

Answer these questions. The answers follow the last question. If you cannot answer these questions correctly, consider reading this section again until you can.

1. Which policy details what users may do with their network access?

   ○ **A.** Privacy

   ○ **B.** Acceptable Use

   ○ **C.** Storage and Retention

   ○ **D.** Secure Disposal

2. When preparing to securely dispose of a hard drive, what is the term for reducing the magnetic flux density of the media to zero?

   ○ **A.** Declassification

   ○ **B.** Destruction

   ○ **C.** Degaussing

   ○ **D.** Overwriting

3. The policy preventing too much power leading to corruption is called the
   _____ policy.

   ○ **A.** Account Provisioning

   ○ **B.** Least Privilege

   ○ **C.** Separation of Duties

   ○ **D.** Acceptable Use

Cram Quiz Answers

1. **B.** The Acceptable Use policy details what users may do with their network access, which generally excludes illegal acts and actions that cost the organization money or public favor. Answer A is incorrect as the Privacy policy covers PII protection requirements and practices. Both C and D deal with information storage and storage device disposal so are not related to network access use.

2. **C.** Degaussing involves exposing the media to a powerful electromagnetic device, erasing all magnetic variation within the media. Answer A is incorrect because declassification is a formal process for assessing the risk involved with discarding information, rather than media sanitization itself. Answer B is incorrect because destruction involves physical destruction of the storage device rather than only magnetic degaussing. Answer D is incorrect because overwriting involves the sequential writing of 1s and 0s to mask previously stored data and does not reduce all magnetic flux in the media to zero.

3. **C.** The separation of duties policy ensures that a single individual is not responsible for all areas of control and compliance over an organizational function, which ensures that proper checks and balances remain in effect. Answer A is incorrect because the account provisioning policy details new account-creation protocols, and answer B is incorrect because the principle of least privilege ensures only that permissions are only sufficient for job requirements without precluding assignment of both control and compliance functions to the same individual. Answer D is incorrect because the acceptable use policy defines only what a user may do with his network access, not what roles he may fulfill.

Explain the Importance of Security-Related Awareness and Training

▶ Security policy training and procedures

▶ Personally identifiable information

▶ Information classification: sensitivity of data (hard or soft)

▶ Data labeling, handling, and disposal

▶ Compliance with laws, best practices, and standards

▶ User habits

▶ Threat awareness

▶ Use of social networking and P2P

Cram**Saver**

If you can correctly answer these questions before going through this section, save time by skimming the Exam Alerts in this section and then completing the Cram Quiz at the end of the section.

1. An email to ALLSTAFF detailing a new email virus improves what aspect of user security awareness?

2. When a user switches between organizational sections, what type of security training does he or she need to cover encryption and using USB thumb drives?

Answers

1. Threat awareness. Threat awareness includes recognizing attacks and requires constant reminders of newly emergent threat agents to remain current.

2. Data handling. Because the policies, procedures, and types of data managed in each organizational section can vary widely, it is important to provide a transferring organizational member with data handling training to ensure her compliance with appropriate protocols ad procedures.

One of the most powerful tools available to a security administrator is the body of network users, who might notice and draw attention to unusual access methods or unexpected changes. This same body of users also creates the greatest number of potential security holes because each user might be unaware of newly emerging vulnerabilities, threats, or required standards of action and access that must be followed. Like a chain, a network is only as secure as its weakest link—and users present a wide variety of bad habits, a vast range of knowledge, and varying intent in access.

User Education

User education is mandatory to ensure that users are made aware of expectations, options, and requirements related to secure access within an organization's network. Education can include many different forms of communication, including the following:

- ▶ New employees and contract agents should be provided education in security requirements as a part of the hiring process.

- ▶ Reminders and security-awareness newsletters, emails, and flyers should be provided to raise general security awareness.

- ▶ General security policies must be defined, documented, and distributed to employees.

- ▶ Regular focus group sessions and on-the-job training should be provided for users regarding changes to the user interface, application suites, and general policies.

- ▶ General online security-related resources should be made available to users through a simple, concise, and easily navigable interface.

> ### ExamAlert
>
> Although all the previously mentioned practices are part of a security-awareness training program, security training during employee orientation combined with yearly seminars is the best choice, as these are active methods of raising security awareness. Email and posters are passive and tend to be less effective.

User training should ensure that operational guidelines, disaster recovery strategies, and operational mandates are clearly conveyed to users and refreshed regularly. Policies may also require refresher training during transfer between organizational components or job duties under the rotation policy. Details such as information classification, sensitivity of data and handling guidelines, legal mandates, best practices, and standards can vary widely between organizational units with the proper protocols for access, storage, and disposal varying accordingly.

User Habits and Expectations

Security awareness training is also key to managing user habits and expectations developed due to the prevalence of computing equipment at home and in their mobile devices.

Passwords

Users must be instructed in the value of their access credentials and the impact that could result from sharing their passwords and logons, using weak passwords (and the ability to identify a strong password), easily guessed passwords and expectations of password expiration schedules to avoid filling up the call center the first Monday morning every 90 days.

Data Handling

User training should address legal or regulatory requirements for accessing, transporting, storing, or disposing of data and data storage devices. This includes encryption systems for mobile and removable storage devices, data access logging requirements under laws such as HIPPA, and review of the retention and destruction policy.

Clean Desk

Training should include details of the organization's clean desk policy, encouraging users to avoid jotting down hard-to-recall passphrases or details from electronic systems that might contain PII. Users should also understand why taping a list of their logons and passwords under their keyboards is a bad idea.

Situational Awareness

User training should encourage situational awareness at all times. Unbadged individuals wandering in secured areas should be challenged, tailgating at check-points (following an authorized individual in closely to avoid having to provide personal authorization credentials) should be prevented, and guidelines for handling other forms of physical and logical security violations must be conveyed and practiced.

Personal Technologies

Common mobile computing devices, removable media storage key fobs; file-sharing systems such as Dropbox, Box.com, or SkyDrive; peer-to-peer transfer services; and even browser-based social media solutions and games can all introduce a range of vulnerabilities and threat agents to an enterprise without

requiring elevated privilege or special equipment. Users must be given training in the proper use of their various personal technologies (or reasons to not
use the technologies). Because this area is constantly evolving, convey
reminders and updates in the regular security-awareness newsletter.

Users must be trained in critical consideration before providing logon credentials to any service, particularly those that bring personal data interaction into
the work-place. Social media services are increasingly used for business purposes, so separation of business and personal accounts become critical in the
event of a legal motion for discovery that could otherwise require access to
personally controlled data resources. Social media services accessed through
encrypted web access also offer a route through which protected information
could be inadvertently disclosed without passing in readable form through
normal boundary content review systems.

Peer-to-peer (P2P) services also present a danger to intellectual property and
system availability protection by allowing direct connections between random
endpoints using a wide variety of protocols and service ports, making firewall
and packet-shaper management much more difficult for technicians and
potentially sharing otherwise secure data stores to unknown parties as in the
case of a misconfigured P2P client such as BitTorrent. P2P encrypted data
streams can also result in contraband content being placed on a system within
an organization without proper review, potentially exposing the organization
to legal action based on the type of contraband.

Threat Awareness and Zero-Day Threats

Emergent viruses, worms, Trojans, rootkits, phishing attacks, and other
threats should be identified and conveyed to users as rapidly as possible before
dozens of calls come in asking why the "I Love You" email didn't show its
attached greeting card properly when opened. Personalized spear-phishing
attacks are becoming more prevalent, requiring vigilance on the part of the
users to avoid the natural response of opening everything that seems to be
coming from their family members, boss, or co-workers. This must be tem-
pered, though, as the million-plus new viral versions every year will rapidly
overwhelm users into a state of helplessness or disinterest in the face of apparent inevitability. When a new Zero-Day threat emerges that has not been
specifically considered in response planning, the same communication channels can be used to alert users of actions being taken by the IT group to correct, recover, repair, or patch systems and data.

Cram Quiz

Answer these questions. The answers follow the last question. If you cannot answer
these questions correctly, consider reading this section again until you can.

1. Which of the following is *not* going to be part of a standard password policy?

   ○ **A.** Establishing a minimum password length

   ○ **B.** Selection of a strong password

   ○ **C.** Establishing password expiration schedules

   ○ **D.** Barring keeping written passwords

2. When conducting data handling training and reviewing disposal practices, what
   consideration must be primary?

   ○ **A.** Breaches of health and safety protocols

   ○ **B.** Remnants of data that may remain accessible

   ○ **C.** Accidental disposal of equipment that is necessary to read archived
   legacy data

   ○ **D.** Disposal costs and penalties arising from regulatory mandates

3. _____ training teaches users not to download links from social media
   sites.

   ○ **A.** Data handling

   ○ **B.** Clean desk

   ○ **C.** Situational awareness

   ○ **D.** Personal technology

4. When an employee discovers someone wandering around a secured area without a badge or escort, which user-awareness training topic should provide them
   with knowledge of the proper response?

   ○ **A.** Data handling

   ○ **B.** Clean desk

   ○ **C.** Situational awareness

   ○ **D.** Personal technology

Cram Quiz Answers

1. **D.** The clean desk policy includes details regarding written residue of passcodes,
   PII, and other sensitive data that might be jotted down during normal business.
   Answers A, B, and C are all incorrect because the question asks which is *not* a
   part of the password policy, and all three would be found in the password policy:
   password length, strength criteria, and password duration before expiration.

2. **A**. Because of the materials involved in the manufacturing and construction of electronic equipment, health, and safety protocols take precedence over the other considerations. Health and safety must always come first. Answer B is incorrect because it is concerned with data confidentiality. Answer C is incorrect because it is concerned with data availability, and answer D is incorrect because it focuses on risks and costs arising from regulation.

3. **D**. Personal technology training should cover social networks, peer-to-peer networking, and mobile technologies owned by the employees but present in the workplace. Answer A is incorrect because the data handling training would be focused on how to manage data stored on organizational systems rather than personal ones. Answer B is incorrect because the clean desk policy provides guidance for data sanitization of the work environment. Answer C is incorrect because situational awareness training involves developing strategies and skills for dealing with physical access violations and similar events rather than addressing which personal technologies are appropriate and how they should be used properly.

4. **C**. Situational-awareness training focuses on strategies and skills for dealing with physical access violations, variations from normal operational routines, and similar events. Answer A is incorrect because data handling training is focused on how to manage data stored on organizational systems rather than how to deal with unauthorized personnel in secure areas. Answer B is incorrect because the clean desk policy provides guidance for data sanitization of the work environment to protect against unauthorized data disclosure should an unauthorized individual gain access. Answer D is incorrect because personal technology training provides strategies for dealing with personal technology and services within the organizational enterprise environment.

What Next?

If you want more practice on this chapter's exam objectives before you move on, remember that you can access all of the Cram Quiz questions on the CD. You can also create a custom exam by objective with the practice exam software. Note any objective you struggle with and go to that objective material in this chapter.

CHAPTER 4

Response and Recovery

This chapter covers the following official CompTIA Security+, SY0-301 exam objectives:

▶ Execute appropriate incident-response procedures

▶ Explain the impact and proper use of environmental controls

▶ Compare and contrast aspects of business continuity

▶ Execute disaster recovery plans and procedures

(For more information on the official CompTIA Security+ Certification exam topics, see the "About the CompTIA Security+ Certification Exam" section in the Introduction.)

The traditional C-I-A Triad of security directives includes maintaining the confidentiality, integrity, and availability of data and services. When any of these have been violated, incident response and recovery procedures must be implemented. This chapter examines incident response and environmental security controls and then examines the requirements for business continuity/continuity of operations and disaster recovery planning.

Planning and testing of those plans is critical prior to an incident in order to ensure that proper policies are in place to preserve organizational value in the face of disaster recovery practices that must focus first on preservation of human life, or in which lines of communication and succession must be well known by those who remain following a large-scale event.

Execute Appropriate Incident Response Procedures

▶ **Basic forensic procedures**

▶ **Damage and loss control**

▶ **Chain of custody**

▶ **Incident response: first responder**

Cram**Saver**

If you can correctly answer these questions before going through this section, save time by skimming the Exam Alerts in this section and then completing the Cram Quiz at the end of the section.

1. Which of the rules of evidence is concerned with using a write-blocker on a hard drive during forensic duplication?

2. Which form of data storage has the greatest volatility from the standpoint of forensic capture?

3. Which rule of evidence involves ensuring data remains authentic and unmodified?

Answers

1. Reliability. The data must be protected against modification to remain verifiably authentic and valid as evidence.

2. CPU registers and caches hold information for nanoseconds and are overwritten automatically millions of times every second during normal system operation.

3. Data must remain authentic and unmodified in order to meet the test for reliability after collection, review, and storage.

First Responders

First responders are the first ones to arrive at the incident scene. The success of data recovery and potential prosecution depends on the actions of the individual who initially discovers a computer incident. How the evidence scene is handled can severely affect the ability of the organization to prosecute if need be. Although police officers are trained to have a good understanding of the limits of the Fourth and Fifth Amendments and applicable laws, many system administrators and network security personnel are not.

The entire work area is a potential crime scene, not just the computer itself. There might be evidence such as removable media, voice-mail messages, or handwritten notes. The work area should be secured and protected to maintain the integrity of the area. Under no circumstances should you touch the computer or should anyone be allowed to remove any items from the scene.

Damage and Loss Control

When the response team has determined that an incident has occurred, the next step in incident analysis involves taking a comprehensive look at the incident activity to determine the scope, priority, and threat of the incident. This aids with researching possible response and mitigation strategies. In keeping with the severity of the incident, the organization can act to mitigate the impact of the incident by containing it and eventually restoring operations to normal.

Depending on the severity of the incident and the organizational policy, incident response functions can take many forms. The response team might send out recommendations for recovery, containment, and prevention to systems and network administrators, who then complete the response steps. The team might perform the remediation actions themselves. The follow-up response can involve sharing information and lessons learned with other response teams and other appropriate organizations and sites.

After the incident is appropriately handled, the organization might issue a report that details the cause of the incident, the cost of the incident, and the steps the organization should take to prevent future incidents.

It is important to accurately determine the cause of each incident so that it can be fully contained and the exploited vulnerabilities can be mitigated to prevent similar incidents from occurring in the future. Forensic analysis of information might require further actions with law enforcement, depending on findings and evidentiary data of interest.

Chain of Custody and Rules of Evidence

Forensics analysis involves establishing a clear chain of custody over the evidence, which is the documentation of all transfers of evidence from one person to another, showing the date, time, and reason for transfer and the signatures of both parties involved in the transfer. In other words, it tells how the evidence made it from the crime scene to the courtroom, including documentation of how the evidence was collected, preserved, and analyzed. Every time data of possible evidentiary value is moved, accessed, manipulated, or reviewed it is critical that the chain of custody be maintained and actions logged.

If you are asked to testify regarding data that has been recovered or preserved, it is critical that you, as the investigating security administrator, be able to prove that no other individuals or agents could have tampered with or modified the evidence. This requires careful collection and preservation of all evidence, including the detailed logging of investigative access and the scope of the investigation. Definition of the scope is crucial to ensure that accidental privacy violations or unrelated exposure do not contaminate the evidence trail. After data is collected, you must secure it in such a manner that you, as the investigating official, can state with certainty that the evidence could not have been accessed or modified during your custodial term.

> ## ExamAlert
>
> In order for evidence to be useful, it must have five properties:
>
> ▶ **Admissible:** Evidence must be able to be used in court or within an organization's practices and so must follow all appropriate legal requirements and guidelines for identification, acquisition, examination, and storage.
>
> ▶ **Authentic:** Evidence must be proven to relate to the incident, with any changes accounted for in evidence review logs.
>
> ▶ **Complete:** In addition to data of evidentiary value, it is critical that evidentiary gathering includes both directly related as well as indirectly related data. An example might include a listing of all accounts logged into a server when an attack occurred, rather than only logging details of the suspect's logon.
>
> ▶ **Reliable:** Evidentiary identification, acquisition, review, and storage practices must ensure that the data remains authentic and unmodified to the best extent possible based on the data's order of volatility.
>
> ▶ **Believable:** Evidence must be clear and easy to understand, but it must be related to original binary or encrypted data through a process that is equally clear, documented, and not subject to manipulation during transition. Raw hexadecimal data is difficult for juries to review, but a chart illustrating the same information must represent the evidentiary data in a manner able to be replicated by another forensic analyst with the same end result.

Basic Forensic Procedures

When a potential security breach must be reviewed, the digital forensics process comes into play. Similar to other forms of forensics, this process requires a vast knowledge of computer hardware, software, and media to protect the chain of custody over the evidence, avoid accidental invalidation or destruction of evidence, and preserve the evidence for future analysis. Computer forensics review involves the application of investigative and analytical techniques to acquire and protect potential legal evidence. Therefore, a professional within this field needs a detailed understanding of the local, regional, national, and even international laws affecting the process of evidence collection and retention, especially in cases involving attacks that may be waged from widely distributed systems located in many separate regions.

ExamAlert

The practice of forensics analysis is a detailed and exacting one. The information provided in this section enables an entering professional to recognize that precise actions must be taken during an investigation. It is crucial that you do not attempt to perform these tasks without detailed training in the hardware, software, network, and legal issues involved in forensics analysis.

The major concepts behind computer forensics are to

▶ Identify the evidence

▶ Determine how to preserve the evidence

▶ Extract, process, and interpret the evidence

▶ Ensure that the evidence is acceptable in a court of law

Each state has its own laws that govern how cases can be prosecuted. For cases to be prosecuted, evidence must be properly collected, processed, and preserved. The corporate world focuses more on prevention and detection, whereas law enforcement focuses on investigation and prosecution.

Documentation

Key to any form of forensic investigation is adherence to standards for the identification, collection, storage, and review of evidence. Chief among these is the creation of a log of all actions taken, including any inferences and causative details used to identify data of potential evidentiary value. This log should support the chain of custody for any evidentiary data, as well as track man hours, expense and details of identification, and contact data for any witnesses and statements provided during an investigation.

Records should be kept of all data and devices collected, including details such as system time offset from a verified time standard, non-standard hardware or equipment configurations, and codecs available for video manipulation and running services (if the system is in operation). Data storage should be duplicated using verified forensic utilities and then only the duplicate reviewed in subsequent investigations to protect the original against modification or corruption.

You can use a full system image to further examine data in an operational state, although you must put protections in place to prevent external communication through wired and wireless connectivity in order to protect against external manipulation or alerting of a suspect. You should generate hashes of all data and applications before and after any deep analysis is performed, allowing validation that the forensic analysis itself has not produced unexpected modifications of evidentiary data.

You should capture screenshots during the investigation and include them in forensic documentation for later reporting or testimony of the process and resulting findings. These should supplement photographs of the scene prior to evidentiary gathering and video of the collection and analysis process itself. Whenever possible, you should capture and preserve network traffic and logs in order to aid in the identification of related processes, remote virtual storage systems, and distributed computing functions that might relate to the investigation.

ExamAlert

Data of potential evidentiary value can be stored in many different forms within a subject system. Some of these storage locations preserve the data even when a system is powered off, whereas others might only hold data for a very brief interval before it is lost or overwritten. Even the process of evaluation can modify or overwrite these volatile storage areas, whereas shutting off a running system might completely wipe all data stored in active memory.

Data capture is highly dependent upon the order of volatility, where capture and examination of more durable storage can eliminate data of potential evidentiary value at more volatile levels.

The order of volatility follows:

▶ **Registers and Caches:** Data stored within the CPU's registers and cache levels might remain only nanoseconds before being overwritten by normal system operations.

▶ **Routing and Process Tables:** Data stored within networking and other active devices can be modified externally by ongoing operations.

▶ **Kernel Statistics:** Data regarding current kernel operations can be in constant transit between cache and main memory.

▶ **Main Memory:** Data stored within the System's RAM storage.

▶ **Temporary File Systems:** Data stored within elements of system memory allocated as temporary file stores, such as a RAM disk, or within virtual system drives.

▶ **Secondary Memory:** Data stored in non-volatile storage such as a hard drive or other form of media that retains data values after a system shutdown.

▶ **Removable Media:** Non-volatile removable media such as backup tape storage media.

▶ **Write-once Storage:** Non-volatile media not subject to later overwrite or modification, such as CD-ROMs and printouts.

Capture of running systems is a specialized practice and should not be attempted by untrained responders.

When collecting data, it is important to do the following:

▶ Document an investigation from initial notification through conclusion.

▶ Locate data any devices of potential evidentiary value.

▶ Identify data of interest.

▶ Establish an order of volatility to identify the first level of data capture desired.

▶ Eliminate external mechanisms of modification.

▶ Collect all data of potential evidentiary value.

▶ Create forensic duplicates of data for review.

▶ Store original data and devices in a manner that preserves integrity.

▶ Perform forensic evaluation and document findings or lack thereof.

▶ Report findings as appropriate.

Cram Quiz

Answer these questions. The answers follow the last question. If you cannot answer these questions correctly, consider reading this section again until you can.

1. Which of the following is not a basic concept of computer forensic analysis?

   ○ **A.** Identify data of potential evidentiary value

   ○ **B.** Determine how best to preserve evidence

   ○ **C.** Determine the guilt of a suspect based on findings

   ○ **D.** Ensure that collected data is acceptable as evidence

2. Why is it important to log a system's time offset against a verified time standard during an investigation?

   ○ **A.** To preserve the chain of custody

   ○ **B.** To ensure the evidence is complete

   ○ **C.** To protect the evidence against modification

   ○ **D.** To locate data supporting the lawyer's case

3. In order to preserve data against modification through the forensic review, which of the following forms of data storage should be examined first?

   ○ **A.** Temporary file storage

   ○ **B.** Main memory

   ○ **C.** Secondary memory

   ○ **D.** Process tables

4. Which of the following steps should be performed first in a forensic investigation?

- ○ **A.** Locate data
- ○ **B.** Establish an order of volatility
- ○ **C.** Collect data
- ○ **D.** Review data

Cram Quiz Answers

1. C. The forensic analysis process might identify information or the lack thereof of interest, but guilt and innocence are determined by the legal system and not part of the forensic review process. Answers A, B, and D are valid because data acquisition, protection, and analysis under the Rules of Evidence are all components of a forensic review.

2. B. Completeness of evidence includes not only the data of interest, but also any related data that might affect conclusions drawn from the investigation. Synchronization of logs, file creation date/time, and logons across multiple systems might require applying calculations to event log timing if the offset varies between systems. Answers A and C are incorrect because the time offset is not involved in maintaining the chain of custody or in protecting the data against modification. Answer D is incorrect because the specific file creation times and other similar details might help to identify timing of actions but will not determine whether logged details support a particular finding.

3. D. The Routing and Process tables are more volatile than the other forms of data storage and might be automatically overwritten during normal operations. Answer A is incorrect because temporary file storage involves file systems caches, whereas answer C is incorrect because secondary memory involves non-volatile media such as a hard-drive. Answer B is incorrect because system RAM holds data uncorrupted until changed by an operation or power loss.

4. A. The first step, after creating initial documentation for the review, is to locate and identify data of interest. Answers B, C, and D are incorrect as the steps presented are in the proper order for a forensic review, although some steps such as the elimination of external mechanisms of modification and creating forensic duplicates are not present.

Explain the Impact and Proper Use of Environmental Controls

▶ HVAC

▶ Fire suppression

▶ EMI shielding

▶ Hot and cold aisles

▶ Environmental monitoring

▶ Temperature and humidity controls

▶ Video monitoring

Cram**Saver**

If you can correctly answer these questions before going through this section, save time by skimming the Exam Alerts in this section and then completing the Cram Quiz at the end of the section.

1. What is the most important asset that must be protected by physical and environmental security controls?

2. What is TEMPEST?

3. Which type of fire extinguisher should be used for burning magnesium fires?

Answers

1. Human life is always the most important asset when planning for physical and environmental safety controls.

2. TEMPEST is a type of shielding used against electromagnetic interference, generally found in military equipment.

3. Class D extinguishers are used for burning combustible metals such as magnesium and sodium.

The Importance of Environmental Controls

Not all incidents arise from attacks, illegal activities, or other forms of directed threats to an enterprise. Many threats emerge due to physical and environmental factors that require additional consideration in planning for security controls.

The location of everything from the actual building to wireless antennas affects security. When picking a location for a building, an organization should investigate the type of neighborhood, population, crime rate, and emergency response times. This helps in the planning of the physical barriers needed, such as fencing, lighting, and security personnel. An organization must also analyze the potential dangers from natural disasters and plan to reduce their effect when possible.

When protecting computers, wiring closets, and other devices from physical damage due to either natural or man made disasters, you must select locations carefully. Proper placement of the equipment should cost a company little money upfront but provide significant protection from possible loss of data due to flooding, fire, or theft.

HVAC

You need to take into consideration the cooling requirements of computer data centers and server rooms when doing facilities planning. The amount of heat generated by some of this equipment is extreme and highly variable. Depending on the size of the space, age, and type of equipment the room contains, energy consumption typically ranges from 20 to 100 watts per square foot. Newer servers, although smaller and more powerful, might consume more energy. Therefore, some high-end facilities with state-of-the-art technology can require up to 400 watts per square foot. These spaces consume many times more energy than office facilities of equivalent size and must be planned for accordingly. Smaller, more powerful IT equipment is considerably hotter than older systems, making heat management a major challenge.

When monitoring the HVAC system, keep in mind that overcooling causes condensation on equipment and too-dry environments lead to excessive static. The area should be monitored for hot spots and cold spots. This is where one exchange is frigid cold under vent and still hot elsewhere. Water or drain pipes above facilities also raise a concern about upper-floor drains clogging, too. One solution is to use rubberized floors above the data center or server room. Above all else, timely A/C maintenance is required.

Fire Suppression

Fire is a danger common to all business environments and one that must be planned for well in advance of any possible occurrence. The first step in a fire-safety program is fire prevention.

The best way to prevent fires is to train employees to recognize dangerous situations and report these situations immediately. Knowing where a fire extinguisher is and how to use it can stop a small fire from becoming a major catastrophe. Many of the newer motion- and ultrasonic-detection systems also include heat and smoke detection for fire prevention. These systems alert the monitoring station of smoke or a rapid increase in temperature. If a fire does break out somewhere within the facility, a proper fire-suppression system can avert major damage. Keep in mind that laws and ordinances apply to the deployment and monitoring of a fire-suppression system. It is your responsibility to ensure that these codes are properly met. In addition, the organization should have safe evacuation procedures and periodic fire drills to protect its most important investment: human life.

Fire requires three main components to exist: heat, oxygen, and fuel. Eliminate any of these components and the fire goes out. A common way to fight fire is with water. Water attempts to take away oxygen and heat. A wet-pipe fire-suppression system is the one that most people think of when discussing an indoor sprinkler system. The term *wet* is used to describe the state of the pipe during normal operations. The pipe in the wet-pipe system has water under pressure in it at all times. The pipes are interconnected and have sprinkler heads attached at regularly spaced intervals. The sprinkler heads have a stopper held in place with a bonding agent designed to melt at an appropriate temperature. After the stopper melts, it opens the valve and allows water to flow from the sprinkler head to extinguish the fire. Keep in mind that electronic equipment and water don't get along well. Fires that start outside electrical areas are well served by water-based sprinkler systems. Also keep in mind that all these systems should have both manual activation and manual shutoff capabilities. You want to be able to turn off a sprinkler system to prevent potential water damage. Most systems are designed to activate only one head at a time. This works effectively to put out fires in the early stages.

Dry-pipe systems work in exactly the same fashion as wet-pipe systems, except that the pipes are filled with pressurized air rather than water. The stoppers work on the same principle. When the stopper melts, the air pressure is released and a valve in the system opens. One of the reasons for using a dry-pipe system is that when the outside temperature drops below freezing, any water in the pipes can freeze, causing them to burst. Another reason for justifying a dry-pipe system is the delay associated between the system activation and the actual water deployment. Because some laws require a sprinkler system even in areas of the building that house electrical equipment, there is enough of a delay that it is feasible for someone to manually deactivate the system before water starts to flow. In such a case, a company could deploy a dry-pipe system and a chemical system together. The delay in the dry-pipe system can be used to deploy the chemical system first and avoid serious damage to the running equipment from a water-based sprinkler system.

Exam**Alert**

Know the difference between the different types of fire-suppression systems (see Figure 4.1):

▶ For Class A fires (trash, wood, and paper), water decreases the fire's temperature and extinguishes its flames. Foam is usually used to extinguish Class B fires, which are fueled by flammable liquids, gases, and greases. Liquid foam mixes with air while passing through the hose and the foam.

▶ Class C fires (energized electrical equipment, electrical fires, and burning wires) are put out using extinguishers based on carbon dioxide or Halon. Halon was once used as a reliable, effective, and safe fire protection tool, but in 1987 an international agreement known as the Montreal Protocol mandated the phase-out of Halons in developed countries by the year 2000 and in less-developed countries by 2010, due to emissions concerns. Therefore, carbon dioxide extinguishers have replaced Halon extinguishers in all but a few locations. Carbon dioxide extinguishers don't leave a harmful residue, making them a good choice for an electrical fire on a computer or other electronic devices.

▶ Class D fires are fires that involve combustible metals such as magnesium, titanium, and sodium. The two types of extinguishing agents for Class D fires are sodium chloride and a copper-based dry powder.

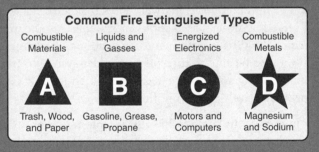

Common Fire Extinguisher Types

Combustible Materials	Liquids and Gasses	Energized Electronics	Combustible Metals
A	**B**	**C**	**D**
Trash, Wood, and Paper	Gasoline, Grease, Propane	Motors and Computers	Magnesium and Sodium

FIGURE 4.1   Labels for common fire extinguisher types.

EMI Shielding

One risk that is often overlooked is electronic and electromagnetic emissions. Electrical equipment generally gives off electrical signals. Monitors, printers, fax machines, and even keyboards use electricity. These electronic signals are said to "leak" from computer and electronic equipment. Shielding seeks to reduce this output. The shielding can be local, cover an entire room, or cover a whole building, depending on the perceived threat. We're going to review two types of shielding: TEMPEST and Faraday cages.

TEMPEST is a code word developed by the U.S. government in the 1950s. It is an acronym built from the Transient Electromagnetic Pulse Emanation Standard. It describes standards used to limit or block electromagnetic emanation (radiation) from electronic equipment. TEMPEST has since grown in its definition to include the study of this radiation. Individual pieces of equipment are protected through extra shielding that helps prevent electrical signals from emanating. This extra shielding is a metallic sheath surrounding connection wires for mouse, keyboard, and video monitor connectors. It can also be a completely shielded case for the motherboard, CPU, hard drive, and video display system. This protection prevents the transfer of signals through the air or nearby conductors, such as copper pipes, electrical wires, and phone wires. You are most likely to find TEMPEST equipment in government, military, and corporate environments that process government/military classified information. Because this can be costly to implement, protecting an area within a building makes more sense than protecting individual pieces of equipment.

A more efficient way to protect a large quantity of equipment from electronic eavesdropping is to place the equipment into a well-grounded metal box of conductive material called a Faraday cage, which is named after its inventor, Dr. Michael Faraday. The box can be small enough for a cell phone or can encompass an entire building. The idea behind the cage is to protect its contents from electromagnetic fields.

The cage surrounds an object with interconnected and well-grounded metal. The metal used is typically a copper mesh that is attached to the walls and covered with plaster or drywall. The wire mesh acts as a net for stray electric signals, either inside or outside the box.

Shielding also should be taken into consideration when choosing cable types and the placement of cable. Coaxial cable was the first type of cable used to network computers. Coaxial cables are made of a thick copper core with an outer metallic shield to reduce interference. Coaxial cables have no physical transmission security and are very simple to tap without being noticed or interrupting regular transmissions. The electric signal, conducted by a single core wire, can easily be tapped by piercing the sheath. It would then be possible to eavesdrop on the conversations of all hosts attached to the segment because coaxial cabling implements broadband transmission technology and assumes many hosts are connected to the same wire. Another security concern of coaxial cable is reliability. Because no focal point is involved, a faulty cable can bring the whole network down. Missing terminators or improperly functioning transceivers can cause poor network performance and transmission errors.

ExamAlert

Twisted-pair cable is used in most of today's network topologies. Twisted-pair cabling is either unshielded (UTP) or shielded (STP). UTP is popular because it is inexpensive and easy to install. UTP consists of eight wires twisted into four pairs. The design cancels much of the overflow and interference from one wire to the next, but UTP is subject to interference from outside electromagnetic sources and is prone to radio frequency interference (RFI) and electromagnetic interference (EMI) as well as crosstalk.

STP is different from UTP in that it has shielding surrounding the cable's wires. Some STP has shielding around the individual wires, which helps prevent crosstalk. STP is more resistant to EMI and is considered a bit more secure because the shielding makes wire-tapping more difficult.

Both UTP and STP are possible to tap, although it is physically a little trickier than tapping coaxial cable because of the physical structure of STP and UTP cable. With UTP and STP, a more inherent danger lies in the fact that it is easy to add devices to the network via open ports on unsecured hubs and switches. These devices should be secured from unauthorized access, and cables should be clearly marked so a visual inspection can let you know whether something is awry. Also, software programs that can help detect unauthorized devices are available.

The plenum is the space between the ceiling and the floor of a building's next level. It is commonly used to run network cables, which must be of plenum-grade. Plenum cable is a grade that complies with fire codes. The outer casing is more fire-resistant than regular twisted-pair cable.

Fiber was designed for transmissions at higher speeds over longer distances. It uses light pulses for signal transmission, making it immune to RFI, EMI, and eavesdropping. Fiber-optic wire has a plastic or glass center, surrounded by another layer of plastic or glass with a protective outer coating. On the downside, fiber is still quite expensive compared to more traditional cabling, it is more difficult to install, and fixing breaks can be costly. As far as security is concerned, fiber cabling eliminates the signal tapping that is possible with coaxial cabling. It is impossible to tap fiber without interrupting the service and using specially constructed equipment. This makes it more difficult to eavesdrop or steal service.

Temperature and Humidity Controls

As mentioned previously, overcooling causes condensation on equipment, and too-dry environments lead to excessive static. In addition to temperature monitoring, humidity should be monitored. Humidity is a measurement of moisture content in the air. A high level of humidity can cause components to rust and degrade electrical resistance or thermal conductivity. A low level of humidity can subject components to electrostatic discharge (ESD), causing damage; at extremely low levels, components might be affected by the air itself. The American Society of Heating, Refrigerating and Air-Conditioning Engineers (ASHRAE) recommends optimal humidity levels in the 40% to 55% range.

Hot-Aisle/Cold-Aisle Separation

Data centers and server farms might make use of an alternating arrangement of server racks, with alternating rows facing opposing directions so that fan intakes drawn in cool air vented to racks facing the cold aisle, and then fan output of hot air is vented to the alternating hot aisles for removal from the data center as shown in Figure 4.2. This data center organization allows greater efficiency in thermal management by allowing for supply ducts to serve all cold aisles and exhaust ducts to collect and draw away heated air.

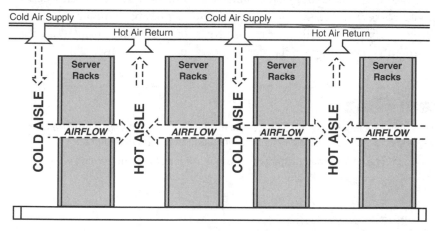

FIGURE 4.2   Simplified hot-aisle/cold-aisle data center layout with overhead HVAC supply and exhaust ducts.

Environmental Monitoring

In order to allow actions to be taken in response to undesirable environmental conditions, it is necessary to put into place environmental monitoring solutions that can raise alerts or trigger automated responses at need. Alerting systems must be able to sustain operations during the event, so a water-sensing monitor should be able to function and raise an alert even when the environment is filled with water.

Monitoring systems must also be able to communicate in the event of service disruption, so that alerts can be passed to responders even if the email server

cluster has shut down due to thermal overload conditions. If the monitoring solution relies on networking for sensor measurement or raising alerts, then environmental issues that degrade or prevent network communications might go unnoticed or alerts may not reach responders in a timely manner.

Video Monitoring

You can monitor physical access through video surveillance systems, although some organizations must deploy adequate signage to make clear whether or not camera systems are monitored or merely present for later prosecution of wrongdoing. Otherwise, individuals who have signaled to the cameras for assistance during an emergency might bring suit against the organization due to the expectation of live monitoring of security cameras. Some video monitoring systems might employ non-visible-spectrum cameras, such as thermal imaging systems able to spot heat blooms and body heat sources even when otherwise concealed. Video monitoring systems should be configured to observe access paths as well as locational areas, but not so that displayed data, password entry, and other similar details become remotely observable.

Cram Quiz

Answer these questions. The answers follow the last question. If you cannot answer these questions correctly, consider reading this section again until you can.

1. Which type of fire extinguisher would be best for putting out burning wires?
   - ○ **A.** Foam
   - ○ **B.** Carbon dioxide
   - ○ **C.** Sodium chloride
   - ○ **D.** Copper powder

2. What is the plenum?
   - ○ **A.** A mesh enclosure designed to block EMI
   - ○ **B.** A mechanism for controlling condensation
   - ○ **C.** A type of dry-pipe fire control system
   - ○ **D.** A mechanism for thermal management

3. The ASHRAE recommends humidity levels in which range?
   - ○ **A.** 25%–40%
   - ○ **B.** 40%–55%
   - ○ **C.** 55%–70%
   - ○ **D.** 70%–85%

4. Which of these is not a concern for environmental monitoring systems?

    ◯ **A.** Able to sustain operations during an environmental disaster

    ◯ **B.** Able to communicate even if the email service was involved

    ◯ **C.** Able to reach responders in a timely manner

    ◯ **D.** Include signage noting live or automated-review only

Cram Quiz Answers

1. **B**. The carbon dioxide extinguisher replaces the Halon extinguisher for putting out electrical (class C) fires. Answer A is incorrect because foam is used for class A fires (trash, wood, and paper). Answers C and D are incorrect because both sodium chloride and copper-based dry powder extinguishers are used for class D (combustible materials) fires.

2. **D**. A plenum is the space below a raised floor or above a drop-ceiling, which can be used in hot-aisle/cold-aisle server rooms to efficiently manage thermal dissipation. Answer A is incorrect because a grounded mesh enclosure for EMI shielding is called a Faraday cage. Answer B is incorrect because management of condensation is handled as part of the HVAC function as air is cooled. Answer C is incorrect because a dry-pipe system is a fire extinguishing system that uses pressurized air as a triggering mechanism for water.

3. **B**. The Air-Conditioning Engineers (ASHRAE) recommendation for optimal humidity levels between 40% and 55% to minimize electrostatic discharge and condensation. Answer A is incorrect because it specifies a range too low that would be dangerous for static discharge, whereas answers C and D are incorrect because they represent too high a humidity level that would be susceptible to the buildup of condensation on cool components and boards.

4. **D**. Video surveillance might require signage noting whether cameras are monitored live or not to avoid a legal complaint if someone tries unsuccessfully to signal for aid during an emergency. Answers A, B, and C are valid concerns because environmental monitoring systems must be able to operate even during a disaster and communicate with responders in a timely manner even if the servers hosting the usual communication services (email, SMS, and so on) are involved in the disaster.

Compare and Contrast Aspects of Business Continuity

▶ Business impact analysis

▶ Removing single points of failure

▶ Business continuity planning and testing

▶ Continuity of operations

▶ Disaster recovery

▶ IT contingency planning

▶ Succession planning

CramSaver

If you can correctly answer these questions before going through this section, save time by skimming the Exam Alerts in this section and then completing the Cram Quiz at the end of the section.

1. Between BC and DR, which is more focused on long-term return to operational capability following an incident?

2. Business contingency plans, business recovery plans, and business resumption plans are all part of what?

3. Is a business impact analysis the same as a risk assessment?

Answers

1. Disaster recovery plans are intended to support the recovery of operational capability in the medium to long term following a disaster or disruption of service, whereas business continuity planning involves maintaining operational capability in the short to midterm, even if in a degraded state.

2. Business continuity plans include requirements for alternative options (contingencies), acquisition (recovery), and return to service (resumption) planning.

3. A risk assessment focuses on the likelihood of a particular threat, but the business impact assessment focuses on the impact to the organization if a particular threat occurs.

Contrasting Business Continuity and Disaster Recovery

Network security and system hardening provide the strongest possible levels of security against directed attacks, but organizational security must also be considered when planning an organization's data security. Continuity of operations planning involves strategies for maintaining operational capability, sometimes in a limited form, until full operational function is restored. Disaster recovery planning involves strategies for recovering after a loss of function and is focused on recovery point objectives (RPOs) and recovery time objectives (RTOs).

For many organizations, downtime is not an option. Organizational security encompasses identifying the critical business needs and the resources associated with those needs. Critical business functions must be designed to continue operating in the event of hardware or other component failure. Critical systems such as servers and Internet availability require redundant hardware. Redundancy planning requires that you prioritize the data and systems that need to be recovered first and then plan backup methods, data replication, and failover systems. Make sure you have redundancy for critical systems, whether it's as simple as a redundant array of independent (or inexpensive) disks (RAID) storage system or as complex as a complete duplicate data center.

> ### ExamAlert
>
> Be familiar with redundancy descriptions indicating potential flaws. Watch for descriptions that include physical details or organizational processes.

Business Continuity Planning

In any planning, safety of human life must be paramount. Business continuity planning involves identification of risks and threats to operation and implementing strategies to mitigate the effect of each. Beyond backup and restoration of data, disaster recovery planning must include a detailed analysis of underlying business practices and support requirements. This is called business continuity planning. Business continuity planning is a more comprehensive approach to provide guidance so that the organization can continue making sales and collecting revenue. As with disaster recovery planning, it covers natural and man made disasters. Business continuity planning should identify required services, such as network access and utility agreements, and arrange for automatic failover of critical services to redundant offsite systems.

Business continuity planning can address the following:

> ▶ **Network connectivity:** In the event that a disaster is widespread or targeted at an ISP or key routing hardware point, an organization's continuity plan should include options for alternative network access, including dedicated administrative connections that might be required for recovery.

▶ **Facilities:** Continuity planning should include considerations for recovery in the event that existing hardware and facilities are rendered inaccessible or unrecoverable. You should include hardware configuration details, network requirements, and utilities agreements for alternative sites (that is, warm and cold sites) in this planning consideration.

▶ **Clustering:** To provide load balancing to avoid functionality loss because of directed attacks meant to prevent valid access, continuity planning might include clustering solutions that allow multiple nodes to perform support while transparently acting as a single host to the user. High-availability clustering might also be used to ensure that automatic failover occurs in the event that hardware failure renders the primary node unable to provide normal service.

▶ **Fault tolerance:** Cross-site replication might be included for high-availability solutions requiring high levels of fault tolerance. Individual servers might also be configured to allow for the continued function of key services even in the case of hardware failure. Common fault-tolerant solutions include RAID solutions, which maintain duplicated data across multiple disks so that the loss of one disk does not cause the loss of data. Many of these solutions might also support the hot-swapping of failed drives and redundant power supplies so that replacement hardware can be installed without ever taking the server offline.

A business recovery plan, business resumption plan, and contingency plan are also considered part of business continuity planning. In the event of an incident, an organization might also need to restore equipment (in addition to data) or personnel lost or rendered unavailable due to the nature or scale of the disaster.

Business Impact Analysis

IT contingency planning for both disaster recovery and operational continuity rely on conducting a business impact analysis (BIA) as part of the overall DR/BC planning process. Unlike a risk assessment, as discussed in Chapter 3, "Risk Management," the BIA is not focused as much on the relative likelihood of potential threats to an organization but instead focuses on the relative impact on critical business functions due to the loss of operational capability due to the threats. Conducting a business impact analysis involves identification of critical business functions and the services and technologies required for each, along with the cost associated with the loss of each and the maximum acceptable outage period.

For hardware-related outages, the assessment should also include the current age of existing solutions along with standards for the expected mean-time-between-failures based on vendor data or accepted industry standards. Strategies for the DR/BC plan are intended to minimize this cost by arranging recovery actions to restore critical functions in the most effective manner based on cost, legal or statutory mandates, and mean time to restore calculations.

Internet Service Providers

Along with power and equipment loss, telephone and Internet communications might be out of service for a while when a disaster strikes. Organizations must consider this factor when formulating a disaster recovery plan. Relying on a single Internet connection for critical business functions could prove disastrous to your business. With a redundant ISP, a backup ISP could be standing by in the event of an outage at the main ISP. Should this happen, traffic is switched over to the redundant ISP. The organization can continue to do business without any interruptions.

Although using multiple ISPs is mostly considered for disaster recovery purposes, it can also relieve network traffic congestion and provide network isolation for applications. As organizations become global, dealing with natural disasters will become more common. Solutions such as wireless ISPs used in conjunction with VoIP to quickly restore phone and data services are being looked at more closely. Organizations might look to ISP redundancy to prevent application performance failure and supplier diversity. For example, businesses that transfer large files can use multiple ISPs to segregate voice and file transfer traffic to a specific ISP. More and more organizations are implementing technologies such as VoIP. When planning deployment, explore using different ISPs for better network traffic performance, for disaster recovery, and to ensure a quality level of service.

Connections

In disaster recovery planning, you might need to consider redundant connections between branches or sites. Internally, for total redundancy, you might need two network cards in computers connected to different switches or hubs. With redundant connections, all devices are connected to each other more than once, to create fault tolerance. A single device or cable failure does not affect the performance because the devices are connected by more than one means. This setup is more expensive because it requires more hardware and cabling. This type of topology can also be found in enterprise-wide networks, with routers being connected to other routers for fault tolerance.

Service Level Agreements

One of the best ways to ensure the availability of replacement parts is through service level agreements (SLAs). These are signed contracts between the organization and the vendors with which they commonly deal. SLAs are covered in greater detail in the next chapter. SLAs can be for services such as access to the Internet, backups, restoration, and hardware maintenance. Should a disaster destroy your existing systems, the SLA can also help you guarantee the availability of computer parts or even entire computer systems.

It is important to understand all equipment warranties, especially if the organization decides against SLAs for computer equipment. Often, opening a computer yourself and replacing the parts voids a warranty if the warranty has not expired.

Also confirm that critical suppliers have strict disaster recovery plans. There's no point in having your equipment in the hands of a company that is struggling to get back on its feet after a disaster or merger.

When evaluating SLAs, the expected uptime and maximum allowed downtime on a yearly basis are considered. Uptime is based on 365 days a year, 24 hours a day. Here is an example:

99.999%	5.3 minutes downtime/year
99.99%	53 minutes downtime/year
99.9%	8.7 hours downtime/year
99%	87 hours downtime/year

Succession Planning

BC planning must also include contingencies for personnel replacement in the event of loss (death, injury, retirement, termination, and so on) or lack of availability. Clear lines of succession and cross-training in critical functions and communications plans for alternative mechanisms of contact to alert individuals as to the need for succession are imperative for meeting RTOs and RPOs.

Cram Quiz

Answer these questions. The answers follow the last question. If you cannot answer these questions correctly, consider reading this section again until you can.

1. Which of the following types of planning assists in preventing loss of service in the event of a server failure?

   ○ **A.** Network connectivity

   ○ **B.** Facilities

   ○ **C.** Clustering

   ○ **D.** Fault tolerance

2. Which of the following is not a consideration for the business impact analysis?

◯   **A.** Identification of critical business functions

◯   **B.** Identification of key services and technologies

◯   **C.** Identification of likelihood of an incident

◯   **D.** Identification of cost associated with an incident

3. How is uptime measured in an SLA?

◯   **A.** Work week (5 days of 7) and work day (8 hours of 24)

◯   **B.** Work week (5 days of 7) and full day (24 hours)

◯   **C.** Full year (365 days) and work day (8 hours of 24)

◯   **D.** Full year (365 days) and full day (24 hours)

4. Which of the following is not a reason for activating succession plans?

◯   **A.** Retraining

◯   **B.** Death

◯   **C.** Retirement

◯   **D.** Injury

Cram Quiz Answers

1. **C.** Clustering allows multiple servers to share operational load or to switch in an alternative following the loss of a single node. Answer A is incorrect because a backup network connection assists in the case of a widespread outage that cuts off normal networking. Answer B is incorrect because facilities planning involves alternatives in the event that a primary site is rendered inaccessible. Answer D is incorrect because fault tolerance addresses redundancy for individual components such as storage or services rather than a node's failover.

2. **C.** Likelihood of an incident's occurrence is part of the risk analysis, rather than the business impact analysis. Answers A, B, and D are not valid because all three represent considerations for the BIA—identifying critical business functions and the key services and technologies required for each, along with the cost associated with loss of service for each.

3. **D.** Service level agreements measure uptime based on the maximum allowed downtime on a yearly basis (365 days, 24 hours/day). Answers A and B are incorrect because the full year must be included in this measure, and answer C is incorrect because all hours in the day must be included in calculating uptime.

4. **A.** Retraining should be a constant part of employee cross-training in support of succession planning. Answers B, C, and D are not valid because death, retirement, and injury represent triggers for activating succession planning to cover for lost skills and human resources.

Execute Disaster Recovery Plans and Procedures

▶ Backup/backout contingency plans or policies

▶ Backups, execution, and frequency

▶ Redundancy and fault tolerance

▶ High availability

▶ Cold site, hot site, warm site

▶ Mean time to restore, mean time between failures, recovery time objectives, and recovery point objectives

Cram**Saver**

If you can correctly answer these questions before going through this section, save time by skimming the Exam Alerts in this section and then completing the Cram Quiz at the end of the section.

1. Which form of recovery site can accommodate the shortest RTO?

2. Which form of RAID does not provide redundancy in the event of a drive's loss?

Answers

1. The hot site allows the shortest recovery time objective (RTO), as it is already running and available 7 days a week, 24 hours per day.

2. RAID 0 spans data storage across multiple drives in order to achieve higher data transfer rates and larger storage volumes without providing redundancy against the loss of a drive.

Disaster Recovery Planning

Too many organizations realize the criticality of disaster recovery planning only after a catastrophic event (such as a hurricane, flood, or terrorist attack). However, disaster recovery is an important part of overall organization security planning for every organization! Natural disasters and terrorist activity can bypass even the most rigorous physical security measures. Common hardware failures and even accidental deletions might require some form of recovery capability. Failure to recover from a disaster might destroy an organization.

Disaster recovery involves many aspects, including the following:

▶ **Impact and risk assessment:** To plan recovery appropriately, a company must determine the scope and criticality of its services and data. In addition, an order (a priority) of recovery must be established.

▶ **Disaster recovery plan:** A disaster recovery plan is a written document that defines how the organization will recover from a disaster and how to restore business with minimum delay. The document also explains how to evaluate risks; how data backup and restoration procedures work; and the training required for managers, administrators, and users. A detailed disaster recovery should address various processes, including backup, data security, and recovery.

▶ **Disaster recovery policies:** These policies detail responsibilities and procedures to follow during disaster recovery events, including how to contact key employees, vendors, customers, and the press. They should also include instructions for situations in which it might be necessary to bypass the normal chain of command to minimize damage or the effects of a disaster.

▶ **Service level agreements:** SLAs are contracts with ISPs, utilities, facilities managers, and other types of suppliers that detail minimum levels of support that must be provided (including in the event of failure or disaster).

Detailed responsibilities and procedures to follow during disaster recovery events should be in place. The procedures must include contact methods. Plans must also be established in case it is necessary to bypass normal access for any reason (perhaps, for instance, to avoid potential sources of failure). Disaster recovery and redundancy require organizations to consider how best to deal with the following issues:

▶ Power in the event of a complete loss of city power

▶ Alternative locations for business operations

▶ Telecommunications restoration

▶ Internet connectivity to continue business operations

▶ Equipment that will be put in place for operations to continue

▶ Replacement software

▶ Data restoration

▶ The contact method for employees and clients

- ▸ The order in which the recovery process should proceed

- ▸ Physical security at current and alternative sites

- ▸ The estimated time to complete the steps in the disaster recovery plan and get the business back to normal

After a "disaster" or other failure situation has been evaluated, and the damage assessed, the company can begin the recovery process. A hard copy of the plan must be available (and key elements of that plan should be removable, such as a vendors list or team member phone numbers). After all, a disaster recovery plan does not do you any good if it is locked in someone's desk drawer and that desk is in a building that has been evacuated or is no longer in existence, as the September 11 attack on the World Trade Center proved.

Alternative Sites

In the beginning stages of the organizational security plan, the organization must decide how it will operate and how it will recover from any unfortunate incidents that affect its ability to conduct business. Redundancy planning encompasses the effects of both natural and man made catastrophes. Often, these catastrophes result from unforeseen circumstances. Hot, warm, and cold sites can provide a means for recovery should an event render the original building unusable. These are discussed individually in the following sections.

Hot Site

A *hot site* is a location that is already running and available 7 days a week, 24 hours a day. These sites allow the company to continue normal business operations, usually within a minimal period of time after the loss of a facility. This type of site is similar to the original site in that it is equipped with all necessary hardware, software, network, and Internet connectivity fully installed, configured, and operational. Data is regularly backed up or replicated to the hot site so that it can be made fully operational in a minimal amount of time in the event of a disaster at the original site. The business can be resumed without significant delay. In the event of a catastrophe, all people need to do is drive to the site, log on, and begin working.

Hot sites are the most expensive to operate and are mostly found in businesses that operate in real time, for whom any downtime might mean financial ruin.

The hot site should be located far enough from the original facility to avoid the disaster striking both facilities. A good example of this is a flood. The range of a flood depends on the category and other factors such as wind and the amount of rain that follows. A torrential flood can sink and wash away buildings and damage various other property, such as electrical facilities. If the hot site is within this range, the hot site is affected, too.

Warm Site

A *warm site* is a scaled-down version of a hot site. The site is generally configured with power, phone, and network jacks. The site might have computers and other resources, but they are not configured and ready to go. In a warm site, the data is replicated elsewhere for easy retrieval. However, you still have to do something to be able to access the data. This "something" might include setting up systems so that you can access the data or taking special equipment over to the warm site for data retrieval. It is assumed that the organization itself will configure the devices, install applications, and activate resources or that it will contract with a third party for these services. Because the warm site is generally office space or warehouse space, the site can serve multiple clients simultaneously. The time and cost for getting a warm site operational is somewhere between a hot and a cold site.

Cold Site

A *cold site* is the weakest of the recovery plan options but also the cheapest. These sites are merely a prearranged request to use facilities if needed. Electricity, bathrooms, and space are about the only facilities provided in a cold site contract. Therefore, the organization is responsible for providing and installing all the necessary equipment. If the organization chooses this type of facility, it will require additional time to secure equipment, install operating systems and applications, and contract services such as Internet connectivity. The same distance factors should be considered when planning a cold site as when planning a hot site.

Choosing a Recovery Site Solution

The type of recovery site an organization chooses depends on the criticality of recovery and budget allocations. Hot sites are traditionally more expensive, but they can be used for operations and recovery testing before an actual catastrophic event occurs. Cold sites are less costly in the short term. However, equipment purchased after such an event might be more expensive or difficult to obtain.

As part of redundancy and recovery planning, an organization can contract annually with a company that offers redundancy services (for a monthly, or otherwise negotiated, service charge). When contracting services from a provider, the organization should carefully read the contract. Daily fees and other incidental fees might apply. In addition, in a large-scale incident, the facility could very well become overextended.

> **ExamAlert**
>
> Be familiar with the various types of site descriptions. Watch for scenarios that require you to choose a hot, warm, or cold site solution.

Utilities

When planning for redundancy, keep in mind that even though the physical building may be spared destruction in a catastrophic event, it can still suffer power loss. If power is out for several days or weeks, your business itself could be in jeopardy. The most common way to overcome this problem is to supply your own power when an emergency scenario calls for it.

Backup Power Generator

Backup power refers to a power supply that runs in the event of a primary power outage. One source of backup power is a gas-powered generator. The generator can be used for rolling blackouts, emergency blackouts, or electrical problems. Most generators can be tied in to the existing electrical grid so that if power is lost, the generator starts supplying power immediately. When selecting a generator, issues to consider include the following:

- ▶ **Power output:** Rated in watts or kilowatts
- ▶ **Fuel source:** Gasoline, diesel, propane, or natural gas
- ▶ **Uptime:** How long the unit can run on one tank of fuel
- ▶ **How unit is started:** Battery or manually with a pull-cord
- ▶ **Transfer switch:** Automatic or manual

Determine how big a generator you need by adding up the wattages required by devices you want turned on at one time. Gasoline-run generators are the least expensive. However, they are louder and have a shorter lifespan than diesel, propane, and natural gas generators.

Uninterruptible Power Supply (UPS)

Power problems can occur in various ways. One of the most obvious is when power strips are daisy-chained. Often, daisy-chained devices do not get enough power. At the other end of the spectrum, daisy-chaining of devices occasionally trips the circuit breakers or starts a fire. Be aware that power issues can quickly burn out equipment. If power is not properly conditioned, it can have devastating effects on equipment. The following list describes some of the power variations that can occur:

▶ **Noise:** Also referred to as electromagnetic interference (EMI) and radio frequency interference (RFI), noise can be caused by lightning, load switching, generators, radio transmitters, and industrial equipment.

▶ **Spikes:** These are instantaneous and dramatic increases in voltage that result from lightning strikes or when electrical loads are switched on or off. They can destroy electronic circuitry and corrupt stored data.

▶ **Surges:** These are short-term increases in voltage commonly caused by large electrical load changes and from utility power-line switching.

▶ **Brownouts:** These are short-term decreases in voltage levels that most often occur when motors are started or are triggered by faults on the utility provider's system.

▶ **Blackouts:** These are caused by faults on the utility provider's system and results in a complete loss of power. Rolling blackouts occur when the utility company turns off the power in a specific area.

To protect your environment from damaging fluctuations in power, always connect your sensitive electronic equipment to power conditioners, surge protectors, and a UPS (uninterruptible power supply, which provides the best protection of all). A UPS is a power supply that sits between the wall power and the computer. In the event of power failure at the wall, the UPS takes over and powers the computer so that you can take action to not lose data (such as saving your work or shutting down your servers).

Three different types of devices are classified as UPSs:

▶ **Standby power supply (SPS):** This is also referred to as an *offline* UPS. In this type of supply, power usually derives directly from the power line until power fails. After a power failure, a battery-powered inverter turns on to continue supplying power. Batteries are charged, as necessary, when line power is available.

▶ **Hybrid or ferroresonant UPS system:** This device conditions power using a ferroresonant transformer. This transformer maintains a constant output voltage even with a varying input voltage and provides good protection against line noise. The transformer also maintains output on its secondary line briefly when a total outage occurs.

- ► **Continuous UPS:** This is also called an *online* UPS. In this type of system, the computer is always running off battery power and the battery is continuously being recharged. There is no switchover time, and these supplies generally provide the best isolation from power-line problems.

You cannot eliminate all risk associated with power problems just by connecting your sensitive electronic equipment to power conditioners, surge protectors, or a UPS. However, you can certainly minimize (if not entirely prevent) the damage such problems can cause.

Redundant Equipment and Connections

The main goal of preventing and effectively dealing with any type of disruption is to ensure availability. Of course, you can use RAID, UPS equipment, and clustering to accomplish this. But neglecting single points of failure can prove disastrous. A single point of failure is any piece of equipment that can bring your operation down if it stops working.

To determine the number of single points of failure in the organization, start with a good map of everything the organization uses to operate. Pay special attention to items such as the Internet connection, routers, switches, and proprietary business equipment. After identifying the single points of failure, perform a risk analysis. In other words, compare the consequences if the device fails to the cost of redundancy. For example, if all your business is web-based, it is a good idea to have some redundancy in the event the Internet connection goes down. However, if the majority of your business is telephone-based, you might look for redundancy in the phone system as opposed to the ISP. In some cases, the ISP might supply both the Internet and the phone services. The point here is to be aware of where your organization is vulnerable and understand what the risk is so that you can devise an appropriate backup plan.

Redundant Array of Inexpensive Disks

Perhaps the biggest asset an organization has is its data. The planning of every server setup should consider how to salvage the data should a component fail. The decision about how to store and protect data is determined by how the organization uses its data. This section examines data-redundancy options.

The most common approach to data availability and redundancy is called RAID. RAID organizes multiple disks into a large, high-performance logical disk. In other words, if you have three hard drives, you can configure them to look like one large drive. Disk arrays are created to stripe data across multiple disks and access them in parallel, which allows the following:

▶ Higher data transfer rates on large data accesses

▶ Higher I/O rates on small data accesses

▶ Uniform load balancing across all the disks

Large disk arrays are highly vulnerable to disk failures. To solve this problem, you can use redundancy in the form of error-correcting codes to tolerate disk failures. With this method, a redundant disk array can retain data for a much longer time than an unprotected single disk. With multiple disks and a RAID scheme, a system can stay up and running when a disk fails and during the time the replacement disk is being installed and data restored. Figure 4.3 shows common types of RAID configurations.

Common RAID Types

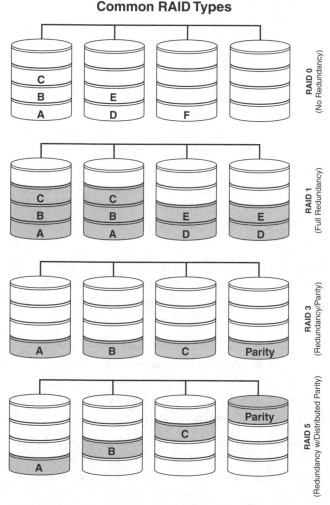

FIGURE 4.3   Common types of RAID configurations.

The two major goals when implementing disk arrays are data striping for better performance and redundancy for better reliability. There are many types of RAID. Some of the more common ones are as follows:

▶ **RAID Level 0 - Striped disk array without fault tolerance:** RAID 0 implements a striped disk array, the data is broken into blocks, and each block is written to a separate disk drive. This requires a minimum of two disks to implement.

▶ **RAID Level 1 - Mirroring and duplexing:** This solution, called mirroring or duplexing, requires a minimum of two disks and offers 100% redundancy because all data is written to both disks. The difference between mirroring and duplexing is the number of controllers. Mirroring uses one controller, whereas duplexing uses one controller for each disk. In RAID 1, disk usage is 50% as the other 50% is for redundancy.

▶ **RAID Level 2 - Hamming Code Error Correcting Code (ECC):** In RAID 2, each bit of a data word is written to a disk. RAID 2 requires the use of extra disks to store an error-correcting code. A typical setup requires 10 data disks and 4 ECC disks. Because all modern disk drives incorporate ECC, this offers little additional protection. No commercial implementations exist today. The controller required is complex, specialized, and expensive, and the performance is not very good.

▶ **RAID Level 3 - Parallel transfer with parity:** In RAID 3, the data block is striped and written on the data disks. This requires a minimum of three drives to implement. In a parallel transfer with parity, data is interleaved bit-wise over the data disks, and a single parity disk is added to tolerate any single disk failure.

▶ **RAID Level 4 - Independent data disks with shared parity disk:** Entire blocks are written onto a data disk. RAID 4 requires a minimum of three drives to implement. RAID 4 is similar to RAID 3 except that data is interleaved across disks of arbitrary size rather than in bits.

▶ **RAID Level 5 - Independent data disks with distributed parity blocks:** In RAID 5, each entire block of the data and the parity is striped. RAID 5 requires a minimum of three disks. Because it writes both the data and the parity over all the disks, it has the best small read, large write performance of any redundancy disk array.

▶ **RAID Level 6 - Independent data disks with two independent parity schemes:** This is an extension of RAID 5 and allows for additional fault tolerance by using two-dimensional parity. This method uses Reed-Solomon codes to protect against up to two disk failures using the bare minimum of two redundant disk arrays.

▶ **RAID Level 10 - High reliability combined with high performance:**
RAID 10 requires a minimum of four disks to implement. This solution
is a striped array that has RAID 1 arrays. Disks are mirrored in pairs for
redundancy and improved performance and then data is striped across
multiple disks for maximum performance.

> **ExamAlert**
>
> Know the different levels of RAID and the number of disks required to implement
> each one.

There are several additional levels of RAID: 7, 50, 53, and 0+1. RAID 7 is a
proprietary solution that is a registered trademark of Storage Computer
Corporation. This RAID has a fully implemented, process-oriented, real-time
operating system residing on an embedded array controller microprocessor.
RAID 50 is more fault tolerant than RAID 5 but has twice the parity overhead
and requires a minimum of six drives to implement. RAID 53 is an implementation of a striped array that has RAID 3 segment arrays. This takes a minimum of five drives, three for RAID 3 and two for striping. RAID 0+1 is a
mirrored array that has RAID 0 segments. RAID 0+1 requires a minimum of
four drives, two for striping and two to mirror the first striped set.

When choosing a method of redundancy, choose a level of RAID that is supported by the operating system. Not all operating systems support all versions
of RAID. For example, Microsoft Windows Servers support RAID levels 0, 1,
and 5. In addition to hardware RAID, software RAID can be used. Software
RAID can be used when the expense of additional drives is not included in the
budget or if the organization is using older servers. Software RAID can provide more flexibility, but it requires more CPU cycles and power to run.
Software RAID operates on a partition-by-partition basis and tends be slightly
more complicated to run.

Another point to remember is that even though you set up the server for
redundancy, you must still back up your data. RAID does not protect you
from multiple disk failures. Regular tape backups enable you to recover from
data loss that results from errors unrelated to disk failure (such as human,
hardware, and software errors). We discuss the different types and methods of
backups later in this chapter.

Servers

It might be necessary to set up redundant servers so that the business can still
function in the event of hardware or software failure. If a single server hosts

vital applications, a simple equipment failure might result in days of downtime as the problem is repaired. In addition, some manufacturers provide redundant power supplies in mission-critical servers.

To ensure availability and reliability, server redundancy is implemented. This means multiple servers are used to perform the same task. For example, if you have a web-based business with more than one server hosting your site, when one of the servers crashes, the requests can be redirected to another server. This provides a highly available website.

If you do not host your own website, confirm whether the vendor you are using provides high availability and reliability.

In today's world, mission-critical businesses demand 100% uptime 24 hours a day 7 days a week. Availability is vital, and many businesses would not be able to function without redundancy. Redundancy can take several forms, such as automatic failover, failback, and virtualization. The most notable advantage of server redundancy, perhaps, is load balancing. In load balancing, the system load is spread over all available servers. This proves especially useful when traffic volume is high. It prevents one server from being overloaded while another sits idle.

Clusters

Another way to increase availability is server clustering. A *server cluster* is the combination of two or more servers so that they appear as one. This clustering increases availability by ensuring that if a server is out of commission because of failure or planned downtime, another server in the cluster takes over the workload.

Backup Techniques and Practices

Fundamental to any disaster recovery plan is the need to provide for regular backups of key information, including user file and email storage; database stores; event logs; and security principal details such as user logons, passwords, and group membership assignments. Without a regular backup process, loss of data through accidents or directed attack could severely impair business processes.

ExamAlert

Any DR/BC plan including contingencies, backup and recovery, or succession must include regular testing of restoration and recovery processes to ensure that personnel are able to transition and that backup media and procedures are adequate to restore lost functionality.

The backup procedures in use might also affect what is recovered following a disaster. Disaster recovery plans should identify the type and regularity of the backup process. The following sections cover the types of backups you can use and different backup schemes.

Backup Types

The different types of backups you can use are full, differential, incremental, and copy. A full backup is a complete backup of all data and is the most time-intensive and resource-intensive form of backup, requiring the largest amount of data storage. In the event of a total loss of data, restoration from a complete backup is faster than other methods. A full backup copies all selected files and resets the archive bit. An *archive bit* is a file attribute used to track incremental changes to files for the purpose of backup. The operating system sets the archive bit any time changes occur, such as when a file is created, moved, or renamed. This method enables you to restore using just one tape. Theft poses the most risk, however, because all data is on one tape—only encryption can protect the data at that point.

A differential backup includes all data that has changed since the last full backup, regardless of whether or when the last differential backup was made, because it doesn't reset the archive bit. This form of backup is incomplete for full recovery without a valid full backup. For example, if the server dies on Thursday, two tapes are needed—the full from Friday and the differential from Wednesday. Differential backups require a variable amount of storage, depending on the regularity of normal backups and the number of changes that occur during the period between full backups. Theft of a differential tape is more risky than an incremental tape because larger chunks of sequential data can be stored on the tape the further away it is from the last full backup.

An incremental backup includes all data that has changed since the last incremental backup, and it resets the archive bit. An incremental backup is incomplete for full recovery without a valid full backup and all incremental backups since the last full backup. For example, if the server dies on Thursday, four tapes are needed—the full from Friday and the incremental tapes from Monday, Tuesday, and Wednesday. Incremental backups require the smallest amount of data storage and require the least amount of backup time, but they can take the most time during restoration. If an incremental tape is stolen, it might not be of value to the offender, but it still represents risk to the company.

A copy backup is similar to a full backup in that it copies all selected files. However, it doesn't reset the archive bit. From a security perspective, the loss of a tape with a copy backup is the same as losing a tape with a full backup.

Backup Schemes

When choosing a backup strategy, a company should look at the following factors:

▶ **How often it needs to restore files:** As a matter of convenience, if files are restored regularly, a full backup might be chosen because it can be done with one tape.

▶ **How fast the data needs to be restored:** If large amounts of data are backed up, the incremental backup method might work best.

▶ **How long the data needs to be kept before being overwritten:** If used in a development arena where data is constantly changing, a differential backup method might be the best choice.

After the backups are complete, they must be clearly marked or labeled so that they can be properly safeguarded. In addition to these backup strategies, organizations employ tape rotation and retention policies. The various methods of tape rotation include the following:

▶ *Grandfather-father-son* backup refers to the most common rotation scheme for rotating backup media. The basic method is to define three sets of backups. The first set, "son," represents daily backups. A second set, "father," is used to perform full backups. The final set of three tapes, "grandfather," is used to perform full backups on the last day of each month.

▶ *Tower of Hanoi* is based on the mathematics of the Tower of Hanoi puzzle. This is a recursive method where every tape is associated with a disk in the puzzle, and the disk movement to a different peg corresponds with a backup to a tape.

▶ *Ten-tape rotation* is a simpler and more cost-effective method for small businesses. It provides a data history of up to two weeks. Friday backups are full backups. Monday through Thursday backups are incremental.

> **Note**
>
> All tape-rotation schemes can protect your data, but each one has different cost considerations. The Tower of Hanoi is more difficult to implement and manage but costs less than the grandfather-father-son scheme.

In some instances, it might be more beneficial to copy or image a hard drive for backup purposes. For example, in a development office, where there might be large amounts of data that changes constantly, instead of spending money on a complex backup system to back up all the developers' data, it might be less expensive and more efficient to buy another hard drive for each developer and have him back up his data that way. If the drive is imaged, it ensures that if a machine has a hard drive failure, a swift way of getting it back up and running again is available.

Another option available for backups is offsite tape storage with trusted third parties. Vendors offer a wide range of offsite tape-vaulting services. These are highly secure facilities that can include secure transportation services, chain-of-custody control for tapes in transit, and environmentally controlled storage vaults.

System Restoration

Disaster recovery planning should include detailed system restoration procedures, particularly in complex clustered and virtualized environments. This planning should explain any needed configuration details that might be required to restore access and network function. These can include items that can either be general or specific.

The procedure for restoring a server hardware failure, for example, is as follows:

1. Upon discovery, a first responder is to notify the on-duty IT manager. If not on the premises, the manager should be paged or reached via cell phone.

2. The IT manager assesses the damage to determine whether the machine can survive on the UPS. If it can, for how long? If it cannot, what data must be protected before the machine shuts down?

3. Because all equipment is under warranty, no cases should be opened without the consent of the proper vendor.

4. The IT manager assigns a technician to contact the vendor for instructions and a date when a replacement part can be expected.

5. A determination is made by the IT manager as to whether the organization can survive without the machine until the replacement part is received.

6. If the machine is a vital part of the business, the IT manager must then notify the head of the department affected by the situation and give an assessment of how and when it will be remedied.

7. The IT manager then finds another machine with similar hardware to replace the damaged server.

8. The damaged machine is shut down properly, if possible; unplugged from the network; and placed in the vendor-assigned work area.

9. The replacement machine is configured by an assigned technician to ensure it meets the specifications listed in the IT department's server configuration manual.

10. The most recent backup is checked out of the tape library by the IT manager. The assigned technician then restores the data.

11. When the technician has determined that the machine is ready to be placed online, the IT manager evaluates it to confirm it meets the procedure specifications.

12. The IT manager puts the replacement server in place. Connectivity must be verified, and then the appropriate department head can be notified that the situation has been remedied.

Also a restoration plan should include contingency planning to recover systems and data even in the event of administration personnel loss or lack of availability. This plan should include procedures on what to do if a disgruntled employee changes an administrative password before leaving. Statistics show that more damage to a network comes from inside than outside. Therefore, any key root-level account passwords and critical procedures should be properly documented so that another equally trained individual can manage the restoration process. This documentation must also include back-out strategies to implement in the event that the most recent backup proves unrecoverable or alternative capacity and type of equipment is all that remains available.

Recovery planning documentation and backup media contain many details that an attacker can exploit when seeking access to an organization's network or data. Therefore, planning documentation, backup scheduling, and backup media must include protections against unauthorized access or potential damage. The data should be protected by at least a password, and preferably encryption. When the backups are complete, they must be clearly labeled so that they can be properly safeguarded. Imagine having to perform a restore for an organization that stores its backup tapes unlabeled in a plastic bin in the server room. The rotation is supposed to be on a two-week basis. When you go to get the needed tape, you discover that the tapes are not marked, nor are they in any particular order. How much time will you spend just trying to find the proper tape? Also, is it a good practice to keep backup tapes in the same room with the servers? What happens if there is a fire?

How backup media is handled is just as important as how it is marked. You certainly don't want to store CDs in a place where they can easily be scratched or store tapes in an area that reaches 110° Fahrenheit during the day. You should ensure that you also have offsite copies of your backups where they are protected from unauthorized access as well as fire, flood, and other forms of environmental hazards that might affect the main facility. Normal backups should include all data that cannot be easily reproduced. Secure recovery services are another method of offsite storage and security that organizations may consider. In military environments, a common practice is to have removable storage media locked in a proper safe or container at the end of the day.

Cram Quiz

Answer these questions. The answers follow the last question. If you cannot answer these questions correctly, consider reading this section again until you can.

1. Which recovery site has only power, telecommunications, and networking active all the time?

   - ○ **A.** Hot site
   - ○ **B.** Cold site
   - ○ **C.** Warm site
   - ○ **D.** Shielded site

2. Which of the following is not a primary consideration for selecting a backup power generator?

   - ○ **A.** Size
   - ○ **B.** Fuel
   - ○ **C.** Power output
   - ○ **D.** Uptime

3. Which of the following describes a short-term decrease in voltage caused by a motor startup?

   - ○ **A.** Blackout
   - ○ **B.** Spike
   - ○ **C.** Surge
   - ○ **D.** Brownout

4. Which type of fault-tolerant RAID configuration provides the lowest disk usage fraction?

    ○ **A.** RAID 0

    ○ **B.** RAID 3

    ○ **C.** RAID 1

    ○ **D.** RAID 5

Cram Quiz Answers

1. **C**. The warm site has basics such as power, networking, and telecommunications active all the time. Although alternative computers may be present, they are not loaded and operating as in a hot site, making answer A incorrect. Answer B is incorrect because a cold site generally only includes power and physical space when not in use. Answer D is incorrect because any of the recovery site types might or might not be shielded against electromagnetic interference.

2. **A**. The physical size of a generator is a secondary concern, restricted only to available physical space at the site. Answers B, C, and D are incorrect as selection of a backup generator includes power output, fuel type, average uptime, startup mechanism, and automatic cutover (transfer).

3. **D**. A brownout is a short-term drop in voltage below established levels due to circuit faults or power insufficiencies caused by large equipment startup. Answer A is incorrect because a blackout is a complete loss of power. Answer B is incorrect because a spike is an instantaneous and dramatic increase in voltage, whereas a surge is a short-term increase in voltage caused by line loading or line switching, making answer C incorrect as well.

4. **C**. RAID 1 (mirroring/duplexing) provides the lowest fraction of total storage for use because every byte of data is written to two devices equally. Answer A is incorrect because RAID 0 does not offer fault protection and spans multiple drives with up to 100% disk usage. RAID 3 and RAID 5 are both incorrect because they both have fault tolerance but have a higher disk use fraction through the use of a parity bit (fixed in RAID 3, distributed in RAID 5) allowing recovery from the loss of a single drive across an array of three or more drives.

What Next?

If you want more practice on this chapter's exam objectives before you move on, remember that you can access all of the Cram Quiz questions on the CD. You can also create a custom exam by objective with the practice exam software. Note any objective you struggle with and go to that objective material in this chapter.

CHAPTER 5

Attacks

This chapter covers the following official CompTIA Security+ Certification exam objectives:

▶ Analyze and differentiate among types of malware

▶ Analyze and differentiate among types of attacks

▶ Analyze and differentiate among types of social engineering attacks

▶ Analyze and differentiate among types of wireless attacks

▶ Analyze and differentiate among types of application attacks

(For more information on the official CompTIA Security+ Certification exam topics, see the "About "About the CompTIA Security+ Certification Exam" section in the Introduction.)

Because networks today have become so complex and mobile, they have many points of entry. These various points can all be vulnerable, leaving an intruder many points of access. With so many ways of getting into the network, the components must be divided into separate elements so that the security process becomes easier to manage. In order to make the best decisions when it comes to securing an environment, it is important that you understand the threats and risks associated with the environment. This section explores those threats, risks, and associated attacks to help you understand everyday potential dangers.

In today's network environment, malicious code, or *malware*, has become a serious problem. The target is not only the information stored on local computers, but also other resources and computers. As a security professional, part of your responsibility is to recognize malicious code and know how to respond appropriately. This section covers the various types of malicious code you might encounter, including viruses, worms, Trojans, spyware, rootkits, botnets, and logic bombs.

Analyze and Differentiate Among Types of Malware

- ▶ Adware
- ▶ Viruses
- ▶ Worms
- ▶ Spyware
- ▶ Trojan

- ▶ Rootkit
- ▶ Backdoor
- ▶ Logic Bomb
- ▶ Botnets

CramSaver

If you can correctly answer these questions before going through this section, save time by skimming the Exam Alerts in this section and then completing the Cram Quiz at the end of the section.

1. How is a virus different from a worm?

2. What are symptoms indicative of a system that contains spyware?

3. What is a botnet, and how does a system become part of a botnet?

Answers

1. Although worms and viruses are similar, the biggest difference is that a worm is able to replicate itself without any user interaction.

2. A system infested with spyware might exhibit various symptoms, such as sluggishness, changes to the web home pages, web pages automatically added to bookmarks, and websites that launch unexpectedly.

3. A botnet consists of a large number of compromised computers that are able to forward transmissions to other computers outside the network. Most computers that are part of a botnet are often compromised via malicious code executed upon the system.

Adware

Advertising-supported software, or *adware*, is another form of spyware. It is an online way for advertisers to make a sale. Companies offer to place banner ads in their products for other companies. In exchange for the ad, a portion of the revenue from banner sales goes to the company that places the ad. However, this novel concept presents some issues for users. These companies also install tracking software on your system, which keeps in contact with the company through your Internet connection. It reports data to the company, such as your general surfing habits and which sites you have visited. And although the company might state that it will not collect sensitive or identifying data from your system, the fact remains that you have software on your PC that is sending information about you and your surfing habits to a remote location.

U.S. federal law prohibits secretly installing software that forces consumers to receive pop-ups that disrupt their computer use. Adware is legitimate only when users are informed up front that they will receive ads. In addition, if the adware gathers information about users, it must inform them. Even though legitimate adware is not illegal, certain privacy issues arise. For instance, although legitimate adware discloses the nature of data collected and transmitted, users have little or no control over what data is being collected and dispersed. Remember, this technology can send more than just banner statistics.

Viruses

A *virus* is a program or piece of code that runs on your computer without your knowledge. It is designed to attach itself to other code and replicate. It replicates when an infected file is executed or launched. It then attaches to other files, adds its code to the application's code, and continues to spread. Even a simple virus is dangerous because it can use all available resources and bring the system to a halt. Many viruses can replicate themselves across networks and bypass security systems.

Viruses are malicious programs that spread copies of themselves throughout a single machine. They infect other machines only if an infected object is accessed and the code is launched by a user on that machine. There are several types of viruses:

- ▶ **Boot sector**: This type of virus is placed into the first sector of the hard drive so that when the computer boots, the virus loads into memory.

- ▶ **Polymorphic**: This type of virus can change form each time it is executed. It was developed to avoid detection by antivirus software.

- ▶ **Macro**: This type of virus is inserted into a Microsoft Office document and emailed to unsuspecting users.

- ▶ **Program**: This type of virus infects executable program files and becomes active in memory.

- ▶ **Stealth**: This type of virus uses techniques to avoid detection, such as temporarily removing itself from an infected file or masking a file's size.

- ▶ **Multipartite**: This type of virus is a hybrid of boot and program viruses. It first attacks a boot sector and then attacks system files or vice versa.

> **ExamAlert**
>
> Viruses have to be executed by some type of action, such as running a program.

Here are a few of the most common viruses:

▶ **Love Bug**: The virus originated in an email titled "I love you." When the attachment was launched, the virus sent copies of the same email to everybody listed in the user's address book. The virus arrived as a Visual Basic Scripting Edition (VBScript) attachment that deleted files, including MP3s, MP2s, and JPGs. It also sent usernames and passwords to the virus author. It infected about 15 million computers and crashed servers around the world.

▶ **Melissa**: Melissa first appeared in March 1999. It is a macro virus, embedded in a Microsoft Word document. When the recipient receives the Word document as an attachment to an email message and opens the document, the virus sends email to the first 50 addresses in the victim's email address book and attaches itself to each message.

▶ **Michelangelo**: Michelangelo is a master boot record virus. It is based on an older virus called Stoned. The Michelangelo virus erases the contents of the infected drive on March 6 (its namesake's birthday) of the current year.

Since 2000, the majority of viruses released are actually worms, which are discussed in the following section.

Worms

Worms are similar in function and behavior to a virus with the exception that worms are self-replicating. A worm is built to take advantage of a security hole in an existing application or operating system and then find other systems running the same software and automatically replicate itself to the new host. This process repeats with no user intervention. After the worm is running on a system, it checks for Internet connectivity. If it finds connectivity, the worm then tries to replicate from one system to the next.

Examples of worms include the following:

▶ **Morris**: This famous worm took advantage of a Sendmail vulnerability and shut down the entire Internet in 1988.

- **Nimda**: This worm infects using several methods, including mass mailing, network share propagation, and several Microsoft vulnerabilities. Its name is *admin* spelled backward.

- **Code Red**: A buffer overflow exploit is used to spread this worm. This threat affects only web servers running Microsoft Windows 2000.

- **Blaster**: This worm made it difficult to patch infected systems as it would restart systems. Blaster exploits a vulnerability in the Remote Procedure Call (RPC) interface.

- **Mydoom**: This was a very fast spreading worm. It spread via email and was used by spammers to send spam.

Worms propagate by using email, instant messaging, file sharing (P2P), and IRC channels. Packet worms spread as network packets and directly infiltrate the RAM of the victim machine, where the code is then executed.

Spyware

Undesirable code sometimes arrives with commercial software distributions. *Spyware* is associated with behaviors such as advertising, collecting personal information, or changing your computer configuration without appropriately obtaining prior consent. Basically, spyware is software that communicates information from a user's system to another party without notifying the user.

Like a Trojan (which is described in the next section), spyware sends information out across the Internet to some unknown entity. In this case, however, spyware monitors user activity on the system, and in some instances includes the keystrokes typed. This logged information is then sent to the originator. The information, including passwords, account numbers, and other private information, will no longer be private.

Here are some indications that a computer may contain spyware:

- The system is slow, especially when browsing the Internet.

- It takes a long time for the Windows desktop to come up.

- Clicking a link does nothing or goes to an unexpected website.

- The browser home page changes, and you might not be able to reset it.

- Web pages are automatically added to your favorites list.

> **ExamAlert**
>
> Spyware monitors user activity on the system and can include keystrokes typed. The information is then sent to the originator of the spyware.

Many spyware eliminator programs are available. These programs scan your machine, similarly to how antivirus software scans for viruses; and just as with antivirus software, you should keep spyware eliminator programs updated and regularly run scans.

Trojans

Trojans are programs disguised as useful applications. Trojans do not replicate themselves like viruses, but they can be just as destructive. Code hidden inside the application can attack your system directly or allow the system to be compromised by the code's originator. The Trojan is typically hidden, so its ability to spread depends on the popularity of the software and a user's willingness to download and install the software. Trojans can perform actions without the user's knowledge or consent, such as collecting and sending data or causing the computer to malfunction. Trojans are often classified by their payload or function. The most common include backdoor, downloader, infostealer, and keylogger Trojans. Backdoor Trojans open a less obvious entry (hence backdoor) into the system, for later access. Downloader Trojans download additional software onto infected systems. This software is most often malicious. Infostealer Trojans attempt to steal information from the infected machine. Keylogger Trojans monitor and send keystrokes typed from the infected machine.

Examples of Trojan horses include the following:

- **Acid Rain**: This is an old DOS Trojan that, when run, deletes system files, renames folders, and creates many empty folders.

- **Nuker**: This Trojan was designed to function as a denial-of-service (DoS) attack against a workstation connected to the Internet.

- **Mocmex**: This Trojan is found in digital photo frames and collects online game passwords.

- **Simpsons**: This Trojan is a self-extracting batch file that attempts to delete files.

- **Vundo**: This Trojan downloads and displays fraudulent advertisements.

Trojans can download other Trojans, which is part of how botnets are controlled, as discussed later in this chapter.

Rootkits

Rootkits were first documented in the early 1990s. Today, rootkits are more widely used and are increasingly difficult to detect on networks. A *rootkit* is a piece of software that can be installed and hidden on a computer mainly for the purpose of compromising the system and getting escalated privileges, such as administrative rights. A rootkit is usually installed on a computer by first obtaining user-level access. After a rootkit has been installed, it enables the attacker to gain root or privileged access to the computer. Root or privileged access could also allow the compromise of other machines on the network.

A rootkit might consist of programs that view traffic and keystrokes, alter existing files to escape detection, or create a back-door on the system.

Exam**Alert**

Rootkits can be included as part of software package, installed by way of an unpatched vulnerability or by the user downloading and installing it.

Attackers are creating more sophisticated programs that update themselves, which makes them that much harder to detect. If a rootkit has been installed, traditional antivirus software can't always detect the malicious programs. Many rootkits run in the background. Therefore, you can usually easily spot them by looking for memory processes, monitoring outbound communications, and checking for newly installed programs.

Kernel rootkits modify the kernel component of an operating system. These newer rootkits can intercept system calls passed to the kernel and can filter out queries generated by the rootkit software. Rootkits have also been known to use encryption to protect outbound communications and piggyback on commonly used ports to communicate without interrupting other applications that use that port. These "tricks" invalidate the usual detection methods because they make the rootkits invisible to administrators and to detection tools.

Many vendors offer applications that can detect rootkits, such as RootkitRevealer. Removing rootkits can be a bit complex because you have to remove the rootkit itself and the malware that the rootkit is using. Often, rootkits change the Windows operating system itself. Such a change might cause the system to function improperly. When a system is infected, the only definitive way to get rid of a rootkit is to completely format the computer's hard drive and reinstall the operating system.

Most rootkits use global hooks for stealth activity. So if you use security tools that can prevent programs from installing global hooks and stop process injection, you can prevent rootkit functioning. In addition, rootkit functionality requires full administrator rights. Therefore, you can avoid rootkit infection by running Windows from an account with lesser privileges.

Botnets

A *bot*, short for robot, is an automated computer program that needs no user interaction. Bots are systems that outside sources can control. A bot provides a spam or virus originator with the venue to propagate. Many computers compromised in this way are unprotected home computers (although many computers in the corporate world are bots, as well). A *botnet* is a large number of computers that forward transmissions to other computers on the Internet. You might also hear a botnet referred to as a *zombie army*.

A system is usually compromised by a virus or other malicious code that gives the attacker access. A bot can be created through a port that has been left open or an unpatched vulnerability. A small program is left on the machine for future activation. The bot master can then unleash the effects of the army by sending a single command to all the compromised machines. A computer can be part of a botnet even though it appears to be operating normally. This is because bots are hidden and usually go undetected unless you are specifically looking for certain activity. The computers that form a botnet can be programmed to conduct a distributed denial-of-service (DDoS) attack, distribute spam, or to do other malicious acts.

Botnets have flooded the Internet. It is estimated that on typical day 40% of the computers connected to the Internet are bots. This problem shows no sign of easing. For example, Storm started out as an email that began circulating on January 19, 2007. It contained a link to a news story about a deadly storm. Fourteen months later, Storm remained the largest, most active botnet on the Internet. Storm was the first to make wide use of peer-to-peer communications. Storm has a self-defense mechanism. When the botnet is probed too much, it reacts automatically and starts a denial-of-service (DoS) attack against the probing entity.

Botnets can be particularly tricky and sophisticated, making use of social engineering. A collection of botnets, known as Zbot, stole millions from banks in four nations. The scammers enticed bank customers to click a link to download an updated digital certificate. This was a ruse, and Zbot installed a program that allowed it to see the next time the user successfully accessed the account. Zbot then automatically completed cash transfers to other accounts while the victims did their online banking.

The main issue with botnets is that they are securely hidden. This enables the botnet masters to perform tasks, gather information, and commit crimes while remaining undetected. Attackers can increase the depth and effect of their crimes by using multiple computers because each computer in a botnet can be programmed to execute the same command.

Logic Bombs

A *logic bomb* is a virus or Trojan horse designed to execute malicious actions when a certain event occurs or a period of time goes by. For a virus to be considered a logic bomb, the user of the software must be unaware of the payload. A programmer might create a logic bomb to delete all his code from the server on a future date, most likely after he has left the company. In several cases recently, ex-employees have been prosecuted for their role in this type of destruction. For example, one of the most high-profile cases of a modern-day logic bomb was the case of Roger Duronio. Duronio was a disgruntled computer programmer who planted a logic bomb in the computer systems of UBS, an investment bank. UBS estimated the repair costs at $3.1 million, and that doesn't include the downtime, lost data, or lost business. The actions of the logic bomb coincided with stock transactions by Duronio, so securities and mail fraud charges were added to the computer crime charges. The logic bomb that he planted on about 1,000 systems deleted critical files and prevented backups from occurring. He was found guilty of leaving a logic bomb on the systems and of securities fraud. He was sentenced to more than eight years in jail and fined $3.1 million.

> **ExamAlert**
>
> A logic bomb is also referred to as *slag code*. It is malicious in intent and usually planted by a disgruntled employee.

During software development, it is a good idea to evaluate the code to keep logic bombs from being inserted. Even though this is a preventive measure, code evaluation will not guarantee a logic bomb won't be inserted after the programming has been completed.

Backdoors

Backdoors are application code functions created intentionally or unintentionally that enable unauthorized access to networked resources. Many times during application development, software designers put in shortcut entry points to allow rapid code evaluation and testing. If not removed before application deployment, such entry points can present the means for an attacker to gain unauthorized access later. Other backdoors might be inserted by the application designers purposefully, presenting later threats to the network if applications are never reviewed by another application designer before deployment.

Cram Quiz

Answer these questions. The answers follow the last question. If you cannot answer these questions correctly, consider reading this section again until you can.

1. Which one of the following is designed to execute malicious actions when a certain event occurs or a specific time period elapses?

   ○ **A.** Logic bomb

   ○ **B.** Spyware

   ○ **C.** Botnet

   ○ **D.** DDoS

2. Which one of the following best describes a polymorphic virus?

   ○ **A.** A virus that infects .exe files

   ○ **B.** A virus that attacks the boot sector and then attacks the system files

   ○ **C.** A virus inserted into a Microsoft Office document such as Word or Excel

   ○ **D.** A virus that changes its form each time it is executed

Cram Quiz Answers

1. **A**. Spyware, botnets, and DDoS are all threats but do not execute malicious code after a specific event or period.

2. **D**. Polymorphic viruses can change their form each time they are run. The other answers describe different types of viruses— program, multipartite, and macro, respectively.

Analyze and Differentiate Among Types of Attacks

- ▶ Man-in-the-Middle
- ▶ DDoS
- ▶ DoS
- ▶ Replay
- ▶ Smurf attack
- ▶ Spoofing
- ▶ Spam
- ▶ Spim

- ▶ Vishing
- ▶ Xmas attack
- ▶ Privilege escalation
- ▶ Malicious insider threat
- ▶ DNS poisoning and ARP poisoning
- ▶ Transitive access
- ▶ Client-side attacks

Cram**Saver**

If you can correctly answer this question before going through this section, save time by skimming the Exam Alerts in this section and then completing the Cram Quiz at the end of the section.

1. Employees internal to an organization might be threats to the organization. Describe the types of insider threats.

Answers

1. The insider threat is typically classified as either a malicious insider or non-malicious insider. The latter is typically unaware of an organization's security policy or is often just trying to accomplish his job. On the other hand, a malicious insider might be motivated by financial gain, be disgruntled, or be looking to gain a competitive advantage.

Man-in-the-Middle

The *man-in-the-middle attack* takes place when an attacker intercepts traffic and then tricks the parties at both ends into believing that they are communicating with each other. This type of attack is possible because of the nature of the three-way TCP handshake process using SYN and ACK packets. Because TCP is a connection-oriented protocol, a three-way handshake takes place when establishing a connection and when closing a session. When establishing a session, the client sends a SYN request, the server sends an acknowledgment and synchronization (SYN-ACK) to the client, and then the client sends an ACK (also referred to as SYN-ACK-ACK), completing the connection. During this process, the attacker initiates the man-in-the-middle attack. The attacker uses a program that appears to be the server to the client and appears to be the client to the server. The attacker can also choose to alter the data or merely eavesdrop and pass it along. This attack is common in Telnet and wireless technologies. It is also generally difficult to implement because of physical routing issues, TCP sequence numbers, and speed. Because the hacker has to be able to sniff both sides of the connection simultaneously, programs such as Juggernaut, T-Sight, and Hunt have been developed to help make the man-in-the-middle attack easier.

If the attack is attempted on an internal network, physical access to the network is required. Be sure that access to wiring closets and switches is restricted; if possible, the area should be locked.

After you have secured the physical environment, you should protect the services and resources that allow a system to be inserted into a session. DNS can be compromised and used to redirect the initial request for service, providing an opportunity to execute a man-in-the-middle attack. You should restrict DNS access to read-only for everyone except the administrator. The best way to prevent these types of attacks is to use encryption and secure protocols.

> **ExamAlert**
>
> A man-in-the-middle attack takes place when a computer intercepts traffic and either eavesdrops on the traffic or alters it.

Replay

In a *replay attack*, packets are captured by using sniffers. After the pertinent information is extracted, the packets are placed back on the network. This type of attack can be used to replay bank transactions or other similar types of data transfer in the hopes of replicating or changing activities, such as deposits or transfers.

Protecting yourself against replay attacks involves some type of time stamp associated with the packets or time-valued, nonrepeating serial numbers. Secure protocols such as IPsec prevent replays of data traffic in addition to providing authentication and data encryption.

Denial of Service

The purpose of a *denial-of-service (DoS)* attack is to disrupt the resources or services that a user would expect to have access to. These types of attacks are executed by manipulating protocols and can happen without the need to be validated by the network. An attack typically involves flooding a listening port on your machine with packets. The premise is to make your system so busy processing the new connections that it cannot process legitimate service requests.

Many of the tools used to produce DoS attacks are readily available on the Internet. Administrators use them to test connectivity and troubleshoot problems on the network, whereas malicious users use them to cause connectivity issues.

Here are some examples of DoS attacks:

▶ **Smurf/smurfing**: This attack is based on the Internet Control Message Protocol (ICMP) echo reply function. It is more commonly known as *ping*, which is the command-line tool used to invoke this function. In this attack, the attacker sends ping packets to the broadcast address of the network, replacing the original source address in the ping packets with the source address of the victim, thus causing a flood of traffic to be sent to the unsuspecting network device.

▶ **Fraggle**: This attack is similar to a Smurf attack. The difference is that it uses UDP rather than ICMP. The attacker sends spoofed UDP packets to broadcast addresses as in the Smurf attack. These UDP packets are directed to port 7 (Echo) or port 19 (Chargen). When connected to port 19, a character generator attack can be run.

▶ **Ping flood**: This attack attempts to block service or reduce activity on a host by sending ping requests directly to the victim. A variation of this type of attack is the ping of death, in which the packet size is too large and the system doesn't know how to handle the packets.

▶ **SYN flood**: This attack takes advantage of the TCP three-way handshake. The source system sends a flood of synchronization (SYN) requests and never sends the final acknowledgment (ACK), thus creating half-open TCP sessions. Because the TCP stack waits before resetting the port, the attack overflows the destination computer's connection buffer, making it impossible to service connection requests from valid users.

▶ **Land**: This attack exploits a behavior in the operating systems of several versions of Windows, UNIX, Macintosh OS, and Cisco IOS with respect to their TCP/IP stacks. The attacker spoofs a TCP/IP SYN packet to the victim system with the same source and destination IP address and the same source and destination ports. This confuses the system as it tries to respond to the packet.

▶ **Teardrop**: This form of attack targets a known behavior of UDP in the TCP/IP stack of some operating systems. The Teardrop attack sends fragmented UDP packets to the victim with odd offset values in subsequent packets. When the operating system attempts to rebuild the original packets from the fragments, the fragments overwrite each other, causing confusion. Because some operating systems cannot gracefully handle the error, the system will most likely crash or reboot.

▶ **Bonk**: This attack affects mostly Windows 95 and NT machines by sending corrupt UDP packets to DNS port 53. The attack modifies the fragment offset in the packet. The target machine then attempts to reassemble the packet. Because of the offset modification, the packet is too big to be reassembled and the system crashes.

▶ **Boink**: This is a Bonk attack that targets multiple ports rather than just port 53.

▶ **Xmas Tree**: A Christmas tree is a packet that makes use of each option for the underlying protocol. Because these packets require more processing, they are often used in what's called a Xmas attack to disrupt service.

DoS attacks come in many shapes and sizes. The first step to protecting yourself from an attack is to understand the nature of different types of attacks in the preceding list. Although there are various security solutions designed specifically to help prevent such attacks, there are other measures that you might consider within your organization. Fundamentally, organizations should ensure they have well-defined processes around such things as auditing, standard operating procedures, and documented configurations. Finally, being well-versed on the nature of the different types of attacks will allow for better decision-making when it comes to attack recognition and implementing controls such as packet filtering and rights management.

Distributed DoS

Another form of attack is a simple expansion of a DoS attack, referred to as a *distributed DoS (DDoS) attack*. Masters are computers that run the client software, and zombies run software. The attacker creates masters, which in turn create a large number of zombies or recruits. The software running on the zombies can launch multiple types of attacks, such as UDP or SYN floods on a particular target. A typical DDoS is shown in Figure 5.1.

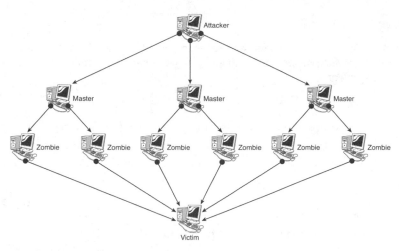

FIGURE 5.1 **A DDoS attack.**

In simple terms, the attacker distributes zombie software that allows the attacker partial or full control of the infected computer system.

Exam**Alert**

When an attacker has enough systems compromised with the installed zombie software, he can initiate an attack against a victim from a wide variety of hosts. The attacks come in the form of the standard DoS attacks, but the effects are multiplied by the total number of zombie machines under the control of the attacker.

Although DDoS attacks generally come from outside the network to deny services, you must also consider the effect of DDoS attacks mounted from inside the network. Internal DDoS attacks allow disgruntled or malicious users to disrupt services without any outside influence.

To help protect your network, you can set up filters on external routers to drop packets involved in these types of attacks. You should also set up another filter that denies traffic originating from the Internet that shows an internal network address. When you do this, the loss of ping and some services and utilities for testing network connectivity are incurred, but this is a small price to pay for network protection. If the operating system allows it, reduce the amount of time before the reset of an unfinished TCP connection. Doing so makes it harder to keep resources unavailable for extended periods of time.

> **Note**
>
> In the case of a DDoS attack, your best weapon is to get in touch quickly with your upstream Internet service provider (ISP) and see whether it can divert traffic or block the traffic at a higher level.

Subscribing to newsgroups and checking security websites daily ensures that you keep up with the latest attacks and exploits. Applying the manufacturer's latest operating system patches or fixes can also help prevent attacks.

DNS Poisoning

DNS poisoning enables a perpetrator to redirect traffic by changing the IP record for a specific domain, thus permitting the attacker to send legitimate traffic anywhere he chooses. This not only sends a requestor to a different website, but also caches this information for a short period, distributing the attack's effect to the server users. DNS poisoning may also be referred to as *DNS cache poisoning* because it affects the information that is cached.

All Internet page requests start with a DNS query. If the IP address is not known locally, the request is sent to a DNS server. There are two types of DNS servers: authoritative and recursive. DNS servers share information, but recursive servers maintain information in cache. This means a caching or recursive server can answer queries for resource records even if it can't resolve the request directly. A flaw in the resolution algorithm allows the poisoning of DNS records on a server. All an attacker has to do is delegate a false name to the domain server along with providing a false address for the server. For example, an attacker creates a hostname hack.hacking.biz. After that, the attacker queries your DNS server to resolve the host hacking.biz. The DNS server resolves the name and stores this information in its cache. Until the zone expiration, any further requests for hacking.biz do not result in lookups but are answered by the server from its cache. It is now possible for the attacker to set your DNS server as the authoritative server for his zone with the domain registrar. If the attacker conducts malicious activity, the attacker can make it appear that your DNS server is being used for these malicious activities.

DNS poisoning can result in many different implications. Domain name servers can be used for DDoS attacks. Malware can be downloaded to an unsuspecting user's computer from the rogue site, and all future requests by that computer will be redirected to the fake IP address. This could be used to build an effective botnet. This method of poisoning could also allow for cross-site scripting exploits, especially because Web 2.0 capabilities allow content to be pulled from multiple websites at the same time.

To minimize the effects of DNS poisoning, check the DNS setup if you are hosting your own DNS. Be sure the DNS server is not open-recursive. An open-recursive DNS server responds to any lookup request without checking where it originates. Disable recursive access for other networks to resolve names that are not in your zone files. You can also use different servers for authoritative and recursive lookups and require that caches discard information except from the com servers and the root servers. From the user perspective, education works best. However, it is becoming more difficult to spot a problem by watching the address bar on the Internet browser. Therefore, operating system vendors are adding more protection. Microsoft Windows User Account Control (UAC) notifies the user that a program is attempting to change the system's DNS settings, thus preventing the DNS cache from being poisoned.

ARP Poisoning

All network cards have a unique 48-bit address that is hard-coded into the network card. For network communications to occur, this hardware address must be associated with an IP address. Address Resolution Protocol (ARP), which operates at Layer 2 (data link layer) of the OSI model, associates MAC addresses to IP addresses. ARP is a lower-layer protocol that is simple and consists of requests and replies without validation. However, this simplicity also leads to a lack of security.

When you use a protocol analyzer to look at traffic, you see an ARP request and an ARP reply, which are the two basic parts of ARP communication. There are also Reverse ARP (RARP) requests and RARP replies. Devices maintain an ARP table that contains a cache of the IP addresses and MAC addresses the device has already correlated. The host device searches its ARP table to see whether there is a MAC address corresponding to the destination host IP address. When there is no matching entry, it broadcasts an ARP request to the entire network. The broadcast is seen by all systems, but only the device that has the corresponding information replies. However, devices can accept ARP replies before even requesting them. This type of entry is known as an unsolicited entry because the information was not explicitly requested.

> **ExamAlert**
>
> Because ARP does not require any type of validation, as ARP requests are sent the requesting devices believe that the incoming ARP replies are from the correct devices. This can allow a perpetrator to trick a device into thinking any IP is related to any MAC address.

In addition, they can broadcast a fake or spoofed ARP reply to an entire network and poison all computers. This is known as *ARP poisoning*. Put simply, the attacker deceives a device on your network, poisoning its table associations of other devices.

ARP poisoning can lead to attacks such as DoS, man-in-the-middle, and MAC flooding. DoS and man-in-the-middle attacks were discussed earlier in this chapter. MAC flooding is an attack directed at network switches. This type of attack is successful because of the nature of the way all switches and bridges work. The amount of space allocated to store source addresses of packets is very limited. When the table becomes full, the device can no longer learn new information and becomes flooded. As a result, the switch can be forced into a hub-like state that will broadcast all network traffic to every device in the network. An example of this is a tool called Macof. Macof floods the network with random MAC addresses. Switches can then get stuck in open-repeating mode, leaving the network traffic susceptible to sniffing. Nonintelligent switches do not check the sender's identity, thereby allowing this condition to happen.

A lesser vulnerability of ARP is port stealing. *Port stealing* is a man-in-the-middle attack that exploits the binding between the port and the MAC address. The principle behind port stealing is that an attacker sends numerous packets with the source IP address of the victim and the destination MAC address of the attacker. This attack applies to broadcast networks built from switches.

ARP poisoning is limited to attacks that are local-based, so an intruder needs either physical access to your network or control of a device on your local network. To mitigate ARP poisoning on a small network, you can use static or script-based mapping for IP addresses and ARP tables. For large networks, use equipment that offers port security. By doing so, you can permit only one MAC address for each physical port on the switch. In addition, you can deploy monitoring tools or an intrusion detection system (IDS) to alert you when suspect activity occurs.

Spoofing

Spoofing is a method of providing false identity information to gain unauthorized access. This is accomplished by modifying the source address of traffic or source of information.

ExamAlert

Spoofing seeks to bypass IP address filters by setting up a connection from a client and sourcing the packets with an IP address that is allowed through the filter.

In blind spoofing, the attacker sends only data and only makes assumptions of responses. In informed spoofing, the attacker can participate in a session and can monitor the bidirectional communications.

Services such as email, web, and file transfer can also be spoofed. Web spoofing happens when an attacker creates a convincing but false copy of an entire website. The false site looks just like the real one; it has all the same pages and links. However, the attacker controls the false site so that all network traffic between the victim's browser and the site goes through the attacker. In email spoofing, a spammer or a computer virus can forge the email packet information in an email so that it appears the email is coming from a trusted host, from one of your friends, or even from your own email address. If you leave your email address at some Internet site or exchange email with other people, a spoofer might be able to use your email address as the sender address to send spam. File-transfer spoofing involves the FTP service. FTP data is sent in clear text. The data can be intercepted by an attacker. The data could then be viewed and altered before sending it on to the receiver. These forms of attacks are often used to get additional information from network users to complete a more aggressive attack.

You should set up a filter that denies traffic originating from the Internet that shows an internal network address. Using the signing capabilities of certificates on servers and clients allows web and email services to be more secure. The use of IPsec can secure transmissions between critical servers and clients. This will help prevent these types of attacks from taking place.

Spam

Just like junk mail clogs our regular mailboxes, spam clogs our email boxes. *Spam* is a term that refers to the sending of unsolicited commercial email. Email spam targets individual users with direct mail messages. Most spam is commercial advertising, often for products such as "get rich quick" schemes, physical enhancements, and cheap medications. More dangerous spam might include hoaxes and may be combined with forms of social engineering discussed in the next section. Spam costs the sender little to send because the actual costs are paid for by the carriers rather than by the sender. Email spam lists are often created by scanning newsgroup postings, stealing Internet mailing lists, or searching the Web for addresses. Spammers use automated tools to subscribe to as many mailing lists as possible. From those lists, they capture addresses or use the mailing list as a direct target for their attacks. State, federal, and international laws regulate spam.

> **Note**
>
> Requesting to be removed from junk email lists often results in more spam because it verifies that you have a legitimate, working email address.

When dealing with spam, follow this advice:

- ▶ Never make a purchase from an unsolicited email.

- ▶ If you do not know the sender of an unsolicited email message, delete it. (Don't be curious and open it.)

- ▶ Do not respond to spam messages and do not click any links within the message (even to "unsubscribe").

- ▶ Do not use the preview function of your email software because if you do, the email message will automatically show as read.

- ▶ When sending email messages to a number of people, use the blind carbon copy (BCC) field to hide their email addresses.

- ▶ Be careful about giving out your email address on websites and newsgroups.

- ▶ Use more than one email address, keeping your personal email address private.

In addition, use software that filters spam. Approximately 75% of the email organizations receive is spam. It is best to filter it before it gets to the users. One method spammers have used to try to circumvent mail filters is sending spam through instant messaging, also known as *spim*. Spim uses bots in order to simulate being a human on the other side of the instant message. In most cases spim, like spam, includes links for which the spammer is trying to market.

Privilege Escalation

Programming errors can result in system compromise, allowing someone to gain unauthorized privileges. Software exploitation takes advantage of a program's flawed code, which then crashes the system and leaves it in a state where arbitrary code can be executed, or an intruder can function as an administrator. This is known as *privilege escalation*.

Perhaps the most popular method of privilege escalation is a buffer overflow attack discussed later in this chapter.

Malicious Insider Threat

Attacks are often thought to be a result of the outside malicious hacker; however, insider threats are a source of many breaches. In many cases, this includes employees who have the right intentions but are unaware of or ignore an organization's security policy. A common example is the well-intentioned employee that uses a personal web-based email account to send home sensitive files to work on later in the evening. These sensitive files have now proliferated unencrypted outside of the organizational network. Another common scenario is the user who brings in USB thumb drives that unknowingly have been infected with malware. Proper training and education are key to help prevent the non-malicious insider threat.

On the other hand, deliberate or malicious insider threats also present a source of attack. These are typically motivated by financial gain, sabotage, and theft in order to gain a competitive advantage.

Cram Quiz

Answer these questions. The answers follow the last question. If you cannot answer these questions correctly, consider reading this section again until you can.

1. You're the security administrator for a bank. The users are complaining about the network being slow. It is not a particularly busy time of the day, however. You capture network packets and discover that hundreds of ICMP packets have been sent to the host. What type of attack is likely being executed against your network?

   ○ **A.** Spoofing

   ○ **B.** Man-in-the-middle

   ○ **C.** DNS kiting

   ○ **D.** Denial of service

2. Which one of the following is not an example of a denial-of-service attack?

   ○ **A.** Fraggle

   ○ **B.** Smurf

   ○ **C.** Gargomel

   ○ **D.** Teardrop

3. Users received a spam email from an unknown source and chose the option in the email to unsubscribe and are now getting more spam as a result. Which one of the following is most likely the reason?

- ○ **A.** The unsubscribe option does not actually do anything.
- ○ **B.** The unsubscribe request was never received.
- ○ **C.** Spam filters were automatically turned off when making the selection to unsubscribe.
- ○ **D.** They confirmed that they are a "live" email address.

Cram Quiz Answers

1. **D.** A ping flood is a DoS attack that attempts to block service or reduce activity on a host by sending ping requests directly to the victim using ICMP. Spoofing involves modifying the source address of traffic or source of information. A man-in-the-middle attack is commonly used to gather information in transit between two hosts. Domain kiting refers to the practice of monopolizing domain names without paying for them.

2. **C.** A Gargomel attack, although cool sounding, does not actually exist. Fraggle, Smurf, and Teardrop are names of specific denial-of-service attacks; therefore, answers A, B, and D are incorrect.

3. **D.** Often an option to opt out of further email does not unsubscribe users, but rather means "send me more spam" because it has been confirmed that the email address is not dormant. This is less likely to occur with email a user receives that he or she opted into in the first place, however. Answers A, B, and C are incorrect because these are less likely and not the best choices.

Analyze and Differentiate Among Types of Social Engineering Attacks

- ▶ Shoulder surfing
- ▶ Dumpster diving
- ▶ Tailgating
- ▶ Impersonation
- ▶ Hoaxes

- ▶ Whaling
- ▶ Vishing
- ▶ Phishing
- ▶ Spear phishing
- ▶ Pharming

CramSaver

If you can correctly answer these questions before going through this section, save time by skimming the Exam Alerts in this section and then completing the Cram Quiz at the end of the section.

1. Phishing, spear-phishing, whaling, vishing, and smishing are commonly used for what purpose, and what are the technical differences between each?

2. Describe several different examples of social engineering attacks.

3. What can an organization do to prevent sensitive information from being divulged via dumpster diving?

Answers

1. Phishing, spear-phishing, whaling, vishing, and smishing are all very similar. Each are techniques commonly used as part of a social engineering ploy. Phishing is commonly done through email across a large audience, whereas spear-phishing targets an individual. Whaling in essence is spear-phishing but instead is directly targeted at a very high-value target. Vishing and smishing are also similar to phishing but use voice and SMS text messaging, respectively.

2. Although there are countless answers, social engineering relies upon extracting useful information by tricking the target. Examples include scenarios that involve impersonating someone else, coercing them into divulging sensitive information without cause for concern, or convincing someone to install a malicious program in order to assist you.

3. The proper disposal of data and equipment should be part of an organization's security policy. Such a policy would likely require ongoing end-user awareness, as well as procedures around the shredding or other proper disposal of sensitive information.

Social Engineering

One area of security planning that is often considered the most difficult to adequately secure is the legitimate user. *Social engineering* is a process by which an attacker might extract useful information from users who are often just tricked into helping the attacker. It is extremely successful because it relies on human emotions. Common examples of social engineering attacks include the following:

▶ An attacker calls a valid user and impersonates a guest, temp agent, or new user asking for assistance in accessing the network or requests details involving the business processes of the organization.

▶ An attacker contacts a legitimate user, posing as a technical aide attempting to update some type of information and asks for identifying user details that can then be used to gain access.

▶ An attacker poses as a network administrator, directing the legitimate user to reset his password to a specific value so that an imaginary update can be applied.

▶ An attacker provides the user with a "helpful" program or agent, through email, a website, or other means of distribution. This program might require the user to enter logon details or personal information useful to the attacker, or it might install other programs that compromise the system's security.

Another form of social engineering has come to be known as *reverse social engineering*. Here, an attacker provides information to the legitimate user that causes the user to believe the attacker is an authorized technical assistant. This might be accomplished by obtaining an IT support badge or logo-bearing shirt that validates the attacker's legitimacy, by inserting the attacker's contact information for technical support in a secretary's Rolodex, or by making himself known for his technical skills by helping people around the office.

Many users would rather ask assistance of a known nontechnical person who they know to be skilled in computer support rather than contact a legitimate technical staff person, who may be perceived as busy with more important matters. An attacker who can plan and cause a minor problem is then able to easily correct this problem, gaining the confidence of the legitimate user while being able to observe operational and network configuration details and logon information, and potentially being left alone with an authorized account logged on to the network.

Exam Alert

Social engineering is a common practice used by attackers, and one that is not easily countered via technology. It is important to understand that the best defense against social engineering is a program of ongoing user awareness and education.

Social engineering is nothing new, and has been around as long as humans. Perhaps you recall face-to-face interactions in which one individual fishes for information in a deceptive way. Most means of social engineering via electronic means are given different names based upon the target and the method used. One of the more common methods of social engineering via electronic means is phishing. *Phishing* is an attempt to acquire sensitive information by masquerading as a trustworthy entity via an electronic communication, usually an email. Phishing attacks rely on a mix of technical deceit and social engineering practices. In the majority of cases, the phisher must persuade the victim to intentionally perform a series of actions that will provide access to confidential information. As scam artists become more sophisticated, so do their phishing email messages. The messages often include official-looking logos from real organizations and other identifying information taken directly from legitimate websites. For best protection, you must deploy proper security technologies and techniques at the client side, the server side, and the enterprise level. Ideally, users should not be able to directly access email attachments from within the email application. However, the best defense is user education.

Other related methods with slightly varying differences include the following:

▶ **Spear phishing**: This is a targeted version of phishing. Whereas phishing often involves mass email, spear phishing might go after a specific individual.

▶ **Whaling**: Whaling is identical to spear phishing except for the "size of the fish." Whaling employs spear phishing tactics but is intended to go after high-profile targets such as an executive within a company.

▶ **Vishing**: Also known as voice phishing, the attacker often uses fake caller ID to appear as a trusted organization and attempts to get the individual to enter account details via the phone.

▶ **Smishing**: Also known as SMS phishing, this involves using phishing methods through text messaging.

▶ **Pharming**: This is a term coined based upon farming and phishing. Pharming does not require the user to be tricked into clicking on a link. Rather farming redirects victims to a bogus website, even if the user correctly entered the intended site. To accomplish this, the attacker employs another attack, such as DNS cache poisoning.

> **ExamAlert**
>
> Phishing combines technical deceit with the elements of traditional social engineering. Be sure to know the different variants of phishing attacks.

Dumpster Diving

As humans, we naturally seek the path of least resistance. Instead of shredding documents or walking them to the recycle bin, they are often thrown in the wastebasket. Equipment sometimes is put in the garbage because city laws do not require special disposal. Because intruders know this, they scavenge discarded equipment and documents, in an act called *dumpster diving*, and extract sensitive information from it without ever contacting anyone in the organization.

In any organization, the potential that an intruder can gain access to this type of information is huge. What happens when employees are leaving the organization? They clean out their desks. Depending on how long the employees have been there, what ends up in the garbage can be a goldmine for an intruder.

Other potential sources of information that are commonly thrown in the garbage include the following:

- ▶ Old company directories
- ▶ Old QA or testing analysis
- ▶ Employee manuals
- ▶ Training manuals
- ▶ Hard drives
- ▶ Floppy disks
- ▶ CDs
- ▶ Printed emails

Proper disposal of data and equipment should be part of the organization's security policy. It is prudent to have a policy in place that requires shredding of all physical documents and secure erasure of all types of storage media before they may be discarded. Secure erasure is often performed via the use of disk-wiping software, which is able to delete the data according to different standards.

Tailgating

Tailgating is a simple yet effective form of social engineering. It involves piggy-backing or following closely behind someone who has authorized physical access within an environment. Tailgating often involves giving off the appearance of being with or part of an authorized group or capitalizing upon people's desire to be polite. A common example is having a secured door held upon by an authorized person when following from behind. Many high-security facilities employ mantraps (an airlock-like mechanism that allows only one person to pass at a time) to provide entrance control and prevent tailgating.

Cram Quiz

Answer these questions. The answers follow the last question. If you cannot answer these questions correctly, consider reading this section again until you can.

1. Which of the following is an effective way to get information in crowded places such as airports, conventions, or supermarkets?

   ○ **A.** Vishing

   ○ **B.** Shoulder surfing

   ○ **C.** Reverse social engineering

   ○ **D.** Phishing

2. At your place of employment you are rushing to the door with your arms full of bags. As you approach, the woman before you scans her badge to gain entrance while holding the door for you, but not without asking to see your badge. What did she just prevent?

   ○ **A.** Phishing

   ○ **B.** Whaling

   ○ **C.** Tailgating

   ○ **D.** Door diving

3. Which one of the following is not a type of phishing attack?

   ○ **A.** Spear phishing

   ○ **B.** Wishing

   ○ **C.** Whaling

   ○ **D.** Smishing

Cram Quiz Answers

1. **B.** Shoulder surfing uses direct observation techniques. It gets its name from looking over someone's shoulder to get information. Answer A is incorrect because vishing uses a phone to obtain information. Answer C is incorrect because reverse social engineering involves an attacker convincing the user that she is a legitimate IT authority, causing the user to solicit her assistance. Answer D is incorrect because phishing is an attempt to acquire sensitive information by masquerading as a trustworthy entity via an electronic communication, usually an email.

2. **C.** Tailgating involves following closely behind someone with authorized physical access in order to gain access to the environment. Answers A and B are incorrect as these describe methods of acquiring sensitive information by masquerading as a trustworthy source. Answer D is also incorrect.

3. **B.** Answers A, C, and D are incorrect, as these all do describe a type of phishing attack. Spear phishing is targeted. Whaling is spear phishing that specifically targets high profile personnel. Smishing is SMS-based phishing.

Analyze and Differentiate Among Types of Wireless Attacks

▶ **Rogue access points**

▶ **Interference**

▶ **Evil twin**

▶ **War driving**

▶ **Bluejacking**

▶ **Bluesnarfing**

▶ **War chalking**

▶ **IV attack**

▶ **Packet sniffing**

Cram**Saver**

If you can correctly answer these questions before going through this section, save time by skimming the Exam Alerts in this section and then completing the Cram Quiz at the end of the section.

1. What is the difference between bluejacking and bluesnarfing?

2. Which of the following describes a pasttime in which wireless networks are marked with a special symbol upon a nearby object?

3. What wireless protocol was subject to an IV attack?

Answers

1. Bluejacking involves sending an unsolicited broadcast message to nearby Bluetooth-enabled devices. On the other hand, bluesnarfing is more nefarious in that, if successful, it enables the attacker to gain unauthorized access to the device. Bluejacking is commonly used as a means to enable bluesnarfing.

2. In combination with war driving, war chalking describes the activity of drawing special symbols on nearby objects to describe the state of existing wireless networks.

3. The Wireless Equivalency Protocol (WEP) was cracked as a result of an IV attack. Specifically, the Initialization Vector (IV) was too short and had a high probability of repeating itself.

Rogue Access Points

Rogue access points refers to situations in which an unauthorized wireless access point has been set up. In organizations, well-meaning insiders might use rouge access points with the best of intentions. However, rogue access points can also serve as a type of man-in-the-middle attack often referred to as an *evil twin*. Because the request for connection by the client is an omnidirectional open broadcast, it is possible for a hijacker to act as an access point (AP) to the client, and as a client to the true network access point, enabling the hijack-er to follow all data transactions with the ability to modify, insert, or delete packets at will. By implementing a rogue access point with stronger signal strength than more remote permanent installations, the attacker can cause a wireless client to preferentially connect to its own stronger nearby connection using the wireless device's standard roaming handoff mechanism. Fortunately, detecting rogue access points is fairly simple through the use of software. A common method to detect rogue access points is through the use of wireless sniffing applications such as AirMagnet or NetStumbler. The latter was com-monly used as the tool of war drivers, which are discussed next.

War Driving

A popular pastime involves driving around with a laptop system configured to listen for open 802.1x APs announcing their SSID broadcasts, which is known as *war driving*. Many websites provide central repositories for identified net-works to be collected, graphed, and even generated against city maps for the convenience of others looking for open access links to the Internet. A modifi-cation of Depression-era symbols is being used to mark buildings, curbs, and other landmarks to indicate the presence of an available AP and its connection details. This so-called *war chalking* uses a set of symbols and shorthand details to provide specifics needed to connect using the AP.

Bluejacking/Bluesnarfing

Mobile devices equipped for Bluetooth short-range wireless connectivity, such as laptops, cell phones, and PDAs, are subject to receiving text and message broadcast spam sent from a nearby Bluetooth-enabled transmitting device in an attack referred to as *bluejacking*. Although typically benign, attackers can use this form of attack to generate messages that appear to be from the device itself, leading users to follow obvious prompts and establish an open Bluetooth connection to the attacker's device. Once paired with the attacker's device, the user's data becomes available for unauthorized access, modification, or deletion, which is a more aggressive attack referred to as *bluesnarfing*.

Packetsniffing

A wireless sniffer includes a hardware or software device capable of capturing the data or packets that traverse across the wireless channel. In situations where traffic being sent across the network is unencrypted, *packetsniffing* enables the attacker to capture the data and decode it from its raw form into readable text.

IV Attack

An *initialization vector* (*IV*) attack is best exemplified by the cracking of Wireless Equivalent Privacy (WEP) encryption. WEP was the original algorithm used to protect wireless networks. An IV is an input to a cryptographic algorithm, which is essentially a random number. Ideally, an IV should be unique and unpredictable. An IV attack can occur when the IV is too short, predictable, or not unique. The attack upon WEP was a result of an IV not long enough, which meant it had a high probability of repeating itself after only a small number of packets. Subsequent wireless encryption algorithms use not only a longer IV, but new protocols, such as Temporal Key Integrity Protocol (TKIP), provide a mechanism to dynamically change keys as the system is used. This combination is able to defeat the IV attack used on WEP.

ExamAlert

In order to prevent an IV attack, an IV must not be repeated with a given key and should appear random.

Cram Quiz

Answer these questions. The answers follow the last question. If you cannot answer these questions correctly, consider reading this section again until you can.

1. What is the term given to a rogue access point in which they serve as a man-in-the-middle from which further attacks can be carried out?

   ○ **A.** War driving

   ○ **B.** Evil twin

   ○ **C.** War twinning

   ○ **D.** Twin driving

2. Which of the following best describes packetsniffing?

   ○ **A.** Packetsniffing allows an attacker to capture and decrypt data into readable text.

   ○ **B.** Packetsniffing allows an attacker to smell which network components are transmitting sensitive data.

   ○ **C.** Packetsniffing allows an attacker to capture and decode data from its raw form into readable text.

   ○ **D.** Packetsniffing allows an attacker to encode and transmit packets to disrupt network services.

3. An initilization vector should be which of the following?

   ○ **A.** Unique and unpredictable

   ○ **B.** Unique and predictable

   ○ **C.** Repeatable and random

   ○ **D.** Repeatable and unique

Cram Quiz Answers

1. **B.** An evil twin is a rogue access point used for malicious purposes, in which the attacker is acting as a man-in-the-middle. War driving refers to the act of traveling around looking for unsecured wireless devices, thus answer A is incorrect. Answers C and D are both incorrect.

2. **C.** Packetsniffing is best described as the process of capturing and decoding data from its raw form into readable text. Answer A is incorrect. Encryption protects against revealing information through packetsniffing. Answers B and D are also incorrect.

3. **A.** An IV should be unique and unpredictable. Answers B, C, and D are incorrect.

Analyze and Differentiate Among Types of Application Attacks

- ▶ Cross-site scripting
- ▶ SQL injection
- ▶ LDAP injection
- ▶ XML injection
- ▶ Directory traversal/ command injection

- ▶ Buffer overflow
- ▶ Zero day
- ▶ Cookies and attachments
- ▶ Malicious add-ons
- ▶ Session hijacking
- ▶ Header manipulation

Cram**Saver**

If you can correctly answer these questions before going through this section, save time by skimming the Exam Alerts in this section and then completing the Cram Quiz at the end of the section.

1. Identify and explain at least two different types of code injection techniques.

2. Why should HTTP headers not be used to transport important and sensitive data?

3. What is the difference between a tracking cookie and a session cookie?

Answers

1. Common code injection techniques include XSS, SQL injection, LDAP injection, and XML injection. XSS involves including client-side script on a website for malicious purpose in order to exploit a vulnerability. SQL, LDAP, and XML injection, like XSS, are similar in that they piggyback malicious code through an input field in the application. SQL injection is targeted at databases, LDAP injection at directories, and XML injection at XML documents and code.

2. HTTP headers can easily be manipulated through the use of proxy software. Because headers originate at the client, the end user can modify the data.

3. A tracking cookie is a particular type of permanent cookie that sticks around. Spyware, for example, would likely use tracking cookies. Session cookies, on the other hand, stay around only for that particular visit to a website.

Browser Threats

The evolution of web network applications, Web 2.0 interactive interfaces, and other browser-based secure and anonymous-access resources available via the HTTP and HTTPS protocols presents an "anytime/anywhere" approach to enterprise network resource availability. As more applications are migrated into the browser, attackers have an increasingly large attack surface area for interception and interaction with user input and for directed attacks against web-based resources. The global nature of the Internet enables attackers to place web-based traps in countries of convenience, where law enforcement efforts are complicated by international legal variance.

> **ExamAlert**
>
> Maintaining operating system, application, and add-on updates helps to reduce the threat posed by many browser-based attack forms. When possible, restricting automatic code execution of JavaScript or ActiveX controls and cookie generation can also strengthen the client's browser security stance.

Browser-based vulnerabilities you should know for the exam include the following:

- ▶ **Session hijacking**: Because browsers access resources on a remote server using a predefined port (80 for HTTP or 443 for HTTPS), browser traffic is easily identifiable by an attacker who may elect to hijack legitimate user credentials and session data for unauthorized access to secured resources. Although Secure Sockets Layer (SSL) traffic is encrypted between endpoints, an attacker who crafts a web proxy with SSL can allow a user to connect securely to this proxy system and then establish a secured link from the proxy to the user's intended resource, capturing plain-text data transport on the proxy system even though the user receives all appropriate responses for a secured connection.

- ▶ **Add-on vulnerabilities**: Active content within websites offers an attractive attack space for aggressors, who might craft special "drivers" required for content access that are in fact Trojans or other forms of malware. Other attackers craft malware to take advantage of unpatched add-ons to directly inject code or gain access to a user's system when a vulnerable browser is directed to an infected website.

- ▶ **Buffer overflows:** Like desktop- and system-based applications, many web browser applications offer an attacker a mechanism for providing input in the form of a crafted uniform resource locator (URL) value. By extending the input values beyond the memory space limitations of the expected input values, an attacker can inject code into adjacent memory space to allow execution of arbitrary code on the web server. Buffer overflows are discussed further next.

Code Injections

Application developers and security professionals need to be aware of the different types of threats from malicious code. Using malicious code injection, attackers can perform a variety of attacks upon systems. These attacks can result in the modification or theft of data. Examples of code injection include the following:

▶ **Cross-Site scripting (XSS)**: By placing malicious client-side script on a website, an attacker can cause an unknowing browser user to conduct unauthorized access activities, expose confidential data, and provide logging of successful attacks back to the attacker without the user being aware of her participation. XSS vulnerabilities can be used to hijack the user's session or to cause the user accessing malware-tainted Site A to unknowingly attack Site B on behalf of the attacker who planted code on Site A.

▶ **SQL injection**: Inserts malicious code into strings, which are later passed to a database server. The SQL server then parses and executes this code.

▶ **LDAP injection**: Some websites perform LDAP queries based upon data provided by the end user. LDAP injection involves changing the LDAP input so that the web app runs with escalated privileges.

▶ **XML injection**: Uses malicious code to compromise XML applications, typically web services. XML injection attempts to insert malicious content into the structure of an XML message to alter the logic of the targeted application.

Directory Traversal

In most instances, surfing the Web presents the users with web pages filled with images and text. Behind these pages, however, is a system of files and directories. Directory traversal allows one to navigate the directories. In most cases this directory structure is restricted; however, an attack using directory traversal enables the attacker to gain access to otherwise restricted files and directories.

As with code injection, directory traversal vulnerabilities are a result of poor input validation. The potential for these types of attacks require the developers to focus on building secure websites and applications.

Header Manipulation

HTTP headers are control data used between the web browser and web server. In most cases websites and applications do not rely upon the headers for important data, yet it was a common practice in the past, and it is still used across many less-secure applications and sites. In cases where a developer chooses to inspect and use the incoming headers, it is important to note that the headers originate at the client. As a result, these headers could easily be modified by the user using freely available proxy software.

Zero-day

A zero-day (or zero-hour or day zero) attack or threat is a computer threat that tries to exploit computer application vulnerabilities that are unknown to others or the software developer, also called zero-day vulnerabilities. Zero-day exploits (actual software that uses a security hole to carry out an attack) are used or shared by attackers before the developer of the target software knows about the vulnerability.

A zero-day attack is more dire and differs from other attacks and vulnerabilities. Most attacks on vulnerable systems involve known vulnerabilities. These include vulnerabilities known by developers, but for which a patch has not been issued. In most cases, however, attacks target known vulnerabilities for which there is a fix or a control, but that is not implemented. In the case of zero-day attacks, the software developer has not even had a chance to distribute a fix for his software.

Buffer Overflows

Buffer overflows cause disruption of service and lost data. This condition occurs when the data presented to an application or service exceeds the storage-space allocation that has been reserved in memory for that application or service. Poor application design might allow the input of 100 characters into a field linked to a variable only capable of holding 50 characters. As a result, the application doesn't know how to handle the extra data and becomes unstable. The overflow portion of the input data must be discarded or somehow handled by the application; otherwise, it could create undesirable results. Because no check is in place to screen out bad requests, the extra data overwrites some portions of memory used by other applications and causes failures and crashes. A buffer overflow can result in the following:

- ▶ Overwriting of data or memory storage.

- ▶ A denial of service due to overloading the input buffer's ability to cope with the additional data.

- ▶ The originator can execute arbitrary code, often at a privileged level.

Services running on Internet-connected computers present an opportunity for compromise using privilege escalation. Some services require special privileges for their operation. A programming error could allow an attacker to obtain special privileges. In this situation, two possible types of privilege escalation exist: a programming error that enables a user to gain additional privileges after successful authentication and a user gaining privileges with no authentication. The following are examples of these types of buffer overflow issues:

- ▶ In the fall of 2002, the Linux Slapper worm infected about 7,000 servers. The worm exploited a flaw in SSL on Linux-based web servers. The premise behind this vulnerability is that the handshake process during an SSL server connection can be made to cause a buffer overflow when a client uses a malformed key.

- ▶ Flaws such as buffer overflows that cause execution stack overwriting in the Java Virtual Machine (JVM). The JVM is the client-side environment supporting Java applets. Improperly created applets can potentially generate a buffer overflow condition, crashing the client system.

In the case of buffer overflows, good quality assurance and secure programming practices could thwart this type of attack. Currently, the most effective way to prevent an attacker from exploiting software is to keep the manufacturer's latest patches and service packs applied and to monitor the Web for newly discovered vulnerabilities.

Cookies

To overcome the limitations of a stateful connection when scaled to global website deployments, the Netscape Corporation created a technology using temporary files stored in the client's browser cache to maintain settings across multiple pages, servers, or sites. These small files are known as *cookies*. They can be used to maintain data such as user settings between visits to the same site on multiple days or to track user browsing habits, such as those used by sites hosting DoubleClick banner advertisements.

Many sites require that browsing clients be configured to accept cookies to store information such as configuration settings or shopping-cart data for electronic commerce sites. Cookies can be used to track information such as the name and IP address of the client system and the operating system and browser client being used. Additional information includes the name of the target and previous URLs, along with any specific settings set within the cookie by the host website.

> ## ExamAlert
>
> Although cookies generally provide benefits to the end users, spyware would be most likely to use a tracking cookie. A *tracking cookie* is a particular type of permanent cookie that sticks around, whereas a *session cookie* stays around only for that particular visit to a website.

If cookies are accessed across many sites, they may be used to track the user's browsing habits and present the user with targeted advertising or content. Many users believe this is a violation of their privacy.

Cookies can also be used to store session settings across multiple actual connections to a web server. This proves helpful when connecting to a distributed server farm, where each page access might be handled by a separate physical server, preventing the use of session variables to maintain details from one page to another.

This is useful in electronic commerce sites where a shopping cart application might add items from multiple pages to a total invoice before being transferred to a billing application. These cookies are also useful to provide custom user configuration settings on subsequent entries to web portals whose content is presented in a dynamic manner.

The danger to maintaining session information is that sites might access cookies stored in the browser's cache that might contain details on the user's e-commerce shopping habits, along with many user details that could possibly include sensitive information identifying the user or allowing access to secured sites.

> ## Note
>
> Clients should regularly clear their browser cookie cache to avoid exposing long-term browsing habits in this way. Where possible, client browsers can also be configured to block third-party cookies, although many online commerce sites require this functionality for their operation.

Cram Quiz

Answer these questions. The answers follow the last question. If you cannot answer these questions correctly, consider reading this section again until you can.

1. Spyware is most likely to use which one of the following types of cookies?

   ○ **A.** Session

   ○ **B.** Transport

   ○ **C.** Tracking

   ○ **D.** Poisonous

2. Which of the following types of attacks can result from the length of variables not being properly checked in the code of a program?

   ○ **A.** Buffer overflow

   ○ **B.** Replay

   ○ **C.** Spoofing

   ○ **D.** Denial of service

3. Which one of the following is a best practice to prevent code injection attacks?

   ○ **A.** Session cookies

   ○ **B.** Input validation

   ○ **C.** Implementing the latest security patches

   ○ **D.** Using unbound variables

Cram Quiz Answers

1. **C.** Whereas cookies generally provide benefits to the end users, spyware would be most likely to use a tracking cookie. A tracking cookie is a particular type of permanent cookie that stays around, whereas a session cookie stays around only for the particular visit to a website. Therefore, answer A is incorrect. Answers B and D are not types of cookies and are incorrect.

2. **A.** Buffer overflows are a result of programming flaws that allow for too much data to be sent. When the program does not know what to do with all this data, it crashes, leaving the machine in a state of vulnerability. Answer B is incorrect because a replay attack records and replays previously sent valid messages. Answer C is incorrect because spoofing involves modifying the source address of traffic or the source of information. Answer D is incorrect because the purpose of a DoS attack is to deny the use of resources or services to legitimate users.

3. **B.** Input validation is the one of the most important countermeasures in order to prevent code injection attacks. Answer B is incorrect, as session cookies pertain to maintaining state within a visit to a website. Answer C is incorrect. Although making sure systems are patched is a good practice, it is not specifically a best practice to prevent code injection attacks. Answer D is incorrect as proper input validation to prevent code injection would rely upon bound variables.

What Next?

If you want more practice on this chapter's exam objectives before you move on, remember that you can access all of the Cram Quiz questions on the CD. You can also create a custom exam by objective with the practice exam software. Note any objective you struggle with and go to that objective material in this chapter.

CHAPTER 6

Deterrents

This chapter covers the following official CompTIA Security+ Certification exam objectives:

▶ Analyze and differentiate among types of mitigation and deterrent techniques

▶ Implement assessment tools and techniques to discover security threats and vulnerabilities

▶ Within the realm of vulnerability assessments, explain the proper use of penetration testing versus vulnerability scanning

(For more information on the official CompTIA Security+ Certification exam topics, see the "About the CompTIA Security+ Certification Exam" section in the Introduction.)

In most situations it is not possible nor even prudent to try to completely eliminate risks. Remember that risk is typically a result of some type of benefit gained. One might be able to eliminate the risk of being involved in a vehicle accident, but this would mean that they never get inside of a vehicle. Of course, however, there is an important benefit derived as a result and thus a tradeoff. Of course, even deciding to walk everywhere instead brings its own risks. Just as one who drives a vehicle buys insurance and wears a seatbelt, for example, organizations look to reduce or mitigate risks when it comes to information security.

Two commonly used assessment methodologies include vulnerability scanning and penetration testing. Both of which provide outputs that assist with the detection of and appropriate response to weaknesses.

Analyze and Differentiate Among Types of Mitigation and Deterrent Techniques

▶ **Manual bypassing of electronic controls**

▶ **Monitoring system logs**

▶ **Physical security**

▶ **Hardening**

▶ **Port security**

▶ **Security posture**

▶ **Reporting**

▶ **Detection controls versus prevention controls**

Cram**Saver**

If you can correctly answer these questions before going through this section, save time by skimming the Exam Alerts in this section and then completing the Cram Quiz at the end of the section.

1. Describe several deterrents used to prevent unauthorized physical access.

2. Aside from the description of an event, what other fields are typical within a system's event log?

3. What are examples of some security deterrents to prevent physical unauthorized access?

Answers

1. Deterrents don't necessarily have to be designed to stop unauthorized access. As the name implies, they need to help deter the access. That is, the potential attacker might think twice about the attempt, especially as even an attacker considers the concept of risk/reward. Common examples include a sign indicating the property is alarmed or protected by a dog. Lighting, locks, dogs, cleared zones around the perimeter, and even life-sized cut-outs of law enforcement officers can make a location appear less inviting to the potential attacker.

2. Although the exact taxonomy might vary by vendor, the various fields one is likely to find within an event include the type of event (for example, error, warning), the time the event occurred, the system from which the event occurred, and an event ID.

3. The purpose of a deterrent is often to stop an event from happening in the first place. Common examples include security guards, dogs, lighting, cameras, and locks.

Manual Bypassing of Electronic Controls

A failure within a security system is always a possibility. As a result, a failsafe mechanism is built in. A system's failsafe describes if it will either fail open or fail closed. In some cases system failures are unintentional, and in other cases the failure might have been caused by malicious activity. In fact, it is sometimes easier to make a security system fail than it is to bypass it while operational. These failures can provide the opportunity for an attacker to gain access or further compromise systems and data. As a result organizations should consider within the design of their security systems that systems fail securely. For example, a system that prevents unauthorized access should default to not allowing access to anyone in the event of a failure.

In some situations, a system might be designed to fail open. This situation is typically seen when security of the overall operation will not be affected. This is common, for example, within systems that transparently monitor or collect data inline—specifically where the loss of that monitoring capability does not outweigh the risk of shutting down the entire system, such as in industrial systems where input and later stages rely on continued production to avoid over-pressure dangers.

Monitoring System Logs

System monitoring is the next method of monitoring. The methodology to perform system monitoring depends on the operating system on the desktop or server. In Microsoft operating systems, the Event Viewer records events in the system event log. Event Viewer enables you to view certain events that occur on the system. Event Viewer maintains three log files: one for system processes, one for security information, and one for applications.

> **ExamAlert**
>
> The security log records security events and is available for view only to administrators. For security events to be monitored, you must enable auditing.

Unlike the security log, the application and system logs are available to all users to view. You can use the application log to tell how well an application is running. The system log shows events that occur on the individual system. You can configure settings such as the size of the file and the filtering of events. Event logging is used for troubleshooting or for notifying administrators of unusual circumstances. It is important to be sure that you have the log file size set properly, that the size is monitored, and that the logs are periodically archived and cleared. Consider carefully where you store log files to make sure that intruders don't have access to them. By doing so, you eliminate the ability for intruders to cover their tracks. Table 6.1 lists the fields and definitions of Windows events.

TABLE 6.1 **Windows Events**

Field Name	Field Description
Type	The type of the event, such as error, warning, or information
Time	The date and time of the local computer at which the event occurred
Computer	The computer on which the event occurred
Provider Type	The type of event that generated the event, such as a Windows event log
Provider Name	The name of the event, such as Application or Security
Source	The application that logged the event, such as MSSQL Server
Event ID	The Windows event number
Description	The description of the event

Of these fields, it is important to note the Event ID and the Description Text fields. The event ID is the easiest way to research the event in the Microsoft Knowledge Base, and the description text usually explains what happened in simple language. Figure 6.1 shows the system event log for a system.

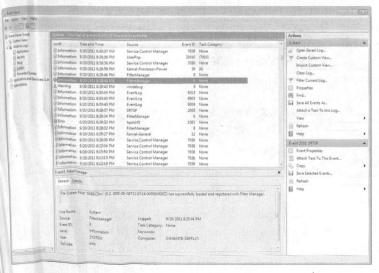

FIGURE 6.1 **Event Viewer.**

There are also built-in and downloadable tools in other operating systems, such as iStat nano for Macintosh systems. iStat nano is a system monitor widget that enables you to view statistics about the system, such as CPU usage, memory usage, hard drive space, bandwidth usage, temperatures, fan speeds, battery usage, uptime, and the top five processes. In addition, third-party programs are available that provide network health monitoring. These programs can monitor the entire network and include devices such as modems, printers, routers, switches, and hubs.

To monitor the health of all systems, you install agents on the machines and then monitor the agents from a central location. For example, Simple Network Management Protocol (SNMP) is an application layer protocol whose purpose is to collect statistics from TCP/IP devices.

Physical Security

When planning security for network scenarios, many organizations overlook physical security. In many smaller organizations, the servers, routers, and patch panels are placed as a matter of convenience because of space restrictions. This can cause security issues. Speaking from experience, this equipment ends up in the oddest places, such as in the coat closet by the receptionist's desk in the lobby, in the room with the copy machine, or in a storage room with a back-door exit that's unlocked most of the time. Securing physical access and ensuring that access requires proper authentication is necessary to avoid accidental exposure of sensitive data to attackers performing physical profiling of a target organization.

When planning physical security, you must consider events such as natural and manmade disasters. If you have space constraints and put the servers in a room with the water heater, how will you deal with the consequences when the water heater springs a leak? How soon will your network be back up and running? If your building is in a flood zone and the most important equipment is in the lowest spot in the building, you need to be prepared when heavy rains come. Manmade disasters can be as simple as a clumsy technician spilling his soda into the most important piece of equipment you have. Many times, these types of scenarios are overlooked until it is too late.

ExamAlert

Be familiar with physical security descriptions indicating potential security flaws. Watch for descriptions that include physical details or organizational processes.

Physical access to a system creates many avenues for a breach in security for several reasons. Many tools can be used to extract password and account information that can then be used to access secured network resources. Given the ability to reboot a system and load software from removable media, attackers might be able to access data or implant Trojan horses and other applications intended to weaken or compromise network security. Unsecured equipment is also vulnerable to social engineering attacks. It is much easier for an attacker to walk into a reception area, say she is there to do some work on the server, and get access to that server in the closet in the front lobby than to get into a physically secured area with a guest sign-in and sign-out sheet. As mentioned earlier, weak physical controls can also amplify the effects of natural and manmade disasters.

Physical security controls parallel the data controls. Mandatory physical access controls are commonly found in government facilities and military installations, where users are closely monitored and very restricted. Because they are being monitored by security personnel and devices, users cannot modify entry methods or let others in. Discretionary physical control to a building or room is delegated to parties responsible for that building or room. In role-based access methods for physical control, groups of people who have common access needs are predetermined and access to different locations is allowed with the same key or swipe card. Users in this model generally have some security training and are often allowed to grant access to others by serving as an escort or by issuing a guest badge. The security department coordinates the secure setup of the facility and surrounding areas, identifies the groups allowed to enter various areas, and allows them access based on their group membership.

When physical security is considered, the most obvious element to control is physical access to systems and resources. Your goal is to allow only trusted use of these resources via positive identification that the entity accessing the systems is someone or something that has permission to do so based on the security model you have chosen. When planning for access control, you pay attention not only to direct physical contact with hosts and network hardware, but also to *line-of-sight access*, which means you need to place systems in such a way that you don't allow an attacker with a telescope or binoculars to spy on typed passwords. You also need to consider areas covered by wireless device transmissions, which may be detected at far greater distances than are useful for two-way network connectivity. Even the location of systems in low-traffic, public, or unmonitored areas may pose security risks.

Access might be controlled by physically securing a system within a locked room or cabinet; attaching the system to fixed, non-movable furniture using locking cables or restraints; and locking the case itself to prevent the removal of key components. Nonstandard case screws are also available to add another layer of security for publicly accessible terminals. Other secured-area considerations include ensuring that air ducts, drop ceilings, and raised floors do not provide unauthorized avenues for physical access. You can have the most secure lock on the door with biometric devices for identification, but if the walls don't go up all the way and ceiling tiles can be removed to access rooms with sensitive equipment in them, someone can easily walk off with equipment and sensitive data.

Frosted or painted glass can be used to eliminate direct visual observation of user actions, and very high-security scenarios may mandate the use of electromagnetic shielding to prevent remote monitoring of emissions generated by video monitors, network switching, and system operation. In addition, many modems and network hardware solutions use raw, transmitted data to illuminate activity indicator lights. Direct observation of these may enable an attacker to remotely eavesdrop on transmitted data using a telescope.

Security guards, surveillance cameras, motion detectors, limited-access zones, token-based and biometric access requirements for restricted areas, and many other considerations may be involved in access control planning. In addition, users must be educated about each measure taken to prevent circumvention to improve ease of normal access. A single propped-open door, a system left logged in when the administrator is away from her desk, or a paper with sensitive data on it thrown in the garbage could undo many layers of protection.

Buildings that house sensitive information and systems usually have an area of cleared land surrounding them. This area is referred to as *no-man's land*. The purpose of this area is to eliminate the possibility of an intruder hiding in the bushes or behind another building. Intruders often *piggyback* their way into a building, meaning they wait for someone with proper access to enter the building and then enter behind before the door closes. Depending on the company policy, the time of day, or the employee, these intruders may never be questioned or escorted out. Having a clear area in the main facility can keep this from happening.

Another common deterrent is a fence or similar device that surrounds the entire building. A fence keeps out unwanted vehicles and people. One factor to consider in fencing is the height. The higher the fence, the harder it is to get over. Another factor to consider is the material the fence is made of. It is much easier to remove wooden slats or cut a chain-link fence with bolt cutters than it is to drill through concrete or block. One final note: If the fence isn't maintained or the area around it isn't well lit, the fence can easily be compromised.

Another physical barrier is a moat. Moats surround part or all of a facility and are excellent physical barriers because they have a low profile and are not as obtrusive as fencing. In this instance, the consideration is the depth and width. As with all physical barriers, the moat must be well maintained.

You can implement the following additional security measures to help deter unauthorized access:

- **Security guards and dogs**: Security guards and dogs can be great deterrents to intruders. It is imperative that they are trained properly. They are often used in combination with other measures.

- **External lighting and cameras**: If areas are brightly lit and have cameras, they are less likely to have unauthorized access attempts.

- **External and internal motion detectors:** Motion detectors can alert security personnel of intruders or suspicious activity on the company's premises. They can be based on light, sound, infrared, or ultrasonic technology. These devices must be properly configured because they are extremely sensitive and can issue false alarms if set too stringently.

- **External doors and windows**: Steel doors are the best deterrent, but steel-reinforced wooden doors work, too. Windows should have locking mechanisms, and building security alarms should monitor the open/closed position of all windows that could pose an entry risk.

- **Mantraps**: A mantrap is a holding area between two entry points that gives security personnel time to view a person before allowing him into the internal building.

- **Locks**: Locks must be easy to operate yet deter intruders. Besides the normal key locks, several different types can be considered. A cipher lock has a punch-code entry system. A wireless lock is opened by a receiver mechanism that reads the card when it is held close to the receiver. A swipe card lock requires a card to be inserted into the lock; many hotels use these. The factors to consider are strength, material, and cost.

- **Biometrics**: Physical security can also integrate biometric methods into a door-lock mechanism. Biometrics can use a variety of methods. See Table 10.1 in Chapter 10, "Authentication and Authorization," for a review of these technologies. When using biometrics, remember that each method has its own degree of error ratios, and some methods might seem invasive to the users and might not be accepted gracefully.

▶ **Door access systems**: Door access systems include biometric access, proximity access, and coded access systems; Disability Discrimination Act (DDA) door entry systems; and modular door entry systems. The type of access used depends on the amount of security needed.

▶ **Video surveillance**: Closed-circuit television (CCTV) is the most common method of surveillance. The video signal is processed and then transmitted for viewing at a central monitoring point. Traditionally, CCTV has been analog; however, recent technologies are taking advantage of the digital format, including IP video surveillance that uses TCP/IP for recording and monitoring.

Exam**Alert**

The exam might include questions about the various physical-barrier techniques. Be sure you are familiar with the methods previously listed.

Physical Security During Building Evacuations

Because a physical security plan should start with an examination of the perimeter of the building, it might also be wise to discuss what happens when an evacuation is necessary. You don't want intruders plundering the building while employees are running haphazardly all over the place. The evacuation process could be a part of the disaster recovery plan and should include some of the following items:

▶ A map of the internal building and all exit areas

▶ Which departments will exit through which doors

▶ What equipment will be shut down and by whom

▶ Who will do a final inspection of each area and make sure it is secure

▶ Where each department, once evacuated, will go and how far away from the building they will be located

▶ Who will notify the proper authorities or agencies of the incident

Make sure that all users understand how these plans function and practice orderly evacuation procedures so that an emergency situation does not leave critical systems unguarded or unsecured. Smoke from a cigarette or a purposefully set flame could create an opportunity for an attacker to gain access to highly secure areas if evacuation planning does not include security considerations.

Hardening

In security terms, *hardening* a system refers to reducing its security exposure and strengthening its defenses against unauthorized access attempts and other forms of malicious attention. A "soft" system is one that is installed with default configurations or unnecessary services, or one that is not maintained to include emerging security updates. There is no such thing as a "completely safe" system, so the process of hardening reflects attention to security thresholds.

Systems installed in default configurations often include many unnecessary services that are configured automatically. These provide many potential avenues for unauthorized access to a system or network. Many services have known vulnerabilities that require specific action to make them more secure, or ones that might just impair system function by causing additional processing overhead. Default configurations also allow for unauthorized access and exploitation. For example, a denial-of-service (DoS) attack against an unneeded web service is one way a nonessential service could potentially cause problems for an otherwise functional system.

Common default-configuration exploits include both services such as anonymous-access FTP servers and network protocols such as the Simple Network Management Protocol (SNMP).

> ## ExamAlert
>
> When presented with a scenario on the exam, you might be tempted to keep all services enabled to cover all requirements. Be wary of this option; it might cause the installation of unnecessary services or protocols.

Many vendors provide regular updates for installed products, managed through automated deployment tools or by manual update procedures carried out by a system user. Regular maintenance is required to meet emerging security threats, whether applying an updated RPM (Redhat Package Manager, a file format used to distribute Linux applications and update packages) by hand or through fully automated "call home for updates" options like those found in many commercial operating systems and applications.

Because of the emergence of blended-threat malware, which targets multiple vulnerabilities within a single attack, all major operating systems and application solutions must be considered in system hardening plans. Automated reverse-engineering of newly released patches has significantly reduced the time from an update's initial release until its first exploits are seen in the wild, down from months to hours before unpatched applications can be targeted.

Types of updates you should be familiar with include the following:

▶ **Hotfixes**: Typically, small and specific-purpose updates that alter the behavior of installed applications in a limited manner. These are the most common type of update.

▶ **Service packs**: Major revisions of functionality or service operation in an installed application. Service packs are the least common type of update, often requiring extensive testing to ensure against service failure in integrated network environments before application. Service packs are usually cumulative, including all prior service packs, hotfixes, and patches.

▶ **Patches**: Like hotfixes, patches are usually focused updates that affect installed applications. Patches are generally used to add new functionality, update existing code operation, or to extend existing application capabilities.

Particular attention should be given to management interfaces and applications. Most hardware and software security solutions provide some type of portal or method to interact with and configure the system. In some cases it may be wise to limit access only to an authorized user that is physically present at the specific system. In lieu of this, additional controls should be put in place such as making sure that all communication is encrypted, strong authentication is used, and only the necessary personnel have access to the systems.

The latter two examples should be considered not only for management interfaces, but also for the hardening of systems in general. Proper password protection is critical. This is often an easy exploit for attackers to mount an attack. Default passwords for systems are easily available. Consider, for example, vendor-supplied default logon/password combinations, such as the Oracle DB default admin: scott/tiger. Many users are aware of the default password phenomenon through the use of home wireless access points in which each specific device shipped with the same username and password. In addition to immediately changing all default passwords, complex passwords or some sort of strong authentication should be used.

Finally, just as unnecessary services should be disabled, so should unnecessary accounts. Some systems include default accounts, which provide an attacker with another option for entry. A more common example are users and administrators that are no longer with the organization or no longer require access to a particular system. Oftentimes, these accounts are left in place. Such accounts should be disabled immediately.

Port Security

Disabling unnecessary services is discussed in the previous section. Each of these services uses a logical port on system. Part of ensuring that service is disabled is through preventing access via the assigned ports. Just as these unnecessary logical ports or services should be disabled, so should physical ports that are not required. Even in the case of ports that are needed, these should still be closely monitored, and possibly have additional layers of controls in place to prevent improper use.

Each device on the network has a MAC address that identifies the network interface. A common control, albeit one that shouldn't be solely relied upon, is MAC limiting and filtering. This control provides further ability to limit what is able to access a network or service. Wireless access points, for example, can easily be configured to only accept connections from specific MAC addresses. The reason that additional measures should be in place is that MAC addresses can easily be spoofed. Although it is a worthy control to prevent the average user from bringing in their own devices, it is not likely to prevent an attacker who wants to gain access.

Devices that need to connect to a network can also be controlled via the IEEE Standard, 802.1X. This should not be confused with 802.11. The former provides standards for port-based access control, whereas 802.11 is specific to wireless technology. 802.1X provides a method for authenticating a device to another system via an authentication server. The standard essentially allows various authentication methods such as RADIUS, digital certificates, and one-time password devices to be used.

Security Posture

A security posture includes an organization's overall plan for protecting itself against threats. This should also include the activities required for the ongoing monitoring and reaction required of security incidents.

An overall approach is to set baseline standards. To establish effective security baselines, enterprise network security management requires a measure of commonality between systems. Mandatory settings, standard application suites, and initial setup configuration details all factor into the security stance of an enterprise network.

Types of configuration settings you should be familiar with include the following:

▶ **Group policies**: Collections of configuration settings applied to a system based on computer or user group membership, which might influence the level, type, and extent of access provided.

▸ **Security templates**: Sets of configurations that reflect a particular role or standard established through industry standards or within an organization, assigned to fulfill a particular purpose. Examples include a "minimum-access" configuration template assigned to limited-access kiosk systems, whereas a "high-security" template could be assigned to systems requiring more stringent logon and access control mechanisms.

▸ **Configuration baselines**: Many industries must meet specific criteria, established as a baseline measure of security. An example of this is the health-care industry, which has a lengthy set of requirements for information technology specified in the Health Insurance Portability and Accountability Act (HIPAA) security standards. Unless the mandated security baseline is met, penalties and fines could be assessed. Security baselines are often established by governmental mandate, regulatory bodies, or industry representatives, such as the PCI requirements established by the credit card industry for businesses collecting and transacting credit information.

To maintain a strong security posture, organizations should also implement plans for continuous security monitoring and remediation. It is important that security monitoring is not just a one-time or isolated event. It needs to be conducted on an ongoing basis. Furthermore, a plan for ongoing security monitoring actually needs to be monitored. That is, it shouldn't just be a system of systematic logging and monitoring. Rather mechanisms and procedures need to be in place to ensure that personnel are actively looking at what's taking place, and that proper alerts and notifications are set up.

Finally, organizations should have a plan for response and remediation. Although the hope is that the controls in place should prevent a breach or damaging attack, this is not always the case. This is especially evident in recent news, in which organizations are breached despite the many controls they had in place. Many of these instances provide ideal case studies in remediation. This includes, for example, how quickly the issue was identified and controlled, how quickly the damage was repaired, and even how effectively the organization dealt with the public and their customers and clients.

Reporting

Proper and effective reporting is critical to the overall health and security of an organization. The use of reporting should be dictated by a policy based upon the overall risk of the infrastructure and data. This will help define what types of reports are required, the frequency of the reports, as well as how often they are examined. Adequate reporting should also include the following mechanisms:

▶ **Alarms**: The purpose of an alarm is to report a critical event that typically requires some type of immediate response. Consider the common analogy of a bank. Each time the safe is accessed might be part of a report that does not necessitate an alarm; however, a broken window after hours is cause for alarm, in which an immediate response can take place.

▶ **Alerts**: An alert is similar to an alarm, but it is less critical and likely does not require an immediate response. Several failed logon attempts, for example, would likely generate an alert. This alert at a minimum should generate a log file, but depending upon the situation, it could also be a notification of some sort to an administrator. Alerts might be used in conjunction with an alarm. For example, several alerts might be correlated together to form a condition that would deem an alarm necessary.

▶ **Trends**: Identifying and understanding trends is vital to detecting and responding to incidents. Furthermore, trends also help prevent the unnecessary response to something that initially might seem warranted but is actually not. Trends become more apparent based upon the time-frame. For example, over a week period there might be an abnormal activity on Sunday. Yet, over a month period it becomes evident that this activity occurs every Sunday, perhaps due to a weekly processing event.

Detection Controls versus Prevention Controls

Consider for a moment the importance of having both detection controls and prevention controls. In a perfect world, we would only need prevention controls. Unfortunately not all malicious activity can be prevented. As a result, it is important that detection controls are part of one's layered security approach. Using our bank analogy from before, even the best protected banks in the world use both. In addition to the locks, bars, and security signs, the bank probably has various detection controls such as motion detectors.

As you might have already guessed, some controls can be both detection controls and preventive controls. A camera (if visible or advertised), for example, not only serves as a detection control (if actively monitored), but it also serves as a deterrent to a would-be attacker, thus being preventive. Although cameras can serve as a deterrent, without active monitoring by a security guard they are likely only useful for later analysis. Security guards, on the other hand, easily serve as both a preventative and detective control. In addition, a security guard can initiate an immediate response to an incident.

Information security intrusions might be physical, such as in the case of an intrusion into a datacenter. In addition, intrusions can occur through the more common means of logical access. An intrusion includes any unauthorized resource access attempt within a secured network. Although it is possible for human monitoring to identify real-time intrusion events within small, tightly controlled networks, it is more likely that a human administrator monitors alerts and notifications generated by intrusion-detection systems (IDSs). These software and hardware agents monitor network traffic for patterns that might indicate an attempt at intrusion, called an *attack signature*, or might monitor server-side logs for improper activity or unauthorized access.

Both passive and active forms of IDS exist:

▸ A passive IDS solution is intended to detect an intrusion, log the event, and potentially raise some form of alert.

▸ An active IDS solution acts to terminate or deny an intrusion attempt by changing firewall or IPsec policy settings automatically before logging the event and raising an alert for human operators.

Both active and passive IDSs must first identify an intrusion before altering the network configuration (in an active system), logging the event, and raising an alert.

In contrast, an intrusion prevention system (IPS) is indented to provide direct protection against identified attacks. Whereas a detection system attempts to identify unauthorized access attempts and generate alerts, a prevention system will provide direct protection against identified attacks. For example, an IPS solution might be configured to automatically drop connections from a range of IP addresses during a DOS attack.

Cram Quiz

Answer these questions. The answers follow the last question. If you cannot answer these questions correctly, consider reading this section again until you can.

1. In order to harden a system, which one of the following is a critical step?
   - ○ **A.** Isolate the system in a below-freezing environment
   - ○ **B.** Disable all unnecessary ports and services
   - ○ **C.** Disable the WWW service
   - ○ **D.** Isolate the system physically from other critical systems

2. Which one of the following is the most common method of video surveillance?
   - ○ **A.** CCTV
   - ○ **B.** IPTV
   - ○ **C.** CTV
   - ○ **D.** ICTV

3. Which one of the following controls is not a physical security measure?
   - ○ **A.** Motion detector
   - ○ **B.** Antivirus software
   - ○ **C.** CCTV
   - ○ **D.** Fence

Cram Quiz Answers

1. **B.** One of the most critical steps in regard to system hardening includes disabling unnecessary ports and services. Answer A is incorrect as keeping systems in below-freezing environments is not considered an approach to system hardening, nor is it even good for the systems. Answer C is incorrect because although the web service might be an unnecessary port, it would not be considered unnecessary if the system was a web server. Answer D is also incorrect as doing such is not a generally accepted critical step for system hardening.

2. **A.** Closed-circuit television (CCTV) is the most common method of video within a security environment. Answer B is incorrect as IPTV refers to broadcast Internet television services. Answers C and D are also incorrect. These are red herring answers which sound closely related to the actual answer.

3. **B.** Answers A, C, and D are all controls used for physical security. Antivirus software is not a physical security control, but a control used to protect computer systems from malware.

Implement Assessment Tools and Techniques to Discover Security Threats and Vulnerabilities

▶ **Vulnerability scanning and interpreting results**

▶ **Tools**

▶ **Risk calculations**

▶ **Assessment types**

▶ **Assessment technique**

Cram**Saver**

If you can correctly answer these questions before going through this section, save time by skimming the Exam Alerts in this section and then completing the Cram Quiz at the end of the section.

1. There is a plethora of software that provides automatic scanning features to help identify vulnerabilities, which sometimes includes built-in knowledge about the vulnerabilities. Why is it still important to properly interpret the results?

2. Describe a "risky" situation in which you engage and discuss the process of risk calculation that you might or might not consciously take. Consider threats, vulnerabilities, likelihood, and even how you might mitigate such risks.

Answers

1. Vulnerabilities need to be considered with an overall structure of risk. Assets being protected vary by organization. In addition, threats and the likelihood of the realization of those threats differ by organization. Finally, vulnerabilities must be considered within the overall goals of the organization. As a result, a vulnerability that correlates to a high risk at one place might be low at another.

2. Every day we engage in various activities that involve some level of risk. These could include such activities from walking to work to engaging in extreme sports. In most of these situations we engage in them as they provide some type of value or pleasure. In most cases, however, we consider the unique circumstances and take steps to mitigate the risks.

Vulnerability Scanning and Interpreting Results

Vulnerability scanning implies the uses of computer software used to test systems for known vulnerabilities or weaknesses. Vulnerability scanning is often part of a much larger vulnerability management program. A variety of tools are available for this purpose. Many of these programs rely upon a database of known security weaknesses to provide knowledge context, whereas others are simply tools in which further context must be applied.

The output of these scanners and tools require careful interpretation. In many cases several factors need to be considered. The interpretation of the results typically result in one of three things:

▶ Doing nothing either because it's a false positive or there is not a significant risk presented to the organization

▶ Fixing or eliminating the vulnerability

▶ Accepting the vulnerability but implementing mitigating controls

Tools

There are a variety of tools that you can use to identify vulnerabilities and that are part of a complete vulnerability management program. These include vulnerability scanners, honeypots, and honeynets. Other tools include protocol analyzers and sniffers, which were introduced in Chapter 1.

Protocol Analyzer

Some operating systems have built-in protocol analyzers. The purpose of the discussion in this chapter is to show how you can use them to detect security-related anomalies. Windows Server operating systems come with a protocol analyzer called Network Monitor. Novell's comparable network-monitoring tool is called LANalyzer. In the UNIX environment, many administrators use the tools that come with the core operating system, such as ps and vmstat. Sun Solaris has a popular utility called iostat that provides good information about I/O performance. You can also use other third-party programs, such as Wireshark, for network monitoring.

> **Note**
> A protocol analyzer is used to capture network traffic and generate statistics for creating reports. When the packets have been captured, you can view the information.

Figure 6.2 shows the information output by the Microsoft Network Monitor.

Some of the basic information recorded is the source address, destination address, headers, and data. Network Monitor detects other installed instances of Network Monitor and identifies the machine name and user account that it is running under. Often, Network Monitor is used in conjunction with

Microsoft System Management Server (SMS) so that it can capture data across routers and resolve IP addresses from names. In addition, you can access the Performance console from within Network Monitor.

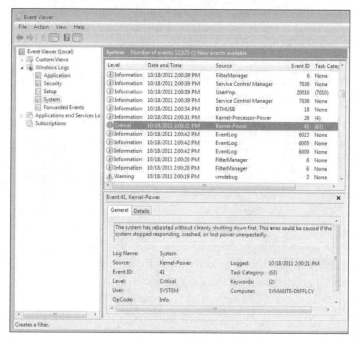

FIGURE 6.2 **Network Monitor.**

You can use Network Monitor to view IPsec communication. It includes parsers for the Internet Security Associate and Key Management Protocol (ISAKMP) Internet Key Exchange (IKE), Authentication Header (AH), and Encapsulating Security Payload (ESP) protocols. Network Monitor cannot parse encrypted portions of IPsec-secured ESP traffic when the encryption is provided by software. It can, however, process the packets if they are being encrypted and decrypted by IPsec-aware network adapters because the packets are already decrypted by the time they reach Network Monitor's parsers.

Sniffer

A sniffer and protocol analyzer are generally accepted as one and the same. As software packages continue to add features, the lines between the two blur. Although the two are considered synonymous, a sniffer can be considered as a tool designed to "sniff" the network capturing packets. In the most simple sense, a sniffer relies upon the user to conduct further analysis and interpretation. On the other hand, the protocol analyzer is able to take those packets and provide further details and context around the captured packets.

Vulnerability Scanner

Another common tool is the vulnerability scanner. A vulnerability scanner is a software utility that scans a range of IP addresses, testing for the presence of known vulnerabilities in software configuration and accessible services. A traditional vulnerability scanner relies upon a database of known vulnerabilities. These automated tools are directed at a targeted system or systems. Unlike a system that tests for open ports, which only test for the availability of services, vulnerability scanners may check for the particular version or patch level of a service to determine its level of vulnerability.

Upon careful examination of the output of vulnerability scans, it is recommended to identify all the false positives and then focus on what's left. Keep in mind that a vulnerability does not necessarily indicate something bad or something that needs to be immediately remediated or even remediated at all. Using an analogy, consider a home as a subject for a vulnerability assessment. A broken dead-bolt lock certainly seems like a vulnerability. Ideally, this might be replaced; however, there are some parts of the world where it is common that nobody locks their doors anyhow. A smashed window is a vulnerability as well. In some cases it might make sense to only mitigate this by covering it with plastic to protect against the elements. Even a perfectly functioning window by itself is a vulnerability! The benefit that that window provides typically outweighs the other option of living without windows. Of course this all depends upon what one is trying to protect and protect against.

> **Note**
>
> Within U.S. governmental agencies, vulnerability may be discussed using the Open Vulnerability Assessment Language (OVAL) sponsored by the Department of Homeland Security's National Cyber Security Division (NCSD). OVAL is intended as an international language for representing vulnerability information using an XML schema for expression, allowing tools to be developed to test for identified vulnerabilities in the OVAL repository.

As you can see in the previous analogy, there isn't necessarily a quick method for determining risk based upon the output of a vulnerability scanner. The relevancy to the business, tradeoffs, as well as identified threats and likelihoods all need to be considered in order to accurately interpret the results of a vulnerability scanner.

Honeypots

Honeypots are often used to identify the level of aggressive attention directed at a network and to study and learn from an attacker's common methods of attack. Honeypots are systems configured to simulate one or more services within an organization's network and left exposed to network access. When attackers access a honeypot system, their activities are logged and monitored by other processes so that the attacker's actions and methods can be later reviewed in detail, while the honeypot distracts the attacker from valid network resources. Honeypots might be simple targets exposed for identification of vulnerability exposure, or they might interact with the attacker to extend access time and allow tracking and logging of an attacker's activities to build better attack profile data.

Honeynets

Honeynets are collections of honeypot systems interconnected to create functional-appearing networks that can be used to study an attacker's behavior within the network. Honeynets make use of specialized software agents to create normal-seeming network traffic. Honeynets and honeypots can be used to distract attackers from valid network content, to study the attacker's methods, and to provide early warning of attack attempts that may later be waged against the more secured portions of the network.

Port Scanner

Port scanners are often part of a more comprehensive vulnerability assessment solution. Port scanners may, however, be standalone in that all they do is scan a range of specific ports to determine what ports are open on a system. The results are valuable to system administrators and attackers alike. Port scanners typically identify one of two states in which the port can be in: open or closed. In addition, some port scanners are able to provide additional information such as the type of operating system running on the targeted system and services running over the ports.

Risk Calculation

Chapter 3, "Risk Management," introduced the important concepts around risk calculation. These concepts are particularly important as related to implementing and interpreting assessment tools. The choice and use of assessment tools and techniques depends upon various interrelated concepts:

- ▶ Threat versus likelihood
- ▶ Risk assessment
- ▶ Threat assessment
- ▶ Vulnerability assessment

Let's consider a simple analogy. If you live in Iowa (a Midwestern state in the middle of the United States, which is more than 1,000 miles from the nearest ocean), how likely are you to be concerned with implementing a program to deal with a hurricane or tsunami? Although there are countless threats when dealing with physical and information security, it is important to consider the likelihood of them actually occurring.

Such considerations are important to conducting an overall risk assessment. Given what you have learned previously about risk, you should understand that various components combined make up one's risk. Therefore, in order to properly understand risk, you must also understand threats and vulnerabilities. Organizations, as part of an overall program, should have identified all relevant threats and their likelihood of occurring to the organization. A hurricane, for example, is a real threat to many coastal communities, but even within that context some are more likely to be hit than others. A financial institution that conducts business online differs in the likelihood of specific threats compared to non-profit organization that maintains a static web presence.

The results of a vulnerability assessment within the context of these other variables now is more actionable. Although the absence of storm shutters exposes a vulnerability, it is not as important to residents in Iowa as it is to a resident in a hurricane-prone home on the coast. Open ports and services (just like doors and windows) present opportunities for attack, yet you must also consider the benefit of what these are providing. A specific vulnerability ultimately correlates to differing levels of risk based upon the organization.

Assessment Technique

When assessing for threats and vulnerabilities as part of an overall risk management program, a variety of techniques exist. Mature risk management programs likely use the following techniques:

> **Baseline reporting**: There is no one-size-fits-all approach to security, even with a single organization across various systems. On the other-hand, it is important to consider a minimum or baseline standard of security. Baseline reporting compares existing implementations against these expected baselines. The goal is to identify those systems that do not meet this minimum level of expected requirements.

> **Code review**: As applications are developed, it is important to make sure that the resulting code is thoroughly and methodically reviewed by someone other than the developers. Many exploited vulnerabilities within software can be prevented. It is considered a good practice within organizations to ensure that developed applications are examined prior

to being released in production or to the general public. These reviews are typically conducted using automated software programs designed to check code, as well as manual human checks in which someone not associated with development combs through the code.

▶ **Determine attack surface**: Given how complex writing code can be, the fact that humans make mistakes, and that technology and threats are constantly evolving, it is important to understand how much opportunity there is for an attack. The attack surface refers to the amount of running code, services, and user-interaction fields and interfaces. An analogy is the story of a sniper who once used a rifle to hit a nickel coin from 100 meters away. Sounds impressive, unless, of course, the target is comprised of thousands of coins! In order to effectively reduce the attack surface to an appropriate level, it is first important to identify just how broad that surface is.

▶ **Architecture review**: An assessment of system architecture considers the entire system. It provides the ability to identify faulty components and interaction between various elements. It also ensures the architecture is consistent with the goals of an organization and the tolerance of risk willing to be accepted. A physical building, for example, needs to adhere to structurally sound engineering methods as all the pieces are put together as well as consideration of the environment. Moreover, the design of the building should correlate to the goals of the occupants as well as the risk. About 2,000 years ago the Roman architect Vitruvius attributed a good building as having durability, utility, and beauty. Certainly within the context of the first two these principles apply to information architecture. Beauty is even important, specifically as it is related to how it is optimized and well-documented and how the complex is simplified. In fact, there are many examples of beauty being a determining factor in software architecture, considering things beyond function and quality. Other examples include a system that anticipates change, and—just like physical architecture—it should delight the users, which includes the developers and testers. This helps ensure a lifecycle of quality and alignment with evolving goals.

▶ **Design review**: Not to be confused with architecture, *design* refers more specifically to the components of the architecture at a more micro level. A review of design considers various elements such as compatibility, modularity, reusability, and, of course, security. Design assessments should not be thought of as a one-time event during initial design. It is important that design be incorporated into a lifecycle process in which design is constantly considered and reviewed. A continuous process of assessing design helps deal with the challenge of evolving threats, new information, and changing organizational goals.

Cram Quiz

Answer these questions. The answers follow the last question. If you cannot answer these questions correctly, consider reading this section again until you can.

1. Which one of the following is used to capture network traffic?
   - ○ **A.** Honeynet
   - ○ **B.** Vulnerability scanner
   - ○ **C.** Honeypot
   - ○ **D.** Protocol analyzer

2. Reviews of architecture, design, and code, as well as baseline reporting and understanding attack surface, are all considered which one of the following?
   - ○ **A.** Control procedure techniques to protect against insider threats
   - ○ **B.** Countermeasures designed to eliminate risk
   - ○ **C.** Techniques for assessing threats and vulnerabilities
   - ○ **D.** Design procedures for creating sustainable and usable applications

3. Which one of the following is not true of port scanners?
   - ○ **A.** They are useful for nefarious purposes.
   - ○ **B.** They can be stand alone or part of a vulnerability assessment solution.
   - ○ **C.** They allow interaction with the attacker to enable logging.
   - ○ **D.** They can provide operating system information.

Cram Quiz Answers

1. **D**. Protocol analyzers and sniffers are tools used to capture network traffic. Answer B is incorrect, as a vulnerability scanner is used to scan and test for known vulnerabilities. Answers A and C are incorrect as these are mechanisms used to trap or deter attackers using an isolated system that appears to be a valuable target.

2. **C**. Each of these are considered assessment techniques, part of an overall risk management program designed to assess threats and vulnerabilities to ensure that systems are designed securely within the goals of an organization. Answers A, B, and D specifically relate to techniques for assessing threats and vulnerabilities.

3. **C**. A system that allows interaction with an attacker to enable logging describes a function of a honeypot. Answers A, B, and D are incorrect in that each of these describe functions of a port scanner.

207

Within the Realm of Vulnerability Assessments, Explain the Proper Use of Penetration Testing versus Vulnerability Scanning

Within the Realm of Vulnerability Assessments, Explain the Proper Use of Penetration Testing versus Vulnerability Scanning

▶ **Penetration testing**

▶ **Vulnerability scanning**

▶ **Black box**

▶ **White box**

▶ **Gray box**

CramSaver

If you can correctly answer these questions before going through this section, save time by skimming the Exam Alerts in this section and then completing the Cram Quiz at the end of the section.

1. Which one of the following provides the best description for a penetration test?

   A. A passive evaluation and analysis of operational weaknesses using tools and techniques that a malicious source might use

   B. An evaluation mimicking real-world attacks in order to identify ways to circumvent security

   C. The monitoring of network communications and examination of header and payload data

   D. A technique used to identify hosts and their associated vulnerabilities

2. What are the differences between a black box, white box, and gray box as they pertain to penetration testing?

Answers

1. **B.** Penetration tests are active evaluations, thus answer A is incorrect. Answer C describes network sniffing, and answer D describes vulnerability scanning. Both of these, however, can be used as part of the penetration process.

2. Each of these refer to testing performed with varying degrees of knowledge about the system or application being tested. Black box testing assumes no knowledge, whereas white box testing provides more transparency about the inner workings. Gray box testing is a combination of both black box and white box testing.

Penetration Testing

In some cases, vulnerability assessments may be complemented by directed efforts to exploit vulnerabilities in an attempt to gain access to networked resources. These are, in essence, "friendly" attacks against a network to test the security measures put into place. Such attacks are referred to as penetration tests or simply *pentests* and may cause some disruption to network operations as a result of the actual penetration efforts conducted. Penetration tests can also mask legitimate attacks by generating false data in IDS systems, concealing aggression that is otherwise unrelated to the officially sanctioned penetration test. Some tools use passive OS fingerprinting. A passive attack attempts to passively monitor data being sent between two parties and does not insert data into the data stream.

Some systems administrators might perform amateur or ad-hoc pentests against networks in an attempt to prove a particular vulnerability exists or to evaluate the overall security exposure of a network. This is a bad practice because it generates false intrusion data; might weaken the network's security level; and might be a violation of privacy laws, regulatory mandates, or business entity guidelines. Although regularly conducted penetration tests may be a good way to assess the effectiveness of an organization's controls, these tests should always be performed within a defined program of governance, which includes the knowledge of senior management.

The high-level components of a penetration test include the following:

▶ **Verify a threat exists**: A penetration tests seeks to exploit vulnerabilities. As a result, it is necessary to first understand a threat and to what extent that threat exists in the first place. A sheep farmer in an isolated location might be less concerned about locking the front door than he or she is about the threat of wolves to the sheep.

▶ **Bypass security controls**: Just as a real attacker would, penetration tests should seek to bypass security controls. Verifying that a battering ram can't penetrate the stone wall is worthless when the gate 100 meters away around the back is left wide-open. Although network firewalls might be protecting the pathways into the network, a rogue wireless access point or modems might present an easier method of entry for an attacker. Another common method of bypassing security controls is to render them ineffective. For example, a DoS attack can be mounted on security controls to overload the control, allowing for potentially easier access.

▶ **Actively test security controls**: Unlike passive techniques, active techniques include direct interaction with a specific target. Passive techniques seek to identify gaps that could lead to missing or misconfigured

209

Within the Realm of Vulnerability Assessments, Explain the Proper Use of Penetration
Testing versus Vulnerability Scanning

security controls. Active techniques, however, seek to identify if controls are implemented properly. Consider a lock on a door. Although passive reviews might show documentation and policies indicating that locks are installed, in an active test someone walks up and tries to open the door.

▶ **Exploit vulnerability**: Executing an attack is the core of a penetration test. Exploiting a vulnerability follows the identification of a potential vulnerability. Unlike vulnerability scanning, penetration tests don't just check for the existence of a potential vulnerability; they attempt to exploit it. A resulting exploit verifies the vulnerability and should lead to mitigation techniques and controls to deal with the security exposure. Most exploited vulnerabilities are likely the result of misconfigurations, kernel flaws, buffer overflow, input validation errors, and incorrect permissions.

Vulnerability Scanning

A penetration test goes beyond vulnerability scanning by actually subjecting a system or network to a real-world attack. Vulnerability scanning, like a port scanner, identifies hosts and open ports, but it takes things a bit further. It looks for specific vulnerabilities and provides information and guidance. As discussed earlier, it is important to note that although vulnerability scanners aid in interpretation, it is very important for the results to be evaluated within the context of one's own business.

> ## Exam**Alert**
>
> The results of a vulnerability scan should be organized based upon the relative security and value associated with each identified threat. As a result, an organization can prioritize what vulnerabilities need to be addressed first.

Vulnerability scanning, unlike penetration testing, does not seek to test or bypass security controls. In addition, after vulnerabilities are discovered by a vulnerability scanner no attempts are made to exploit the weaknesses. When used with a penetration testing program, an effective vulnerability scanner should serve the following purposes:

▶ **Passively testing security controls**: Passive scanning poses minimal risk to the assessed environment. They are designed to not interfere with normal activity or degrade performance. On the other hand, an active scanner is more aggressive, like a penetration test, and is capable of interrupting services.

▶ **Identify vulnerability**: Vulnerability scanners, using their database of vulnerabilities, can quickly identify known vulnerabilities on systems. This includes outdated software versions that contain flaws or even missing patches.

▶ **Identify lack of security controls**: Identifying vulnerabilities provides for the opportunity to remediate the weakness. In some cases, it highlights the needs for further implementation of security controls to mitigate the risk.

▶ **Identify common misconfiguration**: Vulnerability scanners are able to identify many common misconfigurations. Some scanners are even capable of remediation. Checking for misconfigurations is most beneficial when compared against an organization's security policies and standards.

> **ExamAlert**
>
> Although penetration tests are always considered active, vulnerability scans are most often passive attempts to identify weaknesses.

Testing

Penetration testing can be conducted using various techniques. These techniques are commonly known as being one of the following:

▶ Black box

▶ White box

▶ Gray box

Each of these refers to varying degrees of knowledge about the systems or applications being tested. A black box test is conducted with the assessor having no information or knowledge about the inner workings of the system or knowledge of the source code. An easy way to think about this is that one cannot see through or inside the black box. White box testing, also called *clear box* or *glass box*, provides more transparency. Because white box techniques are often more efficient and cost-effective, they are the more commonly used technique. Gray box testing uses a combination of both white and black box techniques. This can be more easily thought of as being translucent.

Within the Realm of Vulnerability Assessments,
Explain the Proper Use of Penetration Testing
versus Vulnerability Scanning

CramQuiz

Cram Quiz

Answer these questions. The answers follow the last question. If you cannot answer
these questions correctly, consider reading this section again until you can.

1. After conducting a vulnerability assessment, which of the following would be the
   best action to perform?

   ○ **A.** Disable all vulnerable systems until mitigating controls can be implemented

   ○ **B.** Contact the network team to shut down all identified open ports

   ○ **C.** Immediately conduct a penetration test against identified
   vulnerabilities

   ○ **D.** Organize and document the results based upon severity

2. You are conducting a penetration test on a software application for a client. The
   client provides you with details around some of the source code and development process. What type of test will you likely be conducting?

   ○ **A.** Black box

   ○ **B.** Vulnerability

   ○ **C.** White box

   ○ **D.** Answer A & C

3. Which of the following would be a reason to conduct a penetration test?

   ○ **A.** To passively test security controls

   ○ **B.** To identify the vulnerabilities

   ○ **C.** To test the adequacy of security measures put in place

   ○ **D.** To steal data for malicious purposes

Cram Quiz Answers

1. **D**. After an assessment, the results should be organized based upon the severity
   of the risk to the organization. Answer A is incorrect. Although in rare situations
   this might be appropriate on a case-by-case basis, this would otherwise be considered extreme. Answer B is incorrect. Many ports are required to be opened
   for a network to function. Answer C is incorrect. Although a penetration test
   might and often does follow a vulnerability scan, it is not necessary to do this
   immediately and certainly not against all identified vulnerabilities.

2. **C**. White box testing is more transparent. Because you are provided with source
   code, you have more knowledge about the system prior to beginning your penetration testing. Answer A is incorrect, as black box testing assumes no prior
   knowledge. Answer B is incorrect as this refers to a weakness.

3. C. A penetration tests helps quantify the adequacy of security measures put in place and to create understanding of the effect that a threat might have against the environment. Answers A and B are incorrect as these describe the purpose of a vulnerability scan. Answer D is incorrect. A penetration test is a "friendly" attack to help safeguard an organization from a real attack. A penetration test, even one that is successful in deeply penetrating an organization, should never maliciously harm critical assets and intellectual property.

What Next?

If you want more practice on this chapter's exam objectives before you move on, remember that you can access all of the Cram Quiz questions on the CD. You can also create a custom exam by objective with the practice exam software. Note any objective you struggle with and go to that objective material in this chapter.

CHAPTER 7

Application Security

This chapter covers the following official CompTIA Security+, SY0-301 exam objectives:

▶ Explain the importance of application security

(For more information on the official CompTIA Security+, SY0-301 exam topics, see the "About the CompTIA Security+, SY0-301 Exam" section in the introduction.)

When establishing operational security baselines, it is important to harden all technologies against as many possible avenues of attack as possible. The three basic areas of hardening are the following:

▶ **Application**: Security of applications and services such as domain name system (DNS), Dynamic Host Configuration Protocol (DHCP), and web servers, and user client-side applications and integration suites.

▶ **Host**: Security of the operating system through hardware and software implementations such as firewalls and anti-malware programs along with logical security involving access control over resources.

▶ **Data**: Security of data on laptops, PCs, removable media, and mobile devices.

These areas are discussed in the next few chapters. Application security has become a major focus of security as we move to a more web-based world, and exploits such as cross-site scripting and SQL injections are an everyday occurrence. Web-based applications and application servers contain a wealth of valuable data. Internally, application servers store a variety of data from web pages to critical data and sensitive information. Regulatory compliance issues make it necessary to have sound procedures in place for the security of application data.

Explain the Importance of Application Security

▶ **Fuzzing**

▶ **Secure coding concepts**

▶ **Cross-site scripting prevention**

▶ **Cross-site Request Forgery (XSRF) prevention**

▶ **Application configuration baseline**

▶ **Application hardening**

▶ **Application patch management**

Cram**Saver**

If you can correctly answer these questions before going through this section, save time by skimming the Exam Alerts in this section and then completing the Cram Quiz at the end of the section.

1. Explain what fuzzing is and how it is used in application security.

2. Explain what steps can be taken to mitigate cross-site scripting (XXS) attacks.

3. Explain what steps can be taken to mitigate cross-site request forgery (XSRF) attacks.

4. Explain what steps can be taken to harden a web-based application.

5. Explain what steps can be taken for proper application patch management.

Answers

1. Fuzzing is a process by which semi-random data is injected into a program or protocol stack for detecting bugs. The idea behind fuzzing is based on the assumption that there are bugs within every program. A systematic discovery approach should find them sooner or later. The data generation part consists of generators. Generators usually use combinations of static fuzzing vectors or totally random data. The vulnerability identification relies on debugging tools.

2. Never insert untrusted data except in allowed locations, use HTML escape before inserting untrusted data into HTML element content, use Attribute escape before inserting untrusted data into HTML common attributes, implement JavaScript escape before inserting untrusted data into HTML JavaScript Data Values, use CSS escape before inserting untrusted data into HTML style property, apply URL escape before inserting untrusted data into HTML URL parameter, use an HTML Policy engine to validate or

Answers

clean user-driven HTML in an outbound way, and prevent DOM-based XSS. In order to help mitigate the effect of an XSS flaw on your website, it is also good practice to set the HTTPOnly flag on the session cookie as well as any custom cookies that are not accessed by your own JavaScript.

3. In order to mitigate this type of attack, the most common solution is to add a token for every POST or GET request that is initiated from the browser to the server. When a user visits a site, the site generates a cryptographically strong, pseudorandom value and sets it as a cookie on the user's machine. The site requires every form submission to include this pseudorandom value as a form value and also as a cookie value. When a POST request is sent to the site, the request is only considered valid if the form value and the cookie value are the same. Another solution is using the unique identifiers that are provided as part of the session management. One extra check can be added to the validation subroutines and the requests modified to include the necessary information.

4. Access control may be accomplished at the operating system or application level by including a requirement for regular update of Secure Sockets Layer (SSL) certifications for secured communications. Regular log review is critical for web servers to ensure that submitted URL values are not used to exploit unpatched buffer overruns or to initiate other forms of common exploits.

5. Proactive patch management is necessary to keep your technology environment secure and reliable. As part of maintaining a secure environment, organizations should have a process for identifying security vulnerabilities and responding quickly. This involves having a comprehensive plan for applying software updates, configuration changes, and countermeasures to remove vulnerabilities from the environment and lessen the risk of computers being attacked. It might include using automated tools that make administrators aware of critical updates and allow them to manage and control installation.

Fuzzing

Just as script kiddies require little talent in order to run exploits, an attacker with moderate skills can reverse engineer executable programs to find major vulnerabilities without ever examining source code. Some of the tools available use a technique called *fuzzing*, which enables an attacker to inject random-looking data into a program to see if it can cause the program to crash.

Exam Alert

Fuzzing is a process by which semi-random data is injected into a program or protocol stack for detecting bugs. The idea behind fuzzing is based on the assumption that there are bugs within every program.

A systematic discovery approach should find application bugs sooner or later. The data generation part consists of generators. Generators usually use combinations of static fuzzing vectors or totally random data. The vulnerability identification relies on debugging tools. Most fuzzers are either protocol/file-format dependent or data-type dependent. New generation fuzzers use genetic algorithms to link injected data and observed impact. OWASP's Fuzz Vector's resource is great for fuzzing methodology and real-life fuzzing vectors examples.

There are several different types of fuzzing:

- ▶ **Application fuzzing:** Attack vectors are within its I/O, such as the user interface, the command-line options, URLs, forms, user-generated content, and RPC requests.

- ▶ **Protocol fuzzing:** Forged packets are sent to the tested application, which can act as a proxy and modify requests on the fly and then replay them.

- ▶ **File format fuzzing:** Multiple malformed samples are generated and then opened sequentially. When the program crashes, debug information is kept for further investigation.

An advantage of fuzzing is that the test design is generally very simple without any presumptions about system behavior. This approach makes it possible to find bugs that would have often been missed by human testing. In some closed application instances, fuzzing might be the only means of reviewing the security quality of the program. The simplicity can be a disadvantage because more advanced bugs will not be found. Additionally if a fuzzer is very protocol-aware, it tends to miss odd errors. A random approach is still a good idea for best results. Fuzzing can add another dimension to normal software-testing techniques.

Secure Coding Concepts

Attacks against software vulnerabilities are becoming more sophisticated. Many times a vulnerability might be discovered that is not addressed by the vendor for quite some time. The vendor decides how and when to patch a vulnerability. As a result, users have become increasingly concerned about the integrity, security, and reliability of commercial software. *Software assurance* is a term used to describe vendor efforts to reduce vulnerabilities, improve resistance to attack, and protect the integrity of their products. Software assurance is especially important in organizations where users require a high level of confidence that commercial software is as secure as possible. Secure software is something that may be achieved when software is created using best practices for secure software development.

The security of software code has come to the forefront in recent years, and coalitions have been formed to improve the security of code. Additionally, there are certifications offered in this software security. The Software Assurance Forum for Excellence in Code (SAFECode) works to identify and promote best practices for developing and delivering more secure and reliable software, hardware, and services. It was founded by EMC Corporation; Juniper Networks, Inc.; Microsoft Corporation; SAP AG; and Symantec Corporation. Organizations like ISC2 offer a certification specifically geared toward secure code design, such as the Certified Secure Software Lifecycle Professional (SSLP). The various stages of secure software include design, coding, source code handling, and testing.

It is important that security is implemented from the very beginning. In the early design phase potential threats to the application must be identified and addressed. You must also take into consideration ways to reduce the associated risks. These objectives can be accomplished through a variety of ways, such as threat modeling and mitigation planning, including analysis of potential vulnerabilities and attack vectors from an attacker's point of view. After the design is complete, the secure programming practices must be implemented. Secure coding skills require the inspection of an application's source code to identify vulnerabilities created by coding errors.

> **ExamAlert**
>
> You should implement secure programming practices that reduce the frequency and severity of errors. You should also perform source code review using a combination of manual analysis and automated analysis tools.

Using automated tools along with manual review can help reduce the vulnerabilities that might be missed using only one method.

After the coding is done and has been reviewed, you must carefully handle the source code. Procedures for secure handling of code include strict change management, tracking, and confidentiality protection of the code. In order to prevent malicious insiders from introducing vulnerabilities, only authorized persons should be permitted to view or modify the code contents. Additional consideration for the protection of code includes protecting the systems and code repositories from unauthorized access. In cases where the development is outsourced, you should conduct internal design and code reviews in order to prevent malicious code from being introduced. The final step in secure code development is testing. In the testing phase, particular attention should be given to validating that the security requirements were met and the design and coding specifications were followed. Testing processes can include the use of testing techniques such as fuzzing and using a variety of inputs to identify possible buffer overflows or other vulnerabilities. Some software vendors submit their products for external testing in addition to doing internal testing because an unbiased, independent test might uncover vulnerabilities that would not be detectable using internal processes.

Error and Exception Handling

Many of the software exploits seen in the past few years were a direct result of poor or incorrect input validation or mishandled exceptions. Common programming flaws include trusting input when designing an application and not performing proper exception checking in the code. These practices allow attacks such as buffer overflows, format string vulnerabilities, and utilization of shell-escape codes. In order to reduce these programming flaws, authentication, authorization, logging and auditing, code dependencies, and error messages and code comment practices should be reviewed.

Authentication strength is vital to the security of the application. You should relinquish common practices such as hardcoding credentials into an application or storing them in cleartext in favor of the practice of encrypting authentication credentials. This is especially important for a web application that uses cookies to store session and authentication information. In web applications or multilayered systems where the identity is often propagated to other contexts, authorization control should form a strong link to the identity through the life cycle of the authenticated session. Logging and auditing should be designed to include configurable logging and auditing capabilities. This will allow the flexibility of collecting detailed information when necessary. Using libraries from established vendors will minimize the risk of unknown vulnerabilities especially when using object-oriented programming that relies on the use of third-party libraries.

You should take care when programming error messages. Although error messages are important to determine the problem, they should not divulge specific system or application information. Because attackers usually gather information before they try to break into an application, outputting detailed error messages can provide an attacker with the necessary information to escalate an attack. Information output in error messages should be on a need-to-know basis. Exception handling should log the error and provide the user with a standard message. You should not use comments in public viewable code that could reveal valuable information about the application or system, especially in web applications where the code and associated comments reside on the browser.

Input Validation

Input validation tests whether an application properly handles input from a source outside the application destined for internal processing.

Exam**Alert**

The most common result of improper input validation is buffer overflow exploitation. Additional types of input validation errors result in format string and denial of service (DoS) exploits.

Application field input should always include a default value and character limitations to avoid these types of exploits. Although software developers can overlook input validation, testing the code by sending varying amounts of both properly and improperly formatted data into the application helps determine if this application is potentially vulnerable to exploits. There are various methods used to test input validation, such as automated testing, session management validation, race condition analysis, cryptographic analysis, and code coverage analysis.

An automated program can randomly perform input validation against the target based on the program's ability to handle input without any established criteria for external interfaces of the application. This means that any component of the application can be tested with randomly generated data without set order or reason. Testing an application for session management vulnerabilities consists of attempting to modify any session state variables to invoke undesirable results from the application. Access can be gained to other communication channels through modified variables, leading to privilege escalation, loss of data confidentiality, and unauthorized access to resources. When there is a window of time between a security operation and the general function it applies to, a window of opportunity is created that might allow security measures to be circumvented. This is known as a race condition. Testing for race conditions attempts to access the file between the time the application creates the file and when the application actually applies the security. Sensitive data, such as passwords and credit card information, are frequently protected by cryptographic methods. Knowing what algorithm an application uses might lead to exploitation of its weaknesses. Additionally if there is strong encryption used, but the vendor implementation is incorrect, the data might not be properly protected and can result in errors such as improper creation or storage of the cryptographic keys and key management. Code coverage analysis is used to verify that proper security measures are taken on all possible paths of code execution. Paths might exist that enable security to be bypassed, leaving the system in a vulnerable state. This type of analysis can be resource intensive and should be done in stages during the development of an application.

Cross-site Scripting Prevention

Web security includes client-side vulnerabilities presented by ActiveX or JavaScript code running within the client's browser; server-side vulnerabilities such as Perl, Active Server Pages (ASP), and common gateway interface (CGI) scripting exploits and buffer overflows used to run undesirable code on the server; and other forms of web-related security vulnerabilities such as those involving the transfer of cookies or unsigned applets. By placing malicious executable code on a website, an attacker can cause an unknowing browser user to conduct unauthorized access activities, expose confidential data, and provide logging of successful attacks back to the attacker without the user being aware of his participation. Cross-site scripting (XXS) vulnerabilities can be used to hijack the user's session or to cause the user accessing malware-tainted Site A to unknowingly attack Site B on behalf of the attacker who planted code on Site A. Much of this scenario stems from accepting untrusted data. From a security perspective, although untrusted data most often comes from an HTTP request, some data that comes from other sources such as databases and web services can be considered untrusted as well. The proper way to treat untrusted data is as though it contains an attack. This concept is extremely important because applications are becoming more interconnected and trusted, opening up the real possibility of an attack being executed downstream.

Traditionally, input validation has been the preferred approach for handling untrusted data. However, input validation is not a great solution for injection attacks because it is typically done before the destination is known and potentially harmful characters must be accepted by applications. Input validation is important and should always be performed, but it is not a complete solution. OWASP has formulated the following rules to prevent XSS in your applications:

▶ Never insert untrusted data except in allowed locations.

▶ Use HTML escape before inserting untrusted data into HTML element content.

▶ Use Attribute escape before inserting untrusted data into HTML common attributes.

▶ Implement JavaScript escape before inserting untrusted data into HTML JavaScript Data Values.

▶ Use CSS escape before inserting untrusted data into HTML style properties.

▶ Apply URL escape before inserting untrusted data into HTML URL parameters.

▶ Use an HTML Policy engine to validate or clean user-driven HTML in an outbound way.

▶ Prevent DOM-based XSS.

In order to help mitigate the effect of an XSS flaw on your website, it is also good practice to set the HTTPOnly flag on the session cookie as well as any custom cookies that are not accessed by your own JavaScript.

Exam Alert

When presented with a question that relates to mitigating the danger of buffer over-flows or XSS attacks, look for answers that relate to input validation. By restricting the data that can be input, application designers can reduce the threat posed by maliciously crafted URL references and redirected web content.

Cross-site Request Forgery Prevention

There are a number of ways in which an end-user can be tricked into loading information from or submitting information to a web application.

Exam Alert

Cross-site Request Forgery (XSRF) is an attack in which the end user executes unwanted actions on a web application while she is currently authenticated.

The attack tricks the victim into loading a page that contains a malicious request usually through sending a link via email or chat. The attacker uses the identity and privileges of the user to execute an undesired function. This can be as simple as changing the victim's email address or as malicious as making purchases on the victim's behalf. A successful attack can compromise end user data and if the targeted end user is the administrator account, this can compromise the entire web application. Although XSRF attacks generally target functions that cause a state change on the server, they can also be used to access sensitive data as in the case of targeting the administrator account.

Most browsers automatically include any credentials associated with the site, such as the user's session cookie and basic authentication credentials, with such requests, so when a user is presently authenticated to the site, the site has no way to distinguish the malicious request from a legitimate user request. Another way this attack can happen is when the XSRF attack is stored on the vulnerable site itself by using an IMG or IFRAME tag in a field that accepts HTML. When an XSRF attack is stored on the site, the victim is more likely to view the page containing the attack because the victim is already authenticated to the site.

Using a secret cookie to mitigate this type of attack does not work well because the secret cookies are submitted with each request. The authentication tokens are submitted whether or not the enduser was tricked into submitting the request. Session identifiers are used to associate the request with a specific session object, not to verify that the end-user intended to submit the request. Only accepting POST requests does not work well either because, although applications can be developed to only accept POST requests, several methods are available whereby an attacker can trick a victim into submitting a forged POST request. For example, a simple form hosted in the attacker's website with hidden values can be triggered automatically by the victim who thinks the form will do something else.

The key element to understanding XSRF is that attackers are betting that users have a validated login cookie for the website already stored in their browser. All they need to do is get that browser to make a request to the website on their behalf. This can be done by either convincing the users to click on a HTML page the attacker has constructed or by inserting arbitrary HTML in a target website that the users visit. In order to mitigate this type of attack, the most common solution is to add a token for every POST or GET request that is initiated from the browser to the server. When a user visits a site, the site generates a cryptographically strong, pseudorandom value and sets it as a cookie on the user's machine. The site requires every form submission to include this pseudorandom value as a form value and also as a cookie value. When a POST request is sent to the site, the request is only considered valid if the form value and the cookie value are the same. Although it sounds easy, the web application that is developed needs to contain another layer of security that handles the random tokens generation and their validation. Another solution is using the unique identifiers that are provided as part of the session management. One extra check can be added to the validation subroutines and the requests modified to include the necessary information.

Application Configuration Baseline

Baselines must be updated on a regular basis and certainly when the network has changed or new technology has been deployed. Application baselining is similar to operating system baselining in that it provides a reference point for normal and abnormal activity. As with operating system hardening, default configurations and passwords must be changed in applications such as database- and web-based applications. Applications must also be maintained in a current state by regularly reviewing applied updates and applying those that are required for the network configuration solutions in use. An initial baseline should be done for both network and application processes so that you can tell whether you have a hardware or software issue. Sometimes applications have memory leaks, or a new version might cause performance issues.

> **ExamAlert**
>
> Established patterns of use by using baselines can be used to identify variations that may identify unauthorized access attempts.

Security monitoring during baselining is important because an ongoing attack during the baselining process could be registered as the normal level of activity. As with operating system hardening, default configurations and passwords must be changed in network hardware such as routers and managed network devices. Routing hardware must also be maintained in a current state by regularly reviewing applied firmware updates and applying those that are required for the network configuration and hardware solutions in use. The sections that follow examine mechanisms for identifying vulnerabilities and hardening vulnerable applications revealed during this process. Failure to update applications on a regular basis or to update auditing can result in an unsecure solution that provides an attacker access to additional resources throughout an organization's network. Additionally, without having a baseline on applications, you may spend a long time trying to figure out what the problem is.

Application Hardening

Each application and service that may be installed within a network must also be considered when planning security for an organization. Applications must be maintained in an updated state through the regular review of hotfixes, patches, and service packs. Many applications, such as antivirus software, require regular updates to provide protection against newly emerging threats.

> **ExamAlert**
>
> Default application administration accounts, standard passwords, and common services installed by default should also be reviewed and changed or disabled as required.

Web Services

Access restrictions to Internet and intranet web services might be required to ensure proper authentication for nonpublic sites, whereas anonymous access might be required for other pages. Access control can be accomplished at the operating system or application level, with many sites including a requirement for regular update of Secure Sockets Layer (SSL) certifications for secured communications.

Regular log review is critical for web servers to ensure that submitted URL values are not used to exploit unpatched buffer overruns or to initiate other forms of common exploits. Many web servers may also be integrated with security add-ins provided to restrict those URLs that may be meaningfully submitted, filtering out any that do not meet the defined criteria. Microsoft's URLScan for the Internet Information Services (IIS) web service is one such filtering add-in.

Email Services

Email servers require network access to transfer Simple Mail Transfer Protocol (SMTP) traffic. Email is often used to transport executable agents, including Trojan horses and other forms of viral software. Email servers might require transport through firewall solutions to allow remote Post Office Protocol 3 (POP3) or Internet Message Access Protocol (IMAP) access or might require integration with VPN solutions to provide secure connections for remote users. User authentication is also of key importance, especially when email and calendaring solutions allow delegated review and manipulation. Inadequate hardware may be attacked through mail bombs and other types of attack meant to overwhelm the server's ability to transact mail messages. Email service hardening also includes preventing SMTP relay from being used by spammers and limiting attachment and total storage per user to prevent denial-of-service attacks using large file attachments.

FTP Services

File Transfer Protocol (FTP) servers are used to provide file upload and download to users, whether through anonymous or authenticated connection. Because of limitations in the protocol, unless an encapsulation scheme is used between the client and host systems, the logon and password details are passed in clear text and might be subject to interception by packet sniffing. Unauthorized parties can also use FTP servers that allow anonymous access to share files of questionable or undesirable content while also consuming network bandwidth and server processing resources.

DNS Services

DNS servers responsible for name resolution may be subject to many forms of attack, including attempts at DoS attacks intended to prevent proper name resolution for key corporate holdings. Planning to harden DNS server solutions should include redundant hardware and software solutions and regular backups to protect against loss of name registrations. Technologies that allow dynamic updates must also include access control and authentication to ensure that registrations are valid. Unauthorized zone transfers should also be restricted to prevent DNS poisoning attacks.

NNTP Services

Network News Transfer Protocol (NNTP) servers providing user access to newsgroup posts raise many of the same security considerations risks as email servers. Access control for newsgroups may be somewhat more complex, with moderated groups allowing public anonymous submission (and authenticated access required for post approval). Heavily loaded servers may be attacked to perform a DoS, and detailed user account information in public newsgroup posting stores like those of the AOL and MSN communities may be exploited in many ways.

File and Print Services

User file-storage solutions often come under attack when unauthorized access attempts provide avenues for manipulation. Files can be corrupted, modified, deleted, or manipulated in many other ways. Access control through proper restriction of file and share permissions, access auditing, and user authentication schemes to ensure proper access are necessary. Network file shares are not secure until you remove default access permissions.

Distributed file system and encrypted file system solutions might require bandwidth planning and proper user authentication to allow even basic access. Security planning for these solutions may also include placing user access authenticating servers close to the file servers to decrease delays created by authentication traffic.

Print servers also pose several risks, including possible security breaches in the event that unauthorized parties access cached print jobs. DoS attacks might be used to disrupt normal methods of business, and network-connected printers require authentication of access to prevent attackers from generating printed memos, invoices, or any other manner of printed materials.

DHCP Services

Dynamic Host Configuration Protocol (DHCP) servers share many of the same security problems associated with other network services, such as DNS servers. DHCP servers might be overwhelmed by lease requests if bandwidth and processing resources are insufficient. This can be worsened by the use of DHCP proxy systems relaying lease requests from widely deployed subnets. Scope address pools might also be overcome if lease duration is insufficient, and short lease duration might increase request traffic. If the operating system in use does not support DHCP server authentication, attackers might also configure their own DHCP servers within a subnet, taking control of the network settings of clients and obtaining leases from these rogue servers. Planning for DHCP security must include regular review of networks for unauthorized DHCP servers.

Data Repositories

Data repositories of any type might require specialized security considerations based on the bandwidth and processing resources required to prevent DoS attacks, removal of default password and administration accounts such as the SQL default sa account, and security of replication traffic to prevent exposure of access credentials to packet sniffing. Placement of authentication, name resolution, and data stores within secured and partially secured zones such as an organization's DMZ may require the use of secured VPN connections or the establishment of highly secured bastion hosts.

> **ExamAlert**
>
> You can use role-based access control to improve security, and eliminating unneeded connection libraries and character sets might help to alleviate common exploits.

Take care to include data repositories beyond the obvious file, email, and database stores. Hardening efforts must also address security of the storage and backup of storage area networks (SANs), network access server (NAS) configurations, and directory services such as Microsoft Active Directory and Novell eDirectory.

Application Patch Management

Organizations sometimes overlook patch installation and management. Because recent worms have the capability of traveling quickly and causing much damage, being proactive in security patch management is necessary to keep your environment secure, reliable, and functional. As part of maintaining a secure environment, organizations should have a process for identifying security vulnerabilities and responding quickly. This involves having a comprehensive plan for applying software updates, configuration changes, and countermeasures to remove vulnerabilities from the environment and lessen the risk of computers being attacked. It might include using automated tools that make administrators aware of critical updates and allow them to manage and control installation.

The term *patch management* describes the method for keeping computers up-to-date with new software releases that are developed after an original software product is installed.

Improperly programmed software can be exploited.

> ## Exam**Alert**
>
> *Software exploitation* is a method of searching for specific problems, weaknesses, or security holes in software code. It takes advantage of a program's flawed code.

The most effective way to prevent an attacker from exploiting software bugs is to keep the latest manufacturer's patches and service packs applied as well as monitor the Web for new vulnerabilities.

Cram Quiz

Answer these questions. The answers follow the last question. If you cannot answer these questions correctly, consider reading this section again until you can.

1. Which of the following is a process by which semi-random data is injected into a program or protocol stack for detecting bugs?

   - ○ **A.** Cross-site scripting
   - ○ **B.** Fuzzing
   - ○ **C.** Input validation
   - ○ **D.** Cross-site request forgery

2. Joe tricks Jane into submitting a request via link in an HTML email. Jane is authenticated with the application when she clicks the link. As a result, money is transferred to Joe's account. Which of the following attacks has occurred?

   - ○ **A.** Buffer overflow
   - ○ **B.** Cross-site scripting
   - ○ **C.** Cross-site request forgery
   - ○ **D.** Input validation error

3. Which of the following are steps to mitigate cross-site request forgery (XSRF) attacks?

   ○ **A.** Hardcode the authentication credentials into the application

   ○ **B.** Always include a default value and character limitations

   ○ **C.** Set the HTTPOnly flag on the session cookie

   ○ **D.** Add a token for every POST or GET request that is initiated from the browser to the server

4. Which of the following are steps to mitigate cross-site scripting (XXS) attacks? (Select two answers.)

   ○ **A.** Set the HTTPOnly flag on the session cookie

   ○ **B.** Always include a default value and character limitations

   ○ **C.** Never insert untrusted data except in allowed locations

   ○ **D.** Hardcode the authentication credentials into the application

5. Which of the following are steps that can be taken to harden DNS services? (Select two answers.)

   ○ **A.** Anonymous access to share files of questionable or undesirable content should be limited.

   ○ **B.** Regular review of networks for unauthorized or rogue servers.

   ○ **C.** Technologies that allow dynamic updates must also include access control and authentication.

   ○ **D.** Unauthorized zone transfers should also be restricted.

1. **B.** Fuzzing is a process by which semi-random data is injected into a program or protocol stack for detecting bugs. The idea behind fuzzing is based on the assumption that there are bugs within every program. Answer A is incorrect because cross-site scripting (XXS) vulnerabilities can be used to hijack the user's session or to cause the user accessing malware-tainted Site A to unknowingly attack Site B on behalf of the attacker who planted code on Site A. Answer C is incorrect because input validation tests whether an application properly handles input from a source outside the application destined for internal processing. Answer D Cross-site Request Forgery (XSRF) is an attack in which the end user executes unwanted actions on a web application while he is currently authenticated.

2. **C.** Cross-site Request Forgery (XSRF) is an attack in which the end user executes unwanted actions on a web application while she is currently authenticated. Answer A is incorrect because a buffer overflow is the direct result of poor or incorrect input validation or mishandled exceptions. Answer B is incorrect because cross-site scripting (XXS) vulnerabilities can be used to hijack the user's session or to cause the user accessing malware-tainted Site A to unknowingly attack Site B on behalf of the attacker who planted code on Site A. Answer D is incorrect because input validation errors are a result of improper field checking in the code.

3. **D**. In order to mitigate cross-site request forgery (XSRF) attacks, the most common solution is to add a token for every POST or GET request that is initiated from the browser to the server. Answer A is incorrect because common practices such as hardcoding credentials into an application are addressed in secure coding practices. Answer B is incorrect because it describes input validation coding practices. Answer C is incorrect because setting the HTTPOnly flag on the session cookie is used to mitigate XXS attacks.

4. **A** and **C**. The first rule of mitigating XXS errors is to never insert untrusted data except in allowed locations. It is also good practice to set the HTTPOnly flag on the session cookie. Answer B is incorrect because it describes input validation coding practices. Answer D is incorrect because common practices such as hardcoding credentials into an application are addressed in secure coding practices.

5. **C** and **D**. Planning to harden DNS server solutions should include redundant hardware and software solutions and regular backups to protect against loss of name registrations. Technologies that allow dynamic updates must also include access control and authentication to ensure that registrations are valid. Unauthorized zone transfers should also be restricted to prevent DNS poisoning attacks. Answer A is incorrect because it is a hardening practice for FTP services. Answer B is incorrect because it is a hardening practice for DHCP services.

What Next?

If you want more practice on this chapter's exam objectives before you move on, remember that you can access all of the Cram Quiz questions on the CD. You can also create a custom exam by objective with the practice exam software. Note any objective you struggle with and go to that objective's material in this chapter.

CHAPTER 8

Host Security

This chapter covers the following official CompTIA Security+, SY0-301 exam objectives:

▶ Carry out appropriate procedures to establish host security

(For more information on the official CompTIA Security+, SY0-301 exam topics, see the "About the CompTIA Security+, SY0-301 Exam" section in the introduction.)

As technology advances, we add more device types to the network. Most organizations have some type of handheld device that connects to the network such as a BlackBerry or an iPhone. With tablets becoming more popular, organizations will not only incorporate them into the network but also will have to determine security policies for these devices, especially when the device belongs to the employee. When dealing with host security issues, two general areas need to be covered. The first one deals with using protocols and software to protect data. This covers software that can help protect the internal network components, such as personal firewalls and antivirus software. The second one addresses the physical components such as hardware, network components, and physical security designs that can be used to secure the devices.

Carry Out Appropriate Procedures to Establish Host Security

▶ Operating system security and settings

▶ Anti-malware

▶ Patch management

▶ Hardware security

▶ Host software baselining

▶ Mobile devices

▶ Virtualization

Cram**Saver**

If you can correctly answer these questions before going through this section, save time by skimming the Exam Alerts in this section and then completing the Cram Quiz at the end of the section.

1. Explain how virtualization is used for host security.

2. Explain what devices can be used for physical security of host machines.

3. Explain what is included in hardening a host operating system.

4. Explain what measures can be taken to secure handheld mobile devices such as cell phones.

5. Explain what is needed to establish effective security baselines for host systems.

6. Explain what procedures should be used to properly protect a host from malware.

Answers

1. The flexibility of being able to run a Windows guest operating on top of a Linux-based host operating system allows security as well as access to both environments without having to dual boot the machine. Virtualization improves enterprise desktop management and control with faster deployment of desktops and fewer support calls due to application conflicts. Virtualization reduces an entire functioning computer down to just a couple of files, which is obviously far easier to manage than the thousands and thousands of files in the Windows directory alone. With virtualization, it is not only practical but also logical to simply discard an old or infected VM in favor of a fresh copy.

Answers

2. Security cables with combination locks can provide physical security and are easy to use. PC Safe Tower and server cages, which have all-steel construction and a lever locking system, are designed to bolt to the floor and prevent theft. A locked cabinet is another alternative for laptop equipment that is not used or does not have to be physically accessed on a regular, daily basis. Vendors provide solutions such as security cabinet lockers that secures CPU towers. The housing is made of durable, heavy-duty steel for strength that lasts.

3. Hardening of the operating system includes planning against both accidental and directed attacks, such as the use of fault-tolerant hardware and software solutions. In addition, it is important to implement an effective system for file-level security, including encrypted file support and secured file system selection that allows the proper level of access control. For example, the Microsoft New Technology File System (NTFS) allows file-level access control, whereas most File Allocation Table (FAT)-based file systems allow only share-level access control. It is also imperative to include regular update reviews for all deployed operating systems to address newly identified exploits and apply security patches, hotfixes, and service packs.

4. A screen lock or passcode is used to prevent access to the phone. Because passwords are one of the best methods of acquiring access, password length is an important consideration for mobile devices. Just like the data on hard drives, the data on mobile devices can be encrypted. Remote wipe allows the handheld's data to be remotely deleted in the event the device is lost or stolen. Mobile voice encryption can allow executives and employees alike to discuss sensitive information without having to travel to secure company locations. In the event a mobile device is lost, GPS tracking can be used to find the location.

5. To establish effective security baselines, enterprise network security management requires a measure of commonality between systems. Mandatory settings, standard application suites, and initial setup configuration details all factor into the security stance of an enterprise network.

6. All host devices must have some type of malware protection. A necessary software program for protecting the user environment is antivirus software. Antivirus software is used to scan for malicious code in email and downloaded files. Anti-spam, anti-spyware software can add another layer of defense to the infrastructure. Pop-up blocking software programs are available through browsers. Desktops and laptops need to have layered security just like servers do. However, many organizations stop this protection at antivirus software, which in today's environment might not be enough to ward off malware, phishing, and rootkits. One of the most common ways to protect desktops and laptops is to use a personal firewall.

Operating System Security and Settings

In security terms, *hardening* a system refers to reducing its security exposure and strengthening its defenses against unauthorized access attempts and other forms of malicious attention. A "soft" system is one that is installed with default configurations or unnecessary services or one that is not maintained to include emerging security updates. There is no such thing as a "completely safe" system, so the process of hardening reflects attention to security thresholds.

Systems installed in default configurations often include many unnecessary services that are configured automatically. These provide many potential avenues for unauthorized access to a system or network. Many services have known vulnerabilities that require specific action to make them more secure or ones that might just impair system function by causing additional processing overhead. Default configurations also allow for unauthorized access and exploitation.

> **Note**
>
> A denial-of-service (DoS) attack against an unneeded web service is one example of how a nonessential service could potentially cause problems for an otherwise functional system.

Common default-configuration exploits include both services such as anonymous-access FTP servers and network protocols such as the Simple Network Management Protocol (SNMP). Others may exploit vendor-supplied default logon/password combinations, such as the Oracle Db default admin: scott/tiger.

> **ExamAlert**
>
> When presented with a scenario on the exam, you might be tempted to keep all services enabled to cover all requirements. Be wary of this option; it might cause the installation of unnecessary services or protocols.

Hardening of the operating system includes planning against both accidental and directed attacks, such as the use of fault-tolerant hardware and software solutions. In addition, it is important to implement an effective system for file-level security, including encrypted file support and secured file system selection that allows the proper level of access control. For example, the Microsoft New Technology File System (NTFS) allows file-level access control, whereas most File Allocation Table (FAT)-based file systems allow only share-level access control.

It is also imperative to include regular update reviews for all deployed operating systems to address newly identified exploits and apply security patches, hotfixes, and service packs. Many automated attacks make use of common vulnerabilities, often ones for which patches and hotfixes are already available but not yet applied. Failure to update applications on a regular basis or to update auditing can result in an unsecure solution that provides an attacker access to additional resources throughout an organization's network.

IP Security (IPsec) and public key infrastructure (PKI) implementations must also be properly configured and updated to maintain key and ticket stores. Some systems may be hardened to include specific levels of access, gaining the C2 security rating required by many government deployment scenarios. The Trusted Computer System Evaluation Criteria (TCSEC) rating of C2 indicates a discretionary access control environment with additional requirements such as individual logon accounts and access logging.

Operating system hardening includes configuring log files and auditing, changing default administrator account names and default passwords, and the institution of account lockout and password policies to guarantee strong passwords that can resist brute-force attacks. File-level security and access control mechanisms serve to isolate access attempts within the operating system environment. Make sure to understand the principle of least privilege which states that every user or service of a system should only operate with the minimal set of privileges required to fulfill their job duty or function.

Security Settings

To establish effective security baselines, enterprise network security management requires a measure of commonality between systems. Mandatory settings, standard application suites, and initial setup configuration details all factor into the security stance of an enterprise network.

Types of configuration settings you should be familiar with include the following:

▶ **Group policies:** Collections of configuration settings applied to a system based on computer or user group membership, which may influence the level, type, and extent of access provided.

▶ **Security templates:** Sets of configurations that reflect a particular role or standard established through industry standards or within an organization, assigned to fulfill a particular purpose. Examples include a "minimum-access" configuration template assigned to limited-access kiosk systems, whereas a "high-security" template could be assigned to systems requiring more stringent logon and access control mechanisms.

▶ **Configuration baselines:** Many industries must meet specific criteria established as a baseline measure of security. An example of this is the health-care industry, which has a lengthy set of requirements for information technology specified in the Health Insurance Portability and Accountability Act (HIPAA) security standards. Unless the mandated security baseline is met, penalties and fines could be assessed. Security baselines are often established by governmental mandate; regulatory bodies; or industry representatives, such as the Payment Card Industry Data Security Standard (PCI DSS) requirements established by the credit card industry for businesses collecting and transacting credit information.

Anti-malware

All host devices must have some type of malware protection. According to the Sophos Security Threat report, the amount of malware affecting computers had almost doubled for the year 2010 as compared to 2009. In 2010, some 95,000 different malware were discovered, with 40% of the malware coming from the social networking sites. According to the "Malicious Mobile Threats Report 2010/2011," a report compiled by the Juniper Networks Global Threat Center (GTC) research facility, the number of Android malware attacks increased 400 % since summer 2010.

Antivirus

A necessary software program for protecting the user environment is antivirus software. Antivirus software is used to scan for malicious code in email and downloaded files. Antivirus software actually works backward. Virus writers release a virus, it is reported, and then antivirus vendors reverse-engineer the code to find a solution. After the virus has been analyzed, the antivirus software can look for specific characteristics of the virus. Remember that for a virus to be successful, it must replicate its code.

The most common method used in an antivirus program is scanning. Scanning searches files in memory, the boot sector, and on the hard disk for identifiable virus code. Scanning identifies virus code based on a unique string of characters known as a signature. When the virus software detects the signature, it isolates the file. Then, depending on the software settings, the antivirus software quarantines it or permanently deletes it. Interception software detects virus-like behavior and then pops up a warning to the user. However, because the software looks only at file changes, it might also detect legitimate files.

In the past, antivirus engines used a heuristic engine for detecting virus structures or integrity checking as a method of file comparison. A false positive occurs when the software classifies an action as a possible intrusion when it is actually a nonthreatening action.

> **Exam Alert**
>
> *Heuristic scanning* looks for instructions or commands that are not typically found in application programs. The issue with these methods is that they are susceptible to false positives and cannot identify new viruses until the database is updated.

Antivirus software vendors update their virus signatures on a regular basis. Most antivirus software connects to the vendor website to check the software database for updates and then automatically downloads and installs them as they become available. Besides setting your antivirus software for automatic updates, you should set the machine to automatically scan at least once a week.

In the event a machine does become infected, the first step is to remove it from the network so that it cannot damage other machines. The best defense against virus infection is user education. Most antivirus software used today is fairly effective, but only if it's kept updated and the user practices safe computing habits, such as not opening unfamiliar documents or programs. Despite all this, antivirus software cannot protect against brand new viruses, and often users do not take the necessary precautions. Users sometimes disable antivirus software because it might interfere with programs that are currently installed on the machine. Be sure to guard against this type of incident.

Anti-spam

Roughly 90% of all email sent during 2010 was spam. Spam is defined several ways, the most common being unwanted commercial email. Although spam may merely seem to be an annoyance, it uses bandwidth, takes up storage space, and reduces productivity. Spam spread on social networking sites has become a big problem, and in late March 2011, a federal court in California held that Facebook postings fit within the definition of "commercial electronic mail message" under the CAN-SPAM Act. The CAN-SPAM act makes it unlawful for persons to initiate the transmission of commercial electronic mail messages that contain materially false or misleading header information.

Anti-spam software can add another layer of defense to the infrastructure. You can install anti-spam software in various ways. The most common methods are at the email server or the email client. When the software and updates are installed on a central server and pushed out to the client machines, this is called a centralized solution. When the updates are left up to the individual users, you have a decentralized environment. The main component of anti-spam software is *heuristic filtering*. Heuristic filtering has a predefined rule set that compares incoming email information against the rule set. The software reads the contents of each message and compares the words in that message against the words in typical spam messages. Each rule assigns a numeric score to the probability of the message being spam. This score is then used to determine whether the message meets the acceptable level set. If many of the same words from the rule set are in the message being examined, it's marked as spam. Specific spam filtering levels can be set on the user's email account. If the setting is high, more spam will be filtered, but it might also filter legitimate email as spam, thus causing false positives.

> **ExamAlert**
>
> It is important to understand that the software can't assign meaning to the words examined. It simply tracks and compares the words used.

Additional settings can be used in the rule set. In general, an email address added to the approved list is never considered spam. This is also known as a whitelist. Using whitelists allows more flexibility in the type of email you receive. For example, putting the addresses of your relatives or friends in your whitelist allows you to receive any type of content from them. An email address added to the blocked list is always considered spam. This is also known as a blacklist. Other factors might affect the ability to receive email on a whitelist. For example, if attachments are not allowed and the email has an attachment, the message might be filtered even if the address is on the approved list.

Anti-spyware

Many spyware eliminator programs are available. These programs scan your machine, similarly to how antivirus software scans for viruses. Just as with antivirus software, you should keep spyware eliminator programs updated and regularly run scans. Configuration options on anti-spyware software allow the program to check for updates on a regularly scheduled basis. The anti-spyware software should be set to load upon start-up and set to automatically update spyware definitions.

Pop-up blockers

A common method for Internet advertising is using a window that pops up in the middle of your screen to display a message when you click a link or button on a website. Although some pop-ups are helpful, many are an annoyance, and others can contain inappropriate content or entice the user to download malware.

There are several variations of pop-up windows. A pop-under ad opens a new browser window under the active window. These types of ads often are not seen until the current window is closed. Hover ads are Dynamic Hypertext Markup Language (DHTML) pop-ups. They are essentially "floating pop-ups" in a web page.

Most online toolbars come with pop-up blockers; various downloadable pop-up blocking software programs are available; and the browsers included with some operating systems, such as Windows, can block pop-ups. Pop-up blockers, just like many of the other defensive software discussed so far, have settings that you can adjust. You might want to try setting the software to medium so that it will block most automatic pop-ups but still allow functionality. Keep in mind that you can adjust the settings on pop-up blockers to meet the organizational policy or to best protect the user environment.

Several caveats apply to using pop-up blockers. There are helpful pop-ups. Some web-based programmed application installers use a pop-up to install software. If all pop-ups are blocked, the user might not be able to install applications or programs. Field help for fill-in forms is often in the form of a pop-up. Some pop-up blockers might delete the information already entered by reloading the page, causing users unnecessary grief. You can also circumvent pop-up blockers in various ways. Most pop-up blockers block only the JavaScript; therefore, technologies such as Flash bypass the pop-up blocker. On many Internet browsers, holding down the Ctrl key while clicking a link will allow it to bypass the pop-up filter.

Host-based Firewalls

Desktops and laptops need to have layered security just like servers. However, many organizations stop this protection at antivirus software, which in today's environment may not be enough to ward off malware, phishing, and rootkits. One of the most common ways to protect desktops and laptops is to use a personal firewall. Firewalls can consist of hardware, software, or a combination of both. This discussion focuses on software firewalls that you can implement into the user environment.

The potential for hackers to access data through a user's machine has grown substantially as hacking tools have become more sophisticated and difficult to detect. This is especially true for the telecommuter's machine. Always-connected computers, typical with cable modems, give attackers plenty of time to discover and exploit system vulnerabilities. Many software firewalls are available, and most operating systems now come with them readily available. You can choose to use the OS vendor firewall or to install a separate one.

Like most other solutions, firewalls have strengths and weaknesses. By design, firewalls close off systems to scanning and entry by blocking ports or nontrusted services and applications. However, they require proper configuration. Typically, the first time a program tries to access the Internet, a software firewall asks whether it should permit the communication. Some users might find this annoying and disable the firewall or not understand what the software is asking and allow all communications. Another caveat is that some firewalls monitor only for incoming connections and not outgoing. Remember that even a good firewall cannot protect you if you do not exercise a proper level of caution and think before you download. No system is foolproof, but software firewalls installed on user systems can help make the computing environment safer. Figure 8.1 shows a picture of the Windows firewall configuration options.

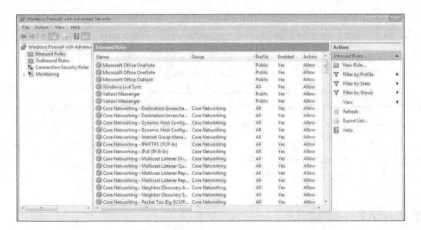

FIGURE 8.1 **Windows firewall configuration options.**

ExamAlert

Monitoring outbound connections is important, so that you protect against malware that "phones home." Without this type of protection, the environment is not properly protected.

Patch Management

Improperly programmed software can be exploited. Software exploitation is a method of searching for specific problems, weaknesses, or security holes in software code. It takes advantage of a program's flawed code. The most effective way to prevent an attacker from exploiting software bugs is to keep the latest manufacturer's patches and service packs applied as well as monitor the Web for new vulnerabilities.

Because of the emergence of blended-threat malware, which targets multiple vulnerabilities within a single attack, all major operating systems and application solutions must be considered in system-hardening plans. Automated reverse engineering of newly released patches has significantly reduced the time from an update's initial release until its first exploits are seen in the wild, down from months to hours before unpatched applications can be targeted.

Types of updates you should be familiar with include the following:

▶ **Hotfixes:** Typically small and specific-purpose updates that alter the behavior of installed applications in a limited manner. These are the most common type of update.

▶ **Service packs:** Major revisions of functionality or service operation in an installed application. Service packs are the least common type of update, often requiring extensive testing to ensure against service failure in integrated network environments before application. Service packs are usually cumulative, including all prior service packs, hotfixes, and patches.

▶ **Patches:** Like hotfixes, patches are usually focused updates that affect installed applications. Patches are generally used to add new functionality, update existing code operation, or extend existing application capabilities.

ExamAlert

To make the patching process easier, Microsoft releases its patches or hotfixes on a monthly schedule. Any system running Microsoft products in your enterprise should be evaluated for the patch requirements.

Because updates are now released on a schedule, it might be easier to put a sensible plan into place. Should an attacker learn of a vulnerability and release an exploit for it before the update date, the hotfix will be posted ahead of schedule if the situation warrants.

The patch management infrastructure of an organization includes all of the tools and technologies that are used to assess, test, deploy, and install software updates. This infrastructure is an essential tool for keeping the entire environment secure and reliable, and therefore it is important that it is managed and maintained properly. When it comes to managing your infrastructure, chances are good that you might have many different types of clients in your network and that they might be at many different levels in regard to the service packs and hot fixes that are applied to them. The most efficient way to update client machines is to use automated processes and products. Many vendors provide regular updates for installed products, managed through automated deployment tools or by manual update procedures carried out by a system user. Regular maintenance is required to meet emerging security threats, whether applying an updated RPM (Redhat Package Manager, a file format used to distribute Linux applications and update packages) by hand or through fully automated "call home for updates" options such as those found in many commercial operating systems and applications.

Systems Management Server (SMS) assists you in security patch management by its ability to scan computers remotely throughout your network and report the results to a central repository. The results can then be assessed and compared to determine which computers need additional patches.

Microsoft maintains the Automatic Updates website, which contains all of the latest security updates. You can configure your Windows host computers to automatically download and install the latest updates on a schedule that you specify. Alternatively, you can choose to download and install the updates yourself. You can configure these settings using Automatic Updates or Windows Update in Windows-based computers. Figure 8.2 shows the Windows update configuration screen.

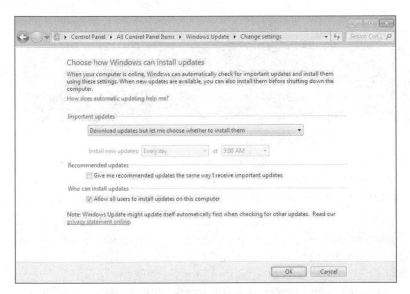

FIGURE 8.2   **Windows update configuration screen.**

Hardware Security

Physical access to a system creates many avenues for a breach in security. Many tools can be used to extract password and account information that can then be used to access secured network resources. Given the ability to reboot a system and load software from a USB drive, attackers might be able to access data or implant Trojan horses and other applications intended to weaken or compromise network security. Unsecured equipment is also vulnerable to social engineering attacks. It is much easier for an attacker to walk into a reception area, say she is there to do some work on the server, and get access to that server in the closet in the front lobby than to get into a physically secured area with a guest sign-in and sign-out sheet.

A more serious threat is theft or loss. Laptops and handheld devices are easy targets for thieves. According to datalossdb.org, stolen laptops account for 18% of all data breaches. In order to prevent theft or loss, you must safeguard the equipment in your organization.

Cable Locks

In order to protect organizational resources and minimize liability costs, it is important for each employee to take responsibility for securing office equipment. Laptops should never be left in an area that is open where anyone can have easy access to them. Laptops, Apple iMacs, and any easily transportable office computers should be physically secured. Security cables with combination locks can provide such security and are easy to use. The cable is used to attach the computer to an immovable object. Computers have one and sometimes two security cable slots. The security cable slots allow you to attach a commercially available antitheft device to the computer. Computer locks commonly use steel cables to secure the PC to a desk. They're most commonly found in computer labs and internet cafés. Laptop locks are meant to protect both privacy and the computer. There are a number of different types of laptop locks: cable locks, case locks, and twist locks. The most common type of anti-theft devices for portable computers usually include a length of metal-stranded cable with an attached locking device and associated key. The cable is looped around an immovable object and the locking device is inserted into a security cable slot. Anti-theft devices differ in design so be sure that it is compatible with the security cable slot on the computer. Never leave a laptop unsecured. If the area is not safe, don't leave a laptop even secured by a cable-locking device. Thieves have driven off with whole ATM machines, so they can find a way to bypass the lock.

Safe

Tower-style computers can also be targets of thieves, not only for a higher resale value than laptops, but also for the data they might hold. For example, financial businesses have been hit hard by theft of desktop computers because they hold a lot of personal data. PC Safe Tower and server cages, which have all-steel construction and a lever locking system, are designed to bolt to the floor. Drive access can be either completely restricted or left available for ease of use.

There are also laptop safe security cases used to protect an organization's computers and data out in the field. For example, Flexysafe Digital makes a safe that is designed for people who take their laptop computers home from work. Also available are high-security laptop safes, which store laptops in a manner similar to bank vault storage. There is individual storage for laptops in locking compartments which can then be additionally secured behind the high-security main safe door when required. The open compartment version offers open shelves (usually one laptop per shelf) for storage that can be secured by the safe's main door. Other computer safe options include types made to securely store laptops and carry cases plus other valuable equipment in reception areas, mobile car safes made to prevent smash and grab attacks, and a home computer safe with an electronic lock similar to the safes provided in hotel rooms.

Locking Cabinets

A locked cabinet is another alternative for laptop equipment that is not used or does not have to be physically accessed on a regular, daily basis. Vendors provide solutions such as a security cabinet locker that secures CPU towers. The housing is made of durable, heavy-duty steel for strength that lasts. The sides and door are ventilated to reduce risk of overheating. Another option is a wood laminate security computer cabinet that provides a computer work-station that can be locked away into a cabinet for space as well as security. Computer cabinets include a keyboard drawer and adjustable top shelf. A slide-out bottom shelf accommodates a CPU and printer. It has built-in cable management grommets. Depending on what needs to be secured, there are computer cabinets designed to hold everything from LCD/LED flat screens to entire systems. This type of security is often used for training rooms where the computers can be secure without the inconvenience of removing them after each training session.

Host Software Baselining

The measure of normal activity is known as a baseline. This gives you a point of reference when something on the computer goes awry. Without a baseline, it is harder to see what is wrong because you don't know what is normal. Baselines must be updated on a regular basis and certainly when the computer has changed or new technology has been deployed. Baselining should be done for both host and application processes so that you can tell whether you have a hardware or software issue. Host software baselining can be done for a variety of reasons, including malware monitoring and creating system images. Generally, the environment needs of an organization fall into a legacy, enterprise, or high-security client. A legacy client has the lowest lockdown level. It is important that there is a good baseline for these computers because of their vulnerability and lack of ability to configure tightened security settings. The enterprise client environment is designed to provide solid security for the organization and allows the use of more restrictive security templates for added security. Using security templates also allows the organization to introduce additional roles on top of the baseline template for easier implementation of these new roles. In a high-security environment, the settings are very restrictive and many applications might not function under this type of configuration. Therefore it is very important to have a baseline.

Mobile Devices

There are specific steps for mitigating mobile attacks. Both enterprise administrators and users alike need to be aware of the growing risks associated with the convenience of having Internet as well as corporate network data in the palm of your hand. Most effective way to secure restricted data is not to store it on mobile devices. In many organizations this does not happen. The comingling of personal and organizational data is inevitable unless there are some safeguards in place, such as keeping sensitive data only on secure servers and accessing it remotely using secure communication techniques outlined in the security policy. Another option is to have the user and organizational data separated on the device. A company called Good Technology provides such a solution. This limits business risk associated with enterprise data on mobile devices by compartmentalizing the data. It leaves employees' private information untouched and enforces policies and compliance at the application level. The risk areas associated with mobile devices are physical risk, including theft or loss, unauthorized access risk, operating system or application risk, network risk, and mobile data storage device risk.

In order to mitigate these risks many of the same protections that apply to computers apply to mobile devices. Safeguards include screen locks, encryption, remote wipes, tracking, and strong passwords.

Screen Lock

A screen lock or passcode is used to prevent access to the phone. Screen locks can be set on just about any mobile device such as BlackBerrys, personal digital assistants (PDAs), and smartphones. This feature is used as a most basic form of security. It is done using a pattern lock or a passcode to secure the handset. It's similar to a password-protected screensaver on a computer. The lock code usually consists of a four-digit code. Screen lock only locks users out of the user interface. It does not encrypt data.

Screen locks should be configured to lock the device screen automatically after a brief period of about 10 or 15 minutes of inactivity. Androids can use a pattern on the screen instead of a password. One caveat, you need your Gmail/Google account credentials to reset the security lock should you forget it, so be sure to set up a valid Gmail/Google account beforehand. There are also a number of applications available on the Android application marketplace that can add additional security measures.

Strong Password

Passwords are one of the first pieces and the best methods of acquiring access; password length is an important consideration for mobile devices. Strong passwords can be derived from events or things the user knows. Password strength is a measure of the difficulty involved in guessing or breaking the password through cryptographic techniques or library-based automated testing of alternative values. A weak password might be very short or only use alphanumeric characters, making decryption simple. A weak password can also be one that is easily guessed by someone profiling the user, such as a birthday; nickname; address; name of a pet or relative; or a common word such as God, love, money, or password.

Organizational policies should include training to educate users to create stronger passwords from events or things the user knows. For example, let's say that the password must be nine characters long and must be a combination of letters, numbers, and special characters. The user went to Fiji on August 8, 2011, with his spouse named Joan. The phrase "Went to Fiji on August 8, 2011 with Joan" can become wtF8811@J. Now you have a complex password that is easy for the user to remember. Alternatively, users can use a phrase that has more than 13 characters so that password-cracking utilities will not be able to crack it. For example, using the password ThisisDiane@sTempPa33w0rd creates a longer string than most programs can crack.

Strong password policies help protect the network from hackers and define the responsibilities of users who have been given access to company resources. You should have all users read and sign security policies as part of their employment process, and you should provide periodic training.

> **Exam**Alert
>
> Using strong passwords lowers overall risk of a security breach, but strong passwords do not replace the need for other effective security controls.

Using static passwords for authentication has a few security flaws because passwords can be guessed, forgotten, or written down. Mobile phones that are capable of running Java applets are becoming more common so a mobile phone can be used as an authentication token. Mobile-OTP is a free authentication solution for Java-capable mobile devices. The solution is based on time synchronous one-time passwords. It consists of a client component and a server component. The server component can easily be plugged into RADIUS to authenticate users. As of 2010, there were more than 30 independent implementations of the Mobile-OTP algorithm, making it a de facto standard for strong mobile authentication.

Device Encryption

Just like the data on hard drives, the data on mobiles can be encrypted but can present some challenges. First, it's difficult to enter complex passwords on small keyboards, and multifactor authentication is unfeasible. The limited processing power of mobiles also means the extra computation required for encryption may cause them to suffer performance issues and the always-on nature of these devices means that encryption can easily break functionality. Another consideration is that due to the variety of devices, a company may have to implement various encryption methods. For example, BlackBerry Enterprise Server can be used to manage built-in data encryption, whereas Windows Mobile devices can use a third-party encryption solution. In addition to built-in tools, here are some third-party encryption programs:

- ▶ Navastream
- ▶ PhoneCrypt
- ▶ Smartphone Encryption
- ▶ Cryptophone
- ▶ Kryptext
- ▶ Secure GSM

Most mobiles have an external media card used for storage. In addition to encryption of the data in the device, the data on the media card needs to be encrypted as well. Mobile Encryption is a feature that enables users to secure sensitive information on Windows Mobile device's removable flash memory storage card. The data is only accessible when the card is installed in a particular mobile device. If the card is ever lost or stolen, the information remains secure because it is encrypted.

Applications such as Good offer a security container that separates company and personal information. The enterprise container is an encrypted envelope that securely houses enterprise data and applications on the device, encrypting all data with strong AES 192-bit encryption. This solution also encrypts any data that's in transit between the device and servers behind the organization's firewall.

Enterprise encryption solutions are also available that encompass a number of different devices. For example, Sophos Mobile Control provides device protection on iOS, Android, and Windows Mobile devices. It can secure mobile devices by centrally configuring security settings and enabling lockdown of unwanted features; and it offers remote over-the-air lock or wipe if a device is lost or stolen in addition to having a self-service portal that allows end users to register new devices and lock or wipe lost or stolen phones.

Remote Wipe/Sanitation

The data stored on a mobile is worth a lot more than the device itself. Mobiles carry a variety of personal and business information, so it's imperative to prevent them from getting into the wrong hands. Many of today's smartphones support a mobile kill switch or remote wipe capability.

ExamAlert

Remote wipe allows the handheld's data to be remotely deleted in the event the device is lost or stolen. All of the major smartphone platforms have this capability. The most common ways to remote wipe are using applications installed on the handset, through an IT management console, or a cloud-based service.

MobileMe is a service offered to Mac users that allows a remote wipe on a lost or stolen iPhone. There is also an option to erase all data on the iPhone after so many failed passcode attempts. The iPhone 3GS includes hardware encryption and all data is encrypted on the fly. This means that for the iPhone 3GS, you don't need to actually wipe the phone's entire contents; remote wiping the encryption key works. Any BlackBerry Enterprise Server (BES) handset can be erased, reset to factory default settings, or set to retain the IT policy it previously had via remote administration. This is done via the Erase Data and Disable Handheld command over the wireless network. By default the device deletes all data after 10 bad password attempts. Microsoft's My Phone Windows Mobile service enables users to locate lost handhelds via GPS and erase their data remotely. To enable remote wipe on enterprise Android phones, the phone must have the Google Apps Device Policy app installed. This is similar in functionality to the remote control features for a BES. In fact, soon Androids and iPhones will be able to be managed through a BES-like solution.

Remote wipes aren't fail-safe. If someone finds the phone before the remote wipe occurs and either takes the device off the network or force-reboots and restores the device, sensitive data can still be recovered. In the case of BlackBerry devices, if the device is turned off or outside the coverage area, the command is queued on the BlackBerry Enterprise Server until the device can be contacted. If a user is removed from the BlackBerry Enterprise Server before the command has reached the smartphone, data will not be erased from the device.

In addition to enterprise or built-in remote wiping tools, third-party products such as SecuWipe can be used to remove sensitive information. This type of product is good as a solution for Windows phones and Pocket PCs. It can securely wipe media cards, and it can be configured to wipe data remotely from a device that has been lost or stolen, automatically wipe the device clean when there is an attempt to insert another SIM card, or disable the phone function.

Voice Encryption

Mobile voice encryption can allow executives and employees alike to discuss sensitive information without having to travel to secure company locations. There are a variety of options available for voice encryption. Secusmart makes microSD flash cards that fit into certain Nokia devices. The software is installed on the phone when the card is first inserted into a device. Another hardware option is what is called embedded encryption. KoolSpan's TrustChip is one such solution. TrustChip consists of three main components:

- ▶ Embedded encryption software on the chip
- ▶ Linux-based management server
- ▶ TrustChip software development kit (SDK)

Kryptos is a secure VoIP application for the iPhone. It utilizes 256-bit AES military-grade encryption to encrypt calls between users. For added security, it uses 1024-bit RSA encryption during the symmetric key exchange. Kryptos can provide VoIP connectivity for secure calls over several networks including 3G, 4G, and Wi-Fi.

One thing to keep in mind when using voice encryption software is that it must be installed on each mobile phone to create a secure connection. You cannot create a secure encrypted connection between a device that has software installed and one that does not. This includes hardware solutions as well. For example, the TrustChip encrypts voice only when the phone calls another TrustChip phone. The user sees an icon on his display that informs him that the call is encrypted.

As with many other solutions, using voice encryption is not an end-all solution. It has been has discovered that 12 commercially available mobile voice encryption products can be intercepted and compromised using a little ingenuity and creativity. Some application can be compromised in as little as 30 minutes. Although some of these applications are not entirely secure, it would take a lot of effort to bypass them. However, the point is, it can be done.

GPS Tracking

In the event a mobile device is lost, you can use GPS tracking to find the location. More commonly, employers use this feature to locate employees via their devices.

> **ExamAlert**
>
> GPS tracking features can be used on company-issued devices for eliminating employees' unauthorized personal use of vehicles and breaks. In the event a mobile device is lost, you can use GPS tracking to find the location.

In the case of serious crimes, such as the hijacking of an armored vehicle, GPS-enabled devices can help locate and recover the stolen vehicle and possibly save the lives of the guards.

There are a number of ways to track the location of a mobile phone. Applications such as FlexiSPY use General Packet Radio Service (GPRS) and allow the GPS coordinates to be downloaded in a variety of formats. This makes it easy to import the coordinates into mapping software or create archives. Executrac Mobile GPS Tracker is a software program that uses a BES and BlackBerry's push technology to allow IT administrators to track devices through a web-based mapping platform, accessible from any computer or cell phone with an Internet connection. iPhone Tracker can reveal any locations visited on phones that have iOS 4.0 installed. Androids can use applications such as My Tracks or InstaMapper.

In addition to applications, there are also services that provide GPS tracking for devices. For example, AccuTracking online GPS cell phone tracking service allows viewing of real-time device locations for about $6.00 per month. Software is installed on the phone, a PC is used to add the device to the vendor's web interface, the phone communicates with the server, and then the device is tracked with viewing done through the vendor website.

Virtualization

Virtualization has many benefits from the data center to the desktop. For example, when working in a development environment, running the new system as a guest avoids the need to reboot the physical computer whenever a bug occurs. A "sandboxed" guest system can also help in computer-security research, which enables the study of the effects of some viruses or worms without the possibility of compromising the host system.

The use of desktop virtualization allows an organization to run multiple OSes, including Windows and Linux, on a single computer. With technology permeating every facet of modern life, the flexibility of being able to run a Windows guest operating on top of a Linux-based host operating system allows an added layer of security as well as access to both environments without having to dual boot the machine.

> **ExamAlert**
>
> Virtualization improves enterprise desktop management and control with faster deployment of desktops and fewer support calls due to application conflicts.

Virtualization reduces an entire functioning computer down to just a couple of files, which is obviously far easier to manage than the thousands and thousands of files found in the Windows directory alone. With virtualization, it is not only practical but also logical to simply discard an old or infected VM in favor of a fresh copy.

Full streaming of an OS is also a new approach to desktop virtualization, which is making its way into the mainstream IT community. A streaming OS provides the same benefit as a virtualized desktop but with more use of the desktop hardware in a traditional manner. With a streaming OS, an end user downloads a complete package, OS, and applications. The benefit is that of a full OS to distributed users who can enjoy the benefits of customization, security, patches, and updates. The trade-off with this architecture is similar to that of other virtualization models: the greater the distance, the slower the performance.

Some good uses of streaming OSes are as follows:

▶ Diskless workstations with a streaming OS that is used for sensitive or classified work environments. With this model, there is no need for lockdown protocols or secure storage for hard drives. The diskless client system increases security, and the network storage aspect allows for indefinite scalability.

▶ OS Streaming could be used quite effectively in an education environment where configuration and maintenance costs can be prohibitive.

▶ OS Streaming, much like a virtual desktop environment, can make the introduction of a new OS much easier. Users can be offered choices allowing for the selection of which OS they want to use based on their needs at that time.

Cram Quiz

Answer these questions. The answers follow the last question. If you cannot answer these questions correctly, consider reading this section again until you can.

1. Which of the follow methods would be the most effective method to physically secure computers that are used in a lab environment?
   - ○ **A.** Security cables
   - ○ **B.** Server cages
   - ○ **C.** Locked cabinet
   - ○ **D.** Hardware locks

2. Which of the following is included in hardening a host operating system?
   - ○ **A.** A policy for antivirus updates
   - ○ **B.** An effective system for file-level security
   - ○ **C.** An efficient method to connect to remote sites
   - ○ **D.** A policy for remote wipe

3. An organization is looking to add a layer of security and improve enterprise desktop management. Which of the following fulfills this requirement?

○ **A.** Roaming profiles

○ **B.** Network storage policies

○ **C.** VPN Remote Access

○ **D.** Desktop virtualization

4. An organization is looking for a mobile solution that will allow executives and employees alike to discuss sensitive information without having to travel to secure company locations. Which of the following fulfills this requirement?

○ **A.** GPS tracking

○ **B.** Remote wipe

○ **C.** Voice encryption

○ **D.** Passcode policy

5. Which of the following is needed to establish effective security baselines for host systems? (Select two correct answers.)

○ **A.** Cable locks

○ **B.** Mandatory settings

○ **C.** Standard application suites

○ **D.** Decentralized administration

6. Which of the following procedures should be used to properly protect a host from malware? (Select two correct answers.)

○ **A.** Web tracking software

○ **B.** Antivirus software

○ **C.** Content filtering software

○ **D.** Pop-up blocking software

Cram Answers

1. **C.** A locked cabinet is an alternative for equipment that is not used or does not have to be physically accessed on a regular, daily basis. Vendors provide solutions such as a security cabinet locker that secures CPU towers. The housing is made of durable, heavy-duty steel for strength. Answer A is incorrect because security cables with combination locks can provide such security and are easy to use but are used mostly to secure laptops and leave the equipment exposed. Answer B is incorrect because PC Safe tower and server cages are designed to bolt to the floor and are meant to be used in an environment that is static. Answer D is incorrect because a hardware lock, also known as a software copy protection dongle, is used for license enforcement.

2. **B**. Hardening of the operating system includes planning against both accidental and directed attacks, such as the use of fault-tolerant hardware and software solutions. In addition, it is important to implement an effective system for file-level security, including encrypted file support and secured file system selection that allows the proper level of access control. Answer A is incorrect because it is a host protection measure, not an OS hardening measure. Answer C is incorrect because this is a secure communication measure. Answer D is incorrect because this is a feature associated with data security, not host hardening.

3. **D**. Virtualization adds a layer of security as well as improving enterprise desktop management and control with faster deployment of desktops and fewer support calls due to application conflicts. Answer A is incorrect because roaming profiles do not add a layer of security. Answer B is incorrect because network storage policies have nothing to do with desktop management. Answer C is incorrect because VPN remote access will not improve enterprise desktop management.

4. **C**. Mobile voice encryption can allow executives and employees alike to discuss sensitive information without having to travel to secure company locations. Answer A is incorrect because in the event a mobile device is lost, GPS tracking can be used to find the location. Answer B is incorrect because remote wipe allows the handheld's data to be remotely deleted in the event the device is lost or stolen. Answer D is incorrect because a screen lock or passcode is used to prevent access to the phone.

5. **B** and **C**. In order to establish effective security baselines, enterprise network security management requires a measure of commonality between the systems. Mandatory settings, standard application suites, and initial setup configuration details all factor into the security stance of an enterprise network. Answer A is incorrect because cable locks have nothing to do with effective security base-lines. Answer D is incorrect because decentralized management does not have anything to do with security baselines.

6. **B** and **D**. All host devices must have some type of malware protection. A necessary software program for protecting the user environment is antivirus software. Antivirus software is used to scan for malicious code in email and downloaded files. Anti-spam, anti-spyware software can add another layer of defense to the infrastructure. Pop-up blocking software programs are available through browsers. Answer A is incorrect because web tracking software merely tracks the sites a person visited. Answer C is incorrect because content filtering is done at the server level to keep host machines from accessing certain content.

What Next?

If you want more practice on this chapter's exam objectives before you move on, remember that you can access all of the Cram Quiz questions on the CD. You can also create a custom exam by objective with the practice exam software. Note any objective you struggle with and go to that objective's material in this chapter.

CHAPTER 9
Data Security

This chapter covers the following official CompTIA Security+, SY0-301 exam objective:

▶ Explain the importance of data security

(For more information on the official CompTIA Security+, SY0-301 exam topics, see the "About the CompTIA Security+, SY0-301 Exam" section in the Introduction.)

Organizations often approach security as a defense strategy targeting the perimeter of the network. This approach might ignore sensitive data stored on the network. The security of organizational data is imperative to prevent attackers from obtaining access to confidential information and to protect sensitive data from employees with high-level access from exploiting this data.

In the next section we discuss the states of data, how they differ, and how to use and protect data in each particular state. But it is also just as important to have some type of data security lifecycle implemented. For example, a data security lifecycle might include stages such as create, store, use, archive, and destroy.

Explain the Importance of Data Security

▶ **Data Loss Prevention (DLP)**

▶ **Data encryption**

▶ **Hardware-based encryption devices**

▶ **Cloud computing**

Cram**Saver**

If you can correctly answer these questions before going through this section, save time by skimming the Exam Alerts in this section and then completing the Cram Quiz at the end of the section.

1. Explain the states of data and how they affect data loss prevention policies.

2. Explain when full disk encryption should be used.

3. Explain what TPM is and how it can be used to secure data.

4. Explain the advantages of using hardware-based USB encryption.

5. Explain how encryption is implemented in a SaaS cloud environment.

Answers

1. Data can generally be considered to be in one of three states: in use, in motion, or at rest. DLP polices and systems are basically designed to detect and prevent unauthorized use and transmission of confidential information based on one of these three states. Protection of data in use is considered to be an endpoint solution and the application is run on end-user workstations or servers in the organization. Protection of data in motion is considered to be a network solution and either a hardware or software solution is installed near the network perimeter to monitor for and flag policy violations. Protection of data at rest is considered to be a storage solution and is generally a software solution that monitors how confidential data is stored.

2. Full disk encryption (FDE), also called whole disk encryption, has gained popularity in recent years to help mitigate the risks associated with lost or stolen laptops and accompanying disclosure laws. Full disk encryption is most useful when you're dealing with a machine that is being taken on the road such as the computers used by traveling executives, sales managers, or insurance agents. Because encryption adds overhead, it's less productive for a computer in a fixed location where there is strong physical access control, unless the data is extremely sensitive and must be protected at all costs.

Answers

3. Answer: TPM refers to a secure cryptoprocessor used to authenticate hardware devices such as PC or laptop. The idea behind TPM is to allow any encryption-enabled application to take advantage of the chip. Therefore, it has many possible applications, such as network access control (NAC), secure remote access, secure transmission of data, whole disk encryption, software license enforcement, digital rights management (DRM), and credential protection. Part of what makes TPM effective is that the TPM module is given a unique ID and master key that even the owner of the system does not control or have knowledge of.

4. No matter how great the encryption algorithm is, if the key is found, the data can be decrypted. When software encryption is used, the key is stored either in the flash memory of the USB drive or on the computer that originated the file encryption. A more secure method is to use a USB drive that stores the encryption key on a separate controller on the device and physically protects the internal contents with a tamper-resistant shell such as the IronKey or LOK-IT. This type of device encrypts all user data stored on the drive using up to 256-bit AES encryption implemented in Cipher Block Chaining (CBC) mode.

5. If using a SaaS environment, the service provider usually encrypts the data. It is essential to inquire where and how the data is encrypted. It some instances, the only encryption provided is basic folder encryption, whereas in other instances data is encrypted using a unique key for every customer. In a SaaS environment, application-level encryption is preferred because the data is encrypted by the application before being stored in the database or file system. The advantage is that it protects the data from the user all the way to storage. To properly secure data stored through a SaaS platform, the organization needs to understand how the provider manages data and the terms of the service contracts.

Data Loss Prevention

One of the biggest challenges for CISOs as well IT security departments is how to keep data from leaving the organization. This can happen as a result of authorized users causing inadvertent data breaches as well as a result of the wrong people having access to sensitive information. When confidential organizational data is exposed, it can severely damage the organization financially and destroy its public image. Many businesses must now adhere to strict regulatory compliance where data security is concerned. As a result, organizations are increasingly turning to data loss prevention (DLP) strategies to protect and control the disclosure of sensitive information.

Data can generally be considered to be in one of three states: in use, in motion, or at rest. DLP systems are basically designed to detect and prevent unauthorized use and transmission of confidential information based on one of these three states. Protection of data in use is considered to be an endpoint solution and the application is run on end-user workstations or servers in the organization. Endpoint systems also can monitor and control access to physical devices such as mobile devices and tablets. Protection of data in motion is considered to be a network solution, and either a hardware or software solution is installed near the network perimeter to monitor for and flag policy violations. Protection of data at rest is considered to be a storage solution and is generally a software solution that monitors how confidential data is stored.

In order for an organization to properly implement a DLP solution, the organization has to understand what kind of sensitive data it has and then perform a risk assessment to determine what happens if data is exposed or gets in the wrong hands. After the sensitive data has been identified and the risk determined, the organization can begin DLP product integration. DLP products include ways to identify confidential or sensitive information. It is important to accurately identify sensitive data in order to lower instances of false positives and negatives.

When evaluating DLP solutions, key content filtering capabilities to look for are high performance, scalability, and the ability to accurately scan nearly anything. High performance is necessary to keep the end user from having lag time and delays. The solution must readily scale as the volume of traffic increases and bandwidth needs increase. The tool should also be able to accurately scan nearly anything.

Using an endpoint solution, here are some examples of when a user can be alerted to security policy violations in order to keep sensitive information from leaving the user's desktop:

► Inadvertently emailing a confidential internal document to external recipients

► Forwarding an email with sensitive information to unauthorized recipients inside or outside of the organization

► Sending attachments such as spreadsheets with personally identifiable information (PII) to an external personal email account

► Accidentally selecting "reply all" and emailing a sensitive document to unauthorized recipients

In addition to DLP, organizations must also address data leakage. Data leakage can occur when a data distributor gives sensitive data to a third party. Sensitive organizational data is sometimes discovered in unauthorized places that can range from wide exposure such as the Internet or in more obscure areas such as on a user's laptop. In order to avoid data leakage, accurate detection and the capability to define granular policies are required of content scanning tools. In order to properly prevent sensitive information from falling into the wrong hands, organizations need to focus on the filtering and blocking of all electronic communications including instant messaging (IM), web-based email, and HTTP traffic.

ExamAlert

You should avoid a high reliance on automated content scanners to correctly interpret the information and apply the right protection because of the possibility that the DLP product will either block non-sensitive data or mistakenly release sensitive data.

Data Encryption

In many situations, encryption can make a huge difference in how secure your environment is. This is true from the workstation level, to the server level, to how data is transferred to and from your business partners. Data encryption has become more and more important in light of the number of data breaches that have occurred in the last few years, which include everything from the 130,000,000 accounts exposed by the Hartland to the 8,000,000 accounts compromised via a NHS lost laptop. Although encryption might be the most practical method of protecting data stored or transmitted electronically, when the data is sensitive, encryption is a necessity. Should a security breach happen that involves sensitive data, failure to have that data encrypted can result in criminal or civil liabilities as well as irreparable harm to the reputation of the organization. There are many different types of data encryption that are covered in the next couple of chapters. Data encryption schemes generally fall into two categories: symmetric and asymmetric. Encryption requires thought and preparation prior to implementation. Consideration should be given to answer the following questions:

▸ How will data encryption affect the performance on the network as well as the servers and workstations attached to that network?

▸ In what ways will the end users interact with encryption? What type of encryption will they experience on an end-user level? What methods of encryption will be needed and in what capacity?

▸ What additional costs will data encryption bring to the organization and the department that manages it? What additional hardware and/or software will be needed?

> ▶ Do the business partners or other organizations we communicate with use encryption? If so, what do they use and how do we integrate with them?

> ▶ How will the encryption algorithm, software, and other methods we implement today scale with what we want to do tomorrow as well as the long-term IT and business goals of our organization?

The answers to these questions help determine how to properly select the encryption methods that best protect the organization's sensitive data.

Full Disk

Full disk encryption (*FDE*), also called whole disk encryption, has gained popularity in recent years to help mitigate the risks associated with lost or stolen laptops and accompanying disclosure laws.

ExamAlert

Whole disk encryption can either be hardware or software based, and, unlike file- or folder-level encryption, whole disk encryption is meant to encrypt the entire contents of the drive (even temporary files and memory).

Full disk encryption involves encrypting the operating system partition on a computer and then booting and running with the system drive encrypted at all times. If the computer is stolen or lost, the OS and all the data on the drive becomes unreadable without the decryption key.

Unlike selective file encryption, which might require the end user to take responsibility for encrypting files, encrypting the contents of the entire drive takes the onus off individual users. It is not unusual for end users to sacrifice security for convenience, especially when they do not fully understand the associated risks. Nevertheless, along with the benefits of whole disk encryption come certain tradeoffs. For example, key management becomes increasingly important; loss of the decryption keys could render the data unrecoverable. In addition, although whole disk encryption might make it easier for an organization to deal with a stolen or otherwise lost laptop, the fact that the entire disk is encrypted could present management challenges, including not being able to effectively control who has unauthorized access to sensitive data.

ExamAlert

The important thing to understand is that after the device is booted and running, it is just as vulnerable as a disk that had no encryption on it.

To effectively use whole disk encryption products, you should also use a preboot authentication mechanism. That is, the user attempting to log on must provide authentication before the actual operating system boots. Thus, the encryption key is decrypted only after another key is input into this preboot environment. Most vendors typically offer different options, such as the following:

▶ Username and password (typically the least secure)

▶ Smart card or smart card–enabled USB token along with a PIN (which provides two-factor functionality and can often be the same token or smart card currently used for access elsewhere)

▶ A Trusted Platform Module to store the decryption key (discussed more later in this chapter)

Full disk encryption is most useful when you're dealing with a machine that is being taken on the road by people such as traveling executives, sales managers, or insurance agents. Because encryption adds overhead, it's less productive for a computer in a fixed location where there is strong physical access control, unless the data is extremely sensitive and must be protected at all costs.

Database

Databases are the largest repository of sensitive information in many organizations. Organizational databases contain data ranging from personally identifiable customer information to intellectual property. Lost or stolen customer data can ultimately result in such severe, permanent damage that the organization goes out of business.

> ### Exam**Alert**
>
> Although database security is a top priority for organizations, traditional database security methods such as firewalls are no longer sufficient to protect organizational data, especially against insider threat. Database encryption can be used to mitigate security breach risk and to comply with regulations.

For example, in the financial sector, organizations must comply with the Payment Card Industry Data Security Standard (PCI-DSS). PCI-DSS creates policies that define what data needs to be encrypted, how it is to be encrypted and defines requirements key management. One of the biggest challenges associated with database encryption is key management. This is especially true for organizations that have to meet policies requiring Federal Information Processing Standard (FIPS) validated key storage. Database encryption is most often accompanied by a centralized method of defining key policy and enforcing key management, creating a center of trust. In the event this trust is breached, the ramifications can be far reaching as mostly recently seen with the RSA breach and subsequent Lockheed Martin attack.

Although a defense in-depth strategy can help, encryption of data should occur both at rest and in transit. For example, application-level encryption can be used to encrypt information before it is stored in the database. This can prevent sensitive database information from being disclosed by either unauthorized access or theft. Database-level encryption by means of encrypting the entire contents written to the database can have unintended consequences such as limiting access control and auditing capabilities, so it is important to evaluate any solution before implementation.

> ### ExamAlert
>
> Database encryption must also be accompanied by key management to provide a high level of security. Other solutions to protect encrypted databases include permission restrictions on database and root administrators as well as restrictions on encryption key administration.

Hardware security modules (HSMs), which are discussed in detail later in the chapter, can provide enforcement of separation of duties for key management by separating database and security administration.

Individual Files

File- or folder-level encryption is different than full disk encryption. In full disk encryption, the entire partition or disk is encrypted. In file- or folder-level encryption, individual files or directories are encrypted by the file system itself. Perhaps one of the most common examples of this type of encryption is the encrypting file system (EFS) available in newer Microsoft operating systems.

> ### ExamAlert
>
> EFS encryption occurs at the file-system level as opposed to the application level. This makes the encryption and decryption process transparent to the user and to the application.

If a folder is marked as encrypted, every file created in or moved to the folder will be encrypted. Applications don't have to understand EFS or manage EFS-encrypted files any differently than unencrypted files. EFS-encrypted files don't remain encrypted during transport if saved to or opened from a folder on a remote server. In other words, the file is decrypted, traverses the network in plaintext, and then, if saved to a folder on a locally encrypted drive, is encrypted locally.

In file-level encryption, typically the file system metadata is not encrypted so anyone who has access to the physical disk can see what data is stored on the disk, even though they cannot access the contents. If EFS is used, metadata such as filenames and ownership are all stored encrypted on the disk while metadata about the storage pool is still stored in the clear. This allows certain information to still be viewable, but not directory information or stored file content.

File-level encryption allows flexible key management, individual management of encrypted files, and shorter memory holding periods for cryptographic keys. Additional uses for file-level encryption include laptops that only periodically hold sensitive data, email attachments, and sensitive information stored on a server in a file that is shared among several employees.

Removable Media

USB flash drives, iPods, and other portable storage devices are pervasive in the workplace and a real threat. They can introduce viruses or malicious code to the network and be used to store sensitive corporate information. Sensitive information is often stored on thumb and external hard drives, which then are lost or stolen. In many instances the banning of these types of devices is not an acceptable solution. For example, in November 2008, thumb drives were banned after thousands of military computers and networks became infected by malicious software. The ban was a major inconvenience for those who relied on thumb drives. Aircraft and vehicle technicians were storing manuals on thumb drives. Medical records of wounded troops were sometimes stored on thumb drives and accompanied patients from field hospitals in foreign countries to their final U.S.-based hospitals. Pilots used thumb drives to transfer mission plans from operations rooms to aircraft computers. These scenarios highlight the importance to finding a way to secure data that is taken outside of a managed environment as opposed to banning the devices entirely. With the capability to carry organizational data on portable storages, encryption is essential. Some disk encryption products only protect the local disk and do not protect USB devices while other encryption products automatically encrypt data copied or written to removable media.

When choosing an enterprise encryption method, it is important to evaluate how it will integrate with any other encryption solutions already in place. For example, most removable media encryption products can be configured to restrict access to devices by means of an authorized list. Some encryption products support a profile approach to creating user permissions such as those in an Active Directory Windows operating system environment. When this type of solution is used, the network authorizes the device, checks the content on the device, and then digitally marks the device before granting access. When evaluating a removable-media encryption product, in addition to authorized device access, access to personal devices, authorized file copy, encryption keys, and ease of use should be evaluated.

USB drives can also be set up to run as portable environments. This option provides a portable virtual environment that allows applications and operating systems to be carried on a USB drive. This eliminates the need to use public kiosks while away from the office. The USB device runs a virtual environment, thereby leaving the original system intact, but there is more of a risk for the data on the USB drive if it is not encrypted. If the USB drive was lost or stolen and it was unencrypted, there would be access to more than just files. The accessible information would include browser history, FTP access, passwords, and email.

All USB flash drives can have their contents encrypted using third-party encryption software. These programs should be evaluated before implementation because many programs, such as TrueCrypt, require the user to have administrative rights on the computer it is run on. In the case where a traveling employee can only take a USB thumb drive, using an encryption method such as FreeOTFE would be a much better solution. FreeOTFE is a free, open source, on-the-fly disk encryption program that can often be run directly from the USB drive without any host machine installation. This enables a user to securely access corporate resources through hotel kiosks without the risk of data being left behind.

Mobile Devices

Handheld devices have become very popular in recent years. Many organizations are now faced with either allowing users to use their personal mobile devices on the network or managing and issuing these devices. From an administrative standpoint, it is simpler to allow the users to use their own devices, but then the organization is faced with figuring out a way to not only separate personal data from corporate data but also how to protect the corporate data. Remember from the last chapter that applications such as Good offer a security container that separates company and personal information, and enterprise encryption solutions are also available that encompass a number of different devices including iOS, Android, and Windows Mobile devices.

Because most smartphones include the capability to have wireless as well as cellular communications, you can take different approaches. Some solutions only include voice encryption and some only provide data encryption. Organizations often implement an end-point solution depending on policy and devices that are used on the network. For example, Pointsec's Mobile Encryption automatically protects data on Symbian, Pocket PC, Palm PC, and Windows Mobile operating systems and includes memory card data encryption. Symantec's Mobile Security Suite offers a combination of mobile security and data protection by including virus protection with encryption of sensitive data and logging file accesses. Some platforms include their own encryption solution. If an organization is using a BlackBerry Enterprise server (BES), devices can be protected via policies. A BES uses a symmetric key encryption algorithm that is designed to protect data in transit between a BlackBerry device and the BES. Standard BlackBerry encryption is designed to encrypt messages that a BlackBerry device sends or that the BlackBerry Enterprise Server forwards to the BlackBerry device. Data protection is a feature available for iOS 4 devices that offer hardware encryption on iPhone 4, iPhone 3GS, iPod touch (third generation or later), and all iPad models.

The factors organizations should consider when evaluating smartphone encryption products include cost, platform support, how the product meets the organizational policy needs, ease of centralized management, and how the encryption is implemented.

Hardware-based Encryption Devices

Due to factors such as the need for a highly secure environment, the unreliability of software, and increased frequency of complex attacks, some organizations turn to the use of hardware-based encryption devices. Hardware-based encryption basically allows IT administrators to move certificate authentication (CA) software components to hardware. Authentication is performed based on the user providing a credential to the hardware on the machine. This provides a hardware-based authentication solution for wireless networks and virtual private networks (VPNs) and eliminates the possibility of users sharing keys.

TPM

The Trusted Computing Group is responsible for the *Trusted Platform Module* (*TPM*) specification.

> ## Exam**Alert**
>
> TPM refers to a secure cryptoprocessor used to authenticate hardware devices such as PC or laptop.

At the most basic level, TPM provides for the secure storage of keys, passwords, and digital certificates. It is hardware based and is typically attached to the circuit board of the system. In addition, TPM can be used to ensure that a system is authenticated and to ensure that the system has not been altered or breached.

TPM is composed of various components. You should be familiar with some key TPM concepts, including the following:

- ▶ **Endorsement key (EK)**: A 2048-bit asymmetric key pair created at the time of manufacturing and that cannot be changed

- ▶ **Storage root key (SRK)**: A 2048-bit asymmetric key pair generated within a TPM and used to provide encrypted storage

- ▶ **Sealed storage**: Protects information by binding it to the system, which means the information can be read only by the same system in a particular described state

- ▶ **Attestation**: Vouching for the accuracy of the system

Computers using a TPM have the ability to create and encrypt cryptographic keys through a process called *wrapping*. Each TPM has a root wrapping key, called the *Storage Root Key* (*SRK*), which is stored within the TPM itself. Additionally, TPM-enabled computers have the ability to create and tie a key to certain platform measurements. This type of key can only be unwrapped when the platform measurements have the same values that they had when the key was created. This process is called *sealing* the key to the TPM. Decrypting it is called *unsealing*. Attestation or any other TPM functions do not transmit personal information of the user.

The idea behind TPM is to allow any encryption-enabled application to take advantage of the chip. Therefore, it has many possible applications, such as network access control (NAC), secure remote access, secure transmission of data, whole disk encryption, software license enforcement, digital rights management

(DRM), and credential protection. Interestingly, part of what makes TPM effective is the TPM module is given a unique ID and master key that even the owner of the system neither controls nor has knowledge of. On the other hand, critics of TPM argue that this security architecture puts too much control into the hands of those who design the related systems and software. So, concerns arise about several issues, including DRM, loss of end-user control, loss of anonymity, and interoperability. If standards and shared specifications do not exist, components of the trusted environment cannot interoperate and trusted computing applications cannot be implemented to work on all platforms. It is also important to understand that TPM can store pre-run-time configuration parameters but does not control the software that is running on a PC. If something happens to the TPM or the motherboard, you need a separate recovery key in order to access your data simply when connecting the hard drive to another computer.

Exam**Alert**

A TPM can offer greater security protection for processes such as digital signing, mission-critical applications, and businesses where high security is required. Trusted modules can also be used in mobile phones and network equipment.

The nature of hardware-based cryptography ensures that the information stored in hardware is better protected from external software attacks. A TPM Management console is incorporated into newer Windows systems such as Windows 7 and Server 2008 R2. This function can be used to administer the TPM security hardware through a TPM Management console and an API called TPM Base Services (TBS). Figure 9.1 shows the TPM console for a Dell with BitLocker enabled.

HSM

A *hardware security module* (*HSM*) can be described as black box combination hardware and software/firmware that is attached or contained inside a computer used to provide cryptographic functions for tamper protection and increased performance.

Exam**Alert**

Basically an HSM is a type of cryptoprocessor that manages digital keys, accelerates cryptographic processes, and provides strong access authentication for critical application encryption keys. HSMs come mainly in the form of slotted cards or external devices that can be attached directly to a network but can also be embedded.

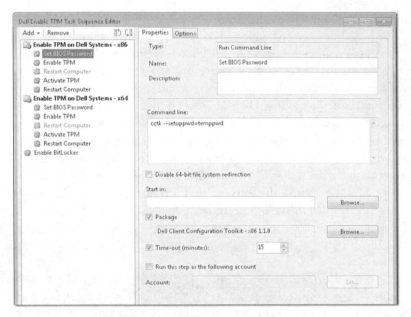

FIGURE 9.1   **TPM console with BitLocker enabled.**

The basic cryptographic operations are the same for the different types of HSMs, but the administration structure and authorization models can vary. Typically, an HSM is installed inside a server box or within an Ethernet cluster. The HSM is then wrapped by the software that provides access to the cryptographic functionality within the HSM. Traditionally, HSMs have been used in the banking sector to secure numerous large, bulk transactions. HSM security requirements were derived from existing ISO, ANSI, federal standards, and accepted best practice recognized by the financial industry. HSMs are also found in PKI deployments to secure CA keys, SSL acceleration, and storing DNSSEC keys along with encrypting zone records.

The PKCS#11 standard provides for access to public and private asymmetric keys, symmetric keys, X.509 certificates, and application data. PKCS#11 is the de facto standard for platform applications, although some newer HSMs include more advanced authentication and authorization models. PKCS#11 was initially designed for accessing smartcards and defines two roles: security officer and user. Each PIN is unique. The security officer PIN is used to manage the user role while the user PIN is used to authorize token usage operations.

As mentioned in the previous section, hardware can better protect encryption keys for several reasons: the application does not directly handle the key; the key does not leave the device; and since the host OS is not storing the key, it cannot be compromised on the host system.

Keep in mind there are two types of HSMs, ones that are PC based, such as PCMCIA cards, and ones that are network based. The main advantages of the network-attached HSM types are similar to the advantages of using a NAS. They are essentially platform independent and can be used simultaneously from several clients. Because HSMs are often part of a mission-critical infrastructure such as a public key infrastructure or online banking application, HSMs can typically be clustered for high availability and some HSMs feature dual power supplies. Host HSM systems are also hardware cryptographic accelerators by nature due to the fact that the keys do not leave devices in an unencrypted form. The HSM must perform the common cryptographic operations so it will accelerate the intense math functions, offering better performance than a normal software-based crypto system.

HSM systems can securely back up their keys either in a wrapped form or externally. Keys protected by HSM are only truly hardware protected if they were generated inside the hardware itself. If a standard software-protected key is imported into an HSM, a non-hardware-protected copy of the key could still exist on old backups.

USB Encryption

As mentioned earlier, sensitive information is often stored on a thumb and external hard drives, which then are lost or stolen. Storing sensitive data on USB drives is always a risk, but many organizations simply cannot ban them. Losing sensitive data can have severe consequences. For example, flash drives carrying sensitive and classified information turned up for sale in a bazaar outside Bagram and a single malware-infected USB stick led to huge compromise of U.S. Central Command's classified and unclassified systems in Iraq. A survey by Ponemon Institute revealed that 51% of respondents said they use USB sticks to store sensitive data, 57% believe others within their organization routinely do it, and 87% said their company has policies against it.

Instead of a software-based solution, organizations can choose to approve or purchase and issue flash drives that have hardware encryption.

ExamAlert

All encryption algorithms used for encrypted flash drives have a single key that is used to both encrypt and decrypt the data.

It is imperative to protect this key because no matter how great the encryption algorithm is, if the key is found, the data can be decrypted. When software encryption is used, the key is stored either in the flash memory of the

USB drive or on the computer that originated the file encryption. A more secure method is to use a USB drive that stores the encryption key on a separate controller on the device and physically protects the internal contents with a tamper-resistant shell such as the IronKey or LOK-IT. This type of device encrypts all user data stored on the drive using up to 256-bit AES encryption implemented in Cipher Block Chaining (CBC) mode. This can help the organization comply with cryptography requirements such as the U.S. Federal Information Processing Standard (FIPS) 140-2 Level 3 requirements. In a drive such as the IronKey, a cryptochip generates the encryption keys used to protect the data when the drive is first activated. The advantage to this solution is that the encryption keys are never stored or loaded onto the PC. The onboard cryptochip manages the keys and performs the encryption routines. USB drive encryption is discussed in further detail late in the chapter.

Another option for USB encryption is biometrics. Transcend's JetFlash220 features a sensor strip that allows users to access protected data by simply scanning their fingerprint. One factor to consider while evaluating this solution is that the fingerprint-scanning portion relies on the host operating system to validate the fingerprint via a software driver. This restricts the use to machines where the driver can be installed and is mainly for Microsoft Windows computers. However, there are USB drives with fingerprint scanners that use controllers that allow access to protected data without any authentication. These drives incorporate a fingerprint scanner that serves as the passcode to the drive, such as the Stealth MXP Bio. It offers an advance fingerprint-recognition technology with 1, 2, or 3 factor authentication; PKI token services; and OATH OTP onboard key generation.

Hard Drive

Hard drive encryption is divided into three main categories: software-based; hardware-based on the storage device itself; and hardware-based elsewhere, such as the CPU or host bus adaptor. With device theft and loss being primary reasons of data loss, it is important that hardware comes loaded with encryption functionality to safeguard confidential data. By now it should be apparent that when hardware-based encryption is implemented correctly, it is superior to software-based encryption. Hardware vendors are now integrating basic encryption functionality on their drives. But hardware-based encryption products can also vary in the level of protection they provide against attacks such as offline parallel attacks or other cryptanalysis attacks. Hardware disk encryption is similar to other hardware-based solutions in that the encryption key is maintained independently from the computer, preventing the memory from being an attack vector.

The Trusted Computing Group (TCG) security subsystem storage standard Opal provides industry-accepted standardization for *self-encrypting drives* (*SEDs*). SEDs automatically encrypt all data in the drive, preventing attackers from accessing the data through the operating system. SED vendors include Seagate Technology; Hitachi, Ltd.; Western Digital; Samsung; and Toshiba.

> **Exam Alert**
>
> With hardware disk encryption, authentication happens on power-up of the drive through either a software pre-boot authentication environment or with a BIOS password. Enhanced firmware and special-purpose cryptographic hardware are built into the hard disks.

The firmware and hardware implement common cryptographic functions. Disk encryption that is embedded in the hard drive provides performance that is very close to that of unencrypted disk drives and to the user; there is no noticeable difference from using an unencrypted disk. Boot drive solutions require a pre-boot authentication component that is available from a number of vendors. The authentication credentials are usually a major potential weakness and some solutions leave the master boot record (MBR) unencrypted. Seagate uses a solution where the authentication software provides the authentication login and then uses a secure and hardened version of Linux to perform the pre-boot authentication. There are also some hardware-based FDE systems that encrypt the entire boot disk, including the MBR. For example, FlagStone hard drives encrypt and decrypt data immediately but come in the form of a direct replacement for the computer's standard hard drive.

Advantages of hardware hard drive encryption include faster setup time, enhanced scalability, improved portability, and better system performance. Disadvantages include lack of management software and weak authentication components. Coupled with the TPM's public key infrastructure (PKI) capability, an SED can achieve very strong authentication. You can use hardware drive encryption to protect data at rest because all the data, even the OS, is encrypted with a secure mode of AES.

Cloud Computing

Cloud computing includes various flavors and uses of technology such as Desktops as a Service and Streaming Operating Systems. The use of these types of environments has a huge potential for a dramatically simplified IT infrastructure with more cost-effective IT management and utilization. But along with that comes the potential for enormous data loss if the data is not properly encrypted. Having highly available cloud data is risky because multiple copies of your data can be in various locations. When you delete files, successful deletion of trace data becomes next to impossible.

Traditional encryption solutions for the purpose of data security protection cannot be adopted for the cloud due to the loss of control of data. Because various kinds of data are stored in the cloud and the need for long-term continuous assurance of data security, verifying the correctness of data stored in the cloud becomes even more challenging. Although encryption is far from a total solution for all cloud data security issues, when used properly and in combination with other controls, it provides effective security. In cloud implementations, encryption might help alleviate the security issues related to multi-tenancy, public clouds, and remote or outsourced hosting. Encrypting data stored in the cloud also helps prevent data from being modified and can reduce the risk of a compromise when sold cloud storage devices still contain organizational information.

The methods used for encryption vary based on the service provider type. Remember from Chapter 1, "Network Design," that cloud computing can be classified as Platform-as-a-Service (PaaS), Software-as-a-Service (SaaS), or Infrastructure-as-a-Service (IaaS). In addition, cloud vendors might have hardware-based solutions in place. In a cloud environment, virtual cryptography-as-a-service deployments are a reality, and some cloud service providers implement a solution with robust security mechanisms, such as centralized key management, granular encryption, and strong access controls. It is best practice to be sure encryption keys are kept secure and separate from the data.

Because PaaS mainly provides the organization with a development platform, encryption implementation depends on the available APIs and development environment. Generally speaking, in cloud implementations data should be encrypted at the application layer rather than within a database due to the complexity involved. Media encryption is managed at the storage layer.

If using a SaaS environment, the service provider usually encrypts the data. It is essential to inquire where and how the data is encrypted. In some instances, the only encryption provided is basic folder encryption; in other instances data is encrypted using a unique key for every customer.

> **ExamAlert**
>
> In a SaaS environment, application-level encryption is preferred because the data is encrypted by the application before being stored in the database or file system. The advantage is that it protects the data from the user all the way to storage.

To properly secure data stored through a SaaS platform, the organization needs to understand how the provider manages data and the terms of the service contracts. When using IaaS, Virtual Private Storage is an option. Virtual Private Storage is a method used to protect remote data when there is not complete control of the storage environment. The organization encrypts the data before sending it off to the cloud provider, allowing control over keys and ACLs. The organization maintains control while still retaining the benefits of cloud-based storage. Many cloud backup solutions use this design. Encrypted virtual machines (VMs) are another option. Encryption of a complete virtual machine on IaaS could be considered media encryption.

Several cloud providers have been moving toward the concept of enabling on-premise HSMs for securing their cloud-hosted applications. This type of environment enables providers to move their applications to the cloud and still keep a root-of-trust within the HSM. The HSM and cloud machines can both live on the same virtual private network, through the use of a virtual private cloud (VPC) environment. This type of solution is mainly found in private datacenters that manage and offload cryptography with dedicated hardware appliances. Using an HSM solution that is properly implemented in a cloud data center can provide the organization a reasonably high level of data protection.

Cram Quiz

Answer these questions. The answers follow the last question. If you cannot answer these questions correctly, consider reading this section again until you can.

1. Your organization is exploring data loss prevention solutions. The proposed solution is an end-point solution. This solution is targeting which of the following data states?

   ○ **A.** In motion

   ○ **B.** In use

   ○ **C.** At rest

   ○ **D.** At flux

2. Which of the following uses a secure cryptoprocessor to authenticate hardware devices such as PC or laptop?

   ○ **A.** Trusted Platform Module

   ○ **B.** Full disk encryption

   ○ **C.** File-level encryption

   ○ **D.** Public key infrastructure

3. Which of the following is one of the biggest challenges associated with database encryption?

- ○ **A.** Weak authentication components
- ○ **B.** Platform support
- ○ **C.** Multi-tenancy
- ○ **D.** Key management

4. Which of the following standards is used in HSMs?

- ○ **A.** PKCS #7
- ○ **B.** PKCS#11
- ○ **C.** AES
- ○ **D.** EFS

5. Which of the following is the preferred type of encryption used in SaaS platforms?

- ○ **A.** Application level
- ○ **B.** HSM level
- ○ **C.** Media level
- ○ **D.** Database level

Cram Answer

1. **B.** Protection of data in use is considered to be an endpoint solution and the application is run on end-user workstations or servers in the organization. Answer A is incorrect because protection of data in motion is considered to be a network solution and either a hardware or software solution is installed near the network perimeter to monitor for and flag policy violations. Answer C is incorrect because protection of data at rest is considered to be a storage solution and is generally a software solution that monitors how confidential data is stored. Answer D is incorrect because there is no such data state.

2. **A.** TPM refers to a secure cryptoprocessor used to authenticate hardware devices such as PC or laptop. The idea behind TPM is to allow any encryption-enabled application to take advantage of the chip. Answer B is incorrect because full-disk encryption involves encrypting the operating system partition on a computer and then booting and running with the system drive encrypted at all times. Answer C is incorrect because in file- or folder-level encryption, individual files or directories are encrypted by the file system itself. Answer D is incorrect because PKI is a set of hardware, software, people, policies, and procedures needed to create, manage, distribute, use, store, and revoke digital certificates.

3. **D.** One of the biggest challenges associated with database encryption is key management. Answer A is incorrect because lack of management software and weak authentication components are associated with hardware hard drive encryption. Answer B is incorrect because cost and platform support are concerns with smartphone encryption products. Answer C is incorrect because multi-tenancy is a security issue related to cloud computing implementations.

4. **B.** The PKCS#11 standard provides for access to public and private asymmetric keys, symmetric keys, X.509 certificates, and application data. PKCS#11 is the de facto standard for platform applications, although some newer HSMs include more advanced authentication and authorization models. Answer A is incorrect because PKCS #7 Cryptographic Message Syntax Standard describes the syntax for data streams, such as digital signatures, that may have cryptography applied to them. Answer C is incorrect because AES is most commonly found on USB drive encryption. Answer D is incorrect because EFS is the encrypting file system available in newer Microsoft operating systems.

5. **A.** In a SaaS environment, application-level encryption is preferred because the data is encrypted by the application before being stored in the database or file system. The advantage is that it protects the data from the user all the way to storage. Answer B is incorrect because an HSM solution is mainly found in private datacenters that manage and offload cryptography with dedicated hardware appliances. Answer C is incorrect because encryption of a complete virtual machine on IaaS could be considered media encryption. Answer D is incorrect because, due to the complexity involved, data should be encrypted at the application layer in cloud implementations rather than being encrypted within a database.

What Next?

If you want more practice on this chapter's exam objectives before you move on, remember that you can access all of the Cram Quiz questions on the CD. You can also create a custom exam by objective with the practice exam software. Note any objective you struggle with and go to that objective's material in this chapter.

CHAPTER 10

Authentication and Authorization

This chapter covers the following official CompTIA Security+ Certification exam objectives:

▶ Explain the fundamental concepts and best practices related to authentication and authorization

▶ Explain the function and purpose of authentication services

(For more information on the official CompTIA Security+ Certification exam topics, see the "About the CompTIA Security+ Certification Exam" section in the Introduction.)

The traditional C-I-A Triad of security directives includes maintaining the confidentiality, integrity, and availability of data and services. In order to protect against unauthorized access or modification and to ensure availability for legitimate access requests, you must put in place a mechanism that allows the identification of an authorized request. This overall process is called access control, although it is actually three subprocesses that must occur in sequence:

1. **Authentication:** Presenting and verifying credentials or keys as authentic

2. **Authorization:** Checking credentials or keys against a list of authorized security principles

3. **Access Control:** Limiting access to resources based on a defined set of allowed actions and areas of access

This chapter focuses on the fundamental concepts and best practices related to authentication and authorization. Chapter 11, "Access Control and Account Management," focuses on the access control function and account management.

> **Note**
>
> The official objective is "Explain the fundamental concepts and best practices related to authentication, authorization, *and access control*." The access control portion of this objective is covered in Chapter 11. All the subobjectives are covered between the two chapters.

Authentication

▶ **Identification versus authentication**

▶ **Authentication (single factor) and authorization**

▶ **Multifactor authentication**

▶ **Biometrics**

▶ **Tokens**

▶ **Common access card**

▶ **Personal identification verification card**

▶ **Smart card**

Authentication Strength

Before authorization can occur for anything other than Anonymous access to public resources, the identity of the account attempting to access a resource must be determined. This process is known as *authentication*. The most common form of authentication is the use of a logon account and password in combination to access resources and services. Access is not possible without both parts required for account authentication.

> **ExamAlert**
>
> The exam might contrast *identification* (the presenting of credentials or keys) with *authentication* (the verification of presented credentials or keys as being valid and present in the authorization system's database).

The relative strength of an authentication system involves the difficulty involved in falsifying or circumventing its process. Anonymous or open access represents the weakest possible form of authentication, whereas the requirement for both a logon identifier and password combination might be considered the simplest form of actual account verification. The highest levels of authentication might involve not only account logon, but also criteria measuring whether the logon is occurring from specific network addresses or whether a security token such as an access smart card is present.

In theory, the strongest security would be offered by identifying biometric (body-measuring) keys unique to a particular user's physical characteristics, such as fingerprints and retinal or iris patterns, combined with other authentication methods involving access passwords or token-based security requiring the possession of a physical smart card key.

> **ExamAlert**
>
> Forms of authentication credentials can be generally broken into four basic categories, depending on what is required to identify the access requester:
>
> ► Something you **know**—passwords, account logon identifiers
>
> ► Something you **have**—smart cards, synchronized shifting keys
>
> ► Something you **are**—fingerprints, retinal patterns, hand geometry
>
> ► Something you **do**—gait and handwriting kinematics
>
> Location-specific logons from a particular GPS zone, time-of-day restrictions, or restricted console terminal requirements can also factor in limiting access to requests

Single versus Multifactor Authentication

Obviously, the needs for authentication are going to be relative to the value assigned to a particular resource's security. Additional authentication layers required for access increase both the administrative overhead necessary for management and the difficulty users have trying to access needed resources. Consider, for example, the differences in authentication requirements for access to a high-security solution such as the Department of Energy's power grid control network as opposed to those needed to access an unprivileged local account in a public kiosk.

In the first scenario, to establish authentication for rightful access, the use of a combination of multiple biometric, token-based, and password-form authentication credentials might be mandatory. You can also use these access methods with even more complex forms of authentication, such as the use of dedicated lines of communication, time-of-day restrictions, synchronized shifting-key hardware encryption devices, and redundant-path comparison. You use these to ensure that each account attempting to make an access request is properly identified. In the second scenario, authentication might be as simple as an automatic anonymous guest logon shared by all visitors.

Each mechanism for authentication provides different levels of identification, security over data during the authentication exchange, and suitability to different authentication methods such as wireless or dial-up network access requests. Multiple authentication factors can be combined to improve the overall strength of the access control mechanism.

A common example of a multi-factor authentication system is used at automated teller machines (ATMs), which require both a "what you have" physical key (your ATM card) in combination with a "what you know" personal identification number (PIN). By combining two or more types of authentication, you improve access security above a single-factor authentication such as your "what you have" car key, which could be used alone without any additional credentials beyond possession of the physical key.

The difficulty involved in gaining unauthorized access increases as more types of authentication are used, although the difficulty for users wanting to authenticate themselves is also increased similarly. Administrative overhead and cost of support also increase with the complexity of the authentication scheme, so a solution should be reasonable based on the sensitivity of data being secured.

> **Exam Alert**
>
> The exam might ask you to distinguish between single-factor and multi-factor authentication solutions. A multi-factor authentication scenario involves two or more of the *types* of authentication (what you know, have, are, or do), not simply multiple credentials or keys of the same type. The common logon/password combination is a single-factor ("what you know") authentication using two keys of the same type.

Common Authentication Forms

This section covers the several forms of authentication you should be familiar with for the exam.

Username and Password

The most common form of authentication combines two "what you know" forms of authentication: a username and a password or pass-phrase. This form is easily implemented across many types of haptic interface, including standard keyboards as well as assistive technology interfaces. If both values match the credentials associated within the authorization system's database, the credentials can be authenticated and authorized for a connection. Password strength is a measure of the difficulty involved in guessing or breaking the password through cryptographic techniques, rainbow tables, or library-based automated brute-force testing of alternative values.

Single Sign-On

Distributed enterprise networks often include many different resources, each of which might require a different mechanism or protocol for authentication and access control. To reduce user support and authentication complexity, a single sign-on (SSO) capable of granting access across multiple services might be desirable. SSO solutions can use a central meta-directory service or can sequester services behind a series of proxy applications as in the service-oriented architecture (SOA) approach.

In the SOA network environment, the client-facing proxy application provides a standard mechanism for interacting with each service (called a Wrapper), handling specialized logon, authentication, and access control functions "behind the scenes" out of sight of the consuming user or service.

Tokens

One of the best methods of "what you have" authentication involves the use of a token, which might either be a physical device or a one-time password issued to the user seeking access. Tokens include solutions such as a chip-integrated smart card or a digital token such as RSA Security's *SecurID* token that provides a numerical key that changes every few minutes and is synchronized with the authentication server. Without the proper key or physical token, access is denied. Because the token is unique and granted only to the user, it is harder to pretend to be (spoof) the properly authorized user. Digital tokens are typically used only one time or are valid for a very short period of time to prevent capture and later reuse. Most token-based access control systems pair the token with a PIN or other form of authentication to protect against unauthorized access using only a lost or stolen token.

Telecommuters might also use an electronic device known as a key fob that provides one part of a three-way match to log in over an unsecure network connection to a secure network. This kind of key fob might have a keypad on which the user must enter a PIN to retrieve an access code, or it could be a display-only device such as a VPN token that algorithmically generates security codes as part of a challenge/response authentication system.

Smart Card

Smart cards are a form of "what you have" authentication that uses a standard wallet-card with an embedded chip that can automatically provide an authenticating cryptographic key to its reader, or it might contain data useful for other forms of authentication, such as biometric measures, which can be too large for volume remote authentication solutions.

> **ExamAlert**
>
> The exam might include questions regarding two new forms of smart card required for U.S. federal service identity verification under the Homeland Security Presidential Directive 12 (HSPD 12):
>
> ▶ **Common Access Card (CAC):** A smart card used in military, reserve officer, and military-contractor identity authentication systems
>
> ▶ **Personal Identity Verification (PIV) Card:** A smart card used for federal employees and contractors

Biometrics

The most unique qualities of an individual can be obtained by measuring and identifying his or her unique physical characteristics in "what you are" forms of bio measurement (biometric) authentication such a fingerprints, retinal patterns, iris patterns, blood-vessel patterns, bone structure, and other forms of physiological qualities unique to each person. Other "what you do" values may be measured, such as voice-pattern recognition, movement kinematics, or high-resolution cardiac patterns, but because these might change based on illness or exertion, they suffer high rates of false rejection (valid attempts at authentication that are returned as failures).

New systems are becoming available to allow authentication of users by their body measurements (biometrics), which are compared to values stored within an authorization system's database to provide authentication only if the biometric values match those previously measured. Another alternative is to store biometric data on smart card tokens, which can then be paired with the requisite physical measurement without requiring a centralized database for comparison. Under this scenario, users must be authenticated within a widely distributed scheme where transactions against a central server storing large and complex biometric values might be difficult.

Table 10.1 describes some of the most common biometric methods.

ExamAlert

Biometric devices are susceptible to false acceptance and false rejection rates.

The *false acceptance rate* (FAR) is a measure of the likelihood that the access system will wrongly accept an access attempt—in other words, allow access to an unauthorized user.

The *false rejection rate* (FRR) is the percentage of identification instances in which false rejection occurs. In false rejection, the system fails to recognize an authorized person and rejects that person as unauthorized.

TABLE 10.1   **A Comparison of Common Biometric Measures**

Method	Process	Issues
Fingerprint	Scans and identifies the swirls and loops of a fingerprint.	Injury, scars, or loss of a finger might create false rejection results. Unless paired with other measures, pattern alone can be easily counterfeited.
Hand/palm Geometry	Measures the length and width of a hand's profile, including hand and bone measures.	Loss of fingers or significant injury might create false rejection results.
Voiceprint	Measures the tonal and pacing patterns of a spoken phrase or passage.	Allergies, illnesses, and exhaustion can distort vocal patterns and create false rejection results.
Facial Recognition	Identifies and measures facial characteristics including eye spacing, bone patterns, chin shape, and forehead size and shape.	Subject to false rejection results if the scanner is not aligned precisely with the scanned face.

TABLE 10.1 **Continued**

Method	Process	Issues
Iris	Scans and identifies the unique patterns in the colored part of the eye that surrounds the pupil.	Lighting conditions, alcohol, and medications can affect the pupil's dilation and present false rejections.
Retina	Scans and identifies the unique blood-vessel and tissue patterns at the back of the eye.	Illness or inaccurate placement of the eye against the scanner's cuff can result in false rejection results.
Blood Vessels	Identifies and measures unique patterns of blood vessels in the hand or face.	Environmental conditions, clothing, and some illnesses can render false rejection results due to measurement inaccuracies.
Signature	Records and measures the speed, shape, and kinematics of a signature provided to an electronic pad.	Variations in personal signature due to attitude, environment, injury, alcohol, or medication might render false rejection results.
Gait	Records and measures the unique patterns of weight shift and leg kinematics during walking.	Variations in gait due to attitude, environment, injury, alcohol, or medication might render false rejection results.

> **ExamAlert**
>
> The exam might include questions regarding the various biometric methods, so be sure you are familiar with each of the descriptions in Table 10.1. Remember that combinations of biometric solutions, such as readers for both hand geometry and blood vessel patterns, remain a single-factor "what you are" authentication solution unless also paired with something else, such as a "what you have" key card.

Certificates

One of the most rigorous forms of authentication involves the use of digital certificates within a public key infrastructure (PKI) to establish encrypted communication streams through unsecured networks. These are not physical papers; they consist of a block of digital information that can be presented to the authentication system automatically from a stored set of credentials or manually through a smart card or token.

Public key systems use an asymmetric cryptographic process in which the encryption and decryption keys are not the same as in a symmetric cryptographic process like that used in Kerberos authentication. More detail on cryptographic systems is presented in Chapter 12, "Cryptography Tools and Techniques."

In public key encryption, public and private keys are generated by a certificate authority (CA), and these keys are returned to the client in the form of digital certificates. The public key is given to those who need to encrypt data and send it to the client. The client then decrypts the data using its private key that only the client has. The public key is used to encrypt a message, and the private key is used to decrypt the results.

This process is depicted in Figure 10.1 where Sally encrypts a message to Bill using Bill's public key. Bill then unencrypts the original message using his private key.

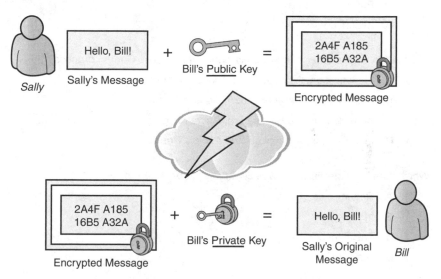

FIGURE 10.1 **Public-key encrypted data transfer from Sally to Bill.**

A registration authority (RA) provides authentication to the CA of the validity of a client's certificate request. One of the most commonly used certification and registration authorities is VeriSign, a vendor specializing in the issuance of X.509 certificates for secure website connections.

Cram Quiz

Answer these questions. The answers follow the last question. If you cannot answer these questions correctly, consider reading this section again until you can.

1. If you have a smart card that contains details of your iris coloring and retinal patterns, which two types of authentication would be involved in a successful access request?

   ○ **A.** What you have and what you do

   ○ **B.** What you do and what you are

   ○ **C.** What you are and what you know

   ○ **D.** What you have and what you are

2. Which type of "what you have" factor is employed by U.S. federal governmental employees and contractors under HSPD 12?

   ○ **A.** Smart card

   ○ **B.** CAC

   ○ **C.** PIV

   ○ **D.** SecurID

3. What is the proper order of operations during the Access Control process?

   ○ **A.** Identification, Authorization, Access Control

   ○ **B.** Authentication, Authorization, Access Control

   ○ **C.** Authorization, Authentication, Accounting

   ○ **D.** Identification, Authentication, Access Control

4. Which biometric measure involves scanning the back of the eye?

   ○ **A.** Retina

   ○ **B.** Iris

   ○ **C.** Facial recognition

   ○ **D.** Signature

Cram Quiz Answers

1. **D**. The smart card is an example of "what you have," and the biometric measures are an example of "what you are." Answer A is incorrect because there are no biometrics relating to "what you do," only simple measurements of bodily configuration. Answer B is incorrect for the same reason—there is no "what you do" metric present. Answer C is incorrect because no PIN or password is employed as a "what you know" factor.

2. **C**. The Personal Identity Verification (PIV) card is used by U.S. federal employees and contractors under HSPD 12. Answer A is incorrect because A, B, and C are all smart card variations but only C is specifically used for federal employees and contractors under HSPD 12. Answer B is incorrect because the Common Access Card (CAC) is used by U.S. military, military reserve, and military contractors. Answer D is incorrect because the RSA SecurID is an example of a time-shifting key token.

3. **B**. The correct order of operations is the authentication of provided credentials or keys, followed by authorization of the presented credentials and finally the application of access controls. Answer A is incorrect because identification involves only the presentation of credentials and not the requirement for verifying those credentials as valid. Answer C is incorrect because the accounting of access is a function of the authentication and authorization service rather than a required operation. Answer D is incorrect because identification is included along with authentication and authorization is missing.

4. **A**. Retinal biometric identification involves the scanning and identification of blood vessels and tissues in the back of the eye. Answer B is incorrect because iris biometric systems analyze only the external colored part of the eye around the pupil. Answer C is incorrect because facial recognition systems measure the overall proportions of facial features and bones. Answer D is incorrect because signature biometric analysis involves the motions and patterns of a written signature rather than those of the back of the eye.

Authorization

- ▶ **RADIUS**
- ▶ **TACACS**
- ▶ **TACACS+**

- ▶ **Kerberos**
- ▶ **LDAP**
- ▶ **XTACACS**

CramSaver

If you can correctly answer these questions before going through this section, save time by skimming the Exam Alerts in this section and then completing the Cram Quiz at the end of the section.

1. Which authentication protocol provides protection against man-in-the-middle data interception attacks?

2. Which of the following protocols provides accounting of access requests and is an open standard: TACACS, TACACS+, or Extended TACACS?

3. Which type of authentication is named for the three-headed dog that guarded the gates to Hades?

Answers

1. The Kerberos protocol supports mutual authentication between two systems, protecting against man-in-the-middle forms of data interception or manipulation by ensuring that both network endpoints are authenticated to one another.

2. The TACACS+ protocol is a replacement for the legacy variations of the TACACS protocol and is not backward compatible. Like RADIUS, the TACACS+ protocol adds accounting of access requests to the authentication and authorization functions of legacy TACACS solutions. TACACS+ is an open standard just as its predecessor, TACACS, whereas XTACACS is a proprietary version created by Cisco.

3. The Kerberos authentication protocol was named for the three-headed dog, Cerberos, that guarded the gates of Hades. It is so-named due to the three-phase process of mutual authentication it uses.

Anonymous Authorization

After authentication of presented access credentials has been accomplished, authorization for access can be performed by testing the authenticated credentials against a database of authorized accounts. In an Anonymous access request such as that to a public website, the authorization process is automatically handled in the background using a predefined service account with specific access rights to information on the server.

Authorization Services

This section presents several services that support authorization you should be familiar with for the exam.

RADIUS

The *Remote Authentication Dial-In User Service (RADIUS)* remote-access control system provides authentication and access control within an enterprise network using UDP transport to a central network access server, which in turn provides credentials for access to resources within the extended enterprise. Developed originally for use in dial-up connectivity over telephonic modems, you might still find RADIUS servers in larger enterprises where logons must span resources located in multiple logon realms.

A protected network segment might implement a virtual private network (VPN) or remote access server (RAS) gateway connection to allow an authenticated external service request to reach a protected server by communicating with a RADIUS server. The requesting account must provide its credentials to the RADIUS server, which then authorizes the access request.

> **ExamAlert**
>
> The RADIUS service provides authentication and authorization functions in addition to network access accounting functions but does not provide further access control.

The RADIUS service is able to forward authentication and authorization requests between authentication domains (called Realms) and so can facilitate cross-enterprise authentication, often as part of a single-sign-on (SSO) solution.

Kerberos

The most basic aspects of authentication within a completely isolated network include only the need to determine the identity of an account (without the third access control subprocess). If a network is physically or logically accessible to external parties that might seek to sniff (capture and examine) data being transacted between systems, the problem arises as to how to keep the authentication keys themselves safe.

Here is an example: A basic File Transfer Protocol (FTP) access session involves the client sending a logon identifier and a password to the FTP server, which accepts or rejects this access. The logon account and password, by default in the FTP protocol, are sent in plain-text form and so are readable by any agent with access to the data as it is transmitted from the client to the server. An unauthorized party, pretending to be the authorized user, might use this information later to gain access to the server.

To avoid sending the open plain-text logon information across an unsecured network, one solution is the symmetric-key authentication protocol known as Kerberos (created by the Athena project at MIT and named for the three-headed dog that guarded Hades). A symmetric key means that both the client and server must agree to use a single key in both the encryption and decryption processes.

> **ExamAlert**
>
> Kerberos is primarily a UDP protocol, although it falls back to TCP for large Kerberos tickets. Kerberos clients send UDP and TCP packets on port 88 and receive replies from the Kerberos servers. Port 88 is the standard port for Kerberos 5. You might also see references to ports 749 and 750 used by earlier versions of Kerberos.

In Kerberos authentication, a client sends its authentication details not to the target server, but rather to a key distribution center (KDC), as follows:

1. The client first contacts a certification authority (CA).

2. The CA creates a time-stamped session key with a limited duration (by default, eight hours) using the client's key and a randomly generated key that includes the identification of the target service.

3. This information is sent back to the client in the form of a ticket-granting ticket (TGT).

4. The client then submits the TGT to a ticket-granting server (TGS).

5. This server then generates a time-stamped key encrypted with the service's key and returns both to the client.

6. The client then uses its key to decrypt its ticket, contacts the server, and offers the encrypted ticket to the service.

7. The service uses its key to decrypt the ticket and verify that the time stamps match and the ticket remains valid.

8. The service contacts the KDC and receives a time-stamped session keyed ticket that it returns to the client.

9. The client then decrypts the keyed ticket using its key. When both agree that the other is the proper account and that the keys are within their valid lifetime, communication is initiated.

> **Exam**Alert
>
> The short lifespan of a ticket ensures that if someone attempts to intercept the encrypted data to try to break its keys, the key will have changed before he or she can reasonably be able to break the key using cryptographic algorithms. The hand-shaking between the client and the KDC and between the service and the KDC provides verification that the current session is valid, without requiring the transmission of logons or passwords between client and service directly.

Kerberos 5 includes support for a process known as mutual authentication, in which both client and server verify that the computer with which they are communicating is the proper system. This process helps to prevent man-in-the-middle attacks, in which an unauthorized party intercepts communications between two systems and pretends to be each to the other, passing some data intact, modifying other data, or inserting entirely new sets of values to accomplish desired tasks.

In mutual authentication, one system creates a challenge code based on a random number and then sends this code to the other system. The receiving system generates a response code using the original challenge code and creates a challenge code of its own, sending both back to the originating system. The originating system verifies the response code as a value and returns its own response code to the second system, generated from the challenge code returned with the first response code. After the second system has verified its returned response code, it notifies the originating system, and both systems consider themselves mutually authenticated.

The strength of Kerberos authentication comes from its time-synchronized connections and the use of registered client and service keys within the KDC. These also create some drawbacks, such as the need to use a standard synchronized time base for all systems involved. Difficulties arise if the KDC is unavailable or the cached client and service credentials were accessed directly from the granting servers. An important advantage of time-stamped credentials is that they help prevent spoofing and replay attacks.

LDAP

The Lightweight Directory Access Protocol (LDAP) provides access to directory services, including those used by the Microsoft Active Directory. LDAP was created as a "lightweight" alternative to earlier implementations of the X.500 Directory Access Protocol and communicates on port 389. Its widespread use influences many other directory systems, including the Directory Service Markup Language (DSML), Service Location Protocol (SLP), and Microsoft Active Directory.

Variations of LDAP share many common vulnerabilities, including the following:

▶ Buffer overflow vulnerabilities may be used to enact arbitrary commands on the LDAP server.

▶ Format string vulnerabilities might result in unauthorized access to enact commands on the LDAP server or impair its normal operation.

▶ Improperly formatted requests may be used to create an effective denial-of-service (DoS) attack against the LDAP server, preventing it from responding to normal requests.

LDAP uses an object-oriented access model defined by the Directory Enabled Networking (DEN) standard, which is based on the Common Information Model (CIM) standard.

TACACS

The *Terminal Access Controller Access Control System (TACACS)* remote-access control system provides authentication and authorization primarily in UNIX networks, where a client service could accept a logon and password from an access requester, forward those credentials to the TACACS server, and receive a response approving the credentials. The original TACACS protocol used either TCP or UDP connectivity over port 49.

Two other variations of this protocol have since been introduced.

XTACACS

A proprietary version of the original TACACS protocol was developed by Cisco and is called the Extended Terminal Access Controller Access Control System (XTACACS) protocol. This protocol extended the original TACACS by adding support for accounting and auditing but has since been displaced by the TACACS+ and RADIUS protocols.

TACACS+

The Extended Terminal Access Controller Access Control System Plus (TACACS+) is a new variation that is not backward-compatible with the legacy TACACS standard. Like RADIUS, the TACACS+ protocol provides authentication and authorization as well as accounting of access requests against a centralized service for authorization of access requests. TACACS+ is similar to RADIUS but uses TCP instead of RADIUS's UDP transport.

IEEE 802.1x

The IEEE 802.1x standard for wireless, port-based access control can be used to provide authentication and authorization but is often paired with a RADIUS or TACACS+ service to facilitate enterprise-wide access management and accounting. Because of the open radio broadcast nature of wireless connectivity, additional transport encryption protocols such as WPA/WPA2 should be used in conjunction with 802.1x authentication to secure communications between the mobile device and the wireless access point (WAP) connected to the secured network. Internet Protocol Security (IPsec) is another common protocol used in conjunction with IEEE 802.1x to provide this functionality.

Cram Quiz

Answer these questions. The answers follow the last question. If you cannot answer these questions correctly, consider reading this section again until you can.

1. Which of the following is not a part of the Kerberos authentication process?

   ○ **A.** Keys must be time-synchronized.

   ○ **B.** The CA creates a session key.

   ○ **C.** The server receives a ticket using port 389.

   ○ **D.** The client receives a ticket using port 749.

2. Which of the following services are used to provide authentication, authorization, and accounting of access requests? (Select all answers that apply.)

   ○ **A.** TACACS+

   ○ **B.** TACACS

   ○ **C.** IEEE 802.1x

   ○ **D.** RADIUS

3. Which of the following services provides the capability of endpoint validation for both client and server?

   ○ **A.** LDAP

   ○ **B.** Kerberos

   ○ **C.** RADIUS

   ○ **D.** XTACACS

4. In a default FTP session, the logon and password can be viewed by direct
inspection of the transferred data. This is an example of _____.

○ **A.** A weak password

○ **B.** Plain-text transport

○ **C.** A wrapper

○ **D.** A man-in-the-middle attack

1. **C**. The server receives communications using ports 88, 749, or 750. Port 389 is
used by the LDAP authentication protocol, not Kerberos. Answers A, B, and D
are all valid statements. The CA creates a time-stamped session key, which
requires synchronization between the time bases of all systems involved and
then returns that key to the client using port 88 or ports 749/750 in older versions of Kerberos.

2. **A** and **D**. Both the RADIUS and TACACS+ services provide authentication,
authorization, and accounting functions. Answer B is incorrect because the outdated version of the TACACS does not support access accounting. Answer C is
incorrect because the IEEE 802.1x specification only provides for authentication
and authorization within wireless networking solutions, and it relies on services
such as RADIUS for accounting and other functions.

3. **B**. Kerberos allows for mutual authentication of connected endpoint systems.
This is useful in guarding against man-in-the-middle attacks. Answers A, C, and
D are all incorrect because the LDAP, RADIUS, and Extended TACACS services
lack support for mutual authentication.

4. **B**. The File Transfer Protocol (FTP) accepts logon information openly using plain-
text transport unless secured through alternative authentication or transport
encryption mechanisms. Answer A is incorrect because a weak password represents one that is easily broken using cryptographic means. Answer C is incorrect
because a wrapper is a programmatic proxy service that is used in SOA environments to isolate a non-standard or weak authentication system from the extended
enterprise by presenting a standard interface and hiding access details "behind
the scenes." Answer D is incorrect because the act of accessing transmitted data
packets is referred to as sniffing, whereas a man-in-the-middle attack involves
inserting a third system between two others so that it can pass along, inspect,
modify, or exclude data during transport between the compromised end systems.

What Next?

If you want more practice on this chapter's exam objectives before you move
on, remember that you can access all of the Cram Quiz questions on the CD.
You can also create a custom exam by objective with the practice exam software. Note any objective you struggle with and go to that objective material
in this chapter.

CHAPTER 11

Access Control and Account Management

This chapter covers the following official CompTIA Security+, SY0-301 exam objectives:

▶ Explain the fundamental concepts and best practices related to access control

▶ Implement appropriate security controls when performing account management

(For more information on the official CompTIA Security+, SY0-301 exam topics, see the "About the CompTIA Security+ Certification Exam" section in the Introduction.)

In order to protect against unauthorized access or modification and to ensure availability for legitimate access requests, you must put a mechanism into place that allows the identification of an authorized request. This overall process is called *access control*.

The previous chapter covered the fundamental concepts related to authentication and authorization. This chapter focuses on the third access control sub-process and best practices for account management.

Explain the Fundamental Concepts and Best Practices Related to Access Control

▶ Least privilege

▶ Separation of duties

▶ ACLs

▶ Access control

▶ Mandatory access control

▶ Discretionary access control

▶ Role/rule-based access control

▶ Implicit deny

▶ Time of day restrictions

▶ Trusted OS

▶ Mandatory vacations

▶ Job rotation

CramSaver

If you can correctly answer these questions before going through this section, save time by skimming the Exam Alerts in this section and then completing the Cram Quiz at the end of the section.

1. What are the three basic forms of access control?

2. What is the mechanism that determines account access rights over a service or resource?

3. Which TCSEC division of access includes all others?

Answers

1. The three basic forms of access control include mandatory access control (MAC), discretionary access control (DAC), and role-based access control (RBAC).

2. The access control list (ACL) includes the underlying data associated with a network resource that defines its related access permissions.

3. The A (Verified) class of access control encompasses all of the other specified classes (B through D).

Access Control Forms

This section examines the methods for controlling access to network resources. Planning for access control might affect the methods used in the authentication process you read about in the previous chapter. For example, if there is a need only for anonymous access to a public read-only HTML document, the simple access control mandates eliminate the need for a complex authentication process.

Access control generally refers to the process of making resources available to accounts that should have access, while limiting that access to only what is required. The forms of access control you need to know include the following:

- ▶ Mandatory access control (MAC)

- ▶ Discretionary access control (DAC)

- ▶ Role-based access control (RBAC)

These types of access control and access control best practices are covered in the following sections. These methods and best practices are based on security criteria set by various efforts. Trusted Computer System Evaluation (TCSEC) and Information Technology Security Evaluation Criteria (ITSEC) are major security criteria efforts. The Common Criteria is based on both TCSEC and ITSEC.

Exam**Alert**

The Trusted Computer System Evaluation Criteria (TCSEC) specification used by many government networks explicitly specifies only the MAC and DAC forms of access control. Because of the color of the original printed manual's cover (DoD 5200.28-STD), the TCSEC is sometimes referred to as the orange book. The TCSEC is the first book in the DoD-published Rainbow series of security criteria, released in 1983. The TCSEC specification identifies levels of security based on the minimum level of access control used in a network environment. The four divisions of access control are the following:

- ▶ A – Verified
- ▶ B – Mandatory
- ▶ C – Discretionary
- ▶ D – Minimal

Category A is the highest level, essentially encompassing all elements of Category B, in addition to formal design and verification techniques.

You should be aware that individual categories are subdivided based on the complexity of implementation. For example, Category C (Discretionary Access Control) contrasts between basic separation of user data and controlling access to resources (C1 – Discretionary Security Protection) from environments using data segmentation, authenticated logons, and logged access audit controls (C2 – Controlled Access Protection).

The designation RBAC is sometimes used to refer to *Rule-Based Access Control* as well as *Role-Based Access Control*.

▶ **Rule-Based** access control includes controls such as those based on time of day, day of the week, specific terminal access, GPS coordinates of the requester, and other factors that might overlay a legitimate account's access request.

▶ **Role-Based** access control is a process by which specific allow/denial rules are assigned to a role and the role is then associated with groups or individuals that inherit its constraints. This process allows changes to be made to the role to automatically encompass all individuals or groups associated with that role.

Mandatory Access Control

The most basic form of access control involves the assignment of labels to resources and accounts (examples include SENSITIVE, SECRET, and PUBLIC). If the labels on the account and resource do not match, the resource remains unavailable in a nondiscretionary manner. This type of access control is called *mandatory access control* (MAC, also referred to as *multilevel access control*) and is often used within governmental systems where resources and access may be granted based on categorical assignment such as classified, secret, or top secret. Mandatory access control applies to all resources within the network and does not allow users to extend access rights by proxy.

> **ExamAlert**
>
> Note that in the Security+ exam the acronym MAC can refer both to mandatory access control and to the Media Access Control sublayer of the data link layer in the OSI model. When the question involves access control, MAC applies to mandatory controls over access rather than Layer 2 networking.

Discretionary Access Control

A slightly more complex system of access control involves the restriction of access for each resource in a discretionary manner. *Discretionary access control (DAC)* scenarios allow individual resources to be made available or secured from access individually. Access rights are configured at the discretion of accounts with authority over each resource, including the ability to extend administrative rights through the same mechanism. In DAC, a security principal (account) has complete control over the objects that it creates or otherwise owns unless restricted through group or role membership. The owner assigns security levels based on objects and subjects and can make his own data available to others at will.

Role-Based Access Control

In a *Role-Based access control (RBAC)* scenario, access rights are first assigned to roles and accounts are then associated with these roles without direct assignment of resource access rights. This solution provides the greatest level of scalability within large enterprise scenarios, where the explicit granting of rights to each individual account could rapidly overwhelm administrative staff, and the potential for accidental granting of unauthorized permissions increases.

RBAC combines some direct access aspects of mandatory access control and varying discretionary access rights based on role membership. Delegation of administration over rights granted through RBAC is itself managed by specialized administration roles, rather than through ownership or direct control over the individual resources as in strictly DAC solutions.

Exam**Alert**

Remember that the exam may include alternative uses for the RBAC acronym that refers to rule-based access controls. In a rule-based access control solution, access rights can vary by account, by time of day, only from a trusted OS, or through other forms of conditional testing. Exam items dealing with conditional testing for access (for example, time-of-day controls) are examining rule-based access control. Items involving assignment of rights to groups for inheritance by group member accounts are focused on role-based access control.

Access Control Lists

The mechanism for assigning Allow/Deny privileges for a particular account or group of accounts involves assigning those rights to an *Access Control List (ACL)*. In its broadest sense, an ACL is the underlying data associated with a network resource that defines its related access permissions. The most common privileges are Read, Write, Read & Execute, Modify, Full Control, and List Folder Contents. ACLs can apply to routers and other devices as well as to individual data resources and services. For purposes of this discussion, the definition is limited to operating system objects. Every operating system object created has a security attribute that matches it to an ACL. The ACL has an entry for each system user that defines the account's access privileges to that object.

Exam Alert

In Microsoft operating systems, each ACL has one or more access control entries (ACEs). These are descriptors that contain the name of a user, group, or role. The access privileges are stated in a string of bits called an *Access Mask*. Generally, the object owner or the system administrator creates the ACL for an object.

ACLs can be broken down further into discretionary access control lists (DACLs) and system access control lists (SACLs). DACL use and SACL use are specific to Microsoft operating systems and are based on ACEs. A DACL identifies who or what is allowed access to the object. If the object does not have a DACL, everyone is granted full access. If the object's DACL has no ACEs, the system denies all access. An SACL enables administrators to log attempts to access the object. Each ACE specifies the types of access attempts that cause the system to generate a record in the security event log.

Implementation of access management is based on one of two models: *centralized* or *decentralized*. Both the group-based and role-based methods of access control have a centralized database of accounts and roles or groups to which the accounts are assigned. This database is usually maintained on a central server that is contacted by the server providing the resource when a user's ACL must be verified for access.

The drawback to the centralized model is scalability. As the company and network grow, it becomes more and more difficult to keep up with the tasks of assigning and managing network resource access and privileges. Decentralized security management is less secure but more scalable. Responsibilities are delegated, and employees at different locations are made responsible for managing privileges within their administrative areas. For example, in Microsoft Active Directory, this can be managed at the Forest, Domain, or Organizational Unit (OU) level. Decentralized management is considered generally less secure because more people are involved in the process and there is a greater possibility for errors.

Exam Alert

In most access control environments, the EXPLICIT DENY wins even when EXPLICIT ALLOW rights are also assigned. In this way, an account that has been granted access rights directly or inherited from group or role membership is blocked from access due to a DENY assignment to the account or its groups or roles. Watch for any access rights questions in which a DENY may be preventing access even when the account has been granted ALLOW access through other assignments.

Access Control Best Practices

A number of best practices exist when developing an access control plan. You should be familiar with the following:

▶ **Implicit deny:** An access control practice wherein resource availability is restricted to only those logons explicitly granted access, remaining unavailable even when not explicitly denied access. This practice is used commonly in Cisco networks, where most ACLs have a default setting of "implicit deny." This ensures that when access is not explicitly granted, it is automatically denied by default.

▶ **Least privilege:** An access control practice wherein a logon is provided only the bare minimum access to resources required to perform its tasks. Whenever confronted by a solution involving the determination of proper levels of access, remember the phrase "less is more." This is a convenient reminder of the security practice known as the *principle of least privilege*, in which an account is granted no more access rights than the bare minimum needed to perform assigned tasks.

▶ **Separation of duties:** An access control practice involving both the separation of logons, such as a day-to-day regular user account and a separate admin account both assigned to the same network admin, and the separation of roles such as security assignment and compliance audit procedures. Separation of account functionality protects the network by ensuring that an inadvertent malware execution during normal unprivileged daily operations cannot attack the network with full administrative privileges possible under the alternative admin-only logon. Separation of role duties ensures that validation is maintained apart from execution to protect the network against fraudulent actions or incomplete execution of security mandates.

▶ **Expiration:** An access control practice to expire accounts and passwords on a regular basis, protecting against brute-force password guessing attacks, and to expire accounts not used after a certain period of time. Unused accounts often retain weak passwords used in initial assignment and might be more susceptible to password-guessing routines using rainbow tables.

▶ **Job rotation:** As an extension of the separation of duties best practice, rotating administrative users between roles both improves awareness of the mandates of each role while also ensuring that fraudulent activity cannot be sustained. This is also the reason that users with administrative access might be required to take mandatory vacations, allowing other

administrators to review standard operating practices and protocols in
place. This is easily remembered by the Latin phrase *Quis custodiet ipsos
custodies?*, which translates to *Who will guard the guardians themselves?*

ExamAlert

The User Account Control (UAC) technology used by the Microsoft Vista and
Windows 7 operating systems ensures that software applications cannot perform
privileged access without additional authorization from the user. Within the
Microsoft environment, lesser accounts may perform privileged processes using the
"run as" option to specify the explicit use of a privileged account from within the
unprivileged account logon. This is similar to the superuser DO (sudo) shell operation under Linux/Unix operating systems.

Cram Quiz

Answer these questions. The answers follow the last question. If you cannot answer
these questions correctly, consider reading this section again until you can.

1. Which of the following are standard forms of access control? (Select all correct
   answers.)

   ○ **A.** DAC

   ○ **B.** MAC

   ○ **C.** RBAC

   ○ **D.** TCSEC

2. Which of the TCSEC criteria specifies a discretionary access control (DAC)
   environment?

   ○ **A.** Division A

   ○ **B.** Division B

   ○ **C.** Division C

   ○ **D.** Division D

3. Which level of access control will "win" if present?

   ○ **A.** Explicit Allow

   ○ **B.** Explicit Deny

   ○ **C.** Implicit Allow

   ○ **D.** Implicit Deny

4. Which access control best practices reduce the potential for malicious impact through legitimate account use? (Select all correct answers.)

- ○ **A.** Least privilege
- ○ **B.** Separation of duties
- ○ **C.** Expiration
- ○ **D.** Job rotation

Cram Answers

1. **A, B**, and **C.** The three forms of access control you are expected to know are discretionary access control (DAC), mandatory access control (MAC), and role-based access control (RBAC). The Trusted Computer System Evaluation Criteria (TCSEC) specifies the levels of security based on the minimum level of access control used in a government network environment, making answer D incorrect.

2. **C.** The TCSEC C level specifies a DAC environment. Division A refers to a verified mandatory access environment, making answer A incorrect. answer B is incorrect because division B refers to a MAC enterprise. Division D involves only minimal security, so answer D is incorrect as well.

3. **B.** A DENY control explicitly assigned overrides all ALLOW access rights, making Answer A incorrect. Answers C and D are incorrect because implicitly derived access rights, such as default settings, are by default overridden by explicit assignments.

4. **A, B**, and **D.** The principle of least privilege ensures that an account has only the minimum rights necessary, whereas both separation of duties and job rotation ensure that accounts are only used for their expected purpose and that incorrect or inappropriate use is discovered during rotation. Expiration involves identification of accounts, either manually or automatically, that have been left active when no longer legitimately necessary, making answer C incorrect.

Implement Appropriate Security Controls when Performing Account Management

▶ **Mitigate issues associated with users with multiple account/roles**

▶ **Account policy enforcement**

▶ **Group-based privileges**

▶ **User assigned privileges**

Cram**Saver**

If you can correctly answer these questions before going through this section, save time by skimming the Exam Alerts in this section and then completing the Cram Quiz at the end of the section.

1. What is the best model for access rights assignment in a large, distributed enterprise?

2. What is the best type of policy to protect against hackers logging in during evening hours when admins are off-duty?

3. Which type of groups are assigned for non-security-related functions?

Answers

1. The *group-based* model is best for large, complex enterprises because each group can have associated access rights that are inherited by individuals and other groups assigned to that group.

2. Time-of-day access control policies prevent logon during off-peak hours, even when using captured legitimate logon credentials.

3. Distribution groups are used for non-security-related groups such as email distribution lists.

Account Provisioning

The creation of new accounts and assignment of appropriate access control settings is referred to as *account provisioning* and requires extensive attention to detail to ensure the C-I-A security constraints are fulfilled. Later changes in access control settings and eventual account removal or de-provisioning present a potential vulnerability to the enterprise due to outdated, unused accounts left in existence as well as the potential for residual access rights retaining permissions on data resources no longer appropriate to a user's new roles.

Logical controls are important to infrastructure security because development of these controls is part of assessing your environment and protecting it to mitigate threats and risks. Insider threats are very real, and the more access someone has, the bigger the threat he or she can become. Logical access controls are used in addition to physical security controls to limit access to data. This design helps ensure the integrity of information, preserve the confidentiality of data, and maintain the availability of information. In addition, it helps the organization conform to laws, regulations, and standards.

The access level that users are given directly affects the level of network protection you have. Even though it might sound strange that the network should be protected from its own users, the internal user has the greatest access to data and the opportunity to either deliberately sabotage it or accidentally delete it.

Security Groups and Roles with Appropriate Rights and Privileges

When dealing with user access, a fine line often exists between sufficient access to get the job done and too much access. In this section, you examine how to manage user access by using groups and group policies. Keep the "least privilege" best practice in mind when comparing access control options.

A user account holds information about the specific user. It can contain basic information such as name, password, and the level of permission the user has in her associated ACLs. It can also contain more specific information, such as the department the user works in, a home phone number, and the days and hours the user is allowed to log on to specific workstations. Groups are created to make the sharing of resources more manageable. A group contains users who share a common need for access to a particular resource; it can be nested in other groups in turn to better aggregate access permissions for multiple roles. Even though the connotations might differ with each operating system, all of these terms still refer to the access that a user or group account is granted or specifically denied.

When working with logical controls, there are two models for assignment of permissions and rights: *user-based* and *group-based*:

▶ **User-Based:** Within a user-based model, permissions are uniquely assigned to each account. One example of this is a peer-to-peer network or a workgroup where access is granted based on individual needs. This access type is also found in government and military situations and in private companies where patented processes and trademark products require protection. User-based privilege management is usually used for specific parts of the network or specific resources. This type of policy is time-consuming and difficult for administrators to handle, plus it does not work well in large environments.

▶ **Group-Based:** Access control over large numbers of user accounts can be more easily accomplished by managing the access permissions on each group, which are then inherited by the group's members. In this type of access, permissions are assigned to groups, and user accounts become members of the groups. Each user account has access based on the combined permissions inherited from its group memberships. These groups often reflect divisions or departments of the company, such as human resources, sales, development, and management. In enterprise networks, groups may also be nested. Group nesting can simplify permission assignment if you know how to use it, or it can complicate troubleshooting when you don't know what was set up or why.

You will find that making groups and assigning users to these groups will make the administration process much easier.

> **ExamAlert**
>
> In Windows environments, Active Directory Services provides flexibility by allowing two types of groups: security groups and distribution groups.
>
> ▶ **Security groups** are used to assign rights and permissions to groups for resource access.
>
> ▶ **Distribution groups** are assigned to a user list for applications or non-security-related functions, such as an email distribution list that functions like a listserv in the Linux/Unix environment.

Default Settings

Certain groups are installed by default. As an administrator, you should know what these groups are and know which accounts are installed by default. In dealing with individual accounts, the administrative account should be used only for the purpose of administering the server. Granting users this type of access is a disaster waiting to happen. An individual using the administrative account can put a company's entire business in jeopardy. By knowing which accounts are installed by default, you can determine which are really needed and which can be disabled, thereby making the system more secure. You should also know which accounts, if any, are installed with blank passwords.

The security settings in many of the newer operating systems do not allow blank passwords. However, there might still be accounts in older operating systems that have a blank password or a well-known default like the *Scott/Tiger* logon in Oracle databases. User rights are applied to security groups to determine what members of that group can do within the scope of a domain or forest. The assignment of user rights is through security options that apply to user accounts.

Although user rights can apply to individual user accounts, they are best administered by using group accounts. The user rights assignment is twofold: It can grant specific *privileges* and it can grant *log-on rights* to users and groups in your computing environment.

> ▶ **Log-on** rights control who and how users log on to the computer, such as the right to log on to a system locally.

> ▶ **Privileges** allow users to perform system tasks, such as the right to back up files and directories.

When working with groups, remember a few key items: No matter what OS you are working with, if you are giving a user FULL access in one group and DENY access in another group, the result is DENY access. However, group permissions are cumulative, so if a user belongs to two groups and one has more liberal access, the user will have the most liberal access, except where the DENY access permission is involved. If a user has difficulty accessing information after he or she has been added to a new group, the first item you might want to check for is conflicting permissions.

Exam**Alert**

When assigning user permissions, if the groups the user is assigned to have liberal access and another group has no access, the result is no access.

Password Policies

Because passwords are one of the best methods of gaining successful access to services and resources, password length, duration, history, and complexity requirements are all important to the security of the network. When setting up user accounts, you should take into account proper planning and policies. Passwords are one of the first pieces of information entered by a user.

Consider the following suggested minimum standards when developing password policies for the exam:

> ▶ Make the password length at least eight characters and require the use of combinations of uppercase and lowercase letters, numbers, and special characters.

> ▶ Lock user accounts out after three to five failed logon attempts. This policy stops programs from deciphering the passwords on locked accounts by repeated brute-force attempts.

▶ Require users to change passwords every 90–180 days, depending on how secure the environment needs to be. Remember that the more frequently users are required to change passwords, the greater the chance that they will write them down.

▶ Configure the server to not allow users to use the same password over and over again. Certain operating systems have settings that do not allow users to reuse a password for a certain length of time or number of password changes.

▶ Never store passwords in an unsecure location or using a reversible form of encryption. Sometimes a company might want a list of server administrative passwords. This list might end up in the wrong hands if not properly secured along with the disaster recovery documentation.

▶ Upon logon, show a logon banner statement to the effect that network access is granted under certain conditions and that all activities might be monitored. This way you can be sure that any legal ramifications are covered and users can be expected to follow security policy protocols.

If you are using Windows servers on your network, you most likely have domains. Domains have their own password policy in addition to the local password policy. These are two different policies, and you need to understand the difference between them. Domain password policies control the complexity and lifetime settings for passwords so that they become more complex and secure. This reduces the likeliness of a successful password attack. Local password policies apply only to local accounts on a system, limiting the effect of compromise to that system alone as long as the same credentials are not used across multiple systems.

ExamAlert

Password policies help secure the network and define the responsibilities of users who have been given access to company resources. You should have all users read and sign security policies as part of their employment process. Domain password policies affect all users in the domain. The effectiveness of these policies depends on how and where they are applied. The three areas that can be configured are password, account lockout, and Kerberos policies. When configuring these settings, keep in mind that you can have only one domain account policy prior to Windows Server 2008.

You can use the account lockout policy to secure the system against attacks by disabling the account after a certain number of attempts, for a certain period of time. Use the Kerberos policy settings for authentication services. In most environments, the default settings should suffice. If you do need to change them, remember that they are applied at the domain level.

Time-of-Day Restrictions and Account Expiration

Besides password restrictions, you can restrict logon hours in many operating systems. By default, all domain users can log on at any time. Many times, it is necessary to restrict logon hours for maintenance purposes. For example, at 11:00 p.m. each evening, the backup is run; therefore, you might want to be sure that everyone is off of the system. Or if databases get re-indexed on a nightly basis, you might have to confirm that no one is changing information or locking records during the re-indexing process.

This is also a good way to be sure that a hacker isn't logging on with stolen passwords during off-peak hours. You can restrict logon hours by days of the week, hours of the day, or both. You can also assign time-of-day restrictions to ensure that employees use computers only during specified hours. This setting is useful for organizations where users require supervision, where security certification requires it, or where employees are mainly temporary or shift workers.

Exam**Alert**

Each OS is different, so the effect of the restrictions differs if the user is currently logged on when the restriction time begins. In a Microsoft environment, whether users are forced to log off when their logon hours expire is determined by the Automatically Log Off Users setting. In other environments, the user might be allowed to stay logged on, but once logged off, the user cannot log back on. The logon schedule is enforced by the Kerberos Group Policy setting Enforce User Logon Restrictions, which is enabled by default in Windows 2003 and later Active Directory environments (including Windows 7 and Windows Server 2008/2008 R2).

The account expires attribute specifies when an account expires. You can use this setting under the same conditions as mentioned previously for the time-of-day restrictions. Temporary or contract workers should have user accounts that are valid only for a certain amount of time. This way, when the account expires it can no longer be used to log on to any service. Statistics show that a large number of temporary accounts are never disabled. Limiting the time an account is active for such employees should be part of the policies and procedures. In addition, user accounts should be audited on a regular basis for de-provisioning or re-provisioning based on role change.

Cram Quiz

Answer these questions. The answers follow the last question. If you cannot answer
these questions correctly, consider reading this section again until you can.

1. Which of the following attributes can be associated with a user account object?
   (Select all correct answers.)

   ○ **A.** Name

   ○ **B.** Password

   ○ **C.** ACLs

   ○ **D.** Authorized hours

2. Which type of password policy will protect against reuse of the same password
   over and over again?

   ○ **A.** Account lock-out

   ○ **B.** Password complexity

   ○ **C.** Expiration

   ○ **D.** Password history

3. A user calls the help desk saying that she changed her password yesterday, did
   not get any email on her mobile phone last night, and cannot log on this morning. Which password policy is most likely at fault for her difficulties?

   ○ **A.** Account lock-out

   ○ **B.** Password complexity

   ○ **C.** Expiration

   ○ **D.** Password history

4. The Programmers group is assigned WRITE-TO and MODIFY permissions to a
   specific file share using domain accounts, whereas the Testers group is given
   only READ and EXECUTE permissions and the Anonymous group is given the
   DENY ALL permission. All Programmers are also Testers. If Sally is made a
   member of the Programmers group, which permissions would Sally have regarding the file share?

   ○ **A.** DENY ALL

   ○ **B.** READ and EXECUTE

   ○ **C.** WRITE-TO and MODIFY

   ○ **D.** READ, WRITE-TO, MODIFY, and EXECUTE

Cram Answers

1. **A, B, C,** and **D.** The user account object can be associated with identifiers and security settings such as name, address, password, phone numbers, department, ACLs, time of day authorizations, and other similar details.

2. **D.** The password history policy prevents reuse of the same passwords over and over again. Account lock-out deactivates an account after a number of failed access attempts, making answer A incorrect. Answer B is incorrect because password complexity is a policy that determines how many types of characters must be used to create a strong password (lower- and uppercase letters, numbers, and symbols being the four general types of characters possible on a standard keyboard). Account expiration policies ensure that unused or no-longer-used accounts are properly disabled, making answer C incorrect.

3. **A.** If the user failed to also change her password on her phone, its repeated attempts to access email during the night would have triggered the account lock-out protections and temporarily disabled her account. Password complexity and history would not lock out her account after successfully changing it, making answers B and D incorrect. Answer C is incorrect because, although account expiration is possible, it is unlikely without specifying this was near the end of her employment.

4. **D.** Sally would inherit the WRITE-TO and MODIFY permissions from her direct assignment to the Programmers group and the READ and EXECUTE permissions from the Testers group through the Programmers group being a member of Testers. Answer A is incorrect because the file share requires domain logons, so the Anonymous group is not involved. Answer B is incorrect because it includes only the permissions granted through inheritance from the Testers group, and answer C is similarly incorrect because it includes only those permissions directly inherited from the Programmers group and fails to include the permissions inherited by the Programmers group in turn from the Testers group.

What Next?

If you want more practice on this chapter's exam objectives before you move on, remember that you can access all of the Cram Quiz questions on the CD. You can also create a custom exam by objective with the practice exam software. Note any objective you struggle with and go to that objective material in this chapter.

CHAPTER 12

Cryptography Tools and Techniques

This chapter covers the following official CompTIA Security+ Certification exam objectives

▶ Summarize general cryptography concepts

▶ Use and apply appropriate cryptographic tools and products

(For more information on the official CompTIA Security+ Certification exam topics, see the "About the CompTIA Security+ Certification Exam" section in the Introduction.)

A cryptosystem or cipher system provides a method for protecting information by disguising (encrypting) it into a format that can be read only by authorized systems or individuals. The use and creation of such systems is called *cryptography*, which is often considered to be both an art and a science.

Cryptography dates back to the ancient Assyrians and Egyptians. In the beginning, the systems of cryptography were manually performed, but during the twentieth century, machine and mechanical cryptography was born. The cryptography that is the focus of this chapter and the exam is modern cryptography, which began with the advent of the computer.

Recently, modern cryptography has become increasingly important and ubiquitous. There has been increasing concern about the security of data, which continues to rapidly grow across information systems and traverse and reside in many different locations. This, combined with more sophisticated attacks and a growing economy around computer-related fraud and data theft, makes the need to protect the data itself even more important than in the past.

One practical way to secure this data is to use cryptography in the form of encryption algorithms applied to data that is passed around networks and to data at rest.

Note

As related to cryptography, an *algorithm* is the mathematical procedure or sequence of steps taken to perform the encryption and decryption. Practically speaking, however, you can think of an algorithm as a cooking recipe, which provides the ingredients needed and step-by-step instructions.

This chapter discusses the concepts of cryptography and many popular encryption methods and their applications. In addition to being able to explain these fundamental cryptography concepts, you will begin to understand how cryptography can be used as a tool to protect and authenticate all types of information and to protect the computers and networks in information security systems.

Summarize General Cryptography Concepts

▶ Symmetric versus asymmetric

▶ Fundamental differences and encryption methods

▶ Transport encryption

▶ Non-repudiation

▶ Hashing

▶ Key escrow

▶ Steganography

▶ Digital signatures

▶ Use of proven technologies

▶ Elliptic curve and quantum cryptography

CramSaver

If you can correctly answer these questions before going through this section, save time by skimming the Exam Alerts in this section and then completing the Cram Quiz at the end of the section.

1. What are the differences between symmetric and asymmetric cryptography?

2. What is the fundamental difference between a block cipher and a stream cipher?

Answers

1. Symmetric cryptography uses a shared key, and asymmetric uses different mathematically related keys. Symmetric key cryptography is more efficient, yet asymmetric cryptography helps overcome the challenges associated with key management and key distribution.

2. Block ciphers operate upon a fixed-length group of bits, which are called blocks. The resulting cipher text corresponds to the input length. Stream ciphers are more efficient and plain-text bits are encrypted one at a time.

Symmetric versus Asymmetric

Symmetric key cryptography is a system that uses a common shared key between the sender and receiver. The primary advantage to such a system is it is easier to implement than an asymmetric system and is typically faster. However, the two parties must first somehow exchange the key securely. Assume, for example, you have a friend located thousands of miles away from you, and to exchange secured messages you send messages back and forth in a secured lockbox; you both have a copy of the key to the lockbox. Although this works, how did you securely deliver the key to your friend? Somehow the key must have be communicated or delivered to your friend, which introduces additional challenges around logistics and ensuring that the key was not compromised in the process. Asymmetric cryptography helps overcome these challenges.

Now imagine a system in which more than two parties are involved. In this scenario, every party participating in communications must have the exact same key to compare the information. If the key is compromised at any point, it is impossible to guarantee that a secure connection has commenced.

> **Note**
>
> Symmetric key algorithms are often referred to as *secret key algorithms*, *private key algorithms*, and *shared secret algorithms*.

Even given the possible risks involved with symmetric key encryption, the method is used often today mainly because of its simplicity and easy deployment. In addition, it is generally considered a strong encryption method as long as the source and destination that house the key information are kept secure.

> **ExamAlert**
>
> A symmetric key is a single cryptographic key used with a secret key (symmetric) algorithm. The symmetric key algorithm uses the same private key for both operations of encryption and decryption.

The asymmetric encryption algorithm has two keys: a public key and a private key. The public key is made available to whoever is going to encrypt the data sent to the holder of the private key. The private key is maintained on the host system or application. Often, the public encryption key is made available in a number of fashions, such as email or centralized servers that host a pseudo address book of published public encryption keys. One of the challenges, however, is ensuring authenticity of the public key. To address this, a public key infrastructure (PKI) is often used. A PKI uses trusted third parties that certify or provide proof of key ownership. PKI is discussed in greater detail in Chapter 13, "Public Key Infrastructure." Figure 12.1 illustrates the asymmetric encryption process.

FIGURE 12.1   An example of asymmetric encryption.

Asymmetric algorithms are often referred to as public key algorithms because of their use of the public key as the focal point for the algorithm.

As an example of asymmetric encryption, think about the secure exchange of an email. When someone wants to send a secure email to someone else, he or she obtains the target user's public encryption key and encrypts the message using this key. Because the message can be unencrypted only with the private key, only the target user can read the information held within. Ideally, for this system to work well, everyone should have access to everyone else's public keys.

Imagine a postal mailbox that enables the letter carrier to insert your mail via an open slot, but only you have the key to get the mail out. This is analogous to an asymmetric system in which the open slot is the public key. If you are concerned about the security of your mail, this is much easier than ensuring every letter carrier has a copy of your mailbox key! The letter carrier is also thankful he or she isn't required to carry hundreds of different keys to complete mail-delivery duties.

ExamAlert

Some general rules for asymmetric algorithms include the following:

▶ The public key can never decrypt a message that it was used to encrypt with.

▶ Private keys should never be able to be determined through the public key (if it is designed properly).

▶ Each key should be able to decrypt a message made with the other. For instance, if a message is encrypted with the private key, the public key should be able to decrypt it.

Public key encryption has proven useful on networks such as the Internet. This is primarily because the public key is all that needs to be distributed. Because nothing harmful can be done with the public key, it is useful over unsecured networks where data can pass through many hands and is vulnerable to interception and abuse. Symmetric encryption works fine over the Internet, too, but the limitations on providing the key securely to everyone that requires it can be difficult. In addition, asymmetric key systems are also used to verify digital signatures, which provide assurance that communications have not been altered and that the communication arrived from an authorized source.

> **ExamAlert**
>
> In an asymmetric key system, each user has a pair of keys: a private key and a public key. Sending an encrypted message requires you to encrypt the message with the recipient's public key. The message in turn gets decrypted by the recipient with his or her private key.

Symmetric encryption uses two primary types of methods for encrypting plain-text data. These include

- **Stream cipher:** The plain-text bits are encrypted a single bit at a time. These bits are also combined with a stream of pseudorandom characters. Stream ciphers are known for their speed and simplicity.

- **Block cipher:** Plain-text is encrypted in blocks, which is a fixed-length group of bits. The block of plain-text is encrypted into a corresponding block of ciphertext. Thus, a 64-bit block of plain-text would output as a 64-bit block of ciphertext.

Transport Encryption

In addition to securing identities and data, encryption is widely used to secure the links between two points. These two points are often referred to as the *client* and the *server*. Without an effective means to protect the transport layer, communications can be exposed. Transport encryption protects communication between the client and the server, preventing the disclosure of sensitive data as well as the manipulation of the data. Another advantage provided by transport encryption is to prevent redirection in which the communication is no longer taking place between the two expected parties. Instead the client may be communicating with an attacker that otherwise appears to be trusted.

There are various types of technologies used to provide transport encryption. These technologies rely upon algorithms already discussed. The next section covers the more common uses and applications of transport encryption.

Nonrepudiation and Digital Signatures

Nonrepudiation is intended to provide, through encryption, a method of accountability that makes it impossible to refute the origin of data. It guarantees that the sender cannot later deny being the sender and that the recipient cannot deny receiving the data. This definition, however, does not factor in the possible compromise of the workstation or system used to create the private key and the encrypted digital signature. The following list outlines four of the key elements that nonrepudiation services provide on a typical client/server connection:

▶ **Proof of origin:** The host gets proof that the client is the originator of particular data or authentication request from a particular time and location.

▶ **Proof of submission:** The client gets proof that the data (or authentication in this case) has been sent.

▶ **Proof of delivery:** The client gets proof that the data (or authentication in this case) has been received.

▶ **Proof of receipt:** The client gets proof that the data (or authentication in this case) has been received correctly.

Digital signatures provide integrity and authentication. In addition, digital signatures provide nonrepudiation with proof of origin. Although authentication and nonrepudiation might appear to be similar, the difference is that with nonrepudiation proof can be demonstrated to a third party.

A sender of a message signs a message using his or her private key. This provides unforgeable proof that the sender did indeed generate the message. Nonrepudiation is unique to asymmetric systems because the private (secret) key is not shared. Remember that in a symmetric system, both parties involved share the secret key, and therefore any party can deny sending a message by claiming the other party originated the message.

Digital signatures attempt to guarantee the identity of the person sending the data from one point to another. The digital signature acts as an electronic signature used to authenticate the identity of the sender and to ensure the integrity of the original content (that it hasn't been changed).

Note

Do not confuse a digital signature with a digital certificate (discussed in the next chapter). In addition, do not confuse digital signatures with encryption. Although digital signatures and encryption use related concepts, their intentions and operations differ significantly. Finally, do not confuse a digital signature with the block of identification information, such as the sender's name and telephone number or digitally created image, often appended to the end of an email.

Digital signatures can easily be transported and are designed so that they cannot be copied by anyone else. This ensures that something signed cannot be repudiated.

A digital signature does not have to accompany an encrypted message. It can simply be used to assure the receiver of the sender's identity and that the message's integrity was maintained. The digital signature contains the digital signature of the certificate authority (CA) that issued the certificate for verification.

The point of this verification is to prevent or alert the recipient to any data tampering. Ideally, if a packet of data is digitally signed, it can only bear the original mark of the sender. If this mark differs, the receiver knows that the packet differs from what it is supposed to be, and either the packet is not unencrypted or is dropped altogether. This works based on the encryption algorithm principles discussed previously. If you cannot determine what the original data was in the encrypted data (in this case, the signature), it becomes much harder to fake the data and actually get it past the receiver as legitimate data.

For example, suppose you need to digitally sign a document sent to your stockbroker. You need to ensure the integrity of the message and assure the stockbroker that the message is really from you. The exchange looks like this:

1. You type the email.

2. Using software built in to your email client, you obtain a hash (which you can think of as digital fingerprint) of the message.

3. You use your private key to encrypt the hash. This encrypted hash is your digital signature for the message.

4. You send the message to your stockbroker.

5. Your stockbroker receives the message. Using his software, he makes a hash of the received message.

6. The stockbroker uses your public key to decrypt the message hash.

7. A match of the hashes proves that the message is valid.

Hashing

A *hash* is a generated summary from a mathematical rule or algorithm and is used commonly as a "digital fingerprint" to verify the integrity of files and messages and to ensure message integrity and provide authentication verification. In other words, hashing algorithms are not encryption methods but offer additional system security via a "signature" for data confirming the original content.

Hash functions work by taking a string (for example, a password or email) of any length and producing a fixed-length string for output. Keep in mind that hashing is one way. Although you can create a hash from a document, you cannot re-create the document from the hash. If this all sounds confusing, the following example should help clear things up. Suppose you want to send an email to a friend, and you also want to ensure that during transit it cannot be read or altered. You would first use software that generates a hash value of the message to accompany the email and then encrypt both the hash and the message. After receiving the email, the recipient's software decrypts the message and the hash and then produces another hash from the received email. The two hashes are then compared, and a match indicates that the message was not tampered with. (Any change in the original message produces a change in the hash.) A Message Authentication Code (MAC) is similar to a hash function but is able to resist forgery and is not open to man-in-the-middle attacks. A MAC can be thought of as an encrypted hash—combining an encryption key and a hashing algorithm. The MAC is a small piece of data known as an authentication tag, which is derived by applying a message or file combined with a secret key to a cryptographic algorithm. The resulting MAC value can ensure the integrity of the data as well as its authenticity, as one in possession of the secret key can subsequently detect whether there are any changes from the original. Specific cryptographic hash functions are covered later in this chapter.

> **Exam Alert**
>
> A message authentication code (MAC) is a bit of a misnomer. Remember that in addition to providing authentication services, as the name suggests, a MAC also provides for data integrity.

Key Escrow

Escrow refers to a trusted third party or broker. A deposit on a new home, for example or a third-party account used to fulfill property tax obligations are examples of escrow. A key escrow then is similar but is specifically used to mitigate key loss or protect entities to ensure agreed upon obligations are fulfilled. Typically the key in escrow should not be released to anybody other than the involved parties without appropriate authorization. Key escrow is a controversial topic given that additional concerns are introduced around the process of the escrow's access to the key and abuse by third parties.

Steganography

Steganography is a word of Greek origin meaning "hidden writing." Steganography is a method for hiding messages so that unintended recipients aren't even aware of any message. Compare this to cryptography, which does not seek to hide the fact a message exists, but rather to just make it unreadable by anyone other than the intended recipients. For example, writing a letter using plain text but in invisible ink is an example of the use of steganography. The content is not scrambled in any way; it is just hidden. Another interesting example, albeit a bit cumbersome, is the historical use of writing a secret message on the scalp of one's bald head, and then allowing the hair to grow back, ultimately to be shaved again upon arrival at the intended recipient.

> **ExamAlert**
>
> Steganography is not cryptography, but the two are related and often used in conjunction with one another. Steganography seeks to hide the presence of a message, whereas the purpose of cryptography is to transform a message from its readable plain text into an unreadable form known as ciphertext.

Of course, steganography is useless if someone other than the intended recipient knows where to look. Therefore, steganography is best used when combined with encryption. This adds an additional layer of security by not even allowing attackers to attempt to crack encryption into a readable form because they don't even know the message exists in the first place. As a result, steganography is not just the stuff of child's play or far-fetched spy movies. In fact, steganography entered into mainstream media with various reports since the terrorist attacks of 9/11—that terrorists may have and are using this practice to secretly hide messages. Modern uses are various, including hiding messages in digital media and digital watermarking. In addition, steganography has been used by many printers, using tiny dots that reveal serial numbers and time stamps.

Use of Proven Technologies

Because of the sensitive nature behind the uses of cryptography, the use of well-known, proven technologies is crucial. Back doors and flaws, for example, can undermine any encryption algorithm, which is why proven algorithms such as those discussed in this chapter should always be considered. Although various vendors might have their own encryption solutions, most of these depend upon well-known, time-tested algorithms, and generally speaking one should be skeptical of any vendor using a proprietary non-proven algorithm.

Kerckhoff's principle (from the nineteenth century) states that a cryptosystem should be secure even if everything about the system is known, except for the key. Proven technologies are well-designed cryptosystems. Systems that require the algorithms to be kept secret not only introduce additional measures around what needs to be protected, but they are often referred to as "security by obscurity."

Elliptic Curve and Quantum Cryptography

Two emerging cryptosystems include Elliptic Curve Cryptography (ECC) and quantum cryptography. ECC is a public-key cryptosystem based upon complex mathematical structures. ECC uses smaller key sizes than traditional public-key cryptosystem. As a result, it is faster and consumes fewer resources, making it more ideal for mobile and wireless devices.

Unlike elliptic curves and other cryptosystems, quantum cryptography does not rely upon mathematics. Quantum cryptography instead relies upon physics. Although slower, the primary advantage provided by quantum cryptography is increased security. Quantum mechanics protects against data being disturbed because one cannot measure the quantum state of the photons. The mere observation of a quantum system changes the system.

Cram Quiz

Answer these questions. The answers follow the last question. If you cannot answer these questions correctly, consider reading this section again until you can.

1. In encryption, when data is broken into a single unit of varying sizes (depending on the algorithm) and the encryption is applied to those chunks of data, what type of algorithm is this?

   ○ **A.** Symmetric encryption algorithm

   ○ **B.** Elliptic curve

   ○ **C.** Block cipher

   ○ **D.** All of the above

2. Which type of algorithm generates a key pair (a public key and a private key) that is then used to encrypt and decrypt data and messages sent and received?

   ○ **A.** Elliptic curve

   ○ **B.** Symmetric encryption algorithms

   ○ **C.** Asymmetric encryption algorithms

   ○ **D.** Paired algorithms

3. When encrypting and decrypting an email using an asymmetric encryption algorithm, you _____.

   ○ **A.** Use the private key to encrypt and only the public key to decrypt

   ○ **B.** Use a secret key to perform both encrypt and decrypt operations

   ○ **C.** Can use the public key to either encrypt or decrypt

   ○ **D.** Can use the public key to either encrypt or decrypt

1. **C.** When data that is going to be encrypted is broken into chunks of data and then encrypted, the type of encryption is called a block cipher. Although many symmetric algorithms use a block cipher, answer A is incorrect because a block cipher is a more precise and accurate term for the given question. Answer B is incorrect because this describes a public key encryption algorithm. Answer D is incorrect.

2. **C.** Although many different types of algorithms use public and private keys to apply their encryption algorithms in their own various ways, algorithms that perform this way are called asymmetric encryption algorithms (or public key encryption). Answer A is incorrect because this is only a type of asymmetric encryption algorithm. Answer B is incorrect because symmetric algorithms use a single key. Answer D is not a type of algorithm, and so it is incorrect.

3. **D.** Answer D provides the only valid statement to complete the sentence. Answer A is incorrect because the public key would be used to encrypt and the private key to decrypt. Answer B is incorrect because this describes symmetric encryption. Answer C is incorrect because the public key cannot decrypt the same data it encrypted.

Use and Apply Appropriate Cryptographic Tools and Products

▶ **WEP versus WPA/WPA2 and Preshared Keys**

▶ **MD5**

▶ **SHA**

▶ **RIPEMD**

▶ **AES**

▶ **DES**

▶ **3DES**

▶ **HMAC**

▶ **RSA**

▶ **RC4**

▶ **One-time-pads**

▶ **CHAP**

▶ **PAP**

▶ **NTLM**

▶ **NTLMv2**

▶ **Blowfish**

▶ **PGP/GPG**

▶ **Whole disk encryption**

▶ **Twofish**

▶ **Comparative strengths of algorithms**

▶ **Use of algorithms with transport encryption**

CramSaver

If you can correctly answer these questions before going through this section, save time by skimming the Exam Alerts in this section and then completing the Cram Quiz at the end of the section.

1. What are examples of symmetric algorithms?

2. SHA-1 and MD5 are examples of what type of cryptographic function?

Answers

1. Examples of common symmetric algorithms include AES, 3DES, Blowfish, Twofish, and RC4.

2. SHA-1 and MD5 are hashing algorithms.

Wireless Encryption Functions

In recent years, there has been the proliferation of wireless local area networks (WLANs) based on the standards defined in IEEE 802.11. One of the earlier algorithms used to secure 802.11 wireless networks is Wired Equivalent Privacy (WEP), which uses the RC4 cipher for confidentiality. However, the WEP algorithm, although still widely used, is no longer considered secure and has been replaced. Temporal Key Integrity Protocol (TKIP) is the security protocol designed to replace WEP and is also known by its later iterations of Wi-Fi Protected Access (WPA) or even WPA2. Similar to WEP, TKIP uses the RC4 algorithm and does not require an upgrade to existing hardware, whereas more recent protocols, such as Counter Mode with Cipher Block Chaining Message Authentication Code Protocol (CCMP), which use the AES algorithm, do require an upgrade.

WPA can either use an authentication server from which keys are distributed, or it can use pre-shared keys. The use of pre-shared keys with WPA is also known as WPA-Personal. This implementation is more ideally suited for smaller environments, where key management is not necessary. The pre-shared key method requires that all devices on the network use the same shared passphrase.

A summary of the three wireless encryption functions that you should be familiar with include the following:

- **WEP:** This is the original wireless encryption standard, which is still commonly seen. It was, however, superseded in 2003 by WPA.

- **WPA:** The successor to WEP in order to provide increased security.

- **WPA2:** This further improved upon WPA and, since 2006, is required for Wi-Fi–certified devices.

In addition, WPA-Personal and WPA-Enterprise target different users and are applicable to both WPA and WPA2. WPA-Personal is designed for home and small office use in that it uses a pre-shared key and does not require a separate authentication server. WPA-Enterprise, on the other hand, is more ideal for larger organizations in that it provides for increased security. This comes with a tradeoff, of course. WPA-Enterprise requires a RADIUS server and is more complicated to set up and maintain.

Cryptographic Hash Functions

Numerous hash functions exist, and many published algorithms are known to be unsecure; however, you should be familiar with the following three hash algorithms:

▶ **Secure Hash Algorithm (SHA, SHA-1, SHA-2, SHA-3):** Hash algorithms pioneered by the National Security Agency and widely used in the U.S. government. SHA-1 can generate a 160-bit hash from any variable-length string of data, making it very secure, but also resource-intensive. Subsequently, four additional hash functions were introduced. These were named after their digest lengths, and included SHA-224, SHA-256, SHA-384, and SHA-512. Together these four hash functions are known as SHA-2. In 2007, a contest was announced to design a hash function (SHA-3) to replace the aging SHA-1 and SHA-2 hash functions.

▶ **Message Digest Series Algorithm (MD2, MD4, MD5):** A series of encryption algorithms created by Ronald Rivest (founder of RSA Data Security, Inc.) designed to be fast, simple, and secure. The MD series generates a hash of up to 128-bit strength out of any length of data.

▶ **RACE Integrity Primitives Evaluation Message Digest (RIPEMD):** RIPEMD was developed within the academic system and is based upon the design of MD4. The more commonly used 160-bit version of the algorithm, RIPEMD-160, performs comparable to SHA-1, though it is less used.

Both SHA and the MD series are similar in design; however, keep in mind that because of the higher bit strength of the SHA algorithm, it will be in the range of 20%–30% slower to process than the MD family of algorithms.

(Exam Alert)

Hashing within security systems is used to ensure the integrity of transmitted messages (that is, to be certain they have not been altered) and for password verification. Be able to identify both the SHA and MD series as hashing algorithms.

The Message Digest Algorithm has been refined over the years (and hence the version numbers). The most commonly used is MD5, which is faster than the others. Both MD4 and MD5 produce a 128-bit hash; however, the hash used in MD4 has been successfully broken. This security breach spurred the development of MD5, which features a redeveloped cipher that makes it stronger than the MD4 algorithm while still featuring a 128-bit hash. Since the mid-2000s, several advances on breaking MD5 have occurred. Although MD5 is still commonly used, U.S. government agencies have stated that MD5 should be considered compromised. Meanwhile, the recommendation is to use the SHA-2 family of hash functions, at least until its successor is formally announced.

In addition to the hashing algorithms just mentioned, you also should be aware of the LAN Manager hash (LM hash or LANMan hash) and the NT LAN Manager hash (NTLM hash, also called the Unicode hash). Both are commonly known as authentication protocols.

LM hash is based on DES encryption (discussed in the next section), but it is not considered effective (and is technically not truly a hashing algorithm) because of design implementation weaknesses. (It's quite easy to crack an LM hash using your average computer system and one of the many cracking tools available.) The two primary weaknesses of LM hash are as follows:

▶ All passwords longer than seven characters are broken down into two chunks, from which each piece is hashed separately.

▶ Before the password is hashed, all lowercase characters are converted to uppercase characters. As a result, the scope of the characters set is greatly reduced, and each half of the password can be cracked separately.

As a result of weaknesses within the LM hash, Microsoft later introduced the NTLM hashing method in early versions of Windows NT. However, the LM hash algorithm was still commonly used by Microsoft operating systems before Windows Vista.

The NTLM hash is an improvement over the LM hash. NTLM hashing makes use of the MD series hashing algorithms and is used on more recent versions of the Windows operating system. NTLM, however, was replaced by NTLM v2, which is more secure. Specifically, NTLM v2 protects against spoofing attacks and adds the ability for a server to authenticate to the client as well.

The Challenge-Handshake Authentication Protocol (CHAP) is another authentication protocol that can be used to provide on-demand authentication within an ongoing data transmission. CHAP is an improvement over Password Authentication Protocol (PAP). PAP is a basic form of authentication during which the username and password are transmitted unencrypted. CHAP uses a one-way hashing function that first involves a service requesting a CHAP response from the client. The client creates a hashed value that is derived using the message digest (MD5) hashing algorithm and sends this value to the service, which also calculates the expected value itself. The server, referred to as the *authenticator*, compares these two values. If they match, the transmission continues. This process is repeated at random intervals during a session of data transaction. CHAP functions over Point-to-Point Protocol (PPP) connections. PPP is a protocol for communicating between two points using a serial interface, providing service at the second layer of the OSI model: the data-link layer. PPP can handle both synchronous and asynchronous connections.

Occasionally, you might find Shiva Password Authentication Protocol (SPAP) implemented. SPAP was designed by Shiva and is an older, two-way reversible encryption protocol that encrypts the password data sent between client and server. A computer running Windows XP Professional, when connecting to a Shiva LAN Rover, uses SPAP, as does a Shiva client that connects to a server running Routing and Remote Access. This form of authentication is more secure than plaintext but less secure than CHAP or MS-CHAP.

HMAC

MACs that are based upon cryptographic hash functions are known as a HMAC (Hash-based Message Authentication Code). The sender of a message uses an HMAC function to produce the MAC. This is a result of using both the message input along with a secret key.

Thus, MACs and HMACs are very similar, but an HMAC provides additional security by adding an additional integrity check to the data being transmitted. For example, SHA-1 can be used to calculate an HMAC, which results in what's called HMAC-SHA1. Or if MD5 is used, it's called HMAC-MD5. Despite the fact MD5 is vulnerable to collision attacks, this should not impede its use with HMAC. Unlike MD5, alone, HMACs are not as affected by collisions.

Symmetric Encryption Algorithms

Earlier in this chapter, you were introduced to the concept of symmetric key encryption, in which a common shared key or identical key is used between the sender and the receiver. Symmetric algorithms can be classified as either block ciphers or stream ciphers. A stream cipher, as the name implies, encrypts the message bit by bit, one at a time. A block cipher encrypts the message in chunks.

Myriad symmetric key algorithms are in use today. The more commonly used algorithms include the following:

- **Data Encryption Standard (DES):** DES was adopted for use by the National Institute of Standards and Technology (NIST) in 1977. DES is a block cipher that uses a 56-bit key and 8 bits of parity on each 64-bit chunk of data. Although it is considered a strong algorithm, it is limited in use because of its relatively short key-length limit.

- **Triple Data Encryption Standard (3DES):** 3DES, also known as Triple-DES, dramatically improves upon the DES by using the DES algorithm three times with three distinct keys. This provides total bit strength of 168 bits. 3DES superseded DES in the late 1990s.

▶ **Advanced Encryption Standard (AES):** Also called Rinjdael, NIST chose this block cipher to be the successor to DES. AES is similar to DES in that it can create keys from 128 bits to 256 bits in length and can perform the encryption and decryption of up to 128-bit chunks of data (in comparison to the 64-bit chunks of the original DES). Similar to 3DES, the data is passed through three layers, each with a specific task, such as generating random keys based on the data and the bit strength being used. The data is then encrypted with the keys through multiple encryption rounds, like DES, and then the final key is applied to the data.

▶ **Blowfish Encryption Algorithm:** Blowfish is a block cipher that can encrypt using any size chunk of data; in addition, Blowfish can also perform encryption with any length encryption key up to 448 bits, making it a flexible and secure symmetric encryption algorithm.

▶ **International Data Encryption Algorithm (IDEA):** Originally created around 1990, IDEA went through several variations before arriving at its final acronym. Originally called the Proposed Encryption Standard (PES), it was later renamed and refined to the Improved Proposed Encryption Standard (IPES). After even more refinement, it was ultimately named IDEA in 1992. In its final form, IDEA is capable of encrypting 64-bit blocks of data at a time and uses a 128-bit-strength encryption key. The use of IDEA has been limited primarily because of software patents on the algorithm, which many believe hinder development, research, and education.

▶ **Rivest Cipher (RC2, RC4, RC5, RC6):** As far as widely available commercial applications go, the Rivest Cipher (RC) encryption algorithms are the most commonly implemented ciphers for encryption security. The RC series (RC2, RC4, RC5, and RC6) are all similarly designed, yet each version has its own take on cipher design, as well as its own capabilities. RC2, RC5, and RC6 are block ciphers, whereas RC4 is a stream cipher.

Table 12.1 compares the algorithms just mentioned (and some lesser-known ones). In addition, notice the differences between the various types of RC algorithms.

TABLE 12.1 **A Comparison of Symmetric Key Algorithms**

Algorithm	Cipher Type	Key Length
DES	Block	56 bits
Triple-DES (3DES)	Block	168 bits
AES (Rinjdael)	Block	128–256 bits
Blowfish	Block	1–448 bits
IDEA	Block	128 bits
RC2	Block	1–2048 bits
RC4	Stream	1–2048 bits
RC5	Block	128–256 bits
RC6	Block	128–256 bits
CAST	Block	128–256 bits
MARS	Block	128–256 bits
Serpent	Block	128–256 bits
Twofish	Block	128–256 bits

ExamAlert

Be sure you understand the differences between various symmetric key algorithms. Note that these are symmetric, and not asymmetric, and be sure to differentiate between stream ciphers and block ciphers. Specifically note that RC4 is the only stream cipher of those mentioned.

Asymmetric Encryption Algorithms

Various asymmetric algorithms have been designed, but few have gained the widespread acceptance of symmetric algorithms. While reading this section about the asymmetric algorithms, keep in mind that some have unique features, including built-in digital signatures (which you learn more about later). Also because of the additional overhead generated by using two keys for encryption and decryption, asymmetric algorithms require more resources than symmetric algorithms.

Popular asymmetric encryption algorithms include the following:

▶ **Rivest, Shamir, and Adleman encryption algorithm (RSA):** RSA, named after the three men who developed it, is a well-known cryptography system used for encryption and digital signatures. In fact, the RSA algorithm is considered by many the standard for encryption and the core technology that secures most business conducted on the Internet. The RSA key length may be of any length, and the algorithm works by multiplying two large prime numbers. In addition, through other operations in the algorithm, it derives a set of numbers: one for the public key and the other for the private key.

▶ **Diffie-Hellman key exchange:** The Diffie-Hellman key exchange (also called exponential key agreement) is an early key exchange design whereby two parties, without prior arrangement, can agree upon a secret key that is known only to them. The keys are passed in a way that they are not compromised, using encryption algorithms to verify that the data is arriving at its intended recipient.

▶ **El Gamal encryption algorithm:** As an extension to the Diffie-Hellman design, in 1985 Dr. El Gamal took to task the design requirements of using encryption to develop digital signatures. Instead of focusing just on the key design, El Gamal designed a complete public key encryption algorithm using some of the key exchange elements from Diffie-Hellman and incorporating encryption on those keys. The resultant encrypted keys reinforced the security and authenticity of public key encryption design and helped lead to later advances in asymmetric encryption technology.

▶ **Elliptic curve cryptography (ECC):** Elliptic curve techniques use a method in which elliptic curves are used to calculate simple but very difficult-to-break encryption keys for use in general-purpose encryption. One of the key benefits of ECC encryption algorithms is that they have a compact design because of the advanced mathematics involved in ECC. For instance, an ECC encryption key of 160-bit strength is, in actuality, equal in strength to a 1024-bit RSA encryption key.

Note

In 2000, RSA Security, Inc. (now known as RSA, The Security Division of EMC) released the RSA algorithm into the public domain. This release allows anyone to create products incorporating their own implementation of the algorithm without being subject to license and patent enforcement.

Throughout this section on different encryption algorithms, you have learned how each type of symmetric and asymmetric algorithm performs. One thing you haven't seen yet is how bit strengths compare to each other when looking at asymmetric and symmetric algorithms in general. The following list reveals why symmetric algorithms are favored for most applications and why asymmetric algorithms are widely considered very secure but often too complex and resource-intensive for every environment:

- ▶ 64-bit symmetric key strength = 512-bit asymmetric key strength

- ▶ 112-bit symmetric key strength = 1792-bit asymmetric key strength

- ▶ 128-bit symmetric key strength = 2304-bit asymmetric key strength

As you can see, a dramatic difference exists in the strength and consequently the overall size of asymmetric encryption keys. For most environments today, 128-bit strength is considered adequate; therefore, symmetric encryption might often suffice. If you want to simplify how you distribute keys, however, asymmetric encryption might be the better choice.

One-time-pads

Throughout history, the common theme among "unbreakable" algorithms is that through practice or theory, they are all breakable. However, one type of cipher has perhaps earned the distinction of being completely unbreakable: one-time pad (OTP). Unfortunately, the OTP currently has the tradeoff of requiring a key as long as the message, thus creating significant storage and transmission costs. Within an OTP, there are as many bits in the key as in the plaintext to be encrypted, and this key is to be random and, as the name suggests, used only once, with no portion of the key ever being reused. Without the key, an attacker cannot crack the ciphertext, even via a brute-force attack in search of the entire key space.

PGP

PGP derives from the Pretty Good Privacy application developed by Phillip R. Zimmerman in 1991 and is an alternative to S/MIME. Basically, it encrypts and decrypts email messages using asymmetric encryptions schemes such as RSA. Another useful feature of the PGP program is that it can include a digital signature that validates that the email has not been tampered with (thus assuring the recipient of the email's integrity).

> **Note**
>
> In the early 1990s, the U.S. government tried to suppress the use of PGP, which was gaining popularity and exposure in the media. The government tried to force the software to be taken down and made unavailable to public consumption. (PGP is the email program that uses encryption and is available to anyone who wants to download it within North America.)
>
> Part of the government's argument against PGP was that it could not control the information people were sending. For example, criminals could use encryption and seemingly be able to hide their online activities and data from the prying eyes of the government. Eventually, the public's right to use encryption (and PGP in particular) won out.

Some systems incorporate a mixed approach, using both asymmetric and symmetric encryption to take advantage of the benefits that each provides. For example, asymmetric algorithms are used at the beginning of a process to securely distribute symmetric keys. From that point on, after the private keys have been securely exchanged, they can be used for encryption and decryption (thus solving the issue of key distribution). PGP is an example of such a system. PGP was originally designed to provide for the encryption and decryption of email and for digitally signing emails. PGP and other similar hybrid encryption systems such as the GNU Privacy Guard (GnuPG or GPG) program follow the OpenPGP format and use a combination of public key and private key encryption.

Further developments of PGP eventually evolved to be part of a company called PGP by the same name. In 2010, Symantec Corporation acquired the PGP Corporation.

Whole Disk Encryption

Often called full disk encryption (FDE), whole disk encryption has gained popularity in recent years to help mitigate the risks associated with lost or stolen laptops and accompanying disclosure laws. Whole disk encryption can either be hardware or software based, and unlike file- or folder-level encryption, whole disk encryption is meant to encrypt the entire contents of the drive (even temporary files and memory).

Unlike selective file encryption, which might require the end user to take responsibility for encrypting files, encrypting the contents of the entire drive takes the onus off individual users. It is not unusual for end users to sacrifice security for convenience, especially when they do not fully understand the associated risks. Nevertheless, along with the benefits of whole disk encryption come certain tradeoffs. For example, key management becomes increasingly important; loss of the decryption keys could render the data unrecoverable. In addition, although whole disk encryption might make it easier for an organization to deal with a stolen or otherwise lost laptop, the fact that the entire disk is encrypted could present management challenges, including not being able to effectively control who has unauthorized access to sensitive data.

To effectively use whole disk encryption products, you should also use a pre-boot authentication mechanism, which means the user attempting to log on must provide authentication before the actual operating system boots. Thus, the encryption key is decrypted only after another key is input into this pre-boot environment. Most vendors typically offer different options, such as the following:

- ▶ Username and password (typically the least secure)

- ▶ Smart card or smart card–enabled USB token along with a PIN (which provides two-factor functionality and can often be the same token or smart card currently used for access elsewhere)

- ▶ A Trusted Platform Module (discussed earlier in Chapter 7, "Application Security," to store the decryption key.)

Use of Algorithms with Transport Encryption

Secure Sockets Layer (SSL) and Transport Layer Security (TLS) are the most widely used cryptographic protocols for managing secure communication between a client and server over the Web. Both essentially serve the same purpose (with TLS being the successor to SSL). Both provide for client- and server-side authentication and for encrypted connection between the two. TLS consists of two additional protocols: the TLS Record Protocol and the TLS Handshake Protocol. The Handshake Protocol allows the client and server to authenticate to one another, and the Record Protocol provides connection security.

The three basic phases of SSL and TLS are as follows:

1. Peer negotiation to decide which public key algorithm and key exchange to use. Usually, the decision is based on the strongest cipher and hash function supported by both systems.

2. Key exchange and authentication occurs. A digital certificate is exchanged, which includes the public encryption key, which is used to generate a session key.

3. Symmetric cipher encryption and message authentication occur. Both parties can generate keys for encryption and decryption during the session as a result of the asymmetric cryptography transaction that occurred in step 2.

SSL and TLS are best known for protecting HTTP (Hypertext Transfer Protocol) web traffic and transactions, commonly known as Hypertext Transfer Protocol over SSL (HTTPS), which is a secure HTTP connection. HTTPS, like HTTP, is used as part of the uniform resource identifier (URI) specified in the address bar of web browsers (https://). When you use HTTPS rather than just plain HTTP, an additional layer is provided for encryption and authentication. Whereas HTTP traffic is usually over port 80, HTTPS traffic typically occurs over port 443.

Exam**Alert**

HTTPS simply combines HTTP with SSL or TLS. The default port for unencrypted HTTP traffic is port 80. The secure version, HTTPS, runs by default over port 443.

Web servers are generally ready to begin accepting HTTP traffic to serve up web pages, but to deploy HTTPS the web server must have a certificate signed by a CA. When a web server is serving content outside of the organization (that is, public-facing sites), the certificate is usually signed by a trusted third-party CA. If the site is used internally only (that is, an intranet), however, a certificate signed by an in-house CA generally suffices. In most cases the use of SSL and TLS is single sided—that is, only the server is being authenticated as valid with a verifiable certificate. For example, when conducting an online banking transaction one can be assured they are at the legitimate site by verifying the server side certificate, whereas the client is verified perhaps by only a username and password. Certificates, however, can also be deployed in a dual-sided scenario in which not only is the server authenticated using a certificate, but the client side is as well. While this certainly can provide for a more secure environment, additional overhead is created, which also includes the fact that a unique client-side certificate now needs to be created and managed for every client rather than just a single server.

Aside from its use with HTTP for web servers, TLS can provide security to many other protocols. It can, for instance, provide the capability to tunnel the connection forming a VPN, providing for easier firewall traversal compared to traditional IPsec VPNs, for example, which we discuss shortly.

Secure Shell

Secure Shell (SSH) provides an authenticated and encrypted session between the client and host computers using public key cryptography. SSH provides a more secure replacement for the common command-line terminal utility Telnet. SSH uses the asymmetric RSA cryptography algorithm to provide both connection and authentication. In addition, data encryption is accomplished using one of several available symmetric encryption algorithms.

The SSH suite encapsulates three secure utilities—slogin, ssh, and scp—derived from the earlier nonsecure UNIX utilities rlogin, rsh, and rcp. Like Telnet, SSH provides a command-line connection through which an administrator can input commands on a remote server. SSH provides an authenticated and encrypted data stream, as opposed to the clear-text communications of a Telnet session. The three utilities within the SSH suite provide the following functionalities:

▶ **Secure Login (slogin):** A secure version of the UNIX Remote Login (rlogin) service, which allows a user to connect to a remote server and interact with the system as if directly connected

▶ **Secure Shell (ssh):** A secure version of the UNIX Remote Shell (rsh) environment interface protocol

▶ **Secure Copy (scp):** A secure version of the UNIX Remote Copy (rcp) utility, which allows for the transfer of files in a manner similar to FTP

Note

Some versions of SSH, including the Secure Shell for Windows Server, include a secure version of FTP (SFTP), along with other common SSH utilities.

IP Security

Layer 2 Tunneling Protocol (L2TP) is an encapsulated tunneling protocol often used to support the creation of VPNs. It is important to understand that L2TP typically provides support along with other protocols. For example, L2TP by itself does not provide for authentication or strong authentication. To meet these needs, L2TP is often combined with IPsec (Internet Protocol Security).

IPsec is a set of protocols widely implemented to support VPNs. It provides for the secure exchange of packets at the IP layer. Therefore, organizations have been able to leverage IPsec to exchange private information over public networks such as the Internet. IPsec can achieve this higher level of assurance for data transport through the use of multiple protocols, including Authentication Header (AH), Encapsulated Secure Payload (ESP), and Internet Key Exchange (IKE). The AH protocol provides data integrity, authentication, and (optionally) anti-replay capabilities for packets. ESP provides for confidentiality of the data being transmitted and also includes authentication capabilities. IKE provides for additional features and ease of configuration. IKE specifically provides authentication for IPsec peers and negotiates IPsec keys and security associations.

Cram Quiz

Answer these questions. The answers follow the last question. If you cannot answer these questions correctly, consider reading this section again until you can.

1. What part of the IPsec protocol provides authentication and integrity but not privacy?

   ○ **A.** Encapsulated security payload

   ○ **B.** Sans-privacy protocol

   ○ **C.** Authentication header

   ○ **D.** Virtual private network

2. Which of the following protocols are used to manage secure communication between a client and a server over the Web? (Select two correct answers.)

   ○ **A.** SSL

   ○ **B.** ISAKMP

   ○ **C.** PGP

   ○ **D.** TLS

3. Which of the following algorithms are examples of a symmetric encryption algorithm? (Choose three answers.)

   ○ **A.** Rijndael

   ○ **B.** Diffie-Hellman

   ○ **C.** RC6

   ○ **D.** AES

4. Which of the following algorithms are examples of an asymmetric encryption algorithm? (Choose three answers.)

   ○ **A.** Elliptic curve

   ○ **B.** 3DES

   ○ **C.** AES

   ○ **D.** RSA

5. Which of the following is a type of cipher that has earned the distinction of being unbreakable?

   ○ **A.** RSA

   ○ **B.** One-time pad

   ○ **C.** 3DES

   ○ **D.** WPA

Cram Quiz Answers

1. **C**. The authentication header (AH) provides authentication so that the receiver
   can be confident of the source the data. It does not use encryption to scramble
   the data, so it cannot provide privacy. Encapsulate security payload (ESP) provides for confidentiality of the data being transmitted and also includes authentication capabilities; therefore, answer A is incorrect. Answer B does not exist,
   and so it is incorrect. A virtual private network makes use of the IPsec protocol
   and is used to secure communications over public networks; therefore, answer D
   is incorrect.

3. **A** and **D**. SSL is the most widely used protocol for managing secure communication between clients and servers on the Web; TLS is similar, and it is considered the successor to SSL. Answer B is incorrect because ISAKMP is a protocol
   common to virtual private networks. Answer C is incorrect because PGP is used
   for the encryption of email.

3. **A**, **C**, and **D**. Because Rijndael and AES are now one in the same, they both can
   be called symmetric encryption algorithms. RC6 is symmetric, too. Answer B is
   incorrect because Diffie-Hellman uses public and private keys, and so it is considered an asymmetric encryption algorithm.

4. **A** and **D**. In this case, both elliptic curve and RSA are types of asymmetric
   encryption algorithms. Although the elliptic curve algorithm is typically a type of
   algorithm incorporated into other algorithms, it falls into the asymmetric family of
   algorithms because of its use of public and private keys, just like the RSA algorithm. Answers B and C are incorrect because 3DES and AES are symmetric
   encryption algorithms.

5. **B**. The one type of cipher that has earned the distinction of being completely
   unbreakable is the one-time pad (OTP). This assumes, however, that the key is
   truly random, is used only once, and is kept secret. Unfortunately, the OTP currently has the tradeoff of requiring a key as long as the message (and thus creates significant storage and transmission costs). Answers A, C, and D are all
   incorrect choices.

What Next?

If you want more practice on this chapter's exam objectives before you move
on, remember that you can access all of the Cram Quiz questions on the CD.
You can also create a custom exam by objective with the practice exam software. Note any objective you struggle with and go to that objective material
in this chapter.

CHAPTER 13

Public Key Infrastructure

This chapter covers the following official CompTIA Security+ Certification exam objectives

▶ Explain the core concepts of public key infrastructure

▶ Implement PKI, certificate management, and associated components

(For more information on the official CompTIA Security+ Certification exam topics, see the "About the CompTIA Security+ Certification Exam" section in the Introduction.)

In Chapter 12, "Cryptography Tools and Techniques," you learned the basic concepts of public and private keys. A public key infrastructure (PKI) makes use of both types of keys and provides the foundation for binding keys to an identity via a certificate authority (CA), thus providing the system for the secure exchange of data over a network through the use of an asymmetric key system. This system for the most part consists of digital certificates and the CAs that issue the certificates. These certificates identify individuals, systems, and organizations that have been verified as authentic and trustworthy.

Recall that *symmetric* key cryptography requires a key to be shared. For example, suppose the password to get into the clubhouse is "open sesame." At some point in time, this key or password needs to be communicated to other participating parties before it can be implemented. PKI provides confidentiality, integrity, and authentication by overcoming this challenge. With PKI, it is not necessary to exchange the password, key, or secret information in advance. This is useful where involved parties have no prior contact or where it is neither feasible nor secure to exchange a secure key.

PKI is widely used to provide the secure infrastructure for applications and networks, including access control, resources from web browsers, secure email, and much more. PKI protects information by providing the following:

▶ Identity authentication

▶ Integrity verification

▶ Privacy assurance

▶ Access authorization

▶ Transaction authorization

▶ Nonrepudiation support

Explain the Core Concepts of Public Key Infrastructure

▶ **Certificate authorities and digital certificates**

▶ **PKI**

▶ **Recovery agent**

▶ **Public key**

▶ **Private keys**

▶ **Registration**

▶ **Key escrow**

▶ **Trust models**

Cram Saver

If you can correctly answer these questions before going through this section, save time by skimming the Exam Alerts in this section and then completing the Cram Quiz at the end of the section.

1. What are the components required in order to implement PKI?

2. What is the purpose of a certificate authority?

3. Why is it best to take a root certificate authority offline?

Answers

1. PKI is comprised of an infrastructure, as the name implies, of hardware, software, policies, and process. All of these components provide for the management and use of digital certificates. Core components include for example, certificate authorities, certificate policies, digital certificates, certificate policies, and certificate practice statements.

2. A certificate authority is a key component of PKI. The primary purpose of a certificate authority is to verify the holder of a digital certificate, issue certificates, and ensure that the holder of a certificate is who they claim to be.

3. Certificate authorities operate upon a hierarchical trust model. Thus, if the root certificate authority is compromised, the entire architecture is compromised. If, on the other hand, the root certificate authority is offline and a subordinate certificate authority is compromised, the root certificate authority can be used to revoke the subordinate.

PKI is comprised of several standards and protocols. These standards and protocols are necessary to allow for interoperability among security products offered by different vendors. Keep in mind, for instance, that digital certificates may be issued by different trusted authorities; therefore, a common language or protocol must exist.

Next, we look at some specific PKI standards. Figure 13.1 illustrates this relationship between standards that apply to PKI at the foundation to the standards that rely on PKI and finally to the applications supported by those standards.

Email	Secure Electronic Commerce	VPN
S/MIME	SSL TLS	IPsec PPTP
PKIX	PKCS	X.509

FIGURE 13.1   **Standards that define PKI up to the applications supported by standards that may rely on PKI.**

The PKIX Working Group of the Internet Engineering Task Force (IETF) is developing Internet standards for PKI based on X.509 certificates with the following focus:

▶ Profiles of X.509 version 3 public key certificates and X.509 version 2 certificate revocation lists (CRLs)

▶ PKI management protocols

▶ Operational protocols

▶ Certificate policies and certificate practice statements (CPSs)

▶ Time-stamping, data-certification, and validation services

Whereas PKIX describes the development of Internet standards for X.509-based PKI, the Public Key Cryptography Standards (PKCS) are the de facto cryptographic message standards developed and published by RSA Laboratories, now part of RSA, The Security Division of EMC. PKCS provides a basic and widely accepted framework for the development of PKI solutions. There were recently 15 documents in the PKCS specification library; however, 2 of the documents have been incorporated into another. These documents are as follows:

- PKCS #1 RSA Cryptography Standard provides recommendations for the implementation of public key cryptography based on the RSA algorithm.

- PKCS #2 no longer exists and has been integrated into PKCS #1.

- PKCS #3 Diffie-Hellman Key Agreement Standard describes a method for using the Diffie-Hellman key agreement.

- PKCS #4 no longer exists and has been integrated into PKCS #1.

- PKCS #5 Password-Based Cryptography Standard provides recommendations for encrypting a data string, such as a private key, with a secret key that has been derived from a password.

- PKCS #6 Extended-Certificate Syntax Standard provides a method for certifying additional information about a given entity beyond just the public key by describing the syntax of a certificate's attributes.

- PKCS #7 Cryptographic Message Syntax Standard describes the syntax for data streams such as digital signatures that may have cryptography applied to them.

- PKCS #8 Private-Key Information Syntax Standard describes syntax for private key information. This includes the private key of a public key cryptographic algorithm.

- PKCS #9 Selected Attribute Types defines certain attribute types of use in PKCS #6, PKCS #7, PKCS #9, and PKCS #10.

- PKCS #10 Certification Request Syntax Standard describes the syntax for a certification request to include a distinguished name, a public key, and an optional set of attributes.

- PKCS #11 Cryptographic Token Interface Standard defines an application programming interface (API) named Cryptoki for devices holding cryptographic information.

- PKCS #12 Personal Information Exchange Syntax Standard specifies a format for storing and transporting a user's private key, digital certificate, and attribute information.

- PKCS #13 Elliptic Curve Cryptography Standard addresses elliptic curve cryptography as related to PKI. As of this writing, PKCS #13 is still under development.

▶ PKCS #14 Pseudo Random Number Generation addresses pseudo random number generation (PRNG), which produces a sequence of bits that has a random-looking distribution. As of this writing, PKCS #14 is still under development.

▶ PKCS #15 Cryptographic Token Information Format Standard establishes a standard for the format of cryptographic information on cryptographic tokens.

Each of the preceding standards documents may be revised and amended periodically, as changes in cryptography occur, and they are always accessible from RSA's website (http://www.rsa.com/rsalabs/). In addition, some have started to move within the control of standards organizations (for example, IETF).

It was stated earlier that PKIX is an IETF working group established to create standards for X.509 PKI. X.509 is an International Telecommunications Union (ITU) recommendation and is implemented as a de-facto standard. X.509 defines a framework for authentication services by a directory.

The X.509 standard additionally defines the format of required data for digital certificates. The preceding chapter briefly introduced you to the contents of a digital certificate; however, it is worth reiterating some of these fields in more detail, which include those required to be compliant to the X.509 standard (see Figure 13.2). These include the following:

▶ **Version**: This identifies the version of the X.509 standard for which the certificate is compliant.

▶ **Serial Number**: The CA that creates the certificate is responsible for assigning a unique serial number.

▶ **Signature Algorithm Identifier**: This identifies the cryptographic algorithm used by the CA to sign the certificate.

▶ **Issuer**: This identifies the directory name of the entity signing the certificate, which is typically a CA.

▶ **Validity Period**: This identifies the time frame for which the private key is valid, if the private key has not been compromised. This period is indicated with both a start and an end time and may be of any duration, but it is often set to one year.

▶ **Subject Name**: This is the name of the entity that is identified in the public key associated with the certificate. This name uses the X.500 standard for globally unique naming and is often called the distinguished name (DN) (for example, CN=John MacNeil, OU=Sales Division, O=Symantec, C=US).

▶ **Subject Public Key Information**: This includes the public key of the entity named in the certificate, as well as a cryptographic algorithm identifier and optional key parameters associated with the key.

FIGURE 13.2   **Details of a digital certificate.**

Currently, there are three versions of X.509. Version 1 has been around since 1988, and although it is the most generic it is also ubiquitous. Version 2, which is not widely used, introduced the idea of unique identifiers for the issuing entity and the subject. Version 3, introduced in 1996, supports an optional Extension field to provide for more informational fields, and thus an extension can be defined by an entity and included in the certificate.

To begin to understand the applications and deployment of PKI, you should understand the various pieces that make up a PKI, including the following:

▶ Certificate authority (CA)

▶ Registration authority (RA)

▶ Digital certificates

▶ Certificate policies

▶ Certificate practice statement (CPS)

▶ Revocation

▶ Trust models

Certificate Authority

Certificate authorities (CAs) are trusted entities and are an important concept within PKI. Aside from the third-party CAs, such as VeriSign (now part of Symantec Corp.), an organization may establish its own CA, typically to be used only within the organization. The CA's job is to issue certificates, to verify the holder of a digital certificate, and to ensure that holders of certificates are who they claim to be. A common analogy used is to compare a CA to a passport-issuing authority. To obtain a passport, you need the assistance of another (for example, a customs office) to verify your identity. Passports are trusted because the issuing authority is trusted.

You have learned about various components and terms that make up PKI, such as digital signatures, public key encryption, confidentiality, integrity, authentication, access control, and nonrepudiation. In the following sections, you learn more about the digital certificates and trust hierarchies involved in PKI.

Registration Authority

Registration authorities (RAs) provide authentication to the CA as to the validity of a client's certificate request; in addition, the RA serves as an aggregator of information. A user, for example, contacts an RA, which in turn verifies the user's identity before issuing the request of the CA to go ahead with issuance of a digital certificate.

Digital Certificates

A digital certificate is a digitally signed block of data that allows public key cryptography to be used for identification purposes. CAs issue these certificates, which are signed using the CA's private key. Most certificates are based on the X.509 standard. Although most certificates follow the X.509 version 3 hierarchical PKI standard, the PGP key system uses its own certificate format. X.509 certificates contain the following information:

- ► Name of the CA
- ► CA's digital signature
- ► Serial number
- ► Issued date

- ► Period of validity
- ► Version
- ► Subject or owner
- ► Subject or owner's public key

The most common application of digital certificates that you have likely used involves websites. Websites that ask for personal information, especially credit card information, use digital certificates (not necessarily all do; however, they should). The traffic from your computer to the website is secured via a protocol called Secure Sockets Layer (SSL), and the web server uses a digital certificate for the secure exchange of information. This is easily identified by a small padlock located in the bottom status bar of most browsers. By clicking this icon, you can view the digital certificate and its details.

Certificate Policies

A certificate policy indicates specific uses applied to a digital certificate and other technical details. Not all certificates are created equal. Digital certificates are issued often following different practices and procedures and are issued for different purposes. Therefore, the certificate policy provides the rules that indicate the purpose and use of an assigned digital certificate. For example, one certificate may have a policy indicating its use for electronic data interchange to conduct e-commerce, whereas another may be issued to only digitally sign documents.

You need to remember that a certificate policy identifies the purpose for which the certificate can be used, but you should also be able to identify the other types of information that can be included within a certificate policy, including the following:

- ▶ Legal issues often used to protect the CA
- ▶ Mechanisms for how users will be authenticated by the CA
- ▶ Key management requirements
- ▶ Instructions for what to do if the private key is compromised
- ▶ Lifetime of the certificate
- ▶ Certificate enrollment and renewal
- ▶ Rules regarding exporting the private key
- ▶ Private and public key minimum lengths

Certificate Practice Statement

A certificate practice statement (CPS) is a legal document created and published by a CA for the purpose of conveying information to those depending on the CA's issued certificates. The information within a CPS provides for the general practices followed by the CA in issuing certificates and customer-related information about certificates, responsibilities, and problem management. It is important to understand that these statements are described in the context of operating procedures and systems architecture, as opposed to certificate policies, discussed previously, which indicate the rules that apply to an issued certificate. A CPS includes the following items:

▶ Identification of the CA

▶ Types of certificates issued and applicable certificate policies

▶ Operating procedures for issuing, renewing, and revoking certificates

▶ Technical and physical security controls used by the CA

> **ExamAlert**
>
> The focus of a certificate policy is on the certificate, whereas the focus of a CPS is on the CA and the way that the CA issues certificates.

Revocation

Just as digital certificates are issued, they can also be revoked. Revoking a certificate invalidates a certificate before its expiration date. Revocation typically occurs because the certificate is considered no longer trustworthy. For example, if a certificate holder's private key is compromised, the certificate is likely to be revoked. Other reasons for revocation include fraudulently obtained certificates or a change in the holder's status, which may indicate less trustworthiness.

One component of a PKI is a mechanism for distributing certificate revocation information, called certificate revocation lists (CRLs). A CRL is used when verification of digital certificate takes place to ensure the validity of a digital certificate.

A newer mechanism for identifying revoked certificates is the Online Certificate Status Protocol (OCSP). A limitation of CRLs is that they must be constantly updated; otherwise, certificates might be accepted despite the fact they were recently revoked. The OSCP, however, checks certificate status in real time instead of relying on the end user to have a current copy of the CRL.

You learn more about revocation as part of the certification life cycle later in this chapter.

Trust Models

Certificate authorities within a PKI follow several models or architectures. The simplest model consists of a single CA. In the single-CA architecture, only one CA exists to issue and maintain certificates. Although this model might benefit smaller organizations because of its administrative simplicity, it has the potential to present many problems. For example, if the CA fails, no other CA can quickly take its place. Another problem can arise if the private key of the CA becomes compromised; in this scenario, all the issued certificates from that CA would then be invalid. A new CA would have to be created, which, in turn, would need to reissue all the certificates.

A more common model, and one that reduces the risks inherent with a single CA, is the hierarchical CA model. In this model, an initial root CA exists at the top of the hierarchy and subordinate CAs reside beneath the root. The subordinate CAs provide redundancy and load balancing should any of the other CAs fail or be taken offline. As a result of this model, you may hear PKI referred to as a trust hierarchy.

A root CA differs from subordinate CAs in that the root CA is usually offline. Remember, if the root CA is compromised, the entire architecture is compromised. If a subordinate CA is compromised, however, the root CA can revoke the subordinate CA.

An alternative to this hierarchical model is the cross-certification model, often referred to as a web of trust. In this model, CAs are considered peers to each other. Such configuration, for example, may exist at a small company that started with a single CA. Then, as the company grew, it continued to implement other single-CA models and then decided that each division of the company needed to communicate with the others and ensure secure exchange of information across the company. To enable this, each of the CAs established a peer-to-peer trust relationship with the others. As you might imagine, such a configuration could become difficult to manage over time.

> **ExamAlert**
>
> The root CA should be taken offline to reduce the risk of key compromise, and the root CA should be made available only to create and revoke certificates for subordinate CAs. A compromised root CA compromises the entire system.

A solution to the complexity of a large cross-certification model is to implement what is known as a bridge CA model. Remember that in the cross-certification model each CA must trust the others. By implementing bridging, however, you can have a single CA, known as the bridge CA, be the central point of trust.

Cram Quiz

Answer these questions. The answers follow the last question. If you cannot answer these questions correctly, consider reading this section again until you can.

1. To check the validity of a digital certificate, which one of the following would be used?

   ○ **A.** Corporate security policy

   ○ **B.** Certificate policy

   ○ **C.** Certificate revocation list

   ○ **D.** Expired domain names

2. Which of the following is not a certificate trust model for the arranging of certificate authorities?

   ○ **A.** Bridge CA architecture

   ○ **B.** Sub-CA architecture

   ○ **C.** Single-CA architecture

   ○ **D.** Hierarchical CA Architecture

3. Which of the following are included within a digital certificate? (Select the correct answers.)

   ○ **A.** User's public key

   ○ **B.** User's private key

   ○ **C.** Information about the user

   ○ **D.** Digital signature of the issuing CA

Cram Quiz Answers

1. **C.** A certificate revocation list (CRL) provides a detailed list of certificates that are no longer valid. A corporate security policy would not provide current information on the validity of issued certificates; therefore, answer A is incorrect. A certificate policy does not provide information on the validity of issued certificates either; therefore, answer B is incorrect. Finally, an expired domain name has no bearing on the validity of a digital certificate; therefore, answer D is incorrect.

2. **B.** Sub-CA architecture does not represent a valid trust model. Answers A, C, and D, however, all represent legitimate trust models. Another common model also exists, called cross-certification; however, it usually makes more sense to implement a bridge architecture over this type of model.

3. **A, C,** and **D.** Information about the user, the user's public key, and the digital signature of the issuing CA are all included within a digital certificate. A user's private key should never be contained within the digital certificate and should remain under tight control; therefore, answer B is incorrect.

Implement PKI, Certificate Management, and Associated Components

▶ **Certificate authorities and digital certificates**

▶ **PKI**

▶ **Recovery agent**

▶ **Public key**

▶ **Private keys**

▶ **Registration**

▶ **Key escrow**

▶ **Trust models**

CramSaver

If you can correctly answer this question before going through this section, save time by skimming the Exam Alerts in this section and then completing the Cram Quiz at the end of the section.

1. Why is it important to consider how private keys are stored when implementing PKI?

Answers

1. The storage of private keys needs to be carefully considered. The private key needs to be protected in order to ensure the validity of certificate authorities and the certificates they issue.

We previously discussed the management structure for digital certificates and the standards and protocols available to use them. In this section, we discuss the management structure for the keys themselves. This review includes the critical elements that you must take into account to properly protect and account for the private key material, which is the most important element of a PKI solution.

Being able to manage digital certificates and key pairs used is critical to any PKI solution. One management method involves the use of a life cycle for digital certificates and their keys. The life cycle is typically based on two documents discussed earlier: the certificate policy and the CPS. The life cycle refers to those events required to create, use, and destroy public keys and the digital certificates with which they are associated. The certificate life cycle comprises the following events:

- **Key generation**: A generator creates a public key pair. Although the CA may generate the key pair, the requesting entity may also generate the pair and provide the public key upon the submission of identity.

- **Identity submission**: The requesting entity submits its identity information to the CA.

- **Registration**: The CA registers the request for a certificate and ensures the accuracy of the identity submission.

- **Certification**: If the identity is validated, the CA creates a certificate and then digitally signs the certificate with its own digital signature.

- **Distribution**: The CA distributes or publishes the digital certificate.

- **Usage**: The entity receiving the certificate is authorized to use the certificate only for its intended use.

- **Revocation and expiration**: The certificate will typically expire and must be withdrawn. Alternatively, the certificate might need to be revoked for various reasons before expiration (for example, if the owner's private key becomes compromised).

- **Renewal**: A certificate can be renewed if requested, as long as a new key pair is generated.

- **Recovery**: Recovery might become necessary if a certifying key is compromised but the certificate holder is still considered valid and trusted. Key recovery is performed by a recovery agent. This agent is an administrative-level user with the ability to decrypt the required key from an escrow database. Key escrow is discussed in further detail shortly.

- **Archiving**: This involves the recording and storing of certificates and their uses.

The preceding list offers a broad view of the certificate life cycle. The following sections delve into more detail about important topics you should understand about key management and the digital certificate life cycle.

Centralized versus Decentralized

There are alternative methods for creating and managing cryptographic keys and digital certificates. These operations may either be centralized or decentralized depending on the organization's security policy.

Centralized key management allows the issuing authority to have complete control over the process. Although this provides for a high level of control, many do not like the idea of a centralized system having a copy of the private key. Whereas the benefit of central control may be seen as an advantage, a centralized system also has disadvantages (for instance, additional required infrastructure, a need to positively authenticate the end entity before transmitting the private key, and the need for a secure channel to transmit the private key).

Decentralized key management allows the requesting entity to generate the key pair and only submit the public key to the CA. Although the CA can still take on the role of distributing and publishing the digital certificate, it can no longer store the private key. Therefore, the entity must maintain complete control over the private key, which is considered one of the most sensitive aspects of a PKI solution. In this scenario, the CA has the additional burden of ensuring that the keys were generated properly and that all key-pair generation policies were followed.

Storage

After the key pairs are generated and a digital certificate has been issued by the CA, both keys must be stored appropriately to ensure their integrity is maintained. However, the key use must still be easy and efficient. The methods used to store the keys may be hardware or software based.

Hardware storage is typically associated with higher levels of security and assurance than software because hardware can have specialized components and physical encasements to protect the integrity of the data stored within. In addition to being more secure, hardware devices are more efficient because they provide dedicated resources to PKI functions. Naturally, however, hardware solutions often have a higher cost than software solutions.

Although software solutions do not have the same level of security as their hardware counterparts, the ability to easily distribute the storage solutions provides for easier administration, transportability, and lower costs.

Because the private key is so sensitive, it requires a higher level of protection than the public key. As a result, you need to take special care to protect private keys, especially the root key for a CA. Remember that if the private key is compromised, the public key and associated certificate are also compromised and should no longer be valid. If the CA's root key becomes compromised, all active keys generated using the CA are compromised and should therefore be revoked and reissued. As a result of this need for increased security over the private keys, hardware solutions are often used to protect private keys.

Even a private key in the possession of an end user should be carefully guarded. At a minimum, this key is protected via a password. An additional safeguard is to provide an additional layer of security by storing the private key on a portable device such as a smart card (thus requiring both possession of the card and knowledge of the password).

Key Escrow

Key escrow occurs when a CA or other entity maintains a copy of the private key associated with the public key signed by the CA. This scenario allows the CA or escrow agent to have access to all information encrypted using the public key from a user's certificate and to create digital signatures on behalf of the user. Therefore, key escrow is a sensitive topic within the PKI community because harmful results might occur if the private key is misused. Because of this issue, key escrow is not a favored PKI solution.

Despite the concerns of the general public about escrow for private use, key escrow is often considered a good idea in corporate PKI environments. In most cases, an employee of an organization is bound by the information security policies of that organization (which usually mandate that the organization has a right to access all intellectual property generated by a user and to any data that an employee generates). In addition, key escrow enables an organization to overcome the large problem of forgotten passwords. Rather than revoke and reissue new keys, an organization can generate a new certificate using the private key stored in escrow.

Expiration

When digital certificates are issued, they receive an expiration date. This validity period is indicated in a specific field within the certificate. Many certificates are set to expire after one year; however, the time period may be shorter or longer depending on specific needs. Open a certificate from within your browser while visiting a secured site (in most web browsers, select the padlock icon from the browser's status bar) and notice the "Valid to" and "Valid from" fields within the certificate (see Figure 13.3).

In the late 1990s, certificate expiration dates in older web browsers became an issue as the year 2000 approached. VeriSign's root certificate, which is embedded into web browsers, had an expiration date of December 31, 1999. When the certificate expired, if the browsers weren't updated, they were unable to correctly verify certificates issued or signed by VeriSign. As a result, many certificates are given expiration dates much further out, up to over 20 years in many cases.

FIGURE 13.3   General information for a digital certificate, including validity period.

Revocation

As you learned earlier in this chapter, when a certificate is no longer valid, certificate revocation occurs. There are many reasons why this might occur— for example, a private key might become compromised, the private key is lost, or the identifying credentials are no longer valid. Revoking a certificate is just not enough, however. The community that trusts these certificates must be notified that the certificates are no longer valid. This is accomplished via a certificate revocation list (CRL) or the Online Certificate Status Protocol (OCSP).

Status Checking

Both OSCP and CRLs are used to verify the status of a certificate. Three basic status levels exist in most PKI solutions: valid, suspended, and revoked. The status of a certificate can be checked by going to the CA that issued the certificate or to an agreed upon directory server that maintains a database indicating the status level for the set of certificates. In most cases, however, the application (such as a web browser) will have a function available that initiates a check for certificates.

Suspension

Certificate suspension occurs when a certificate is under investigation to determine whether it should be revoked. This mechanism allows a certificate to stay in place, but it is not valid for any type of use. Like the status checking that occurs with revoked certificates, users and systems are notified of suspended certificates in the same way. The primary difference is that new credentials will not need to be retrieved; it is only necessary to be notified that current credentials have had a change in status and are temporarily not valid for use.

Recovery

Key recovery is the process of using a recovery agent to restore a key pair from a backup and re-create a digital certificate using the recovered keys. Unlike in the case of a key compromise, this should be done only if the key pair becomes corrupted but they are still considered valid and trusted. Although it is beneficial to back up an individual user's key pair, it is even more important to back up the CA's keys in a secure location for business continuity and recovery purposes.

M of N Control

M of N control as it relates to PKI refers to the concept of backing up the public and private keys across multiple systems. This multiple backup provides a protective measure to ensure that no one individual can re-create his or her key pair from the backup. The backup process involves a mathematical function to distribute that data across a number of systems. A typical setup includes multiple personnel with unique job functions, and from different parts of the organization, to discourage collusion for the purpose of recovering keys without proper authority.

Renewal

As mentioned previously, every certificate is issued with an expiration date. When the certificate expires, a new certificate needs to be reissued. So long as the certificate holder's needs or identity information has not changed, the process is relatively simple. After the issuing CA validates the entity's identity, a new certificate can be generated based on the current public key.

Destruction

Destruction of a key pair and certificate typically occurs when the materials are no longer valid. Care should be taken when destroying a key pair. If the key pair to be destroyed is used for digital signatures, the private key portion should be destroyed first to prevent future signing activities with the key. If the materials were used for privacy purposes only, however, it might be necessary to archive a copy of the private key. You might need it later to decrypt archived data that was encrypted using the key. In addition, a digital certificate associated with keys that are no longer valid should be added to the CRL regardless of whether the key is actually destroyed or archived.

Key Usage

Digital certificates and key pairs can be used for various purposes, including privacy and authentication. The security policy of the organization that is using the key or the CA will define the purposes and capabilities for the certificates issued.

To achieve privacy, a user will require the public key of the individual or entity he or she wants to communicate with securely. This public key is used to encrypt the data that is transmitted, and the corresponding private key is used on the other end to decrypt the message.

Authentication is achieved by digitally signing the message being transmitted. To digitally sign a message, the signing entity requires access to the private key.

In short, the key usage extension of the certificate specifies how the private key can be used—either to enable the exchange of sensitive information or to create digital signatures. In addition, the key usage extension can specify that an entity can use the key for both the exchange of sensitive information and for signature purposes.

Multiple Key Pairs

In some circumstances, dual or multiple key pairs might be used to support distinct and separate services. For example, an individual in a corporate environment may require one key pair just for signing and another just for encrypting messages. Another example is the reorder associate who has one key pair to be used for signing and sending encrypted messages and might have another restricted to ordering equipment worth no more than a specific dollar amount. Multiple key pairs require multiple certificates because the X.509 certificate format does not support multiple keys

Cram Quiz

Answer these questions. The answers follow the last question. If you cannot answer
these questions correctly, consider reading this section again until you can.

1. In a decentralized key management system, the user is responsible for which
   one of the following functions?

   ○ **A.** Creation of the private and public key

   ○ **B.** Creation of the digital certificate

   ○ **C.** Creation of the CRL

   ○ **D.** Revocation of the digital certificate

2. Which of the following is not true regarding the expiration dates of certificates?

   ○ **A.** Certificates may be issued for a week.

   ○ **B.** Certificates are issued only at one-year intervals.

   ○ **C.** Certificates may be issued for 20 years.

   ○ **D.** Certificates must always have an expiration date.

Cram Quiz Answers

1. **A**. In a decentralized key system, the end user generates his or her own key pair.
   The other functions, such as the creation of the certificate, CRL, and the revocation of the certificate, are still handled by the certificate authority; therefore,
   answers B, C, and D are incorrect.

2. **B**. Digital certificates contain a field indicating the date to which the certificate is
   valid. This date is mandatory, and the validity period can vary from a short period of
   time up to a number of years; therefore, answers A, C, and D are true statements.

What Next?

If you want more practice on this chapter's exam objectives before you move
on, remember that you can access all of the Cram Quiz questions on the CD.
You can also create a custom exam by objective with the practice exam software. Note any objective you struggle with and go to that objective's material
in this chapter.

Practice Exam 1

CompTIA Security+ SY0-301

The multiple-choice questions provided here help you determine how prepared you are for the actual exam and which topics you need to review further. Write down your answers on a separate sheet of paper so you can take this exam again if necessary. Compare your answers against the answers and explanations that follow.

Exam Questions

1. An organization is looking for a filtering solution that will help eliminate some of the recent problems it has had with viruses and worms. Which of the following best meets this requirement?

   ○ **A.** Intrusion detection

   ○ **B.** Malware inspection

   ○ **C.** Load balancing

   ○ **D.** Internet content filtering

2. Which risk management response is being implemented when a company purchases insurance to protect against service outage?

   ○ **A.** Acceptance

   ○ **B.** Avoidance

   ○ **C.** Mitigation

   ○ **D.** Transference

3. A collection of compromised computers running software installed by a Trojan horse or a worm is referred to as what?

   ○ **A.** Zombie

   ○ **B.** Botnet

   ○ **C.** Herder

   ○ **D.** Virus

4. Adding a token for every POST or GET request that is initiated from the browser to the server can be used to mitigate which of the following attacks?

   ○ **A.** Buffer overflow

   ○ **B.** Cross-site request forgery (XSRF)

   ○ **C.** Cross-site scripting

   ○ **D.** Input validation error

5. Which of the following is one of the biggest challenges associated with database encryption?

   ○ **A.** Multi-tenancy

   ○ **B.** Key management

   ○ **C.** Weak authentication components

   ○ **D.** Platform support

6. Which form of access control enables data owners to extend access rights to other logons?

- ○ **A.** MAC
- ○ **B.** DAC
- ○ **C.** Role-based (RBAC)
- ○ **D.** Rule-based (RBAC)

7. In a decentralized key management system, the user is responsible for which one of the following functions?

- ○ **A.** Creation of the private and public key
- ○ **B.** Creation of the digital certificate
- ○ **C.** Creation of the CRL
- ○ **D.** Revocation of the digital certificate

8. What is the name given to the system of digital certificates and certificate authorities used for public key cryptography over networks?

- ○ **A.** Protocol Key Instructions (PKI)
- ○ **B.** Public Key Extranet (PKE)
- ○ **C.** Protocol Key Infrastructure (PKI)
- ○ **D.** Public Key Infrastructure (PKI)

9. If Sally wants to send a secure message to Mark using public-key encryption but is not worried about sender verification, what does she need in addition to her original message text?

- ○ **A.** Sally's private key
- ○ **B.** Sally's public key
- ○ **C.** Mark's private key
- ○ **D.** Mark's public key

10. Which of the following methods would be the most effective method to physically secure laptops that are used in an environment such as an office?

- ○ **A.** Security cables
- ○ **B.** Server cages
- ○ **C.** Locked cabinet
- ○ **D.** Hardware locks

11. Which of the following serves the purpose of trying to lure a malicious attacker into a system?

    O   **A.** Honeypot

    O   **B.** Pot of gold

    O   **C.** DMZ

    O   **D.** Bear trap

12. What is the recommended range of humidity level according to the ASHRAE?

    O   **A.** 10%–20%

    O   **B.** 30%–40%

    O   **C.** 40%–55%

    O   **D.** 55%–65%

13. Which of the following is a network protocol that supports file transfers and is a combination of RCP and SSH?

    O   **A.** HTTPS

    O   **B.** FTPS

    O   **C.** SFTP

    O   **D.** SCP

14. You want to implement a technology solution for a small organization that can function as a single point of policy control and management for access to Internet content. Which of the following should you choose?

    O   **A.** Proxy gateway

    O   **B.** Circuit-level gateway

    O   **C.** Application-level gateway

    O   **D.** Web security gateway

15. You have recently had security breaches in the network. You suspect they might be coming from a telecommuter's home network. Which of the following devices would you use to require a secure method for employees to access corporate resources while working from home?

    O   **A.** A router

    O   **B.** A VPN concentrator

    O   **C.** A firewall

    O   **D.** A network-based IDS

16. At which layer of the OSI model does the Internet Protocol Security protocol function?

    ◯ **A.** Network layer

    ◯ **B.** Presentation layer

    ◯ **C.** Session layer

    ◯ **D.** Application layer

17. When troubleshooting SSL, which two layers of the OSI model are of most value?

    ◯ **A.** Application layer and Presentation layer

    ◯ **B.** Presentation layer and Session layer

    ◯ **C.** Application layer and Transport layer

    ◯ **D.** Physical layer and Data Link layer

18. Which of the three principles of security is supported by an iris biometric system?

    ◯ **A.** Confidentiality

    ◯ **B.** Integrity

    ◯ **C.** Availability

    ◯ **D.** Vulnerability

19. _____ describes the potential that a weakness in hardware, software, process, or people will be identified and taken advantage of.

    ◯ **A.** Vulnerability

    ◯ **B.** Exploit

    ◯ **C.** Threat

    ◯ **D.** Risk

20. Which of the following is not a principal concern for first responders to a hacking incident within a corporation operating in the United States?

    ◯ **A.** Whether EMI shielding is intact

    ◯ **B.** Whether data is gathered properly

    ◯ **C.** Whether data is protected from modification

    ◯ **D.** Whether collected data is complete

21. Which rule of evidence within the United States involves Fourth Amendment protections?

    ◯ **A.** Admissible

    ◯ **B.** Complete

    ◯ **C.** Reliable

    ◯ **D.** Believable

22. A user has downloaded trial software and subsequently downloads a key generator in order to unlock the trial software. The user's antivirus detection software now alerts the user that the system is infected. Which one of the following best describes the type of malware infecting the system?

    ○ **A.** Logic bomb

    ○ **B.** Trojan

    ○ **C.** Adware

    ○ **D.** Worm

23. Which of the following is a coordinated effort in which multiple machines attack a single victim or host with the intent to prevent legitimate service?

    ○ **A.** DoS

    ○ **B.** Masquerading

    ○ **C.** DDoS

    ○ **D.** Trojan horse

24. What is the name given to the activity that consists of collecting information that will be later used for monitoring and review purposes?

    ○ **A.** Logging

    ○ **B.** Auditing

    ○ **C.** Inspecting

    ○ **D.** Vetting

25. Which of the following are not methods for minimizing a threat to a web server? (Choose the two best answers.)

    ○ **A.** Disable all non-web services

    ○ **B.** Ensure Telnet is running

    ○ **C.** Disable nonessential services

    ○ **D.** Enable logging

26. The organization is concerned about bugs in commercial off-the-shelf (COTS) software. Which of the following might be the only means of reviewing the security quality of the program?

    ○ **A.** Fuzzing

    ○ **B.** Cross-site scripting

    ○ **C.** Input validation

    ○ **D.** Cross-site request forgery

27. Which of the following is an attack in which the end user executes unwanted actions on a web application while he is currently authenticated?

   ○ **A.** Buffer overflow

   ○ **B.** Input validation error

   ○ **C.** Cross-site scripting

   ○ **D.** Cross-site request forgery

28. Which of the follow methods would be the most effective method to physically secure computers that are used in a lab environment that operates on a part-time basis?

   ○ **A.** Security cables

   ○ **B.** Server cages

   ○ **C.** Locked cabinet

   ○ **D.** Hardware locks

29. Which of the following methods would be the most effective to physically secure tower-style computers in a financial organization?

   ○ **A.** Security cables

   ○ **B.** Server cages

   ○ **C.** Locked cabinet

   ○ **D.** Hardware locks

30. Your organization is exploring data loss prevention solutions. The proposed solution is an end-point solution. This solution is targeting which of the following data states?

   ○ **A.** In motion

   ○ **B.** At rest

   ○ **C.** In use

   ○ **D.** At flux

31. Which of the following uses a secure crypto-processor to authenticate hardware devices such as PC or laptop?

   ○ **A.** Public Key Infrastructure

   ○ **B.** Full disk encryption

   ○ **C.** File-level encryption

   ○ **D.** Trusted Platform Module

32. Which process involves verifying keys as being authentic?

- ○ **A.** Authorization
- ○ **B.** Authentication
- ○ **C.** Access control
- ○ **D.** Verification

33. Which category of authentication includes smart cards?

- ○ **A.** Something you know
- ○ **B.** Something you have
- ○ **C.** Something you are
- ○ **D.** Something you do

34. Which of the following is not a division of access control as defined by the Orange Book?

- ○ **A.** Discretionary
- ○ **B.** Limited
- ○ **C.** Mandatory
- ○ **D.** Verified

35. Which division of TCSEC access control includes the subdivisions Controlled Access Protection and Discretionary Security Protection?

- ○ **A.** Division A
- ○ **B.** Division B
- ○ **C.** Division C
- ○ **D.** Division D

36. Which of the following is a hybrid cryptosystem?

- ○ **A.** IDEA
- ○ **B.** MD5
- ○ **C.** RSA
- ○ **D.** PGP

37. Which of the following is the type of algorithm used by MD5?

- ○ **A.** Block cipher algorithm
- ○ **B.** Hashing algorithm
- ○ **C.** Asymmetric encryption algorithm
- ○ **D.** Cryptographic algorithm

38. To check the validity of a digital certificate, which one of the following would be used?

   ○ **A.** Corporate security policy

   ○ **B.** Certificate policy

   ○ **C.** Certificate revocation list

   ○ **D.** Expired domain names

39. What is the acronym for the de facto cryptographic message standards developed by RSA Laboratories?

   ○ **A.** PKIX

   ○ **B.** X.509

   ○ **C.** PKCS

   ○ **D.** Both A and C

40. Which of the following is true of digital signatures? (Choose the two best answers.)

   ○ **A.** They use the skipjack algorithm.

   ○ **B.** They can be automatically time-stamped.

   ○ **C.** They allow the sender to repudiate that the message was sent.

   ○ **D.** They cannot be imitated by someone else.

41. What is the recommended best model of privilege management in a large extended enterprise?

   ○ **A.** DACLs

   ○ **B.** User-based

   ○ **C.** SACLs

   ○ **D.** Group-based

42. Which authorization protocol is generally compatible with TACACS?

   ○ **A.** LDAP

   ○ **B.** RADIUS

   ○ **C.** TACACS+

   ○ **D.** XTACACS

43. Your organization is exploring data loss prevention solutions. The proposed solution is a software storage solution that monitors how confidential data is stored. This solution is targeting which of the following data states?

   ○ **A.** In motion

   ○ **B.** At rest

   ○ **C.** In use

   ○ **D.** At flux

44. Which of the following is needed to establish effective security baselines for host systems? (Select two correct answers.)

- ○ **A.** Cable locks
- ○ **B.** Mandatory settings
- ○ **C.** Standard application suites
- ○ **D.** Decentralized administration

45. Which of the following types of attacks is executed by placing malicious executable code on a website?

- ○ **A.** Buffer overflow
- ○ **B.** Cross-site request forgery (XSRF)
- ○ **C.** Cross-site scripting (XXS)
- ○ **D.** Input validation error

46. Which of the following are examples of protocol analyzers? (Select all correct answers.)

- ○ **A.** Metasploit
- ○ **B.** Wireshark
- ○ **C.** SATAN
- ○ **D.** Network Monitor

47. Which one of the following is not an example of a type of virus?

- ○ **A.** Boot sector
- ○ **B.** Macro
- ○ **C.** Stealth
- ○ **D.** Multiparisite

48. Which form of cabling is least susceptible to EM interference?

- ○ **A.** STP
- ○ **B.** UTP
- ○ **C.** Co-axial
- ○ **D.** Fiber-optic

49. Which of the following is not a factor used in asset identification?

- ○ **A.** Methods of access
- ○ **B.** Original and replacement costs
- ○ **C.** Maintenance costs
- ○ **D.** Profit generated

50. It is suspected that some recent network compromises are originating from the use of SNMP. Which of the following UDP port traffic should be monitored? (Choose two correct answers.)

    ○ **A.** 161

    ○ **B.** 139

    ○ **C.** 138

    ○ **D.** 162

51. You are implementing network access for several internal business units that work with sensitive information on a small organizational network. Which of the following would best mitigate risk associated with users improperly accessing other segments of the network without adding additional switches?

    ○ **A.** Log analysis

    ○ **B.** Access Control Lists

    ○ **C.** Network segmentation

    ○ **D.** Proper VLAN management

52. Your organization is exploring data loss prevention solutions. The proposed solution is a software network solution installed near the network perimeter to monitor for and flag policy violations. This solution is targeting which of the following data states?

    ○ **A.** In motion

    ○ **B.** At rest

    ○ **C.** In use

    ○ **D.** At flux

53. What is the first step in performing a basic forensic analysis?

    ○ **A.** Ensure that the evidence is acceptable in a court of law

    ○ **B.** Identify the evidence

    ○ **C.** Extract, process, and interpret the evidence

    ○ **D.** Determine how to preserve the evidence

54. Which of the following is not true regarding expiration dates of certificates?

    ○ **A.** Certificates may be issued for a week.

    ○ **B.** Certificates are issued only at yearly intervals.

    ○ **C.** Certificates may be issued for 20 years.

    ○ **D.** Certificates must always have an expiration date.

55. Which of the following statements are true when discussing physical security? (Select all correct answers.)

  ○ **A.** Physical security attempts to control access to data from Internet users.

  ○ **B.** Physical security attempts to control unwanted access to specified areas of a building.

  ○ **C.** Physical security attempts to control the effect of natural disasters on facilities and equipment.

  ○ **D.** Physical security attempts to control internal employee access into secure areas.

56. Which type of authorization provides no mechanism for unique logon identification?

  ○ **A.** Anonymous

  ○ **B.** Kerberos

  ○ **C.** TACACS

  ○ **D.** TACACS+

57. Which is the best rule-based access control constraint to protect against unauthorized access when admins are off-duty?

  ○ **A.** Least privilege

  ○ **B.** Separation of duties

  ○ **C.** Account expiration

  ○ **D.** Time of day

58. Which of the following protocols supports DES, 3DES, RC2, and RSA2 encryption along with CHAP authentication, but was not widely adopted?

  ○ **A.** S-HTTP

  ○ **B.** S/MIME

  ○ **C.** HTTP

  ○ **D.** PPTP

59. A new switch has been implemented in areas where there is very little physical access control. Which of the following would the organization implement as a method for additional checks in order to prevent unauthorized access?

  ○ **A.** Loop protection

  ○ **B.** Flood guard

  ○ **C.** Implicit deny

  ○ **D.** Port security

60. There have been some sporadic connectivity issues on the network. Which of the following is the best choice to investigate these issues?

- ○ **A.** Protocol analyzer
- ○ **B.** Circuit-level gateway logs
- ○ **C.** Spam filter appliance
- ○ **D.** Web application firewall logs

61. Which of the following types of attacks can be done by either convincing the users to click on an HTML page the attacker has constructed or insert arbitrary HTML in a target website that the users visit?

- ○ **A.** Buffer overflow
- ○ **B.** Cross-site request forgery (XSRF)
- ○ **C.** Cross-site scripting (XXS)
- ○ **D.** Input validation error

62. Which of the following standards is used in HSMs?

- ○ **A.** PKCS #11
- ○ **B.** PKCS #7
- ○ **C.** AES
- ○ **D.** EFS

63. Which of the following algorithms is not an example of a symmetric encryption algorithm?

- ○ **A.** Rijndael
- ○ **B.** Diffie-Hellman
- ○ **C.** RC6
- ○ **D.** AES

64. Which of the following best describes the process of encrypting and decrypting data using an asymmetric encryption algorithm?

- ○ **A.** Only the public key is used to encrypt, and only the private key is used to decrypt.
- ○ **B.** The public key is used to either encrypt or decrypt.
- ○ **C.** Only the private key is used to encrypt, and only the public key is used to decrypt.
- ○ **D.** The private key is used to decrypt data encrypted with the public key.

65. Which one of the following defines APIs for devices such as smart cards that contain cryptographic information?

- ○ **A.** PKCS #11
- ○ **B.** PKCS #13
- ○ **C.** PKCS #4
- ○ **D.** PKCS #2

66. Which of the following are steps that can be taken to harden FTP services?

- ○ **A.** Anonymous access to share files of questionable or undesirable content should be limited.
- ○ **B.** Regular review of networks for unauthorized or rogue servers.
- ○ **C.** Technologies that allow dynamic updates must also include access control and authentication.
- ○ **D.** Unauthorized zone transfers should also be restricted.

67. A situation in which a program or process attempts to store more data in a temporary data storage area than it was intended to hold is known as a what?

- ○ **A.** Buffer overflow
- ○ **B.** Denial of service
- ○ **C.** Distributed denial of service
- ○ **D.** Storage overrun

68. TEMPEST deals with which form of environmental control?

- ○ **A.** HVAC
- ○ **B.** EMI shielding
- ○ **C.** Humidity
- ○ **D.** Cold-aisle

69. Which of the following is included in hardening a host operating system?

- ○ **A.** A policy for antivirus updates
- ○ **B.** A policy for remote wipe
- ○ **C.** An efficient method to connect to remote sites
- ○ **D.** An effective system for file-level security

70. Which of the following is the preferred type of encryption used in SaaS platforms?

- ○ **A.** Application level
- ○ **B.** Database level
- ○ **C.** Media level
- ○ **D.** HSM level

71. Several organizational users are experiencing network and Internet connectivity issues. Which of the following would be most helpful in troubleshooting where the connectivity problems might exist?

- ○ **A.** SSL
- ○ **B.** IPsec
- ○ **C.** SNMP
- ○ **D.** Traceroute

72. An organization has an access control list implemented on the border router, but it appears that unauthorized traffic is still being accepted. Which of the following would the organization implement to improve the blocking of unauthorized traffic?

- ○ **A.** Loop protection
- ○ **B.** Flood guard
- ○ **C.** Implicit deny
- ○ **D.** Port security

73. An asset is valued at $12,000; the threat exposure factor of a risk affecting that asset is 25%; and the annualized rate of occurrence is 50%. What is the SLE?

- ○ **A.** $1,500
- ○ **B.** $3,000
- ○ **C.** $4,000
- ○ **D.** $6,000

74. Which form of fire suppression functions best in an Alaskan fire of burning metals?

- ○ **A.** Dry-pipe sprinkler
- ○ **B.** Wet-pipe sprinkler
- ○ **C.** Carbon dioxide
- ○ **D.** Dry powder

75. While performing regular security audits, you suspect that your company is under attack and someone is attempting to use resources on your network. The IP addresses in the log files belong to a trusted partner company, however. Assuming an attack, which of the following might be occurring?

- ○ **A.** Replay
- ○ **B.** Authorization
- ○ **C.** Social engineering
- ○ **D.** Spoofing

76. Which mandatory access control label is appropriate for generally available data?

- ○ **A.** ANONYMOUS
- ○ **B.** PUBLIC
- ○ **C.** SENSITIVE
- ○ **D.** SECRET

77. After a new switch was implemented, some sporadic connectivity issues on the network have occurred. The issues are suspected to be device related. Which of the following would the organization implement as a method for additional checks in order to prevent issues?

- ○ **A.** Loop protection
- ○ **B.** Flood guard
- ○ **C.** Implicit deny
- ○ **D.** Port security

78. Which of the following is an example of a false negative result?

- ○ **A.** An authorized user is granted access to a resource.
- ○ **B.** An unauthorized user is granted access to a resource.
- ○ **C.** An authorized user is refused access to a resource.
- ○ **D.** An unauthorized user is refused access to a resource.

79. Which of the following is the best choice for encrypting large amounts of data?

- ○ **A.** Asymmetric encryption
- ○ **B.** Symmetric encryption
- ○ **C.** Elliptical curve encryption
- ○ **D.** RSA encryption

80. You want to be sure that the FTP ports that are required for a contract worker's functionality have been properly secured. Which of the following ports would you check?

- ○ **A.** 25/110/143
- ○ **B.** 20/21
- ○ **C.** 137/138/139
- ○ **D.** 161/162

81. Security guards are a form of which specific type of control?

    ○   **A.** Management

    ○   **B.** Technical

    ○   **C.** Physical

    ○   **D.** Access

82. Which utility allows for the compilation of a list of systems, devices, and network hardware?

    ○   **A.** Port scanner

    ○   **B.** Vulnerability scanner

    ○   **C.** Protocol analyzer

    ○   **D.** Network mapper

83. Which one of the following is not considered a physical security component?

    ○   **A.** VPN tunnel

    ○   **B.** Mantrap

    ○   **C.** Fence

    ○   **D.** CCTV

84. A physical security plan should include which of the following? (Select all correct answers.)

    ○   **A.** Description of the physical assets being protected

    ○   **B.** The threats from which you are protecting against and their likelihood

    ○   **C.** Location of a hard disk's physical blocks

    ○   **D.** Description of the physical areas where assets are located

85. Never inserting untrusted data except in allowed locations can be used to mitigate which of the following attacks? (Select two answers.)

    ○   **A.** Buffer overflow

    ○   **B.** Cross-site request forgery (XSRF)

    ○   **C.** Cross-site scripting

    ○   **D.** Input validation error

86. An organization is looking to add a layer of security and improve enterprise desktop management. Which of the following fulfills this requirement?

    ○   **A.** Virtualization

    ○   **B.** Network storage policies

    ○   **C.** VPN remote access

    ○   **D.** Roaming profiles

87. Which of the following is a program that uses SSH to transfer files?

    ○ **A.** S-HTTP

    ○ **B.** S/MIME

    ○ **C.** SFTP

    ○ **D.** HTTPS

88. Which one of the following best describes the type of attack designed to bring a network to a halt by flooding the systems with useless traffic?

    ○ **A.** DoS

    ○ **B.** Ping of death

    ○ **C.** Teardrop

    ○ **D.** Social engineering

89. The process of making an operating system more secure by closing known vulnerabilities and addressing security issues is known as which of the following?

    ○ **A.** Handshaking

    ○ **B.** Hardening

    ○ **C.** Hotfixing

    ○ **D.** All of the above

90. An organization is looking for a mobile solution that allows both executives and employees to discuss sensitive information without having to travel to secure company locations. Which of the following fulfills this requirement?

    ○ **A.** GPS tracking

    ○ **B.** Voice encryption

    ○ **C.** Remote wipe

    ○ **D.** Passcode policy

91. Users received a spam email from an unknown source and chose the option in the email to unsubscribe and are now getting more spam as a result. Which one of the following is most likely the reason?

    ○ **A.** The unsubscribe option does not actually do anything.

    ○ **B.** The unsubscribe request was never received.

    ○ **C.** Spam filters were automatically turned off when making the selection to unsubscribe.

    ○ **D.** They confirmed that their addresses are "live."

92. Which form of data storage is the most subject to modification?

- ○ **A.** Main memory
- ○ **B.** Write-once memory
- ○ **C.** Routing tables
- ○ **D.** Secondary memory

93. Which of the following is not an example of multifactor authentication?

- ○ **A.** Logon and password
- ○ **B.** Smart card and PIN
- ○ **C.** RFID chip and thumbprint
- ○ **D.** Gait and iris recognition

94. Which of the following is an example of role-based access control criteria?

- ○ **A.** GPS coordinates
- ○ **B.** Trusted OS
- ○ **C.** Members of the Administrators group
- ○ **D.** Time of day

95. The sender of data is provided with proof of delivery, and neither the sender nor receiver can deny either having sent or received the data. What is this called?

- ○ **A.** Nonrepudiation
- ○ **B.** Repetition
- ○ **C.** Nonrepetition
- ○ **D.** Repudiation

96. Which of the following are steps that can be taken to harden DHCP services?

- ○ **A.** Anonymous access to share files of questionable or undesirable content should be limited.
- ○ **B.** Regular review of networks for unauthorized or rogue servers.
- ○ **C.** Technologies that allow dynamic updates must also include access control and authentication.
- ○ **D.** Unauthorized zone transfers should also be restricted.

97. Which of the fields included within a digital certificate identifies the directory name of the entity signing the certificate?

- ○ **A.** Signature Algorithm Identifier
- ○ **B.** Issuer
- ○ **C.** Subject Name
- ○ **D.** Subject Public Key Information

98. Which of the following rights assignments overrides all others in a DAC or RBAC environment?

   ○ **A.** Implicit DENY

   ○ **B.** Implicit ALLOW

   ○ **C.** Explicit ALLOW

   ○ **D.** Explicit DENY

99. Which type of biometric authentication involves identification of the unique patterns of blood vessels at the back of the eye?

   ○ **A.** Facial recognition

   ○ **B.** Iris

   ○ **C.** Retina

   ○ **D.** Signature

100. Which version of X.509 supports an optional Extension field?

   ○ **A.** Version 1

   ○ **B.** Version 2

   ○ **C.** Version 3

   ○ **D.** Answers B and C

Answers to Practice Exam 1

Answers at a Glance

1. B	35. C	68. B
2. D	36. D	69. D
3. B	37. B	70. A
4. B	38. C	71. D
5. B	39. C	72. C
6. B	40. B and D	73. B
7. A	41. D	74. D
8. D	42. D	75. D
9. D	43. B	76. B
10. A	44. B and C	77. A
11. A	45. C	78. C
12. C	46. B and D	79. B
13. D	47. D	80. B
14. D	48. D	81. C
15. B	49. A	82. D
16. A	50. A and D	83. A
17. C	51. D	84. A, B, and D
18. A	52. A	85. A and D
19. C	53. B	86. A
20. A	54. B	87. C
21. A	55. B, C and D	88. A
22. B	56. A	89. B
23. C	57. D	90. B
24. A	58. A	91. D
25. B and D	59. D	92. C
26. A	60. A	93. A
27. D	61. B	94. C
28. C	62. A	95. A
29. B	63. B	96. B
30. C	64. D	97. B
31. D	65. A	98. D
32. B	66. A	99. C
33. B	67. A	100. C
34. B		

Answers with Explanations

Question 1

Answer B is correct. A malware inspection filter is basically a web filter applied to traffic that uses the HTTP protocol. The body of all HTTP requests and responses is inspected. Malicious content is blocked while legitimate content passes through unaltered. Answer A is incorrect because intrusion-detection systems are designed to analyze data, identify attacks, and respond to the intrusion. Answer C is incorrect because load balancers are servers configured in a cluster to provide scalability and high availability. Answer D is incorrect because Internet content filters use a collection of terms, words, and phrases that are compared to content from browsers and applications.

Question 2

Answer D is correct. The liability of risk is transferred through insurance policies. Answer A is incorrect because accepting a risk is to do nothing in response. Risk avoidance involves simply terminating the operation that produces the risk, making answer B incorrect. Answer C is not correct because mitigation applies a solution that results in a reduced level of risk or exposure.

Question 3

Answer B is correct. Answers A and C are incorrect but are related to a botnet in that a zombie is one of many computer systems that make up a botnet, whereas a bot herder is the controller of the botnet. Answer D is incorrect. A virus is a program that infects a computer without the knowledge of the user.

Question 4

Answer B is correct. In order to mitigate cross-site request forgery (XSRF) attacks, the most common solution is to add a token for every POST or GET request that is initiated from the browser to the server. Answer A is incorrect because buffer overflows are associated with input validation. Answer C is incorrect because setting the HTTPOnly flag on the session cookie is used to mitigate XXS attacks. Answer D is incorrect because input validation tests whether an application properly handles input from a source outside the application destined for internal processing.

Question 5

Answer B is correct. One of the biggest challenges associated with database encryption is key management. Answer A is incorrect because multi-tenancy is a security issue related to cloud computing implementations. Answer C is incorrect because lack of management software and weak authentication components are associated with hardware hard drive encryption. Answer D is incorrect because cost and platform support are concerns with smartphone encryption products.

Question 6

Answer B is correct. Discretionary access control (DAC) systems enable data owners to extend access rights to other logons. Mandatory access control (MAC) systems require assignment of labels to extend access, making answer A incorrect. Answers C and D are incorrect because both RBAC access control forms rely on conditional assignment of access rules either inherited (role-based) or by environmental factors such as time of day or secured terminal location (rule-based).

Question 7

Answer A is correct. In a decentralized key system, the end user generates his or her own key pair. The other functions, such as creation of the certificate, CRL, and the revocation of the certificate, are still handled by the certificate authority; therefore, answers B, C, and D are incorrect.

Question 8

Answer D is correct. Public Key Infrastructure describes the trust hierarchy system for implementing a secure public key cryptography system over TCP/IP networks. Answers A, B, and C are incorrect because these are bogus terms.

Question 9

Answer D is correct. Sally needs Mark's public key to encrypt her original message in a form that only Mark can decrypt. Neither of Sally's keys is needed because the originator does not need to be validated, making answers A and B incorrect. Answer C is incorrect because Mark's private key is used for decrypting the encrypted message to reveal Sally's original message.

Question 10

Answer A is correct. Security cables with combination locks can provide such security and are easy to use. They are used mostly to secure laptops and leave the equipment exposed. Answer B is incorrect because PC Safe tower and server cages are designed to bolt to the floor and are meant to be in an environment that is static. Answer C is incorrect because a locked cabinet is an alternative for equipment that is not used or does not have to be physically accessed on a regular, daily basis. Vendors provide solutions such as a security cabinet locker that secures CPU towers. The housing is made of durable, heavy-duty steel for strength. Answer D is incorrect because a hardware lock is used for license enforcement.

Question 11

Answer A is correct. A honeypot is used to serve as a decoy and lure a malicious attacker. Answers B and D are incorrect answers and are not legitimate terms for testing purposes. Answer C is incorrect because a DMZ is an area between the Internet and the internal network.

Question 12

Answer C is correct. The American Society of Heating, Refrigerating and Air-Conditioning Engineers (ASHRAE) recommends optimal humidity levels in the 40% to 55% range, making answers A, B, and D incorrect. Very low levels of humidity can promote the buildup of electrostatic charges that can harm sensitive electronic components. Very high levels of humidity can promote condensation on chilled surfaces and introduce liquid into operating equipment.

Question 13

Answer D is correct. The Secure Copy Protocol (SCP) is a network protocol that supports file transfers. SCP is a combination of RCP and SSH. It uses the BSD RCP protocol tunneled through the Secure Shell (SSH) protocol to provide encryption and authentication. Answer A is incorrect because HTTPS is used for secured web-based communications. Answer B is incorrect. FTPS, also known as FTP Secure and FTP-SSL, is a FTP extension that adds support for TLS and SSL. Answer C is incorrect because SFTP, or secure FTP, is a program that uses SSH to transfer files. Unlike standard FTP, it encrypts both commands and data, preventing passwords and sensitive information from being transmitted in the clear over the network.

Question 14

Answer D is correct. Web security gateways offer a single point of policy control and management for web-based content access. Answer A is too generic to be a proper answer. Answer B is incorrect because a circuit-level gateway's decisions are based on source and destination addresses. Answer C is incorrect because an application-level gateway understands services and protocols.

Question 15

Answer B is correct. A VPN concentrator is used to allow multiple users to access network resources using secure features that are built into the device and are deployed where the requirement is for a single device to handle a very large number of VPN tunnels. Answer A is incorrect because a router forwards information to its destination on the network or the Internet. A firewall protects computers and networks from undesired access by the outside world; therefore, answer C is incorrect. Answer D is incorrect because network-based intrusion-detection systems monitor the packet flow and try to locate packets that are not allowed for one reason or another and might have gotten through the firewall.

Question 16

Answer A is correct. IPsec validation and encryption function at the network layer of the OSI model. Answers B, C, and D are incorrect because IPsec functions at a lower level of the OSI model.

Question 17

Answer C is correct. SSL connections occur between the application and transport layers. Answer A is incorrect because the Secure Sockets Layer SSL operates at a deeper level. Answer B is incorrect because the Secure Sockets Layer transport effectively fills the same role as these OSI model layers. Answer D is incorrect because the data has been abstracted beyond the level at which SSL operates.

Question 18

Answer A is correct. Confidentiality involves protecting against unauthorized access, which biometric authentication systems support. Integrity is concerned with preventing unauthorized modification, making answer B incorrect. Answer C is not correct because availability is concerned with ensuring that access to services and data is protected against disruption. Answer D is incorrect because a vulnerability is a failure in one or more of the C-I-A principles.

Question 19

Answer C is correct. A threat is the potential that a vulnerability will be identified and exploited. Answer A is incorrect because a vulnerability is the weakness itself and not the likelihood that it will be identified and exploited. Answer B is incorrect because an exploit is the mechanism of taking advantage of a vulnerability rather than its likelihood of occurrence. Answer D is incorrect because risk is the likelihood that a threat will occur and the measure of its effect.

Question 20

Answer A is correct. EMI shielding is important to protecting data and services against unauthorized interception as well as interference but is not a principal concern for first responders following an incident. First responders must ensure that data is collected correctly and protect it from modification using proper controls, ensuring a clear chain of evidence, making answers B and C incorrect. Answer D is incorrect because a first responder might be the only agent able to ensure that all data is collected before being lost due to volatility of storage.

Question 21

Answer A is correct. Admissibility involves collecting data in a manner that ensures its viability in court, including legal requirements such as the Fourth Amendment protections against unlawful search and seizure. Answers B and C are incorrect because data must be collected completely and protected against modification to ensure reliability, but these are not concerns of the Fourth Amendment. Answer D is incorrect because believability focuses on evidence being understandable, documented, and not subject to modification during transition.

Question 22

Answer B is correct. Trojans are programs disguised as something useful. In this instance, the user was likely illegally trying to crack software, and in the process infect the system with malware. Although answers A, C, and D are types of malware, they are not the best choices.

Question 23

Answer C is correct. A distributed denial of service (DDoS) is similar to a denial-of-service (DoS) attack in that they both try to prevent legitimate access to services. However, a DDoS is a coordinated effort among many computer systems; therefore, answer A is incorrect. Masquerading involves using someone else's identity to access resources; therefore, answer B is incorrect. A Trojan horse is a program used to perform hidden functions; therefore, answer D is incorrect.

Question 24

Answer A is correct. Logging is the process of collecting data to be used for monitoring and auditing purposes. Auditing is the process of verification that normally involves going through log files; therefore, answer B is incorrect. Typically, the log files are frequently inspected, and inspection is not the process of collecting the data; therefore, answer C is incorrect. Vetting is the process of thorough examination or evaluation; therefore, answer D is incorrect.

Question 25

Answers B and D are correct. Having Telnet enabled presents security issues and is not a primary method for minimizing threat. Logging is important for secure operations and is invaluable when recovering from a security incident. However, it is not a primary method for reducing threat. Answer A is incorrect because disabling all non-web services might provide a secure solution for minimizing threats. Answer C is incorrect because each network service carries its own risks; therefore, it is important to disable all nonessential services.

Question 26

Answer A is correct. In some closed application instances, fuzzing might be the only means of reviewing the security quality of the program. Answer B is incorrect because cross-site scripting (XXS) vulnerabilities can be used to hijack the user's session or to cause the user accessing malware-tainted Site A to unknowingly attack Site B on behalf of the attacker who planted code on Site A. Answer C is incorrect because input validation tests whether an application properly handles input from a source outside the application destined for internal processing. Answer D, Cross-site Request Forgery (XSRF), is an attack in which the end user executes unwanted actions on a web application while she is currently authenticated.

Question 27

Answer D is correct. Cross-site Request Forgery (XSRF) is an attack in which the end user executes unwanted actions on a web application while he is currently authenticated. Answer A is incorrect because a buffer overflow is a direct result of poor or incorrect input validation or mishandled exceptions. Answer B is incorrect because input validation errors are a result of improper field checking in the code. Answer C is incorrect because cross-site scripting (XXS) vulnerabilities can be used to hijack the user's session or to cause the user accessing malware-tainted Site A to unknowingly attack Site B on behalf of the attacker who planted code on Site A.

Question 28

Answer C is correct. A locked cabinet is an alternative for equipment that is not used or does not have to be physically accessed on a regular, daily basis. Vendors provide solutions such as a security cabinet locker that secures CPU towers. The housing is made of durable, heavy-duty steel for strength. Answer A is incorrect because security cables with combination locks can provide such security and are easy to use but are used mostly to secure laptops and leave the equipment exposed. Answer B is incorrect because PC Safe tower and server cages are designed to bolt to the floor and are meant to be in an environment that is static. Answer D is incorrect because a hardware lock is used for license enforcement.

Question 29

Answer B is correct. Products such as PC Safe tower and server cages are designed to bolt to the floor and are meant to be in an environment that is static. For example, financial businesses have been hit hard by theft of desktop computers because they hold a lot of personal data. Answer A is incorrect because security cables with combination locks can provide such security and are easy to use and are used mostly to secure laptops and leave the equipment exposed. Answer C is incorrect because a locked cabinet is an alternative for equipment that is not used or does not have to be physically accessed on a regular, daily basis. Answer D is incorrect because a hardware lock, also known as a software protection dongle, is used for license enforcement.

Question 30

Answer C is correct. Protection of data in use is considered to be an endpoint solution and the application is run on end-user workstations or servers in the organization. Answer A is incorrect because protection of data in motion is considered to be a network solution and either a hardware or software solution is installed near the network perimeter to monitor for and flag policy violations. Answer B is incorrect because protection of data at rest is considered to be a storage solution and is generally a software solution that monitors how confidential data is stored. Answer D is incorrect because there is no such data state.

Question 31

Answer D is correct. TPM refers to a secure crypto-processor used to authenticate hardware devices such as PC or laptop. The idea behind TPM is to allow any encryption-enabled application to take advantage of the chip. Answer A is incorrect because Public Key Infrastructure (PKI) is a set of hardware, software, people, policies, and procedures needed to create, manage, distribute, use, store, and revoke digital certificates. Answer B is incorrect because full-disk encryption involves encrypting the operating system partition on a computer and then booting and running with the system drive encrypted at all times. Answer C is incorrect because in file- or folder-level encryption, individual files or directories are encrypted by the file system itself.

Question 32

Answer B is correct. Authentication involves the presentation and verification of credentials of keys as being authentic. Answer A is incorrect because authorization involves checking authenticated credentials against a list of authorized security principles. Once checked, resource access is allowed or limited based on Access Control constraints, making answer C incorrect. Answer D is incorrect because verification of credentials occurs during authentication (as being authentic) and authorization (as being authorized to request resource access) and is not a recognized access control process.

Question 33

Answer B is correct. Something you have includes smart cards, tokens, and keys. Something you know includes account logons, passwords, and PINs, making answer A incorrect. Answers C and D are incorrect because both something you are and something you do involve measures of personal biological qualities and do not require an external device such as a smart card or key.

Question 34

Answer B is correct. "Limited" is not an access control designation within the Trusted Computer System Evaluation Criteria (TCSEC) document DoD

5200.28-STD, often referred to as the "Orange Book." The four divisions are Mandatory, Discretionary, Minimal, and Verified— making answers A, C, and D incorrect.

Question 35

Answer C is correct. Discretionary access control (C-level) includes subdivisions Discretionary Security Protection (C1) and Controlled Access Protection (C2) based on details such as data segmentation and logging. These are not subdivisions of the Minimal (D-level), Mandatory (B-level), or Verified (A-level) access control divisions—making answers A, B, and D incorrect.

Question 36

Answer D is correct. Pretty Good Privacy (PGP) is a hybrid cryptosystem that makes use of the incorrect choices, A, B, and C. IDEA is a symmetric encryption cipher, RSA is an asymmetric cipher, and MD5 is a hash.

Question 37

Answer B is correct. Although the Message Digest (MD) series of algorithms is classified globally as a symmetric key encryption algorithm, the correct answer is hashing algorithm, which is the method that the algorithm uses to encrypt data. Answer A in incorrect because a block cipher divides the message into blocks of bits. Answer C is incorrect because MD5 is a symmetric key algorithm, not an asymmetric encryption algorithm (examples of this include RC6, Twofish, and Rijndael). Answer D is incorrect because cryptographic algorithm is a bogus term.

Question 38

Answer C is correct. A certificate revocation list (CRL) provides a detailed list of certificates that are no longer valid. A corporate security policy would not provide current information on the validity of issued certificates; therefore, answer A is incorrect. A certificate policy does not provide information on invalid issued certificates, either; therefore, answer B is incorrect. Finally, an expired domain name has no bearing on the validity of a digital certificate; therefore, answer D is incorrect.

Question 39

Answer C is correct. The Public Key Cryptography Standards (PKCS) are the de facto cryptographic message standards developed and maintained by RSA Laboratories, a division of the RSA Security Corporation. PKIX describes the development of Internet standards for X.509-based digital certificates; therefore, answers A, B, and D are incorrect.

Question 40

Answers B and D are correct. Digital signatures offer several features and capabilities. This includes being able to ensure the sender cannot repudiate that he or she used the signature. In addition, non-repudiation schemes are capable of offering time stamps for the digital signature. Answer A is incorrect. The Skipjack algorithm was developed for use with a chipset developed by the U.S. government. Skipjack provides only for encryption. Answer C is incorrect, as a key feature of digital signatures is to provide for non-repudiation.

Question 41

Answer D is correct. Group-based privilege management is generally the best model for assignment of rights and denials in large extended enterprise environments, as a user's rights can be easily reviewed by examining its group membership. Answer B is incorrect because user-based privilege management requires significant overhead to provision and de-provision individual permissions and can leave unauthorized access rights after personnel transfer between organizational roles or locales. Answers A and C are incorrect because both discretionary (DACLs) and system access control lists (SACLs) are produced as the result of privilege assignment and not models of management.

Question 42

Answer D is correct. The Extended Terminal Access Controller Access Control System (XTACACS) protocol is a proprietary form of the TACACS protocol developed by Cisco and is compatible in many cases. Neither LDAP nor RADIUS is affiliated with the TACACS protocol, making answers A and B incorrect. Answer C is incorrect because the newer TACACS+ is not backward-compatible with its legacy equivalent.

Question 43

Answer B is correct. Protection of data at rest is considered to be a storage solution and is generally a software solution that monitors how confidential data is stored. Answer C is incorrect because protection of data in use is considered to be an endpoint solution and the application is run on end-user workstations or servers in the organization. Answer A is incorrect because protection of data in motion is considered to be a network solution and either a hardware or software solution is installed near the network perimeter to monitor for and flag policy violations. Answer D is incorrect because there is no such data state.

Question 44

Answers B and C are correct. In order to establish effective security baselines, enterprise network security management requires a measure of commonality between the systems. Mandatory settings, standard application suites, and initial setup configuration details all factor into the security stance of an enterprise network. Answer A is incorrect because cable locks have nothing to do with effective security baselines. Answer D is incorrect because decentralized management does not have anything to do with security baselines.

Question 45

Answer C is correct. Cross-site scripting (XXS) vulnerabilities can be used to hijack the user's session or to cause the user accessing malware-tainted Site A to unknowingly attack Site B on behalf of the attacker who planted code on Site A. Answer A is incorrect because a buffer overflow is a direct result of poor or incorrect input validation or mishandled exceptions. Answer B is incorrect. The key element to understanding XSRF is that attackers are betting that users have a validated login cookie for the website already stored in their browsers. Answer D is incorrect because input validation errors are a result of improper field checking in the code.

Question 46

Answers B and D are correct. Windows Server operating systems come with a protocol analyzer called Network Monitor. Third-party programs such as Wireshark can also be used for network monitoring. Metasploit is a framework used for penetration testing, and SATAN is a network security testing tool; therefore, answers A and C are incorrect.

Question 47

Answer D is correct. Answers A, B, and C each represent a different type of virus. Multiparisite is not a type of computer virus; however, a multipartite is a type of virus that describes a hybrid of a boot sector and program virus.

Question 48

Answer D is correct. Fiber-optic cabling is least subject to electromagnetic (EM) interference because its communications are conducted by transmitting pulses of light over glass, plastic, or sapphire transmission fibers. Twisted-pair (shielded STP as well as unshielded UTP) copper cables provide minimal shielding against interference but can function as antenna picking up nearby EM sources when extended over long cable runs, making answers A and B incorrect. Answer C is incorrect because, although co-axial cables limit EM interference by encasing one conductor in a sheath of conductive material, they are still conductive and not as resistant as purely optical forms of communication.

Question 49

Answer A is correct. Methods of access are identified during the risk and threat assessment rather than during asset identification. Asset identification involves original and replacement costs along with maintenance costs and profits generated by the asset. Consequently, answers B, C, and D are incorrect.

Question 50

Answers A and D are correct. UDP ports 161 and 162 are used by SNMP. Answer B is incorrect because UDP uses port 139 for network sharing. Answer C is incorrect because port 138 is used to allow NetBIOS traffic for name resolution.

Question 51

Answer D is correct. VLANs provide a way to limit broadcast traffic in a switched network. This creates a boundary and, in essence, creates multiple, isolated LANs on one switch. Answer A is incorrect because logging is the process of collecting data to be used for monitoring and auditing purposes. Answer B is incorrect because access control generally refers to the process of making resources available to accounts that should have access while limiting that access to only what is required. Answer C is incorrect because access network segmentation is used for interconnected networks where one compromised system on one network can easily spread to other networks.

Question 52

Answer A is correct. Protection of data in motion is considered to be a network solution, and either a hardware or software solution is installed near the network perimeter to monitor for and flag policy violations. Answer B is incorrect because protection of data at rest is considered to be a storage solution and is generally a software solution that monitors how confidential data is stored. Answer C is incorrect because protection of data in use is considered to be an endpoint solution and the application is run on end-user workstations or servers in the organization. Answer D is incorrect because there is no such data state.

Question 53

Answer B is correct. It is necessary to first identify the evidence that is available to be collected. Answer A is incorrect because protecting the data's value as evidence must come after the type and form of evidence is known. Extraction, preservation, processing, and interpretation of evidence also follow the identification of data types and storage that must be collected, making answers C and D incorrect.

Question 54

Answer B is correct. Digital certificates contain a field indicating the date to which the certificate is valid. This date is mandatory, and the validity period can vary from a short period of time up to a number of years; therefore, answers A, C, and D are incorrect.

Question 55

Answers B, C, and D are correct. Natural disasters, unwanted access, and user restrictions are all physical security issues. Preventing Internet users from getting to data is data security, not physical security; therefore, answer A is incorrect.

Question 56

Answer A is correct. During anonymous access, such as requests to a public FTP server, unique identify of the requester is not determined and so cannot be used for personalized logon identification. Answers B, C, and D are incorrect because authorization services such as Kerberos, TACACS, and its replacement TACACS+ all verify access requests against a list of authorized credentials and so can log individual visits and identify access request logons.

Question 57

Answer D is correct. Time of day rules prevent administrative access requests during off-hours when local admins and security professionals are not on duty. Answer A is incorrect because least privilege is a principle of assigning only those rights necessary to perform assigned tasks. Answer B is incorrect because separation of duties aids in identification of fraudulent or incorrect processes by ensuring that action and validation practices are performed separately. Answer C is incorrect because account expiration protocols ensure that individual accounts do not remain active past their designated lifespan but do nothing to ensure protections are enabled during admin downtime.

Question 58

Answer A is correct. An alternative to HTTPS is the Secure Hypertext Transport Protocol (S-HTTP), which was developed to support connectivity for banking transactions and other secure web communications. S-HTTP was not adopted by the early web browser developers (for example, Netscape and Microsoft) and so remains less common than the HTTPS standard. Additionally, S-HTTP encrypts individual messages so it cannot be used for VPN security. Answer B is incorrect. S/MIME is used to encrypt electronic mail transmissions over public networks. Answer C is incorrect because HTTP is used for unsecured web-based communications. Answer D is incorrect because Point-to-Point Tunneling Protocol (PPTP) is a network protocol that enables the secure transfer of data from a remote client to a private enterprise server by creating a virtual private network (VPN) across TCP/IP-based data networks.

Question 59

Answer D is correct. Port security is a Layer 2 traffic control feature on Cisco Catalyst switches. It enables individual switch ports to be configured to allow only a specified number of source MAC addresses coming in through the port. Answer A is incorrect because the loop guard feature makes additional checks in Layer 2 switched networks. Answer B is incorrect because a flood guard is a firewall feature to control network activity associated with denial-of-service attacks (DoS). Answer C is incorrect because implicit deny is an access control practice wherein resource availability is restricted to only those logons explicitly granted access.

Question 60

Answer A is correct. Protocol analyzers help you troubleshoot network issues by gathering packet-level information across the network. These applications capture packets and can conduct protocol decoding, putting the information into readable data for analysis. Answer B is incorrect because a circuit-level gateway filters based on source and destination addresses. Answer C is incorrect because all-in-one spam filter appliances allow for checksum technology, which tracks the number of times a particular message has appeared, and message authenticity checking, which uses multiple algorithms to verify authenticity of a message. Answer D is incorrect because a web application firewall is software or a hardware appliance used to protect the organization's web server from attack.

Question 61

Answer B is correct. The key element to understanding XSRF is that attackers are betting that users have a validated login cookie for the website already stored in their browsers. All they need to do is get the browsers to make a request to the website on their behalf. This can be done by either convincing the users to click on an HTML page the attacker has constructed or inserting arbitrary HTML in a target website that the users visit. Answer A is incorrect because a buffer overflow is a direct result of poor or incorrect input validation or mishandled exceptions. Answer C is incorrect because cross-site scripting (XXS) vulnerabilities can be used to hijack the user's session or to cause the user accessing malware-tainted Site A to unknowingly attack Site B on behalf of the attacker who planted code on Site A. Answer D is incorrect because input validation errors are a result of improper field checking in the code.

Question 62

Answer A is correct. The PKCS #11 standard provides for access to public and private asymmetric keys, symmetric keys, X.509 certificates, and application data. PKCS #11 is the de facto standard for platform applications, although some newer HSMs include more advanced authentication and authorization models. Answer B is incorrect because PKCS #7 Cryptographic Message Syntax Standard describes the syntax for data streams such as digital signatures that may have cryptography applied to them. Answer C is incorrect because AES is most commonly found on USB drive encryption. Answer D is incorrect because EFS is the encrypting file system available in newer Microsoft operating systems.

Question 63

Answer B is correct. Diffie-Hellman uses public and private keys, so it is considered an asymmetric encryption algorithm. Because Rijndael and AES are now one in the same, they both can be called symmetric encryption algorithms; therefore, answers A and D are incorrect. Answer C is incorrect because RC6 is symmetric, too.

Question 64

Answer D is correct. When encrypting and decrypting data using an asymmetric encryption algorithm, you use only the private key to decrypt data encrypted with the public key. Answers A and B are both incorrect because in public key encryption, if one key is used to encrypt, you can use the other to decrypt the data. Answer C is incorrect because the public key is not used to decrypt the same data it encrypted.

Question 65

Answer A is correct. PKCS #11, the Cryptographic Token Interface Standards, defines an API named Cryptoki for devices holding cryptographic information. Answer B is incorrect because PKCS #13 is the Elliptic Curve Cryptography Standard. Both answers C and D are incorrect because PKCS #4 and PKCS #2 no longer exist and have been integrated into PKCS #1, RSA Cryptography Standard.

Question 66

Answer A is correct. Anonymous access to share files of questionable or undesirable content should be limited for proper FTP server security. Answer B is incorrect because it is a hardening practice for DHCP services. Answers C and D are incorrect because they are associated with hardening DNS service.

Question 67

Answer A is correct. A buffer overflow occurs when a program or process attempts to store more data in a buffer than the buffer was intended to hold. The overflow of data can flow over into other buffers overwriting or deleting data. A denial of service is a type of attack in which too much traffic is sent to a host, preventing it from responding to legitimate traffic. A distributed denial of service is similar, but it is initiated through multiple hosts; therefore, answers B and C are incorrect. Although answer D sounds correct, it is not.

Question 68

Answer B is correct. TEMPEST protections involve the hardening of equipment against EMI broadcast and sensitivity. Answers A and C are incorrect because HVAC controls include temperature and humidity management techniques to manage evolved heat in the data center and to minimize static charge buildup. Answer D is incorrect because hot-aisle/cold-aisle schemes provide thermal management for data centers by grouping air intakes on cold aisles and air exhausts on designated hot aisles, making HVAC more effective.

Question 69

Answer D is correct. Hardening of the operating system includes planning against both accidental and directed attacks, such as the use of fault-tolerant hardware and software solutions. In addition, it is important to implement an effective system for file-level security, including encrypted file support and secured file system selection that allows the proper level of access control. Answer A is incorrect because it is a host protection measure, not an OS hardening measure. Answer B is incorrect because this is a feature associated with data security, not host hardening. Answer C is incorrect because this is a secure communication measure.

Question 70

Answer A is correct. In an SaaS environment, application-level encryption is preferred because the data is encrypted by the application before being stored in the database or file system. The advantage is that it protects the data from the user all the way to storage. Answer B is incorrect because in cloud implementations data should be encrypted at the application layer rather than within a database due to the complexity involved, and media encryption is managed at the storage layer. Answer C is incorrect because encryption of a complete virtual machine on IaaS could be considered media encryption. Answer D is incorrect because an HSM solution is mainly found in private datacenters that manage and offload cryptography with dedicated hardware appliances.

Question 71

Answer D is correct. Traceroute uses an ICMP echo request packet to find the path between two addresses. Answer A is incorrect because SSL is a public key-based security protocol that is used by Internet services and clients for authentication, message integrity, and confidentiality. Answer B is incorrect because Internet Protocol Security (IPsec) authentication and encapsulation standard is widely used to establish secure VPN communications. Answer C is incorrect because SNMP is an application layer protocol whose purpose is to collect statistics from TCP/IP devices. SNMP is used for monitoring the health of network equipment, computer equipment, and devices such as uninterruptible power supplies (UPSs).

Question 72

Answer C is correct. Implicit deny is an access control practice wherein resource availability is restricted to only those logons explicitly granted access. Answer A is incorrect because the loop guard feature makes additional checks in Layer 2 switched networks. Answer B is incorrect because a flood guard is a firewall feature to control network activity associated with denial of service attacks (DoS). Answer D is incorrect because port security is a Layer 2 traffic control feature on Cisco Catalyst switches. It enables individual switch ports to be configured to allow only a specified number of source MAC addresses coming in through the port.

Question 73

Answer B is correct. The single loss expectancy (SLE) is the product of the value ($12,000) and the threat exposure (.25) or $3,000. Answer A is incorrect because $1,500 represents the annualized loss expectancy (ALE), which is the product of the SLE and the annualized rate of occurrence (ARO). Answers C and D are incorrect calculated values.

Question 74

Answer D is correct. Combustible metal fires (Class D) require sodium chloride and copper-based dry powder extinguishers. Although dry-pipe would be preferable to wet-pipe sprinklers in regions that experience very low temperatures such as Alaska, water is only appropriate for wood, paper, and trash fires (Class A), making answers A and B incorrect. Answer C is incorrect because carbon dioxide and Halon extinguishers are useful for fires involving live electric wiring (Class C) and would not be used for burning metals.

Question 75

Answer D is correct. The most likely answer is spoofing because this enables an attacker to misrepresent the source of the requests. Answer A is incorrect because this type of attack records and replays previously sent valid messages.

Answer B is incorrect because this is not a type of attack but is instead the granting of access rights based on authentication. Answer C is incorrect because social engineering involves the nontechnical means of gaining information.

Question 76

Answer B is correct. The PUBLIC label can be applied to generally available data within MAC access control environments. Answer A is incorrect because the ANONYMOUS method of authorization is not available in MAC environments because it lacks logon identification. Answers C and D are incorrect because the SENSITIVE and SECRET labels indicate access control limitations that are more restrictive than PUBLIC.

Question 77

Answer A is correct. The loop guard feature makes additional checks in Layer 2 switched networks. Answer B is incorrect because a flood guard is a firewall feature to control network activity associated with denial-of-service attacks (DoS). Answer C is incorrect because implicit deny is an access control practice wherein resource availability is restricted to only those logons explicitly granted access. Answer D is incorrect because port security is a Layer 2 traffic control feature on Cisco Catalyst switches. It enables individual switch ports to be configured to allow only a specified number of source MAC addresses coming in through the port.

Question 78

Answer C is correct. A false negative result involves access refusal for an authorized user, which makes answer D incorrect. Answers A and B are incorrect because they represent granted resource access.

Question 79

Answer B is correct. Public key encryption is not usually used to encrypt large amounts of data, but it does provide an effective and efficient means of sending a secret key from which to do symmetric encryption thereafter, which provides the best method for efficiently encrypting large amounts of data. Therefore, answers A, C, and D are incorrect.

Question 80

Answer B is correct. Ports 20 and 21 are used for FTP. Answer A is incorrect because these ports are used for email. Answer C is incorrect because these NetBIOS ports are required for certain Windows network functions such as file sharing. Answer D is incorrect because these ports are used for SNMP.

Question 81

Answer C is correct. Physical controls include facility design details such as layout, door, locks, guards, and surveillance systems. Management controls include policies and procedures, whereas technical controls include access control systems, encryption, and data classification solutions, making answers A and B incorrect. Access controls include all three classifications: management, technical, and physical, making answer D incorrect because the question asks for a specific type.

Question 82

Answer D is correct. A network mapper identifies all devices within a network segment. Port scanners check service ports on a single device, making answer A incorrect. Answer B is incorrect because vulnerability scanners look for particular vulnerabilities associated with versions of software or services. Answer C is incorrect because protocol analyzers examine network traffic and identify protocols and endpoint devices in the identified transactions.

Question 83

Answer A is correct. A VPN tunnel is an example of data security—not physical security. Mantrap, fence, and CCTV are all components of physical security; therefore, answers B, C, and D are incorrect.

Question 84

Answers A, B, and D are correct. A physical security plan should be a written plan that addresses your current physical security needs and future direction. With the exception of answer C, all the answers are correct and should be addressed in a physical security plan. A hard disk's physical blocks pertain to the file system.

Question 85

Answers A and D are correct. A buffer overflow is a direct result of poor or incorrect input validation or mishandled exceptions, and input validation errors are a result of improper field checking in the code. Answer B is incorrect because Cross-site Request Forgery (XSRF) is an attack in which the end user executes unwanted actions on a web application while he or she is currently authenticated. Answer C is incorrect because cross-site scripting (XXS) vulnerabilities can be used to hijack the user's session or to cause the user accessing malware-tainted Site A to unknowingly attack Site B on behalf of the attacker who planted code on Site A.

Question 86

Answer A is correct. Virtualization adds a layer of security as well as improves enterprise desktop management and control with faster deployment of desktops and fewer support calls due to application conflicts. Answer B is incorrect because network storage policies have nothing to do with desktop management. Answer C is incorrect because VPN remote access does not improve enterprise desktop management. Answer D is incorrect because roaming profiles do not add a layer of security.

Question 87

Answer C is correct. SFTP, or secure FTP, is a program that uses SSH to transfer files. Unlike standard FTP, it encrypts both commands and data, preventing passwords and sensitive information from being transmitted in the clear over the network. Answer A is incorrect because S-HTTP is an alternative to HTTPS, which was developed to support connectivity for banking transactions and other secure web communications. Answer B is incorrect. S/MIME is used to encrypt electronic mail transmissions over public networks. Answer D is incorrect because HTTPS is used for secured web-based communications.

Question 88

Answer A is correct. A DoS attack (or denial of service) is designed to bring down a network by flooding the system with an overabundance of useless traffic. Although answers B and C are both types of DoS attacks, they are incorrect because DoS more accurately describes "a type of attack." Answer D is incorrect because social engineering describes the nontechnical means of obtaining information.

Question 89

Answer B is correct. Hardening refers to the process of securing an operating system. Handshaking relates the agreement process before communication takes place; therefore, answer A is incorrect. A hotfix is just a security patch that gets applied to an operating system; therefore, answer C is incorrect. Hardening is the only correct answer; therefore, answer D is incorrect.

Question 90

Answer B is correct. Mobile voice encryption can allow executives and employees alike to discuss sensitive information without having to travel to secure company locations. Answer A is incorrect because in the event a mobile device is lost, GPS tracking can be used to find the location. Answer C is incorrect because remote wipe allows a handheld's data to be remotely deleted in the event the device is lost or stolen. Answer D is incorrect because a screen lock or passcode is used to prevent access to the phone.

Question 91

Answer D is correct. Often an option to opt out of further email does not unsubscribe users; instead it means, "send me more spam," because it has been confirmed that the email address is not dormant. This is less likely to occur with email a user receives that he or she opted into in the first place, however. Answers A, B, and C are incorrect because these are less likely and not the best choices.

Question 92

Answer C is correct. Only CPU registers and caches are more volatile than routing and process tables, making answers A, B, and D incorrect as well.

Question 93

Answer A is correct. Both logon and password represent a form of "what you know" authentication. Answers B, C, and D are all incorrect because they represent paired multifactor forms of authentication. A smart card and PIN represent what you have and know, and an RFID chip and thumbprint link what you have with what you are. Gait is a measure of what you do, and iris details are an example of what you are.

Question 94

Answer C is correct. Role-based access control involves assignment of access rights to groups associated with specific roles, with accounts inheriting rights based on group membership. Answers A and B are incorrect, as requirements for access only from specific locations or only from systems running a trusted OS are examples of rule-based access controls. Time of day restrictions are also rule-based access controls, making answer D incorrect.

Question 95

Answer A is correct. Nonrepudiation means that neither party can deny either having sent or received the data in question. Both answers B and C are incorrect. And repudiation is defined as the act of refusal; therefore, answer D is incorrect.

Question 96

Answer B is correct. Regular review of networks for unauthorized or rogue servers is a practice used to harden DHCP services. Answer A is incorrect because anonymous access to share files of questionable or undesirable content should be limited for proper FTP server security. Answers C and D are incorrect because they are associated with hardening DNS servers.

Question 97

Answer B is correct. The Issuer field identifies the name of the entity signing the certificate, which is usually a certificate authority. The Signature Algorithm Identifier identifies the cryptographic algorithm used by the CA to sign the certificate; therefore, answer A is incorrect. The Subject Name is the name of the end entity identified in the public key associated with the certificate; therefore, answer C is incorrect. The Subject Public Key Information field includes the public key of the entity named in the certificate, including a cryptographic algorithm identifier; therefore, answer D is incorrect.

Question 98

Answer D is correct. An explicit DENY overrides all other access grants in a discretionary access control environment. Explicit rights assignments function in combination with inherited implicit rights in all other cases, making answers A, B, and C incorrect.

Question 99

Answer C is correct. Retinal biometric systems identify unique patterns of blood vessels in the back of the eye. Facial recognition systems identify fixed spacing of key features of the face such as bones, eyes, and chin shape, making answer A incorrect. Answer B is incorrect because iris scanning involves identification of unique patterns in the outer colored part of the eye. Answer D is incorrect because signature analysis is a form of biometric authentication recording the speed, shape, and unique kinematics of a personal written signature.

Question 100

Answer C is correct. Version 3 of X.509, which was introduced in 1996, supports an optional Extension field used to provide for more informational fields. Version 1 is the most generic and did not yet incorporate this feature; therefore, answer A is incorrect. Version 2 did introduce the idea of unique identifiers, but not the optional Extension field; therefore, answers B and D are incorrect.

Practice Exam 2

CompTIA Security+ SY0-301

The multiple-choice questions provided here help you determine how prepared you are for the actual exam and which topics you need to review further. Write down your answers on a separate sheet of paper so you can take this exam again if necessary. Compare your answers against the answers and explanations that follow.

Exam Questions

1. In which of the following types of architecture is the user responsible for the creation of the private and public key?

   ○ **A.** Decentralized key management

   ○ **B.** Centralized key management

   ○ **C.** Revocation key management

   ○ **D.** Multilevel key management

2. Which of the following standards ensures privacy between communicating applications and clients on the Web and has been designed to replace SSL?

   ○ **A.** Secure Sockets Layer 2

   ○ **B.** Point-to-Point Tunneling Protocol

   ○ **C.** Transport Layer Security

   ○ **D.** Internet Protocol Security

3. Lynn needs access to the Accounting order-entry application but keeps getting an error that indicates inadequate access permissions. Bob assigns Lynn's account to the Administrator's group to overcome the error until he can work on the problem. Which access control constraint was violated by this action?

   ○ **A.** Implicit denial

   ○ **B.** Least privilege

   ○ **C.** Separation of duties

   ○ **D.** Account expiration

4. An authentication system relies on an RFID chip embedded in a plastic key together with the pattern of blood vessels in the back of an authorized user's hand. What types of authentication are being employed in this system?

   ○ **A.** Something you have and something you are

   ○ **B.** Something you do and something you know

   ○ **C.** Something you know and something you are

   ○ **D.** Something you do and something you have

5. In which of the following types of encryption does authentication happen on power-up of the drive through either a software pre-boot authentication environment or with a BIOS password?

   ○ **A.** TPM

   ○ **B.** HSM

   ○ **C.** Hard disk encryption

   ○ **D.** File-level encryption

6. Which of the following methods can be used to locate a device in the event it is lost or stolen?

   ○ **A.** GPS tracking

   ○ **B.** Voice encryption

   ○ **C.** Remote wipe

   ○ **D.** Passcode policy

7. Which of the following is a step that can be taken to harden data?

   ○ **A.** Anonymous access to share files of questionable or undesirable content should be limited.

   ○ **B.** Technologies that allow dynamic updates must also include access control and authentication.

   ○ **C.** Secure storage and backup of storage area networks (SANs).

   ○ **D.** Unauthorized zone transfers should also be restricted.

8. Which one of the following is a holding area between two entry points that gives security personnel time to view a person before allowing him into the internal building?

   ○ **A.** Mantrap

   ○ **B.** Biometric

   ○ **C.** Honeypot

   ○ **D.** Honeynet

9. Bluejacking and bluesnarfing make use of which wireless technology?

   ○ **A.** Wi-Fi

   ○ **B.** Bluetooth

   ○ **C.** BluFi

   ○ **D.** All of the above

10. If an organization takes a full backup every Sunday morning and a daily differential backup each morning, what is the fewest number of backups that must be restored following a disaster on Friday?

   ○ **A.** 1

   ○ **B.** 2

   ○ **C.** 5

   ○ **D.** 6

11. Which risk reduction policy does not aid in identifying internal fraud?

- ○ **A.** Mandatory vacations
- ○ **B.** Least privilege
- ○ **C.** Separation of duties
- ○ **D.** Job rotation

12. Due to organizational requirements, strong encryption cannot be used. Which of the following is the most basic form of encryption that can be used on 802.11-based wireless networks to provide privacy of data sent between a wireless client and its access point?

- ○ **A.** Wireless Application Environment (WAE)
- ○ **B.** Wireless Session Layer (WSL)
- ○ **C.** Wired Equivalent Privacy (WEP)
- ○ **D.** Wireless Transport Layer Security (WTLS)

13. Which of the following methods of cloud computing enables the client to literally outsource everything that would normally be in a typical IT department?

- ○ **A.** SaaS
- ○ **B.** DaaS
- ○ **C.** PaaS
- ○ **D.** IaaS

14. You are the administrator of an organization with 15,000 users. Which internal address range and subnet mask should you use on the network?

- ○ **A.** 10.1.1.1/255.0.0.0
- ○ **B.** 172.16.1.1/255.255.0.0
- ○ **C.** 192.168.1.1/255.255.255.0
- ○ **D.** 192.168.10.1/255.255.255.0

15. You have a network on which there are mixed vendor devices and are required to implement a strong authentication solution for wireless communications. Which of the following would best meet your requirements? (Select two.)

- ○ **A.** EAP
- ○ **B.** WEP
- ○ **C.** LEAP
- ○ **D.** PEAP

16. Which of the following includes a packet number (PN) field and produces a message integrity code (MIC) providing data origin authentication and data integrity for the packet payload data?

   ○ **A.** ICMP

   ○ **B.** CCMP

   ○ **C.** WEP

   ○ **D.** WPA

17. Which risk management response is being implemented when a company decides to close a little-used legacy web application identified as vulnerable to SQL Injection?

   ○ **A.** Acceptance

   ○ **B.** Avoidance

   ○ **C.** Mitigation

   ○ **D.** Transference

18. A video surveillance system is a form of which type of access control?

   ○ **A.** Quantitative

   ○ **B.** Management

   ○ **C.** Technical

   ○ **D.** Physical

19. Which element of business continuity planning (BCP) is most concerned with hot site/cold site planning?

   ○ **A.** Network connectivity

   ○ **B.** Facilities

   ○ **C.** Clustering

   ○ **D.** Fault tolerance

20. What aspect of disaster recovery planning details training required for managers, administrators, and users?

   ○ **A.** Impact and risk assessment

   ○ **B.** Disaster recovery plan

   ○ **C.** Disaster recovery policies

   ○ **D.** Service level agreements

21. A man-in-the-middle attack takes advantage of which of the following?

   ○ **A.** TCP handshake

   ○ **B.** UDP handshake

   ○ **C.** Juggernaut

   ○ **D.** All of the above

22. Which of the following best describes the reason that a requesting device might believe that incoming ARP replies are from the correct devices?

- ○ **A.** ARP requires validation.
- ○ **B.** ARP does not require validation.
- ○ **C.** ARP is connection-oriented.
- ○ **D.** ARP is connectionless.

23. Which of the following describes a network of systems designed to lure an attacker away from another critical system?

- ○ **A.** Bastion host
- ○ **B.** Honeynet
- ○ **C.** Vulnerability system
- ○ **D.** Intrusion-detection system

24. Which one of the following is not a component of a penetration test?

- ○ **A.** Verify a threat exists
- ○ **B.** Bypass security controls
- ○ **C.** Actively test security controls
- ○ **D.** Exploit vulnerability
- ○ **E.** Remediate vulnerability

25. An organization has had a rash of malware infections. Which of the following can help mitigate the number of successful attacks?

- ○ **A.** Application baselining
- ○ **B.** Patch management
- ○ **C.** Network monitoring
- ○ **D.** Input validation

26. In which of the following phases should code security first be implemented?

- ○ **A.** Testing
- ○ **B.** Review
- ○ **C.** Implementation
- ○ **D.** Design

27. Which of the following helps track changes to the environment when an organization needs to keep legacy machines?

- ○ **A.** Virtualization
- ○ **B.** Network storage policies
- ○ **C.** Host software baselining
- ○ **D.** Roaming profiles

28. An organization is looking for a basic mobile solution that will be used to prevent access to users' phones. Which of the following fulfills this requirement?

- ○ **A.** GPS tracking
- ○ **B.** Voice encryption
- ○ **C.** Remote wipe
- ○ **D.** Passcode policy

29. EFS is an example of which of the following?

- ○ **A.** Full disk encryption
- ○ **B.** File-level encryption
- ○ **C.** Media-level encryption
- ○ **D.** Application-level encryption

30. Which of the following is the most useful when you're dealing with data that is stored in a shared cloud environment?

- ○ **A.** Full disk encryption
- ○ **B.** File-level encryption
- ○ **C.** Media-level encryption
- ○ **D.** Application-level encryption

31. If Bob wants to send a secure message to Val using public-key encryption without sender validation, what does Val need?

- ○ **A.** Bob's private key
- ○ **B.** Bob's public key
- ○ **C.** Val's private key
- ○ **D.** Val's public key

32. Which category of authentication includes your ATM card?

- ○ **A.** Something you are
- ○ **B.** Something you do
- ○ **C.** Something you know
- ○ **D.** Something you have

33. Which is the best access control constraint to protect against accidental unauthorized access?

- ○ **A.** Implicit denial
- ○ **B.** Least privilege
- ○ **C.** Separation of duties
- ○ **D.** Account expiration

34. Morgan is a member of the Accounting, Executive Assistants, Billing, and Users groups. Accounting members are allowed VIEW and CHANGE rights over a folder on the file server. Executive Assistants are allowed only VIEW permissions on the same folder, whereas Billing group members can VIEW and WRITE new files. Users have a default implicit DENY for this folder. What is Morgan's access to this folder?

- ○ **A.** DENY
- ○ **B.** VIEW
- ○ **C.** VIEW and CHANGE
- ○ **D.** VIEW, CHANGE, and WRITE

35. What type of algorithm is SHA-1?

- ○ **A.** Asymmetric encryption algorithm
- ○ **B.** Digital signature
- ○ **C.** Hashing algorithm
- ○ **D.** Certificate authority

36. Which of the following is true of Pretty Good Privacy (PGP)? (Choose the two best answers.)

- ○ **A.** It uses a web of trust.
- ○ **B.** It uses a hierarchical structure.
- ○ **C.** It uses public key encryption.
- ○ **D.** It uses private key encryption.

37. Which one of the following best identifies the system of digital certificates and certification authorities used in public key technology?

- ○ **A.** Certificate practice system (CPS)
- ○ **B.** Public key exchange (PKE)
- ○ **C.** Certificate practice statement (CPS)
- ○ **D.** Public key infrastructure (PKI)

38. Which of the following is not a certificate trust model for the arranging of certificate authorities?

- ○ **A.** Bridge CA architecture
- ○ **B.** Sub-CA architecture
- ○ **C.** Single-CA architecture
- ○ **D.** Hierarchical CA architecture

39. Which of the following procedures should be used to properly protect a host from malware? (Select two correct answers.)

   ○ **A.** Pop-up blocking software

   ○ **B.** Antivirus software

   ○ **C.** Content filtering software

   ○ **D.** Web tracking software

40. Which of the following are advantages of honeypots and honeynets? (Select all correct answers.)

   ○ **A.** Attackers are diverted to systems that they cannot damage.

   ○ **B.** Administrators are allotted time to decide how to respond to an attack.

   ○ **C.** Attackers' actions can more easily be monitored and resulting steps taken to improve system security.

   ○ **D.** Well-defined legal implications exist.

   ○ **E.** They provide a structure that requires fewer security administrators.

41. You are setting up an FTP server that needs to be accessed by both the employees and external contractors. What type of architecture should you implement?

   ○ **A.** VLAN

   ○ **B.** DMZ

   ○ **C.** NAT

   ○ **D.** VPN

42. A CA with multiple subordinate CAs would use which of the following PKI trust models?

   ○ **A.** Cross-certified

   ○ **B.** Hierarchical

   ○ **C.** Bridge

   ○ **D.** Linked

43. Which of the following are types of updates applied to systems? (Select all correct answers.)

   ○ **A.** Hotfix

   ○ **B.** Service packs

   ○ **C.** Patches

   ○ **D.** Coldfix

44. Which type of UPS is also termed an "online" UPS?

    ○ **A.** SPS

    ○ **B.** Ferroresonant

    ○ **C.** Generator

    ○ **D.** Continuous

45. What is a potential concern to weaker encryption algorithms as time goes on? (Choose the best answer.)

    ○ **A.** Performance of the algorithm worsens over time.

    ○ **B.** Keys generated by users start to repeat on other users' systems.

    ○ **C.** Hackers using distributed computing might be able to finally crack a logarithm.

    ○ **D.** All options are correct.

46. Which of the following is not a common quality of quantitative risk analysis?

    ○ **A.** Difficult for management to understand

    ○ **B.** Less precise

    ○ **C.** Labor intensive

    ○ **D.** Time consuming

47. Which of the following should be implemented if the organization wants to monitor unauthorized transfer of confidential information?

    ○ **A.** Content filter

    ○ **B.** Proxy server

    ○ **C.** Protocol analyzer

    ○ **D.** Packet-filtering firewall

48. Which is the only access control mechanism that does not reduce the likelihood of users employing the same password for organizational systems and personal online services?

    ○ **A.** No reuse of last 100 passwords

    ○ **B.** Expiration every 60 days

    ○ **C.** Password length at least 14 characters

    ○ **D.** Password complexity requiring case-less alphanumeric characters

49. Which of the following is a method that can be used to prevent data from being accessed in the event the device is lost or stolen?

- ○ **A.** GPS tracking
- ○ **B.** Voice encryption
- ○ **C.** Remote wipe
- ○ **D.** Passcode policy

50. A certificate authority discovers it has issued a digital certificate to the wrong person. What needs to be completed?

- ○ **A.** Certificate practice statement (CPS)
- ○ **B.** Revocation
- ○ **C.** Private key compromise
- ○ **D.** Fraudulent practices statement (FPS)

51. You are setting up a switched network in which each department requires a logical separation. Which of the following meets these requirements?

- ○ **A.** DMZ
- ○ **B.** VPN
- ○ **C.** VLAN
- ○ **D.** NAT

52. Which of the following is the most useful when you're dealing with machines that are being taken on the road by traveling executives, sales managers, or insurance agents?

- ○ **A.** Full disk encryption
- ○ **B.** File-level encryption
- ○ **C.** Media-level encryption
- ○ **D.** Application-level encryption

53. Which type of biometric authentication system is not subject to false rejection due to illness or minor injury?

- ○ **A.** Fingerprint
- ○ **B.** Voiceprint
- ○ **C.** Facial recognition
- ○ **D.** Retina

54. If an asset is valued at 100,000, the threat exposure factor of a risk affecting that asset is 25%, and the annualized rate of occurrence is 20%. What is the ALE?

- ○ **A.** $5,000
- ○ **B.** $20,000
- ○ **C.** $25,000
- ○ **D.** $45,000

55. What is the minimal level of alternative site that includes live networking?

- ○ **A.** Cold
- ○ **B.** Warm
- ○ **C.** Hot
- ○ **D.** Remote

56. Which of the following statements is true about SSL?

- ○ **A.** SSL provides security for both the connection and the data after it is received.
- ○ **B.** SSL only provides security for the connection, not the data after it is received.
- ○ **C.** SSL only provides security for the data when it is received, not the connection.
- ○ **D.** SSL does not provide security for either the connection or the data after it is received.

57. Which of the following services/protocols operate on Port 53?

- ○ **A.** DNS
- ○ **B.** SCP
- ○ **C.** HTTPS
- ○ **D.** SMB

58. Which utility allows the identification of all devices conducting network traffic both to and from a network segment?

- ○ **A.** Port scanner
- ○ **B.** Vulnerability scanner
- ○ **C.** Protocol analyzer
- ○ **D.** Network mapper

59. Which of the following is commonly used in the banking sector to secure numerous large, bulk transactions?

- ○ **A.** Full disk encryption
- ○ **B.** HSM
- ○ **C.** TPM
- ○ **D.** File-level encryption

60. What is the default Kerberos session key duration?

- ○ **A.** 3 minutes
- ○ **B.** 30 minutes
- ○ **C.** 3 hours
- ○ **D.** 8 hours

61. Which of the following algorithms is now known as the Advanced Encryption Standard?

- ○ **A.** Rijndael
- ○ **B.** 3DES
- ○ **C.** RC6
- ○ **D.** Twofish
- ○ **E.** CAST

62. Which of the following services/protocols operate on Port 22?

- ○ **A.** DNS
- ○ **B.** HTTPS
- ○ **C.** SCP
- ○ **D.** SMB

63. Which of the following best describes a host intrusion detection system?

- ○ **A.** Examines the information exchanged between machines
- ○ **B.** Collects and analyzes data that originates on the local machine
- ○ **C.** Controls the information coming in and out of the host machine
- ○ **D.** Attempts to prevent network attacks in real time

64. What best describes the difference between phishing and whaling?

- ○ **A.** They are the same.
- ○ **B.** Whaling makes use of the voice channel, whereas phishing uses email.
- ○ **C.** Whaling uses SMS, whereas phishing uses email.
- ○ **D.** Whaling is similar to phishing but specifically targets high-profile individuals.

65. Which of the following is not focused on recovering after loss of function?

○ **A.** RTO

○ **B.** DRP

○ **C.** RPO

○ **D.** BCP

66. Which form of access control relies on labels for access control management?

○ **A.** MAC

○ **B.** DAC

○ **C.** Role-based (RBAC)

○ **D.** Rule-based (RBAC)

67. Which password standard provides the best opportunity to detect and react to a high-speed brute-force password attack?

○ **A.** Password length

○ **B.** Account lockout

○ **C.** Password expiration

○ **D.** Logon banner

68. Which of the following is not one of the vulnerabilities of LDAP authentication services?

○ **A.** Buffer overflow vulnerabilities can be used to enact arbitrary commands on the LDAP server.

○ **B.** Loss of time synchronization between the service, client, and KDC prevents communication.

○ **C.** Format string vulnerabilities might result in unauthorized access to enact commands on the LDAP server or impair its normal operation.

○ **D.** Improperly formatted requests might be used to create an effective denial-of-service (DoS) attack against the LDAP server.

69. Which of the following types of attacks is characterized by client-side vulnerabilities presented by ActiveX or JavaScript code running within the client's browser?

○ **A.** Buffer overflow

○ **B.** Cross-site request forgery (XSRF) attacks

○ **C.** Cross-site scripting

○ **D.** Input validation error

70. Which of the following is a hardware solution typically attached to the circuit board of the system used for greater security protection for processes such as digital signing, mission-critical applications, and businesses where high security is required?

- ○ **A.** Full disk encryption
- ○ **B.** HSM
- ○ **C.** TPM
- ○ **D.** File-level encryption

71. What is the name given to the system of digital certificates and certificate authorities used for public key cryptography over networks?

- ○ **A.** Protocol Key Instructions (PKI)
- ○ **B.** Public Key Extranet (PKE)
- ○ **C.** Protocol Key Infrastructure (PKI)
- ○ **D.** Public Key Infrastructure (PKI)

72. The new biometric authentication system has been identified as having a high FAR. What does this mean?

- ○ **A.** Authorized users are being allowed access.
- ○ **B.** Unauthorized users are being allowed access.
- ○ **C.** Authorized users are being denied access.
- ○ **D.** Unauthorized users are being denied access.

73. Which of the following provide a "sandboxed" system that can be used to investigate malware?

- ○ **A.** Virtualization
- ○ **B.** Network storage
- ○ **C.** Host software baselining
- ○ **D.** Application baselining

74. Which one of the following is an indication that a system might contain spyware?

- ○ **A.** The system is slow, especially when browsing the Internet.
- ○ **B.** It takes a long time for the Windows desktop to come up.
- ○ **C.** Clicking a link does nothing or goes to an unexpected website.
- ○ **D.** All of the above.

75. Which of the following models is useful for individuals and businesses that want to have the right to access a certain applications without having to purchase a full license?

- ○ **A.** PaaS
- ○ **B.** IaaS
- ○ **C.** SaaS
- ○ **D.** DaaS

76. You are conducting a penetration test on an application for a client. The client provides you with no details about the source code and development process. What type of test will you likely be conducting?

- ○ **A.** Black box
- ○ **B.** White box
- ○ **C.** Vulnerability
- ○ **D.** Answers A and C

77. Which type of power variation includes short-term decreases in voltage levels?

- ○ **A.** Spikes
- ○ **B.** Surges
- ○ **C.** Brownouts
- ○ **D.** Blackouts

78. Which of the following is the most effective method that can be used to prevent data from being accessed in the event the device is lost or stolen?

- ○ **A.** GPS tracking
- ○ **B.** Device encryption
- ○ **C.** Remote wipe
- ○ **D.** Passcode policy

79. What is the highest division of TCSEC access control that allows resource owners to extend access to other logons?

- ○ **A.** Division A
- ○ **B.** Division B
- ○ **C.** Division C
- ○ **D.** Division D

80. When a certificate authority revokes a certificate, notice of the revocation is distributed via what?

- ○ **A.** Certificate revocation list
- ○ **B.** Certificate policy
- ○ **C.** Digital signature
- ○ **D.** Certificate practice statement

81. In which of the following types of fuzzing are forged packets sent to the tested application and then replayed?

- ○ **A.** Application fuzzing
- ○ **B.** Protocol fuzzing
- ○ **C.** File format fuzzing
- ○ **D.** Web page fuzzing

82. Which of the following describes a type of algorithm where data is broken into several units of varying sizes (dependent on algorithm) and encryption is applied to those chunks of data?

- ○ **A.** Symmetric encryption algorithm
- ○ **B.** Elliptic curve
- ○ **C.** Block cipher
- ○ **D.** All the options are correct.

83. Which form of media sanitization might be required for flash-based solid state drives to be considered fully sanitized?

- ○ **A.** Declassification
- ○ **B.** Degaussing
- ○ **C.** Destruction
- ○ **D.** Overwriting

84. Which of the following is the best measure to prevent divulging sensitive information through dumpster diving? (Select two.)

- ○ **A.** A firewall
- ○ **B.** Antivirus software
- ○ **C.** Proper disposal policy
- ○ **D.** Training and awareness

85. What is the last step in the access control process?

- ○ **A.** Identification
- ○ **B.** Authentication
- ○ **C.** Authorization
- ○ **D.** Access control

86. Which of the following are used to verify the status of a certificate? (Select two correct answers.)

- ○ **A.** OSCP
- ○ **B.** CRL
- ○ **C.** OSPF
- ○ **D.** ACL

87. Buffer overflows, format string vulnerabilities, and utilization of shell-escape codes can be mitigated by which of the following practices?

- ○ **A.** Fuzzing
- ○ **B.** Testing
- ○ **C.** Input validation
- ○ **D.** Browser initiated token request

88. Which one of the following controls are physical security measures? (Select all correct answers.)

- ○ **A.** Motion detector
- ○ **B.** Antivirus software
- ○ **C.** CCTV
- ○ **D.** Fence

89. Michael is a member of the Accounting, Executive Assistants, Billing, and Users groups. Accounting members are allowed VIEW and CHANGE rights over a folder on the file server. Executive Assistants are allowed only VIEW permissions on the same folder, whereas Billing group members can VIEW and WRITE new files. Users have an explicit DENY for this folder. What is Michael's access to this folder?

- ○ **A.** DENY
- ○ **B.** VIEW
- ○ **C.** VIEW and CHANGE
- ○ **D.** VIEW, CHANGE, and WRITE

90. Which of the following would best mitigate the risks associated with allowing organizational network access required by the terms of a joint project with a business partner?

    ○ **A.** Proper VLAN management

    ○ **B.** Access Control Lists

    ○ **C.** Network segmentation

    ○ **D.** Log analysis

91. Which of the following does not describe techniques for assessing threats and vulnerabilities?

    ○ **A.** Understanding attack surface

    ○ **B.** Baseline reporting

    ○ **C.** Reviews of architecture, design, and code

    ○ **D.** System hardening

92. Which of the following statements best describes nonrepudiation?

    ○ **A.** A set of mathematical rules used in encryption

    ○ **B.** A means of proving that a transaction occurred

    ○ **C.** A method of hiding data in another message

    ○ **D.** A drive technology used for redundancy and performance improvement

93. Which of the following provides government-grade security by implementing the AES encryption algorithm and 802.1x-based authentication?

    ○ **A.** WPA2

    ○ **B.** WEP

    ○ **C.** WPA

    ○ **D.** WAP

94. Which of the following is a cloud-based security solution mainly found in private datacenters?

    ○ **A.** VPC

    ○ **B.** HSM

    ○ **C.** TPM

    ○ **D.** PKI

95. Which of the following provide a method for mitigating ARP poisoning?

    ○ **A.** Use a device that offers port security

    ○ **B.** Use a static map of IP address to MAC address

    ○ **C.** Answers A and B

    ○ **D.** None of the above

96. What is the minimum number of drives necessary to provide a RAID 5 redundant with distributed parity disk array?

- ○ **A.** 1
- ○ **B.** 2
- ○ **C.** 3
- ○ **D.** 5

97. Which of the following describes a simple form of social engineering in which an unauthorized individual follows closely behind someone who has authorized physical access to an environment?

- ○ **A.** Tailgating
- ○ **B.** Piggybacking
- ○ **C.** Answers A and B
- ○ **D.** None of the above

98. Which of the three principles of security is supported by an offsite tape backup system?

- ○ **A.** Confidentiality
- ○ **B.** Integrity
- ○ **C.** Availability
- ○ **D.** Sanitization

99. Which type of authorization provides a mechanism for validation of both sender and receiver?

- ○ **A.** Anonymous
- ○ **B.** Kerberos
- ○ **C.** TACACS
- ○ **D.** RADIUS

100. An executive from ABC Corp receives an email from a Vice President of XYZ Corp, which is a prestigious partner organization of ABC Corp. This email was formatted using XYZ's corporate logo, images and text from their website (checked by the executive before opening the included form). After clicking on the provided link, the executive was asked to verify his credentials for access to a confidential report about ABC Corp but after he filled out the form, the executive received only a referral to XYZ's site. What type of attack was used in this scenario?

- ○ **A.** Smishing
- ○ **B.** Phishing
- ○ **C.** Vishing
- ○ **D.** Spear phishing

Answers to Practice Exam 2

Answers at a Glance

1. A	35. C	68. B
2. C	36. A and C	69. C
3. B	37. D	70. C
4. A	38. B	71. D
5. C	39. A and B	72. B
6. A	40. A, B, and C	73. A
7. C	41. B	74. D
8. A	42. B	75. C
9. B	43. A, B, and C	76. A
10. B	44. D	77. C
11. B	45. C	78. B
12. C	46. B	79. C
13. D	47. A	80. A
14. B	48. D	81. B
15. A and D	49. C	82. C
16. B	50. B	83. C
17. B	51. C	84. C and D
18. D	52. A	85. D
19. B	53. C	86. A and B
20. B	54. A	87. C
21. A	55. B	88. A, C, and D
22. B	56. B	89. A
23. B	57. A	90. C
24. E	58. C	91. D
25. B	59. B	92. B
26. D	60. D	93. A
27. C	61. A	94. A
28. D	62. C	95. C
29. B	63. B	96. C
30. D	64. D	97. C
31. C	65. D	98. C
32. D	66. A	99. B
33. A	67. B	100. D
34. D		

Answers with Explanations

Question 1

Answer A is correct. In a decentralized key-management scheme, the user creates both the private and public key and then submits the public key to the CA to allow it to apply its digital signature after it has authenticated the user. Answer B is incorrect because centralized key management allows the organization to have complete control over the creation, distribution, modification, and revocation of the electronic credentials that it issues. Answers C and D are incorrect because they are nonexistent terms.

Question 2

Answer C is correct. Transport Layer Security (TLS) is a network protocol that replaces Secure Sockets Layer (SSL) to provide security communication security over networks. Answer A is incorrect, as such a thing was never developed. Answers B and D are incorrect as these describe methods for implementing VPNs and are were not designed to replace SSL.

Question 3

Answer B is correct. Least privilege is a principle of assigning only those rights necessary to perform assigned tasks. By making Lynn a member of the Administrators group, Bob not only bypassed the application's access control protocols, but may also have granted Lynn access to additional application features or administrative-only tools that often lack the same safeguards as user-level APIs. Answer A is incorrect because the default assignment of an implicit denial is overridden by explicit grants of access aids in protected resources against accidental access and is not directly violated by this action because Lynn's account now has full Administrator rights assigned. Answer C is incorrect because separation of duties is focused on ensuring that action and validation practices are performed separately. Answer D is incorrect because account expiration protocols ensure that individual accounts do not remain active past their designated lifespan, but Lynn's account is current and enabled so it is unaffected.

Question 4

Answer A is correct. The RFID-enabled key is a form of "something you have," and the blood vessel biometric signature is a form of "something you are." Answers B and C are incorrect because there are no "something you know" requirements, such as the input of a personal identification number (PIN) or password. Answer D is incorrect because the pattern of blood vessels is not a "something you do" form of biometric measure.

Question 5

Answer C is correct. With hard disk encryption, authentication happens on power-up of the drive through either a software pre-boot authentication environment or with a BIOS password. Enhanced firmware and special-purpose cryptographic hardware are built into the hard disks. Answer A is incorrect because TPM refers to a secure crypto processor used to authenticate hardware devices such as PC or laptop. Answer B is incorrect because a hardware security module (HSM) can be described as black box combination hardware and software/firmware that is attached or contained inside a computer used to provide cryptographic functions for tamper protection and increased performance. Answer D is incorrect because in file- or folder-level encryption, individual files or directories are encrypted by the file system itself.

Question 6

Answer A is correct. In the event a mobile device is lost, GPS tracking can be used to find the location. Answer B is incorrect because mobile voice encryption can allow executives and employees alike to discuss sensitive information without having to travel to secure company locations. Answer C is incorrect because remote wipe allows the handheld's data to be remotely deleted in the event the device is lost or stolen. Answer D is incorrect because a screen lock or passcode is used to prevent access to the phone.

Question 7

Answer C is correct. Hardening efforts for data repositories must address security of the storage and backup of storage area networks (SANs), network access server (NAS) configurations, and directory services such as Microsoft Active Directory and Novell eDirectory. Answer A is incorrect because it is associated with FTP server security. Answer B is incorrect because it is associated with hardening DNS service. Answer D is incorrect because it is a hardening practice for DHCP services.

Question 8

Answer A is incorrect. A mantrap is a physical security control that is a holding area between two entry points that gives security personnel time to view a person before allowing him into the internal building. Biometrics typically incorporate something about the person, such as retina scan or fingerprint, to allow access, thus answer B is incorrect. Answers C and D are also incorrect as these describe controls not related to physical security.

Question 9

Answer B is correct. Both bluejacking and bluesnarfing refer to types of attacks over the short-range Bluetooth technology. Answers A, C, and D are incorrect.

Question 10

Answer B is correct. With a differential backup scheme, only the last Full and last Differential backup need to be restored, making answer C incorrect as well. Daily full backups would require only the last full backup, making answer A incorrect in this configuration. Answer D would be correct in an Incremental rather than a Differential backup setting, where the last Full and all intervening Incremental backups must be restored for recovery.

Question 11

Answer B is correct. Although least privilege can aid in protecting against internal fraud, it does not particularly aid in identifying it if occurring. Mandatory vacations, job rotation, and separation of duties such as monetary processing and validation all provide cross-checks that can aid in the identification of ongoing fraudulent operations, making answers A, C, and D incorrect.

Question 12

Answer C is correct. WEP is the most basic form of encryption that can be used on 802.11-based wireless networks to provide privacy of data sent between a wireless client and its access point. Answer A is incorrect. Wireless Application Environment (WAE) specifies the framework used to develop applications for mobile devices, including cell phones, data pagers, and PDAs. Answers B and D are incorrect. Wireless Session Layer (WSL), Wireless Transport Layer (WTL), and Wireless Transport Layer Security (WTLS) are the specifications that are included in the WAP standard.

Question 13

Answer D is correct. Infrastructure-as-a-Service (IaaS) is the delivery of computer infrastructure in a hosted service model over the Internet. This method of cloud computing enables the client to literally outsource everything that would normally be in a typical IT department. Answer A is incorrect because Software-as-a-Service (SaaS) is the delivery of a licensed application to customers over the Internet for use as a service on demand. Answer B is incorrect because Desktop-as-a-Service (DaaS), also called virtual desktop or hosted desktop services, is the outsourcing of a virtual desktop infrastructure (VDI) to a third-party service provider. Answer C is incorrect. Platform-as-a-Service (PaaS) is the delivery of a computing platform, often an operating system with associated services, that is delivered over the Internet without downloads or installation.

Question 14

Answer B is correct. In a Class B network, valid host IDs are from 172.16.0.0 to 172.31.255.255. Answer A is incorrect because it is a Class A address and provides too many available addresses. Valid host IDs are from 10.0.0.1 to 10.255.255.254. Answers C and D are incorrect because they both are Class C addresses and do not provide enough host addresses.

Question 15

Answers A and D are correct. The IEEE and IETF specify 802.1X and EAP as the standard for secure wireless networking, and Protected EAP (PEAP) is standards based. PEAP was jointly developed by Microsoft, RSA Security, and Cisco Systems. It is an IETF open standard, and Protected EAP (PEAP) is standards based. PEAP provides mutual authentication and uses a certificate for server authentication by the client, and users have the convenience of entering password-based credentials. Answer B is incorrect because WEP is the most basic form of encryption that can be used on 802.11-based wireless networks to provide privacy of data sent between a wireless client and its access point. Answer C is incorrect because LEAP is a Cisco-proprietary protocol.

Question 16

Answer B is correct. In order to provide for replay protection, a packet number (PN) field is used. CCMP produces a message integrity code (MIC) that provides data origin authentication and data integrity for the packet payload data. Answer A is incorrect because ICMP is a network troubleshooting protocol. Answer C is incorrect because WEP is the most basic form of encryption that can be used on

802.11-based wireless networks. Answer D is incorrect because WPA protects networks by incorporating a set of enhanced security features. WPA-protected networks require users to enter a passkey in order to access a wireless network.

Question 17

Answer B is correct. Risk avoidance involves simply terminating the operation that produces the risk, such as when shutting down a vulnerable site. Answer A is incorrect because accepting a risk is to do nothing in response, except to document the risk-management decision and obtain senior management sign-off. Answer C is not correct because mitigation applies a solution that results in a reduced level of risk or exposure. Answer D is incorrect because the liability or cost associated with a risk is transferred through insurance policies and other such legal means.

Question 18

Answer D is correct. Physical controls include facility design details such as layout, door, locks, guards, and electronic surveillance systems. Quantitative risk analysis involved the use of numerical metrics and is used to identify and sort risks rather than to control risk, making answer A incorrect. Answer B is incorrect because Management controls include policies and procedures. Answer C is incorrect because technical controls include access control systems, encryption, and data classification solutions.

Question 19

Answer B is correct. Facilities continuity planning is focused around alternative site management, hardware, and service contracts. Network connectivity BC planning involves establishing alternative network access paths and dedicated recovery administrative connections, making answer A incorrect. High-availability clustered servers ensure that automatic failover occurs in the event that the primary service node(s) is unable to perform normal service functions, making answer C incorrect. Fault tolerance, particularly in the area of storage devices, supports individual server operational continuity in the face of hardware device failure, making answer D incorrect. In SAN storage systems, redundant storage network connections similarly ensure continuous resource access for devices in the storage area network.

Question 20

Answer B is correct. The disaster recovery plan documents how organizations will recover from a disaster. It includes risk evaluations, restoration procedures application, and training required. Answer A is incorrect because the impact and risk assessment details on recovery scope, priority, and order of restoration. Answer C is incorrect because the disaster recovery policies detail responsibilities and procedures to follow during disaster recovery events. Service-level agreements are contracts with suppliers and vendors that detail minimum levels of support, making answer D incorrect.

Question 21

Answer A is correct. TCP is a connection-oriented protocol, which uses a three-way handshake to establish and close a connection. Answers B, C, and D are incorrect. A man-in-the-middle attack takes advantage of this handshake by inserting itself in the middle. UDP is a connectionless protocol and does not use a handshake to establish a connection. Juggernaut describes a program that helps make man-in-the-middle attacks easier.

Question 22

Answer B is correct. ARP is a protocol used for mapping IP addresses to MAC addresses. It does not require validation, thus answer A is incorrect. Answers C and D are incorrect because connection-oriented and connectionless are used to describe communications between two endpoints in which a message is sent with or without prior arrangement.

Question 23

Answer B is correct. Honeynets are collections of honeypot systems interconnected to create networks that appear to be functional and that can be used to study an attacker's behavior within the network. A bastion host is the first line of security that a company allows to be addressed directly from the Internet; therefore, answer A is incorrect. Answer C is incorrect because it is a made-up term. Answer D is incorrect because an IDS is used for intrusion detection.

Question 24

Answer E is correct. Answers A, B, C, and D represent the high-level components of a penetration test. Remediating vulnerabilities is not part of a penetration test. Some testers, however, might provide information or ideas about remediating vulnerabilities.

Question 25

Answer B is correct. Proactive patch management is necessary to keep your technology environment secure and reliable. Answer A is incorrect because application baselining is similar to operating system baselining in that it provides a reference point for normal and abnormal activity. Answer C is incorrect because network monitoring is used to check network activity. Answer D is incorrect because input validation errors are a result of improper field checking in the code.

Question 26

Answer D is correct. It is important that security is implemented from the very beginning. In the early design phase, potential threats to the application must be identified and addressed. Ways to reduce the associated risks must also be taken into consideration. Therefore, answers A, B, and C are incorrect.

Question 27

Answer C is correct. Host software baselining can be done for a variety of reasons including malware monitoring and creating system images. Generally, the environment needs of an organization will fall into a legacy, enterprise, or high security client. Answer A is incorrect because virtualization adds a layer of security as well as improves enterprise desktop management and control with faster deployment of desktops and fewer support calls due to application conflicts. Answer B is incorrect because network storage policies have nothing to do with desktop management. Answer D is incorrect because roaming profiles do not add a layer of security.

Question 28

Answer D is correct. A screen lock or passcode is used to prevent access to the phone. Answer A is incorrect because in the event a mobile device is lost, GPS tracking can be used to find the location. Answer B is incorrect because mobile voice encryption can allow executives and employees alike to discuss sensitive information without having to travel to secure company locations. Answer C is incorrect because remote wipe allows the handheld's data to be remotely deleted in the event the device is lost or stolen.

Question 29

Answer B is correct. In file- or folder-level encryption, individual files or directories are encrypted by the file system itself. Perhaps one of the most common examples of this type of encryption is the encrypting file system (EFS) available in newer Microsoft operating systems. Answer A is incorrect because full disk encryption is most useful when you're dealing with a machine that is being taken on the road by people such as traveling executives, sales managers, or insurance agents. Answer C is incorrect because media encryption is used for USB flash drives, iPods, and other portable storage devices. Answer D is incorrect because application-level encryption is used in cloud implementations.

Question 30

Answer D is correct. In a cloud environment, application-level encryption is preferred because the data is encrypted by the application before being stored in the database or file system. The advantage is that it protects the data from the user all the way to storage. Answer A is incorrect because full disk encryption is most useful when you're dealing with a machine that is being taken on the road by people such as traveling executives, sales managers, or insurance agents. Answer B is incorrect because in file- or folder-level encryption, individual files or directories are encrypted by the file system itself. Answer C is incorrect because media encryption is used for USB flash drives, iPods, and other portable storage devices.

Question 31

Answer C is correct. Val needs her own private key to decrypt the message Bob encrypted with her public key. Neither of Bob's keys is needed because the originator does not need to be validated, making answers A and B incorrect. Answer D is incorrect because Val's public key is used to encrypting the original message before transmission.

Question 32

Answer D is correct. "Something you have" includes ATM cards, smart cards, and keys. "Something you know" includes logons, passwords, and PINs, making answer C incorrect. Answers A and B are incorrect because both "something you are" and "something you do" are biometric measures present even without your ATM card.

Question 33

Answer A is correct. The default assignment of an implicit denial, overridden by explicit grants of access, aids in protected resources against accidental access during normal network operations. Answer B is incorrect because least privilege is a principle of assigning only those rights necessary to perform assigned tasks. Answer C is incorrect because separation of duties is focused on ensuring that action and validation practices are performed separately. Answer D is incorrect because account expiration protocols ensure that individual accounts do not remain active past their designated lifespan, but they do nothing to protect against accidental resource availability for currently enabled accounts.

Question 34

Answer D is correct. Morgan inherits explicit VIEW and CHANGE from her Accounting group membership and explicit WRITE from her Billing group membership, overriding the default implicit DENY from the Users group. Answer A is incorrect because the default implicit DENY is overridden by explicit assignments inherited through group membership. Answer B is incorrect because it lacks both CHANGE and WRITE permissions, and answer C is incorrect because it lacks the WRITE permission inherited from the Billing group.

Question 35

Answer C is correct. SHA-1 is a cryptographic hash function and is an updated version of the original Secure Hash Algorithm (SHA). Answer A is incorrect because this is an algorithm that uses a public and private key pair and is not associated with SHA-1. Answer B is incorrect because a digital signature is not an encryption algorithm. Answer D is incorrect because a certificate authority accepts or revokes certificates.

Question 36

Answers A and C are correct. PGP uses a web of trust rather than the hierarchical structure. It also uses public key encryption. Based on this, answers B and D are incorrect.

Question 37

Answer D is correct. PKI represents the system of digital certificates and certificate authorities. Answers A, B, and C are incorrect. A CPS is a document created and published by a CA that provides for the general practices followed by the CA. Answers A and B are fictitious terms.

Question 38

Answer B is correct. Sub-CA architecture does not represent a valid trust model. Answers A, C, and D, however, all represent legitimate trust models. Another common model also exists, called cross-certification; however, it usually makes more sense to implement a bridge architecture over this type of model.

Question 39

Answers A and B are correct. All host devices must have some type of malware protection. A necessary software program for protecting the user environment is antivirus software. Antivirus software is used to scan for malicious code in email and downloaded files. Anti-spam and anti-spyware software can add another layer of defense to the infrastructure. Pop-up blocking software programs are available through browsers. Answer C is incorrect because content filtering is done at the server level to keep host machines from accessing certain content. Answer D is incorrect because web tracking software merely tracks the sites a person visited.

Question 40

Answers A, B, and C are correct. All except answers D and E are advantages of honeypots and honeynets. Currently, the legal implications of using such systems are not that well defined, and the use of these systems typically requires more administrative resources.

Question 41

Answer B is correct. A DMZ is a small network between the internal network and the Internet that provides a layer of security and privacy. Answer A is incorrect. The purpose of a VLAN is to unite network nodes logically into the same broadcast domain regardless of their physical attachment to the network. Answer C is incorrect because NAT acts as a liaison between an internal network and the Internet. Answer D is incorrect because a VPN is a network connection that allows you access via a secure tunnel created through an Internet connection.

Question 42

Answer B is correct. A PKI structure with a single CA and multiple subordinate CAs would benefit the most from a hierarchical structure. This is because it allows the top CA to be the root CA and control trust throughout the PKI. Answer A is incorrect because a cross-certified model is where CAs have a trust relationship with each other; they trust certificates from other CAs. Answer C is incorrect because a bridge is a central point for a cross-certified model. Answer D is incorrect because linked is not a PKI trust model.

Question 43

Answers A, B, and C are correct. Each of these describes types of updates that can be applied to a system. Answer D is incorrect.

Question 44

Answer D is correct. A continuous UPS, which can also be called an "online" UPS, is constantly running on battery, which is always being charged as long as service power is available. It has no cutover time in the event of power loss. A standby power supply (SPS) uses line power until an interruption, where a battery-powered inverter turns on to provide power, making answer A incorrect. Answer B is incorrect because a hybrid/ferroresonant UPS is designed to maintain line voltage during variation and briefly after an outage instead of continuously. Answer C is incorrect because a backup power generator is not a type of uninterruptable power supply (UPS) because it must be started to begin providing power.

Question 45

Answer C is correct. As computers get faster, so does the ability for hackers to use distributed computing as a method of breaking encryption algorithms. With computer performance, in some cases, increasing by 30%–50% a year on average, this could become a concern for some older algorithms. Answer A is incorrect because weak keys exhibit regularities, and the weakness has nothing to do with performance. Answer B is incorrect because the weakness in keys comes from a block cipher regularity in the encryption of secret keys. The keys do not repeat themselves on other machines. Answer D is incorrect because there is only one correct answer.

Question 46

Answer B is correct. Qualitative risk assessments tend to be less precise than quantitative assessments. Quantitative risk assessments tend to be more difficult for management to understand properly without additional explanation, require intensive labor to gather all of the necessary measurements, and are time consuming to produce and keep up-to-date, making answers A, C, and D incorrect.

Question 47

Answer A is correct. Internet content filters use a collection of terms, words, and phrases that are compared to content from browsers and applications. This type of software can filter content from various types of Internet activity and applications, such as instant messaging, email, and office documents. It can be used to monitor and stop the disclosure of the organization's proprietary or confidential information. Answer B is incorrect. When a proxy server receives a request for an Internet service, it passes through filtering requirements and checks its local cache of previously downloaded web pages. Because web pages are stored locally, response times for web pages are faster and traffic to the Internet is substantially reduced. Answer C is incorrect. Protocol analyzers help you troubleshoot network issues by gathering packet-level information across the network. These applications capture packets and decode the information into readable data for analysis. Answer D is incorrect; a packet-filtering firewall filters packets based on IP addresses, ports, or protocols and is a simple, good first line of defense.

Question 48

Answer D is correct. Because many systems allow passwords of higher complexity than this requirement, users may tend to use the same password at work as for other online services. Answers A and B are incorrect because the combination of rapid expiration of individual passwords and protections against their reuse tend to prevent the use of the same passwords at work and elsewhere where password turnover rates and reuse might be less dynamic. Answer C is incorrect because requiring a password of greater length than the common standard eight characters encourages users to create more complex passwords that are different from their normal, simpler passwords.

Question 49

Answer C is correct. A remote wipe allows the handheld's data to be remotely deleted in the event the device is lost or stolen. Answer A is incorrect because in the event a mobile device is lost, GPS tracking can be used to find the location. Answer B is incorrect because mobile voice encryption can allow executives and employees alike to discuss sensitive information without having to travel to secure company locations. Answer D is incorrect because a screen lock or passcode is used to prevent access to the phone.

Question 50

Answer B is correct. There are numerous reasons why a certificate might need to be revoked (including a certificate being issued to the incorrect person). A CPS is a published document from the CA describing their policies and procedures for issuing and revoking certificates; therefore, answer A is incorrect. A private key compromise is actually another reason to perform revocation of a certificate; therefore, answer C is incorrect. Answer D is incorrect because this is a bogus term.

Question 51

Answer C is correct. The purpose of a VLAN is to unite network nodes logically into the same broadcast domain regardless of their physical attachment to the network. Answer A is incorrect because a DMZ is a small network between the internal network and the Internet that provides a layer of security and privacy. Answer B is incorrect because a virtual private network (VPN) is a network connection that allows you access via a secure tunnel created through an Internet connection. Answer D is incorrect because NAT acts as a liaison between an internal network and the Internet.

Question 52

Answer A is correct. Full disk encryption is most useful when you're dealing with machines that are being taken on the road by traveling executives, sales managers, or insurance agents. Answer B is incorrect because in file- or folder-level encryption, individual files or directories are encrypted by the file system itself. Answer C is incorrect because media encryption is used for USB flash drives, iPods, and other portable storage devices. Answer D is incorrect because application-level encryption does not protect the data stored on the machines.

Question 53

Answer C is correct. Facial recognition systems measure relative spacing between underlying features such as the bone structure and eye placement, requiring more than a minor injury to modify this biometric signature. Fingerprint signatures can be modified by minor cuts, abrasions, and exposure to chemicals, making answer A incorrect. Both voiceprint and retinal signatures can be modified due to illness and injury, making answers B and D incorrect.

Question 54

Answer A is correct. The annualized loss expectancy (ALE) is the product of the SLE (value times exposure factor) and the ARO or $20% of 100,000 × 25% = $5,000. Answer B is incorrect because $20,000 represents the asset value times ARO. Answer C is incorrect because the value times the exposure factor represents the single loss expectancy (SLE) rather than the annual loss expectancy (ALE). Answer D is simply an incorrectly calculated value.

Question 55

Answer B is correct. A warm site generally includes power, phone, and networking. It might include computers that are not yet set up or kept fully up-to-date. Cold sites generally have little more than space, restrooms, and electricity until activated, making answer A incorrect. Hot sites are locations that are fully operational and include all aspects of operational requirements, making answer C incorrect. Alternative sites (hot, warm, or cold) should be remote enough to be outside of the zone of involvement during a disaster event, making answer D incorrect.

Question 56

Answer B is correct. Secure Sockets Layer (SSL) provides security only for the connection, not the data after it is received. The data is encrypted while it is being transmitted, but when received by the computer, it is no longer encrypted. Therefore, answers A, C, and D are incorrect.

Question 57

Answer A is correct. DNS uses port 5. Answer B is incorrect because SCP operates on Port 22. Answer C is incorrect because HTTPS uses port 443. Answer D is incorrect SMB uses port 445.

Question 58

Answer C is correct. Protocol analyzers examine network traffic and identify protocols and endpoint devices in the identified transactions. Port scanners check service ports on a single device, making answer A incorrect. Answer B is incorrect because vulnerability scanners look for vulnerabilities associated with particular versions of software or services. Answer D is incorrect because a network mapper identifies all devices within a network segment and would not identify endpoint devices beyond that address space.

Question 59

Answer B is correct. Traditionally, HSMs have been used in the banking sector to secure numerous large, bulk transactions. Answer A is incorrect because full disk encryption is most useful when you're dealing with a machine that is being taken on the road by people such as traveling executives, sales managers, or insurance agents. Answer C is incorrect because TPM refers to a secure crypto-processor used to authenticate hardware devices such as PC or laptop. Answer D is incorrect because in file- or folder-level encryption, individual files or directories are encrypted by the file system itself.

Question 60

Answer D is correct. The default Kerberos session key duration is eight hours, making answers A, B, and C incorrect.

Question 61

Answer A is correct. Rijndael was the winner of the new AES standard. Although RC6 and Twofish competed for selection, they were not chosen. 3DES and CAST did not participate; therefore, answers B, C, D, and E are incorrect.

Question 62

Answer C is correct. SCP operates on Port 2. Answer A is incorrect because DNS uses port 5. Answer B is incorrect because HTTPS uses port 443. Answer D is incorrect because SMB uses port 445.

Question 63

Answer B is correct. A HIDS collects and analyzes data that originates on the local machine. Answer A is incorrect; a NIDS tries to locate packets not allowed on the network that the firewall missed and looks at the information exchanged between machines. Answer C is incorrect because firewalls control the information that gets in and out of the host machine. Answer D is incorrect; intrusion prevention differs from intrusion detection in that it actually prevents attacks in real time instead of only detecting the occurrence.

Question 64

Answer D is correct. Although they are very similar, they differ in the scope of the target. Answer B is incorrect and refers to vishing, which is essentially phishing but using the phone. Answer C is incorrect as this describes smishing, which uses SMS.

Question 65

Answer D is correct. Business continuity planning (BCP)/continuity of operations (COO) is focused on maintaining continued service availability even if in a limited form. Recovery time objectives (RTOs) and recovery point objectives (RPOs) are components of Disaster Recovery Planning (DRP) focusing on recovery after a loss of function, making answers A, B, and C incorrect.

Question 66

Answer A is correct. Mandatory access control (MAC) systems require assignment of labels such as PUBLIC, SECRET, and SENSITIVE to provide resource access. Answer B is incorrect because discretionary access control (DAC) systems allow data owners to extend access rights to other logons based on explicit assignments or inherited group membership. Answers C and D are incorrect because both RBAC access control forms rely on conditional assignment of access rules either inherited (role-based) or by environmental factors such as time of day or secured terminal location (rule-based).

Question 67

Answer B is correct. By locking an account after a limited number of failed attempts, administrative action is necessary to unlock the account and can raise awareness of repeated unauthorized access attempts while reducing the overall number of tests that can be attempted. Answers A and C are incorrect because both password length and password expiration can aid in complicating slow "brute-force" testing of sequential passwords if performed only a few times per day to avoid notice, but they provide only limited protection against high-bandwidth brute-force attempts to guess passwords. Password complexity (including mixed-case letters, numbers, and symbols) provides more protection than length alone because the number of variations possible for each character rapidly expands the number of total tests that must be completed. Answer D is incorrect because logon banners detail legal repercussions following unauthorized access but provide no barrier against a brute-force attack.

Question 68

Answer B is correct. Kerberos is a time-synchronized protocol that relies on a common time base for session ticket lifetime verification. LDAP is not a ticket-based or a lifetime-based protocol. Answers A, C, and D are incorrect because all three are vulnerabilities of some LDAP service variations.

Question 69

Answer C is correct. Cross-site scripting (XXS) vulnerabilities can be used to hijack the user's session or to cause the user accessing malware-tainted Site A to unknowingly attack Site B on behalf of the attacker who planted code on Site A. Answer A is incorrect because a buffer overflow is a direct result of poor or incorrect input validation or mishandled exceptions. Answer B is incorrect. The key element to understanding XSRF is that attackers are betting that users have a validated login cookie for the website already stored in their browsers. Answer D is incorrect because input validation errors are a result of improper field checking in the code.

Question 70

Answer C is correct. At the most basic level, a Trusted Platform Module (TPM) provides for the secure storage of keys, passwords, and digital certificates, and it is hardware-based (typically attached to the circuit board of the system). Answer A is incorrect because full disk encryption is a software solution and is most useful when you're dealing with a machine that is being taken on the road by people such as traveling executives, sales managers, or insurance agents. Answer B is incorrect because a hardware security module (HSM) can be described as black box combination hardware and software/firmware that is attached or contained inside a computer used to provide cryptographic functions for tamper protection and increased performance. Answer D is incorrect because in file- or folder-level encryption, individual files or directories are encrypted by the file system itself.

Question 71

Answer D is correct. Public Key Infrastructure describes the trust hierarchy system for implementing a secure public key cryptography system over TCP/IP networks. Answers A, B, and C are incorrect because these are bogus terms.

Question 72

Answer B is correct. The false acceptance rate (FAR) is a measure of unauthorized biometric signatures being accepted as valid. Answers A and D are incorrect because they represent valid biometric operations. Answer C is incorrect because denial of authorized signatures is measured as the false rejection rate (FRR).

Question 73

Answer A is correct. A virtualized "sandboxed" guest system can help in computer-security research, which enables the study of the effects of some viruses or worms without the possibility of compromising the host system. Answer B is incorrect because network storage has nothing to do with desktop management. Answer C is incorrect because host software baselining can be done for a variety of reasons including malware monitoring and creating system images. Answer D is incorrect because application baselining is used to monitor changes in application behavior.

Question 74

Answer D is correct. Each of these represents common symptoms of a computer that has had spyware installed.

Question 75

Answer C is correct. Software-as-a-Service (SaaS) is the delivery of a licensed application to customers over the Internet for use as a service on demand. Answer A is incorrect. Platform-as-a-Service (PaaS) is the delivery of a computing platform, often an operating system with associated services, that is delivered over the Internet without downloads or installation. Answer B is incorrect because Infrastructure-as-a-Service (IaaS) is the delivery of computer infrastructure in a hosted service model over the Internet. Answer D is incorrect because Desktop-as-a-Service (DaaS), also called virtual desktop or hosted desktop services, is the outsourcing of a virtual desktop infrastructure (VDI) to a third-party service provider.

Question 76

Answer A is correct. Black box testing does not provide any information about the environment. Answer B is incorrect as white box testing is more transparent, and would provide details around the particular application. A vulnerability test and penetration test are separate items, thus Answer C is incorrect. Answer D is also incorrect.

Question 77

Answer C is correct. A brownout is a short-term decrease in voltage, often occurring when motors are started or due to provider faults. Both spikes and surges are increases of voltage, making Answers A and B incorrect. Blackouts involve a complete loss of power rather than simply a reduction of voltage, making Answer D incorrect.

Question 78

Answer B is correct. Just like the data on hard drives, the data on mobiles can be encrypted. Answer A is incorrect because in the event a mobile device is lost, GPS tracking can be used to find the location. Answer C is incorrect. A remote wipe allows the handheld's data to be remotely deleted in the event the device is lost or stolen. Answer D is incorrect because a screen lock or passcode is used to prevent access to the phone.

Question 79

Answer C is correct. Discretionary access control (C-level) gives owner discretionary control over resource access control. Answers A and B are incorrect because Mandatory (B-level) or Verified (A-level) access control divisions restrict access based on additional constraints beyond owner assignment. Answer D is incorrect because the Minimal (D-level) division is more permissive than the higher Discretionary division.

Question 80

Answer A is correct. Certificate revocation lists are used to identify revoked certificates; however, they are being replaced by the Online Certificate Status Protocol (OSCP), which provides certificate status in real time. Answers B and D are both incorrect because these terms relate to the policies and practices of certificates and the issuing authorities. Answer C is incorrect because a digital signature is an electronic signature used for identity authentication.

Question 81

Answer B is correct. In protocol fuzzing, forged packets are sent to the tested application, which can act as a proxy and modify requests on the fly and then replay them. Answer A is incorrect because in an application fuzzing attack vectors are within its I/O, such as the user interface, the command-line options, URLs, forms, user-generated content, and RPC requests. Answer C is incorrect because in file format fuzzing, multiple malformed samples are generated and then opened sequentially. Answer D is incorrect because web page fuzzing is not a real term.

Question 82

Answer C is correct. When data that is going to be encrypted is broken into chunks of data and then encrypted, the type of encryption is called a block cipher. Although many symmetric algorithms use a block cipher, Answer A is incorrect because block cipher is a more precise and accurate term for the given question. Answer B is incorrect because elliptic curve is a type of asymmetric encryption algorithm. Answer D is an incorrect choice because only one answer is correct.

Question 83

Answer C is correct. In some forms of non-ferric solid state storage devices, only destruction may provide full data sanitization. Answer A is incorrect because declassification is a formal process for assessing the risk associated with discarding information, rather than a sanitization process itself. Answer B is incorrect because non-ferric solid state data storage might not react to powerful magnetic fields used during degaussing. Answer D is incorrect because overwriting in a solid state device operates differently than in magnetic storage media and might not completely wipe all data.

Question 84

Answers C and D are correct. Dumpster diving describes a physical means of acquiring sensitive data, often by digging through discarded material. A policy that clearly describes an organization's stance on proper disposal of data and equipment along with user training and awareness are key measures that should be taken to prevent the disclosure of sensitive data through dumpster diving. Answers A and B are incorrect and cannot prevent a physical attack on materials.

Question 85

Answer D is correct. Only after credentials have been provided, authenticated, and authorized will access control list (ACL) values be assigned based on explicit and inherited grant and denial constraints. Answer A is incorrect because identification involves only the presentation of credentials and not the requirement for verifying those credentials as valid. Answers B and C are incorrect because both authentication and authorization must occur before access control constraints can be applied to an access request.

Question 86

Answers A and B is correct. The Online Certificate Status Protocol (OCSP) and the certificate revocation list (CRL) are used to verify the status of digital certificates. OSPF is a routing protocol; therefore, Answer C is incorrect. An ACL is used to define access control; therefore, Answer D is incorrect.

Question 87

Answer C is correct. Input validation tests whether an application properly handles input from a source outside the application destined for internal processing. Answer A is incorrect because fuzzing allows an attacker to inject random-looking data into a program to see if it can cause the program to crash. Answer B is incorrect because testing is too generic or a term. Answer D is incorrect because it a method used to mitigate Cross-site Request Forgery (XSRF) attacks.

Question 88

Answers A, C, and D are correct. Motion detectors, CCTV, and fencing are all controls used for physical security. Antivirus is not a physical security control, but a control used to protect computer systems from malware, thus Answer B is incorrect.

Question 89

Answer A is correct. The explicit assignment of DENY overrides all other assignments, making Answers B, C, and D incorrect.

Question 90

Answer C is correct. With interconnected networks, the potential for damage greatly increases because one compromised system on one network can easily spread to other networks. Networks that are shared by partners, vendors, or departments should have clear separation boundaries. Answer A is incorrect because VLANs are a logical separation of a physical network. Answer B is incorrect because access control generally refers to the process of making resources available to accounts that should have access, while limiting that access to only what is required. Answer D is incorrect because logging is the process of collecting data to be used for monitoring and auditing purposes.

Question 91

Answer D is correct. System hardening refers to reducing a system's security exposure and strengthening its defenses against unauthorized access attempts and other forms of malicious attention. Answers A, B, and C, on the other hand, are specific techniques to assess for threats and vulnerabilities.

Question 92

Answer B is correct. Nonrepudiation means that neither a sender nor a receiver can deny sending or receiving a message or data. Answer A is incorrect because it describes an algorithm. Answer C is incorrect because it describes steganography. Answer D is incorrect because it describes RAID.

Question 93

Answer A is correct. WPA2 is based on the IEEE 802.11i standard and provides government-grade security by implementing the AES encryption algorithm and 802.1x-based authentication. Answer B is incorrect because the WEP standard was proven to be unsecure and has been replaced by the newer WPA standards. Answer C is incorrect because the early WPA standard has been superseded by the WPA2 standard, implementing the full 802.11i-2004. Answer D is incorrect because a WAP refers to a wireless access point, which is the wireless network hardware that functions in the place of a wired switch.

Question 94

Answer A is correct. The HSM and cloud machines can both live on the same virtual private network through the use of a virtual private cloud (VPC) environment. This type of solution is mainly found in private datacenters that manage and offload cryptography with dedicated hardware appliances. Answer B is incorrect because traditionally HSMs have been used in the banking sector to secure numerous large, bulk transactions. Answer C is incorrect because TPM refers to a secure crypto-processor used to authenticate hardware devices such as a PC or laptop. Answer D is incorrect because Public Key Infrastructure (PKI) is a set of hardware, software, people, policies, and procedures needed to create, manage, distribute, use, store, and revoke digital certificates.

Question 95

Answer C is correct. A device that offers port security is ideal for larger networks; however, you may also create a static or script-based mapping. Answer D is incorrect.

Question 96

Answer C is correct. The minimum number of drives in a RAID 5 array is three, making Answers B and D incorrect. A single drive does not provide fault tolerance, making Answer A incorrect.

Question 97

Answer C is correct. Both tailgating and piggybacking describe a simple method to gain unauthorized access to an environment by closely following behind someone with authorized access. Answer D is incorrect.

Question 98

Answer C is correct. Availability is concerned with ensuring that access to services and data is protected against disruption, including disasters and other events that could require recovering from offsite backup media. Answer A is incorrect because confidentiality involves protecting against unauthorized access. Integrity is concerned with preventing unauthorized modification, making Answer B incorrect. Answer D is incorrect because sanitization involves the destruction or overwriting of data to protect confidentiality.

Question 99

Answer B is correct. Kerberos authentication enables validation of both end-points and can help protect against interception attacks such as the "man-in-the-middle." Anonymous connections do not even allow verification of the access requestor, making answer A incorrect. Answers C and D are incorrect because neither TACACS nor RADIUS services provide mutual endpoint validation.

Question 100

Answer D is correct. This is an example of a spear phishing attack, which uses fraudulent email in order to obtain access to data of value (here, the executive's credentials) from a targeted organization. Answer A is incorrect because while phishing attacks involve email, spear phishing attacks are targeted and cus-tomized to a selected target. The questions description of the images, links and report all indicate a very targeted attack. Answer B is incorrect because Smishing attacks are conducted using SMS messages. Answer C is similarly incorrect because vishing attacks employ telephone or VoIP audio communications.

Glossary

A

acceptable use An organization's policy that provides specific detail about what users may do with their network access, including email and instant messaging usage for personal purposes, limitations on access times, and the storage space available to each user.

access control list (ACL) In its broadest sense, an access control list is the underlying data associated with a network resource that defines the access permissions. The most common privileges include the ability to read, write to, delete, and execute a file.

accounting The tracking of users' access to resources primarily for auditing purposes.

ActiveX A Microsoft-developed, precompiled application technology that can be embedded in a web page in the same way as Java applets.

Address Resolution Protocol (ARP) A protocol that allows the resolution of a device's assigned IP address into its MAC hardware address.

Address Resolution Protocol (ARP) poisoning This can allow a perpetrator to trick a device into thinking any IP is related to any MAC address. In addition, they can broadcast a fake or spoofed ARP reply to an entire network and poison all computers.

Advanced Encryption Standard (AES) A symmetrical 128-bit block encryption system that replaces the legacy DES standard.

algorithm A set of sequenced steps that are repeatable. In encryption, the algorithm is used to define how the encryption is applied to data.

Annualized Loss Expectancy (ALE) The expected cost per year arising from a risk's occurrence. It is calculated as the product of the single loss expectancy (SLE) and the annualized rate of occurrence (ARO).

Annualized Rate of Occurrence (ARO) The number of times a given risk will occur within a single year.

anomaly-based monitoring A subset of behavior-based monitoring that stores normal system behavior profiles and triggers an alarm when some type of unusual behavior occurs.

anti-spam A software program that can add another layer of defense to the infrastructure by filtering out undesirable email.

antivirus A software program used for protecting the user environment that scans for email and downloadable malicious code.

applet Java-based mini-program that executes when the client machine's browser loads the hosting web page.

application logging Application logging has become a major focus of security as we move to a more web-based world and exploits such as cross-site scripting and SQL injections are an everyday occurrence.

asset A company or personal resource that has value.

Asymmetric key A pair of key values—one public and the other private—used to encrypt and decrypt data, respectively. Only the holder of the private key can decrypt data encrypted with the public key, which means anyone who obtains a copy of the public key can send data to the private key holder in confidence.

attack signature A signature that identifies a known method of attack.

auditing The tracking of user access to resources, primarily for security purposes.

authentication The process of identifying users.

Authentication Header (AH) A component of the IPsec protocol that provides integrity, authentication, and anti-replay capabilities.

authorization The process of identifying what a given user is allowed to do.

availability Ensures any necessary data is available when it is requested.

B

back door A method of gaining access to a system or resource that bypasses normal authentication or access control methods.

backup technique A defined method to provide for regular backups of key information, including user files and email storage, database stores, event logs, and security principal details such as user logons, passwords, and group membership assignments.

baseline This measure of normal activity is used as a point to determine abnormal system and network behaviors.

behavior-based IDS A detection method that involves a user noticing an unusual pattern of behavior, such as a continually operating hard drive or a significantly slowed level of performance.

behavior-based monitoring The use of established patterns of baseline operations to identify variations that might identify unauthorized access attempts.

biometrics Authentication based on some part of the human anatomy (retina, fingerprint, voice, and so on).

BIOS Basic Input/Output System is the firmware code run upon start of a system.

block cipher Transforms a message from plaintext (unencrypted form) to ciphertext (encrypted form) one piece at a time, where the block size represents a standard chunk of data that is transformed in a single operation.

botnet A large number of computers that forward transmissions to other computers on the Internet. You might also hear a botnet referred to a *zombie army*.

business continuity plan A plan that describes a long-term systems and services replacement and recovery strategy, designed for use when a complete loss of facilities occurs. A business continuity plan prepares for automatic failover of critical services to redundant offsite systems.

C

centralized key management Involves a certificate authority generating both public and private key pairs for a user and then distributing them to the user.

certificate An electronic document that includes the user's public key and the digital signature of the certificate authority (CA) that has authenticated her. The digital certificate can also contain information about the user, the CA, and attributes that define what the user is allowed to do with systems she accesses using the digital certificate.

certificate authority (CA) A system that issues, distributes, and maintains current information about digital certificates. Such authorities can be private (operated within a company or an organization for its own use) or public (operated on the Internet for general public access).

Certificate Enrollment Protocol (CEP) A proprietary Cisco protocol that allows Cisco IOS-based routers to communicate with certificate authorities.

certificate life cycle The period of time a certificate is valid. Issued certificates expire at the end of their lifetime and can be renewed.

Certificate Management Protocol (CMP) A protocol used for advanced PKI management functions. These functions include certificate issuance, exchange, invalidation, revocation, and key commission.

certificate policy A statement that governs the usage of digital certificates.

certificate practice statement (CPS) A document that defines the practices and procedures a CA uses to manage the digital certificates it issues.

certificate revocation The act of invalidating a digital certificate.

certificate revocation list (CRL) A list generated by a CA that enumerates digital certificates that are no longer valid and the reasons they are no longer valid.

certificate suspension The act of temporarily invalidating a certificate while its validity is being verified.

chain of custody The documentation of all transfers of evidence from one person to another, showing the date, time, and reason for transfer, and the signatures of both parties involved in the transfer. Chain of custody also refers to the process of tracking evidence from a crime scene to the courtroom.

Challenge Handshake Authentication Protocol (CHAP) A widely used authentication method in which a hashed version of a user's password is transmitted during the authentication process.

change management This term indicates that a formal process to schedule, implement, track, and document changes to policies, configurations, systems, and software is used in an organization.

cipher A method for encrypting text, the term cipher is also used to refer to an encrypted message (although the term *ciphertext* is preferred).

code of ethics A formal list of rules governing personal and professional behavior that is adopted by a group of individuals or organizations. Many security certifications, including Security+, require their holders to adhere to a code of ethics that's designed to foster ethical and legal behavior and discourage unethical or illegal behavior.

cold site A remote site that has electricity, plumbing, and heating installed, ready for use when enacting disaster recovery or business continuity plans. At a cold site, all other equipment, systems, and configurations are supplied by the company enacting the plan.

Computer Emergency Response Team (CERT) The team of experts who respond to security incidents, also referred to as a CIRT or CSIRT.

Computer Incident Response Team (CIRT) The team of experts who respond to a computer security incident. Also referred to as a CSIRT (Computer Security Incident Response Team) or a CERT.

confidentiality Involves a rigorous set of controls and classifications associated with sensitive information to ensure that such information is neither intentionally nor unintentionally disclosed.

cookies Temporary files stored in the client's browser cache to maintain settings across multiple pages, servers, or sites.

countermeasures Methods used in some scenarios to provide automatic response in the event of intrusion detection.

cross-certification When two or more CAs choose to trust each other and issue credentials on each other's behalf.

Cross-Site Request Forgery (XSRF) A web attack that exploits existing site trust, such as unexpired banking session cookies, to perform actions on the trusting site using the already-existing trusted account.

cross-site scripting (XSS) Malicious executable code placed on a website that allows an attacker to hijack a user session to conduct unauthorized access activities, expose confidential data, and provide logging of successful attacks back to the attacker.

cryptographic module Any combination of hardware, firmware, or software that implements cryptographic functions such as encryption, decryption, digital signatures, authentication techniques, and random number generation.

cryptography A process that provides a method for protecting information by disguising (encrypting) it into a format that can be read only by authorized systems or individuals.

D

Data Loss Prevention (DLP) Security services that identify, monitor, and protect data during use, storage, or transfer between devices. DLP software relies on deep inspection of data and transactional details for unauthorized access operations.

decentralized key management Key management that occurs when a user generates a public and private key pair and then submits the public key to a certificate authority for validation and signature.

deflection Redirecting or misdirecting attackers to secured segmented areas, allowing them to assume they have been successful while preventing access to secured resources.

degaussing A method of removing recorded magnetic fields from magnetic storage media by applying strong cyclic magnetic pulses, thereby erasing the content and making the media unreadable.

demilitarized zone (DMZ) Also called the *neutral zone*, a DMZ is an area in a network that allows limited and controlled access from the public Internet.

denial of service (DoS)   A type of attack that denies legitimate users access to a server or services by consuming sufficient system resources or network bandwidth or by rendering a service unavailable.

dictionary attack   An attack in which software is used to compare hashed data, such as a password, to a word in a hashed dictionary. This is repeated until matches are found in the hash, with the goal being to match the password exactly to determine the original password that was used as the basis of the hash.

digital certificate   *See* certificate.

digital signature   A hash encrypted to a private key of the sender that proves user identity and authenticity of the message. Signatures do not encrypt the contents of an entire message. A digital signature uses data to provide an electronic signature that authenticates the identity of the original sender of the message or data.

disaster recovery   Actions to be taken in case a business is hit with a natural or manmade disaster.

discretionary access control (DAC) A distributed security method that allows users to set permissions on a per-object basis.

distributed denial of service (DDoS) A DDoS attack originates from multiple systems simultaneously thereby causing even more extreme consumption of bandwidth and other resources than a DoS attack.

DMZ   *See* demilitarized zone.

Domain Name Service (DNS)   The service responsible for translation of hierarchical human-readable named addresses into their numerical IP equivalents.

Domain Name Service (DNS) kiting DNS kiting refers to the practice of taking advantage of the Add Grace Period to monopolize domain names without even paying for them. How domain kiting works is that a domain name is deleted during the five-day AGP and immediately reregistered for another five-day period.

Domain Name Service (DNS) poisoning   DNS poisoning allows a perpetrator to redirect traffic by changing the IP record for a specific domain, thus permitting the attacker to send legitimate traffic anywhere he chooses. This not only sends a requestor to a different website but also caches this information for a short period, distributing the attack's effect to the server users.

dry-pipe fire suppression   A sprinkler system with pressurized air in the pipes. If a fire starts, a slight delay occurs as the pipes fill with water. This system is used in areas where wet-pipe systems might freeze.

due care   Assurance that the necessary steps are followed to satisfy a specific requirement, which can be an internal or external requirement, as in an agency regulation.

dumpster diving   Scavenging discarded equipment and documents and extracting sensitive information from them without ever contacting anyone in the company.

Dynamic Host Configuration Protocol (DHCP)   A broadcast protocol capable of automatically obtaining an IP address and other network settings such as DNS and WINS settings from an available pool of addresses managed by the DHCP server.

E

elliptic curve cryptography (ECC)   A method in which elliptic curve equations are used to calculate encryption keys for use in general-purpose encryption.

Encapsulating Security Payload (ESP)   Used to provide confidentiality, data origin authentication, connectionless integrity, an anti-replay service, and traffic flow confidentiality.

encryption algorithm   A mathematical formula or method used to scramble information before it is transmitted over unsecure media. Examples include RSA, DH, IDEA, Blowfish, MD5, and DSS/DSA.

environment   The physical conditions that affect and influence growth, development, and survival. Used in the security field to describe the surrounding conditions of an area to be protected.

escalation   The upward movement of privileges when using network resources or exercising rights (such as moving from read permissions to write).

evidence   Any hardware, software, or data that can be used to prove the identity and actions of an attacker.

Extensible Markup Language (XML)   A flexible markup language is based on standards from the World Wide Web Consortium. XML is used to provide widely accessible services and data to end users, exchange data among applications, and capture and represent data in a large variety of custom and standard formats.

extranet   A special internetwork architecture wherein a company's or organization's external partners and customers are granted access to some parts of its intranet and the services it provides in a secure, controlled fashion.

F

Faraday cage   A metal enclosure used to conduct stray EMEs (electromagnetic emissions) to ground, thereby eliminating signal leakage and the ability of external monitors or detectors to "read" network or computer activity. A Faraday cage can be very small or encompass an entire building, and it is generally used only when security concerns are extremely high (as in national defense, classified areas, or highly sensitive commercial environments).

Federal Information Processing Standard (FIPS)   A standard created by the U.S. government for the evaluation of cryptographic modules. It consists of four levels that escalate in their requirement for higher security levels.

File Transfer Protocol (FTP) A client-server data file transfer service for TCP networks, capable of anonymous or authenticated access.

firewall A hardware device or software application designed to filter incoming or outgoing traffic based on predefined rules and patterns. Firewalls can filter traffic based on protocol uses, source or destination addresses, and port addresses; they can even apply state-based rules to block unwanted activities or transactions.

forensics As related to security, forensics is the process of analyzing and investigating a computer crime scene after an attack has occurred and of reconstructing the sequence of events and activities involved in such an attack.

G

Graphic Processing Unit (GPU) A specialized CPU chip optimized for graphic rendering, vector, or stream processing. Current General Purpose Graphic Processing Unit (GPGPU) chips can contain hundreds of cores capable of independent processing and are increasingly used in high-performance computing (HPC) systems.

Group Policy Group Policy can be used for ease of administration in managing the environment of users in a Microsoft network. This can include installing software and updates or controlling what appears on the desktop. The Group Policy object (GPO) is used to apply a group policy to users and computers.

guideline Specific information about how standards should be implemented. A guideline is generally not mandatory, thus acting as a kind of flexible rule used to produce a desired behavior or action. A guideline allows freedom of choice on how to achieve the behavior.

H

hard disk drive (HDD) A magnetic medium for data storage that employs one or more spinning disks covered by a magnetic coating written to and read from by a read/write head that moves above the surface to access data storage in concentric circular tracks.

hash value The resultant output or data generated from an encryption hash when applied to a specific set of data. If computed and passed as part of an incoming message and then recomputed upon message receipt, such a hash value can be used to verify the received data when the two hash values match.

hashing A methodology used to calculate a short, secret value from a data set of any size (usually for an entire message or for individual transmission units). This secret value is recalculated independently on the receiving end and compared to the submitted value to verify the sender's identity.

Heating, Ventilation and Air Conditioning (HVAC) A form of environmental control that warms, cools, and transports air for the purpose of thermal and humidity regulation.

honeypot A decoy system designed to attract hackers. A honeypot usually has all its logging and tracing enabled, and its security level is lowered on purpose. Likewise, such systems often include deliberate lures or bait, in hopes of attracting would-be attackers who think there are valuable items to be attained on these systems.

host-based IDS (HIDS) Host-based intrusion-detection systems (HIDSs) monitor communications on a host-by-host basis and try to filter malicious data. These types of IDSs are good at detecting unauthorized file modifications and user activity.

Host-based IPS (HIPS) A software intrusion-detection system capable of reacting to and preventing or terminating unauthorized access within a single host system.

hot site A site that is immediately available for continuing computer operations if an emergency arises. It typically has all the necessary hardware and software loaded and configured, and it is available 24/7.

Hypertext Transfer Protocol (HTTP) A client-server protocol for network transfer of information between a web server and a client browser over the World Wide Web (WWW).

Hypertext Transfer Protocol over Secure Sockets Layer (HTTPS) A protocol used in a secured connection encapsulating data transferred between the client and web server that occurs on port 443.

hypervisor A hypervisor controls how access to a computer's processors and memory is shared. A hypervisor

or virtual machine monitor (VMM) is a virtualization platform that provides more than one operating system to run on a host computer at the same time.

I

identity proofing Identity proofing is an organizational process that binds users to authentication methods. Identity proofing gives the organization assurance that the user performing an authentication is the legitimate user. This is the main component of authentication life cycle management.

incident Any violation or threatened violation of a security policy.

incident response A clear action plan on what each response team member needs to do and when it has to be done in the event of an emergency or a security incident.

Infrastructure as a Service (IaaS) A cloud computing model in which hardware, storage, and networking components are virtualized and provided by an outsourced service provider.

integrity Involves a monitoring and management system that performs integrity checks and protects systems from unauthorized modifications to data, system, and application files. When applied to messages or data in transit, integrity checks rely on calculating hash or digest values before and after transmission to ensure nothing changed between the time the data was sent and the time it was received.

Internet Control Message Protocol (ICMP) A transport protocol within the TCP/IP suite that operates separately from TCP or UDP transfer. ICMP is intended for passing error messages and is used for services such as PING and TRACEROUTE.

Internet Key Exchange (IKE) A method used in the IPsec protocol suite for public key exchange, security association parameter negotiation, identification, and authentication.

Internet Protocol Security (IPsec) Used for encryption of TCP/IP traffic, IPsec provides security extensions to IPv4. IPsec manages special relationships between pairs of machines, called security associations.

Internet Security Associate and Key Management Protocol (ISAKMP) Defines a common framework for the creation, negotiation, modification, and deletion of security associations.

Internet Service Provider (ISP) An organization that provides last-mile connectivity between the public Internet backbone and an end-user's facility. ISPs often manage their own DNS name resolution services and specific IP address ranges through DHCP automatic client address leasing.

intranet A portion of the information technology infrastructure that belongs to and is controlled by the company in question.

intrusion Malicious activity such as denial-of-service attacks, port scans, or attempts to break into computers.

intrusion-detection system (IDS) A sophisticated network-protection system designed to detect attacks in progress but not to prevent potential attacks from occurring (although many IDSs can trace attacks back to an apparent source; some can even automatically notify all hosts through which attack traffic passes that they are forwarding such traffic).

K

Kerberos authentication Kerberos defines a set of authentication services and includes the Authentication Service (AS) Exchange protocol, the Ticket-Granting Service (TGS) Exchange protocol, and the Client/Server (CS) Exchange protocol.

Key Distribution Center (KDC) A cryptographic system service that handles authentication of an access request by providing a client ticket based on a server's key and then verifying that ticket when submitted to the appropriate server.

key escrow Key escrow occurs when a CA or other entity maintains a copy of the private key associated with the public key signed by the CA.

key exchange A technique in which a pair of keys is generated and then exchanged between two systems (typically a client and server) over a network connection to allow a secure connection to be established between them.

key management The methods for creating and managing cryptographic keys and digital certificates.

knowledge-based detection
Knowledge-based detection relies on the identification of known attack signatures and events that should never occur within a network.

L

Layer 2 Tunneling Protocol (L2TP)
A technology used with a VPN to establish a communication tunnel between communicating parties over unsecure media. L2TP permits a single logical connection to transport multiple protocols between a pair of hosts. L2TP is a member of the TCP/IP protocol suite and is defined in RFC 2661; a framework for creating virtual private networks that uses L2TP appears in RFC 2764.

Lightweight Directory Access Protocol (LDAP) A TCP/IP protocol that allows client systems to access directory services and related data. In most cases, LDAP is used as part of management or other applications or in browsers to access directory services information.

logic bomb A piece of software designed to do damage at a predetermined point in time or in response to some type of condition (for example, "disk is 95% full") or event (for example, some particular account logs in or some value the system tracks exceeds a certain threshold).

logical tokens A method of access controls used in addition to physical security controls to limit access to data.

M

M of N Control The process of backing up a private key material across multiple systems or devices. This provides a protective measure to ensure that no one individual can re-create his key pair from the backup.

man in the middle An attack in which a hacker attempts to intercept data in a network stream and then inserts her own data into the communication with the goal of disrupting or taking over communications. The term itself is derived from the insertion of a third party—the proverbial "man in the middle"—between two parties engaged in communications.

mandatory access control (MAC)
A centralized security method that doesn't allow users to change permissions on objects.

mantrap A two-door configuration in a building or office that can lock unwanted individuals in a secured area, preventing them from entering other areas or even from exiting wherever it is they're being held.

message The content and format a sender chooses to use to communicate with some receiver across a network, an intranet, an extranet, or the Internet.

message digest The output of an encryption hash that's applied to some fixed-size chunk of data. A message digest provides a profound integrity check because even a change to 1 bit in the target data also changes the resulting digest value. This explains why digests are included so often in network transmissions.

misuse Misuse is typically used to refer to unauthorized access by internal parties.

multifactor authentication Multifactor authentication involves the use of two or more different forms of authentication. What you know (logon, password, PIN), what you have (keycard, SecurID number generator), or what you are (biometrics) constitute different forms.

mutual authentication A situation in which a client provides authentication information to establish identity and related access permissions with a server and in which a server also provides authentication information to the client to ensure that illicit servers cannot masquerade as genuine servers.

N

National Institute of Standards & Technology (NIST) An agency within the U.S. Department of Commerce responsible for developing measurement standards, including standards for cyber security best practices, monitoring, and validation.

network access control (NAC) NAC offers a method of enforcement that helps ensure computers are properly configured. The premise behind NAC is to secure the environment by examining the user's machine and, based on the results, grant access accordingly.

Network Address Translation (NAT) TCP/IP protocol technology that maps internal IP addresses to one or more external IP addresses through a NAT server of some type. NAT enables the conservation of public IP address space by mapping private IP addresses used in an internal LAN to one or more external public IP addresses to communicate with the external world. NAT also provides address-hiding services thus adding both security and simplicity to network addressing.

network-based IDS (NIDS) Network-based IDSs monitor the packet flow and try to locate packets that might have gotten through the firewall and that are not allowed for one reason or another. They are best at detecting DoS attacks and unauthorized user access.

network-based IPS (NIPS) A device or software program designed to sit inline with traffic flows and prevent attacks in real-time.

Network Time Protocol (NTP) A UDP protocol used for device clock synchronization providing a standard time base over variable-latency networks, which is critical for time-synchronized encryption and access protocols such as Kerberos.

O

One Time Pad (OTP) Within an OTP, there are as many bits in the key as there are in the plaintext to be encrypted, and as the name suggests, this key is to be random and used only once, with no portion of the key ever being reused.

Online Certificate Status Protocol (OCSP)   An Internet protocol defined by the IETF that is used to validate digital certificates issued by a CA. OCSP was created as an alternative to certificate revocation lists (CRLs) and overcomes certain limitations of CRL.

Open Vulnerability Assessment Language (OVAL)   A community open standard for transfer of information regarding security tools and services, focusing on vulnerabilities, patch states, and configuration states.

OSI model   The Open Systems Interconnect model is a logically structured model that encompasses the translation of data entered at the application layer through increasingly more abstracted layers of data, resulting in the actual binary bits passed at the physical layer.

P

passive detection   A method of intrusion detection that has an IDS present in the network in a silent fashion; it does not interfere with communications in progress.

Password Authentication Protocol (PAP)   A legacy cleartext authentication protocol for remote server access that does not support stronger authentication mechanisms.

pattern matching   A network-analysis approach that compares each individual packet against a database of signatures. The inherent weakness in this method is that such patterns must be known (and definitions in place) before they can be used to recognize attacks or exploits.

performance baseline   *See* baseline.

performance monitoring   The act of using tools to monitor changes to system and network performance.

personally identifiable information (PII)   Privacy-sensitive information that identifies or can be used to identify, contact, or locate the person to whom such information pertains.

Plain Old Telephone Service (POTS)   Traditional audio circuit-switched telephone services, which predated modern broadband network connectivity using audio MODulator/DEModulator (MODEM) endpoint devices for remote data access. Still used in many rural and underdeveloped areas lacking a broadband infrastructure.

Point-to-Point Tunneling Protocol (PPTP)   A TCP/IP technology used to create virtual private networks (VPN) or remote-access links between sites or for remote access. PPTP is generally regarded as less secure than L2TP and is used less frequently for that reason.

policy   A broad statement of views and positions. A policy that states high-level intent with respect to a specific area of security is more properly called a security policy.

pop-up blocker   A program used to block a common method for Internet advertising, using a window that pops up in the middle of your screen to display a message when you click a link or button on a website.

Port Address Translation (PAT)   A form of network address translation (NAT) that allows redirection of IP packet address port information during transfer.

Pretty Good Privacy (PGP) A shareware encryption technology for communications that utilizes both public and private encryption technologies to speed up encryption without compromising security.

Private Branch Exchange (PBX) An audio telephone exchange that serves an organization or facility and provides connectivity between external public telephone exchanges and internal business telephone services.

private key In encryption, this is the key used to unencrypt a message.

privilege escalation A method of software exploitation that takes advantage of a program's flawed code. Usually, this crashes the system and leaves it in a state where arbitrary code can be executed or an intruder can function as an administrator.

privilege management The process of controlling users and their capabilities on a network.

probability Used in risk assessment, probability measures the likelihood or chance that a threat will actually exploit some vulnerability.

procedure A procedure specifies how policies will be put into practice in an environment (that is, it provides necessary how-to instructions).

Protected Extensible Authentication Protocol (PEAP) An encrypted form of the EAP authentication protocol, which couples EAP with transport encryption to protect credentials during transfer.

protocol analyzer Protocol analyzers help troubleshoot network issues by gathering packet-level information across the network. These applications capture packets and decode the information into readable data for analysis.

Public Branch Exchange (PBX) A telephone switch used on a company's or organization's premises to create a local telephone network. Using a PBX eliminates the need to order numerous individual phone lines from a telephone company and permits PBX owners to offer advanced telephony features and functions to their users.

public key A key that is made available to whoever is going to encrypt the data sent to the holder of a private key.

Public Key Cryptography Standards (PKCS) The de facto cryptographic message standards developed and published by RSA Laboratories.

public key infrastructure (PKI) A paradigm that encompasses certificate authorities and X.509 certificates used with public encryption algorithms to distribute, manage, issue, and revoke public keys. Public key infrastructures typically also include registration authorities to issue and validate requests for digital certificates, a certificate-management system of some type, and a directory in which certificates are stored and can be accessed. Together, all these elements make up a PKI.

Public Key Infrastructure based on X.509 Certificates (PKIX) A working group of the Internet Engineering Task Force (IETF) focused on developing Internet standards for certificates.

R

Rapid application development (RAD) An accelerated software development methodology that involves progressive elaboration and iterative development of software prototypes in favor of extensive pre-planning.

receiver The party that receives a message from its sender.

Recovery Time Objective (RTO) A measure of the time in which a service should be restored during disaster recovery operations.

redundancy planning The process of planning for continuing service in the event of failure by providing more than one of the same components or services.

redundant array of inexpensive disks (RAID) A redundant array of inexpensive disks is an organization of multiple disks into a large, high-performance logical disk to provide redundancy in the event of a disk failure.

Remote Access Server (RAS) Software or hardware systems that facilitate remote data access over digital networks, forming the backbone to virtualized and remote administrative services.

Remote Authentication Dial-In User Services (RADIUS) An Internet protocol used for remote-access services. It conveys user authentication and configuration data between a centralized authentication server and a remote-access server (RADIUS client) to permit the remote access server to authenticate requests to use its network access ports.

removable storage This is a small, high-capacity, removable device that can store information such as an iPod, thumb drive, or cell phone.

replay An attack that involves capturing valid traffic from a network and then retransmitting that traffic at a later time to gain unauthorized access to systems and resources.

restoration The process whereby data backups are restored into the production environment.

retention policy Documentation of the amount of time an organization will retain information.

risk The potential that a threat might exploit some vulnerability.

role A defined behavior for a user or group of users based on some specific activity or responsibilities. (For example, a tape backup administrator is usually permitted to back up all files on one or more systems; that person might or might not be allowed to restore such files, depending on the local security policies in effect.)

role-based access control (RBAC)

A security method that combines both MAC and DAC. RBAC uses profiles. Profiles are defined for specific roles within a company, and then users are assigned to such roles. This facilitates administration in a large group of users because when you modify a role and assign it new permissions, those settings are automatically conveyed to all users assigned to that role.

rollback A process used to undo changes or transactions when they do not complete, when they are suspected of being invalid or unwanted, or when they cause problems.

rootkit A piece of software that can be installed and hidden on a computer mainly for the purpose of compromising the system.

round A selection of encrypted data that is split into two or more blocks of data. Each block of data is then run through an encryption algorithm that applies an encryption key to each block of data individually, rather than applying encryption to the entire selection of data in a single operation.

router A device that connects multiple network segments and routes packets between them. Routers split broadcast domains.

rule-based access control (RBAC)

A rule-based access control method is an extension of access control that includes stateful testing to determine whether a particular request for resource access may be granted. When a rule-based method is in force, access to resources might be granted or restricted based on conditional testing.

S

Secure Hypertext Transfer Protocol (S-HTTP) An alternative to HTTPS is the Secure Hypertext Transport Protocol developed to support connectivity for banking transactions and other secure web communications.

Secure/Multipurpose Internet Mail Extensions (S/MIME) An Internet protocol governed by RFC 2633 and used to secure email communications through encryption and digital signatures for authentication. It generally works with PKI to validate digital signatures and related digital certificates.

Secure Shell (SSH) A protocol designed to support secure remote login, along with secure access to other services across an unsecure network. SSH includes a secure transport layer protocol that provides server authentication, confidentiality (encryption), and integrity (message digest functions), along with a user-authentication protocol and a connection protocol that runs on top of the user-authentication protocol.

Secure Sockets Layer (SSL) An Internet protocol that uses connection-oriented, end-to-end encryption to ensure that client/server communications are confidential (encrypted) and meet integrity constraints (message digests). Because SSL is independent of the application layer, any application protocol can work with SSL transparently. SSL can also work with a secure transport layer protocol, which is why the term SSL/TLS appears frequently. *See also* Transport Layer Security.

security association (SA) A method in IPsec that accounts for individual security settings for IPsec data transmission.

security baseline Defined in a company's or organization's security policy, a security baseline is a specific set of security-related modifications to and patches and settings for systems and services in use that underpins technical implementation of security.

security groups A logical boundary that helps enforce security policies.

security policies Documentation of the goals and elements of an organization's systems and resources.

sender The party that originates a message.

sequence number A counting mechanism in IPsec that increases incrementally each time a packet is transmitted in an IPsec communication path. It protects the receiver from replay attacks.

service level agreement (SLA) A contract between two companies or a company and individual that specifies, by contract, a level of service to be provided by one company to another. Supplying replacement equipment within 24 hours of loss of that equipment or related services is a simple example of an SLA.

Short Message Service (SMS) A text-based mobile communication system with message size originally limited to 160 characters per message.

signature-based monitoring A signature-based monitoring method is sometimes considered a part of the misuse-detection category. This type of monitoring method looks for specific byte sequences or signatures that are known to appear in attack traffic. The signatures are identified through careful analysis of the byte sequence from captured attack traffic.

Simple Mail Transport Protocol (SMTP) relay An exploitation of SMTP relay agents used to send out large numbers of spam messages.

Simple Network Management Protocol (SNMP) A UDP-based application layer Internet protocol used for network management, SNMP is governed by RFCs 2570 and 2574. In converting management information between management consoles (managers) and managed nodes (agents), SNMP implements configuration and event databases on managed nodes that can be configured to respond to interesting events by notifying network managers.

Single Loss Expectancy (SLE) The expected cost per instance arising from a risk's occurrence. It is calculated as the product of the asset value and the risk's exposure factor (a percentage of loss if a risk occurs).

single sign-on (SSO)   The concept or process of using a single logon authority to grant users access to resources on a network regardless of what operating system or application is used to make or handle a request for access. The concept behind the term is that users need to authenticate only once and can then access any resources available on a network.

smart card   A credit card-size device that contains an embedded chip. On this chip, varying and multiple types of data can be stored, such as a driver's license number, medical information, passwords, or other authentication data, and even bank account data.

sniffer   A hardware device or software program used to capture and analyze network data in real time. Because such a device can typically read and interpret all unencrypted traffic on the cable segment to which it is attached, it can be a powerful tool in any competent hacker's arsenal.

social engineering   The process of using human behavior to attack a network or gain access to resources that would otherwise be inaccessible. Social engineering is a term that emphasizes the well-known fact that poorly or improperly trained individuals can be persuaded, tricked, or coerced into giving up passwords, phone numbers, or other data that can lead to unauthorized system access, even when strong technical security measures can otherwise prevent such access.

Software as a Service (SaaS)   A cloud computing model in which software applications are virtualized and provided by an outsourced service provider.

Software Development Life Cycle (SDLC)   A formal structured process for software development, proceeding in phases from initiation through design, implementation, and maintenance and ending with retirement. Different models can be used to facilitate traditional (Waterfall) and accelerated (Agile) programming styles.

spam   A term that refers to the sending of unsolicited commercial email.

spoofing   A technique for generating network traffic that contains a different (and usually quite specific) source address from that of the machine actually generating the traffic. Spoofing is used for many reasons in attacks: It foils easy identification of the true source; it permits attackers to take advantage of existing trust relationships; and it deflects responses to attacks against some (usually innocent) third party or parties.

spyware   Software that communicates information from a user's system to another party without notifying the user.

standard   This term is used in many ways. In some contexts, it refers to best practices for specific platforms, implementations, OS versions, and so forth. Some standards are mandatory and ensure uniform application of a technology across an organization. In other contexts, a standard might simply describe a well-defined rule used to produce a desired behavior or action.

steganography A word of Greek origin meaning hidden writing, which can be further described as both an art and a science for simply hiding messages so that unintended recipients wouldn't even be aware of any message.

storage policy A policy defining the standards for storing each classification level of data.

switch A hardware device that manages multiple, simultaneous pairs of connections between communicating systems. Switches split collision domains but can also provide greater aggregate bandwidth between pairs or groups of communicating devices because each switched link normally gets exclusive access to available bandwidth.

symmetric key A single encryption key that is generated and used to encrypt data. This data is then passed across a network. After that data arrives at the recipient device, the same key used to encrypt that data is used to decrypt it. This technique requires a secure way to share keys because both the sender and receiver use the same key (also called a shared secret because that key should be unknown to third parties).

system logging The process of collecting system data to be used for monitoring and auditing purposes.

system monitoring A method of monitoring used to analyze events that occur on individual systems.

T

Terminal Access Controller Access-Control System Plus (TACACS+) An authentication, access control, and accounting standard that relies on a central server to provide access over network resources, including services, file storage, and network routing hardware.

threat A danger to a computer network or system (for example, a hacker or virus represents a threat).

token A hardware- or software-based system used for authentication wherein two or more sets of matched devices or software generate matching random passwords with a high degree of complexity.

Transmission Control Protocol/ Internet Protocol (TCP/IP) hijacking A process used to steal an ongoing TCP/IP session for the purposes of attacking a target computer. Essentially, hijacking works by spoofing network traffic so that it appears to originate from a single computer, when in actuality it originates elsewhere so that the other party in the communication doesn't realize another computer has taken over an active communications session.

Transport Layer Security (TLS) An end-to-end encryption protocol originally specified in ISO Standard 10736 that provides security services as part of the transport layer in a protocol stack.

Trojan A form of malware that appears to be useful software but has code hidden inside that attacks your system directly or allows the system to be infiltrated by the originator of the code when it is executed. A Trojan horse is software hidden inside other software and is commonly used to infect systems with viruses, worms, or remote-control software.

Trusted Platform Module (TPM) A secure crypto-processor used to authenticate hardware devices such as PC or laptop.

U–V

uninterruptible power supply (UPS) A power supply that sits between the wall power and the computer. In the event of power failure at the wall, the UPS takes over and powers the computer so that you can take action before data loss occurs.

Universal Resource Locator (URL) A character string representing an Internet location and the protocol required for accessing resources at that address. A browser address of "HTTP://example.com" establishes a connection to the example.com address using the Hypertext Transport Protocol (HTTP), whereas "FTP://example.com" connects to the same address using the File Transfer Protocol (FTP).

User Acceptance Testing (UAT) One of the final phases in the SDLC, user acceptance testing provides validation that software meets the scope mandates to the user's satisfaction.

video surveillance A surveillance method using closed-circuit television (CCTV), with which the picture is viewed or recorded as a means of security.

virtual local area network (VLAN) A software technology that allows for the grouping of network nodes connected to one or more network switches into a single logical network. By permitting logical aggregation of devices into virtual network segments, VLANs offer simplified user management and network resource access controls for switched networks.

virtual private network (VPN) A popular technology that supports reasonably secure, logical, private network links across some unsecure public network infrastructure, such as the Internet. VPNs are more secure than traditional remote access because they can be encrypted and because VPNs support tunneling (the hiding of numerous types of protocols and sessions within a single host-to-host connection).

virtualization technology A technology developed to allow a guest operating system to run along with a host operating system while using one set of hardware.

virus A piece of malicious code that spreads to other computers by design, although some viruses also damage the systems on which they reside. Viruses can spread immediately upon reception or implement other unwanted actions, or they can lie dormant until a trigger in their code causes them to become active. The hidden code a virus executes is called its payload.

Voice over IP (VoIP) A mechanism for the transfer of audio communication over digital transport services. This provides point-to-point communications over the Internet or can be integrated with POTS telephony services in services like the popular Skype system.

vulnerability   A weakness in hardware or software that can be used to gain unauthorized or unwanted access to or information from a network or computer.

W

warm site   A backup site that has some of the equipment and infrastructure necessary for a business to begin operating at that location. Typically, companies or organizations bring their own computer systems and hardware to a warm site, but that site usually already includes a ready-to-use networking infrastructure and also might include reliable power, climate controls, lighting, and Internet access points.

Web Application Framework (WAF)   A software-development framework for dynamic data-driven web applications and services.

wet-pipe fire suppression   A sprinkler system with pressurized water in its pipes. If a fire starts, the pipes release water immediately and offer the fastest and most effective means of water-based fire suppression.

whole disk encryption   Whole disk encryption can either be hardware- or software-based and is meant to encrypt the entire contents of the drive. This can include even temporary files and memory.

Wi-Fi   Short term for Wireless Fidelity communication standard.

Wi-Fi Protected Access (WPA)   A transport wireless transport security service implementing TKIP 128-bit encryption in place of the weaker legacy WEP encryption standard.

Wired Equivalent Privacy (WEP)   A security protocol used in IEEE 802.11 wireless networking, WEP is designed to provide security equivalent to that found in regular wired networks. This is achieved by using basic symmetric encryption to protect data sent over wireless connections so that sniffing of wireless transmissions doesn't produce readable data and so that drive-by attackers cannot access a wireless LAN without additional effort and attacks.

Wireless Application Protocol (WAP)   A long-range mobile equipment communications used by server-side processes to perform functions needed within the website.

Wireless Intrusion Detection System (WIDS)   A network intrusion-detection system monitoring wireless data communications. These types of IDSs are good at detecting unauthorized file modifications and user activity for mobile data connections.

Wireless Intrusion Prevention System (WIPS)   An intrusion-detection system capable of reacting to and preventing or terminating unauthorized access across wireless data transport mechanisms.

wireless local area networks (WLANs)   A networking technology that uses high-frequency radio waves rather than wires to communicate between nodes.

Wireless Transport Layer Security (WTLS)   WTLS defines a security level for applications based on the Wireless Application Protocol (WAP). As its acronym indicates, WTLS is based on transport layer security (TLS) but has been modified to work with the low-bandwidth, high-latency, and limited-processing capabilities found in many wireless networking implementations. WTLS also provides authentication, data integrity, and confidentiality mechanisms, all based on encryption methods using shared 56- or 128-bit symmetric keys.

worm   A special type of virus designed primarily to reproduce and replicate itself on as many computer systems as possible, a worm does not normally alter files but rather remains resident in a computer's memory. Worms typically rely on access to operating system capabilities that are invisible to users.

X–Y–Z

X.500 directory   A standard that regulates global, distributed directory services databases; it's also known as a white pages directory (because lookup occurs by name, rather than by job role or other categorized information, as in a yellow pages type of system).

X.509 digital certificate   A digital certificate that uniquely identifies a potential communications party or participant. Among other things, an X.509 digital certificate includes a party's name and public key, but it can also include organizational affiliation, service or access restrictions, and a host of other access- and security-related information.

Index

Numbers

3DES (Triple Data Encryption Standard), 46, 328

802.1X, 20-21

A

acceptable use policies, 83

access control, 295

  account expiration, 301

  account provisioning, 304-305

  ACLs, 299-301

  best practices, 296, 301-303

  centralized management, 300

  DAC, 298

  decentralized access management, 300

  default user account settings, 306-307

  group-based access, 306

  MAC, 298

  physical security

    during building evacuations, 191

    fences, 189

    line-of-sight access, 188-189

    moats, 190

    no-man's land, 189

  principle of least privilege, 301

  RBAC, 299

  Rule-Based, 297

  separation of duties, 301

  UAC, 302

  user accounts

    expiring, 309

    passwords, 307-308

    time-of-day restrictions, 309

  user-based access, 305

X-Y-Z